IN SEARCH
OF THE
PHOENICIANS

IN SEARCH
OF THE
PHOENICIANS

JOSEPHINE CRAWLEY QUINN

PRINCETON UNIVERSITY PRESS

PRINCETON AND OXFORD

Published by Princeton University Press, 41 William Street, Princeton, New Jersey 08540

In the United Kingdom: Princeton University Press, 6 Oxford Street, Woodstock, Oxfordshire OX20 1TR

press.princeton.edu

Cover art: Joseph Mallord William Turner, *The Decline of the Carthaginian Empire, 1817* © Tate Modern, 2017

First paperback printing, 2019
Paper ISBN 978-0-691-19596-4
Cloth ISBN 978-0-691-17527-0

Library of Congress Control Number: 2017935146

British Library Cataloging-in-Publication Data is available

This book has been composed in Linux Libertine O

Printed on acid-free paper. ∞

Printed in the United States of America

For Christopher

CONTENTS

ILLUSTRATIONS

ABBREVIATIONS

All abbreviations are as in *The Oxford Classical Dictionary* (4th ed., 2012), except the following:

ANET[3] Pritchard, James B., ed. 1969. *Ancient Near Eastern Texts Relating to the Old Testament*. 3rd ed. Princeton, NJ: Princeton University Press.

AT Wiseman, Donald J. 1953. *The Alalakh Tablets*. London: British Institute of Archaeology at Ankara.

BMC Hill, George F. 1910. *Catalogue of the Greek Coins of Phoenicia*. London: Trustees of the British Museum.

BMCV Wroth, Warwick W. 1911. *Catalogues of the coins of the Vandals, Ostrogoths and Lombards and of the empires of Thessalonica, Nicaea and Trebizond in the British Museum*. London: Trustees of the British Museum.

C. Ord. Ptol.[2] Lenger, Marie-Thérèse. 1980. *Corpus des ordonnances des Ptolémées*. 2nd ed. Brussels: Palais des académies.

C. Ptol. Sklav. Scholl, Reinhold. 1990. *Corpus der ptolemäischen Sklaventexte*. Stuttgart: Franz Steiner.

DNWSI Hoftijzer, Jacob, and Karel Jongeling. 1995. *Dictionary of the North-West Semitic Inscriptions*. Leiden: Brill.

EH Berthier, André, and René Charlier. 1955. *Le sanctuaire punique d'El-Hofra à Constantine*. Paris: Arts et métiers graphiques.

Enc. Berb. *Encyclopédie berbère*. 1984–2010. Aix-en-Provence: Édisud; 2010– . Leuven: Peeters.

IEphesos Wankel, Hermann, Helmut Engelmann, Johannes Nollé, et al. 1979–84. *Die Inschriften von Ephesos*. Bonn: Habelt.

IGLS Jalabert, Louis, René Mouterde et al. 1929–. *Inscriptions grecques et latines de la Syrie*. Paris: P. Geuthner.

IKition Yon, Marguerite. 2004. *Kition-Bamboula V: Kition dans les textes. Testimonia littéraires et épigraphiques et corpus des inscriptions*. Paris: Éditions recherche sur les civilisations.

IPergamon Fränkel, Max. 1890–95. *Die Inschriften von Pergamon*. Berlin: W. Spemann.

IPT Levi della Vida, Giorgio and Maria Giulia Amadasi Guzzo. 1987. *Iscrizioni puniche della Tripolitania (1927–1967)*. Rome: "L'Erma" di Bretschneider.

IRT Ward-Perkins, John B. and Joyce M. Reynolds. 1953. *Inscriptions of Roman Tripolitania*. Rome and London: British School at Rome.

KAI[5] Donner, Herbert, and Wolfgang Röllig. 2002. *Kanaanäische und aramäische Inschriften*. 5th ed. Wiesbaden: Harrassowitz.

KTU[3] Dietrich, Manfried, Oswald Loretz, and Joaquín Sanmartín. 2013. *Die keilal-phabetischen Texte aus Ugarit, Ras Ibn Hani und anderen Orten.* 3rd ed. Münster: Ugarit-Verlag.

ODNB Matthew, Henry C. G., and Bryan Harrison. 2004. *Oxford Dictionary of National Biography.* New ed. Oxford: Oxford University Press.

PPG[3] Friedrich, Johannes, Wolfgang Röllig, Maria Giulia Amadasi Guzzo, and Werner Mayer. 1999. *Phönizisch-punische Grammatik.* 3rd ed. Rome: Pontificio Istituto Biblico.

RÉS *Répertoire d'épigraphie sémitique.* 1900–1968. Paris: Imprimerie nationale.

RPC Burnett, Andrew, Michel Amandry, Pere Pau Ripollés Alegre, Ian Carradice, and Marguerite S. Butcher. 1992– . *Roman Provincial Coinage.* London: British Museum Press.

TDOT Botterweck, G. Johannes, Helmer Ringgren, and Heinz-Josef Fabry. 1974– . *Theological Dictionary of the Old Testament.* Grand Rapids, MI: Eerdmans.

TSSI Gibson, John C. L. 1971–82. *Textbook of Syrian Semitic Inscriptions.* Oxford: Clarendon Press.

TWOT Harris, R. Laird, Gleason Archer, and Bruce Waltke. 1980. *Theological Wordbook of the Old Testament.* Chicago: Moody Press.

INTRODUCTION

I want to begin a long way from Phoenicia: in Ireland, at the end of Brian Friel's play *Translations*, which was first performed at the Guildhall in Derry in 1980.[1] We are in a schoolroom in Baile Beag, the "small town" in County Donegal in which Friel set many of his plays. The year is 1833, shortly after the British have established a system of National Schools, with English as the language of instruction, as an alternative to these more informal "hedge schools" that taught in Irish. Even more recently a group of British soldiers have arrived in Baile Beag as part of the new Ordnance Survey of Ireland, which is replacing every Irish place name with an English equivalent, and a lieutenant called George Yolland has gone missing after a dance. The wrath of the British Army descends on the town as a whole, and Captain Lancey has just announced that unless information as to the whereabouts of the young man is forthcoming within twenty-four hours, all the livestock in the town will be shot, and that twenty-four hours later the settlement itself will be razed to the ground. Amidst the ensuing panic, the old schoolmaster Hugh O'Donnell remains on stage with his old students Maire and Jimmy Jack, and a few drinks inside him. He leaves his pupils and the audience with the Roman poet Virgil's description of Carthage, translating from Latin into Irish as he goes:

> *Urbs antiqua fuit*—there was an ancient city which, 'tis said, Juno loved above all the lands. And it was the goddess's aim and cherished hope that here should be the capital of all nations—should the fates perchance allow that. Yet in truth she discovered that a race was springing from Trojan blood to overthrow some day these Tyrian towers—a people *late regum belloque superbum*—kings of broad realms and proud in war who would come forth for Lybia's downfall—such was—such was the course—What the hell's wrong with me? Sure I know it backways. I'll begin again . . .[2]

What are these lines from book 1 of the *Aeneid* doing in a play about the experience of British imperialism in Ireland? Friel is alluding here to an Irish intellectual fashion popular in Hugh's younger days that postulated ancient Phoenician settlement on the island and influence on its culture, with some scholars even tracing the Irish language back to Phoenician. This theory encouraged people to interpret the British colonial occupation of Ireland in terms of the great struggle between noble Carthage and savage

Rome. And what's awful here, what makes Hugh stumble in his translation, is that Virgil's lament for Phoenician Carthage is in Latin; the story of the conquered can only be told in the language of the conqueror. Friel's play was of course written in English.[3]

It is not only Friel's evocation of Irish Phoenicianism in his closing scene that makes *Translations* a good place for us to start: the play as a whole highlights the contingency of collective identity. When the English soldiers arrive, many of the townspeople offer them hospitality and even guarded friendship, more shocked to discover that the soldiers speak neither Irish, nor Latin, nor Greek, than by their mission to rename Irish places. There are mutterings of discontent, and rumors of serious resistance offstage, but these are prompted by the practical irritations of British rule, and the towns-people relate much more to their immediate surroundings than to Ireland as a whole. Hugh himself is attached to Irish among other languages, and his fondness for the traditions and history of Ireland is colored by alcohol and compromised by his ambition to take a job at one of the new National Schools. At the end of the play, he reminisces with Jimmy Jack about how they marched together for twenty-three miles to Sligo to take part in the 1798 rebellion of the United Irishmen against the British: "Two young gallants with pikes across their shoulders and the *Aeneid* in their pockets," but then "in Phelan's pub" homesickness overtook them, "the desiderium nostrorum—the need for our own." They turned around and marched back. "Our pietas, James, was for older, quieter things."[4]

The only person who maintains a strongly resistant attitude to the British on what seems to be principle is Hugh's son Manus, an ambiguous character, superficially sympathetic, but also weak, jealous, and perhaps by the end of the play a murderer. His brother Owen, by contrast, just back from several years in Dublin and proud of his command of English, enthusiastically assists the renaming project. For him it is an exercise in modernizing a backward and somewhat embarrassing corner of his country's and his own past—until Captain Lancey's announcement convinces him that he has made a terrible mistake. Owen's Irish roots and affiliation emerge only under the pressure of a brutal foreign army, and his change of heart is jarring: a complex situation fades swiftly for him to black and white. The horrific turn of events does not affect everyone the same way. For most of Friel's characters, being Irish is a sentiment based more on present circumstance than nature or conviction, when it is felt at all. Whatever the contingent reasons in this particular colonial context for their specific self-conceptions, they remind us of the dangers of stamping ethnic labels on people who may themselves have felt ambivalent about or simply uninterested in them, people whose own collective identities came, went, and in some cases never rose above the level of their own towns or even families. The Phoenicians, I will suggest in this book, constitute just such a case.

The ancient Phoenicians have been credited with discovering everything from the pole star to the Cornish cream tea, and there is no doubt that sailors, traders, and settlers from the narrow strip of coast below Mount Lebanon that the Greeks labeled Phoenicia had a disproportionate impact on the ancient Mediterranean. Their heyday came after the collapse of the great powers of Hittite Anatolia, Kassite Babylonia, and Mycenaean Greece around 1200 BCE: merchants from Levantine ports including Tyre, Sidon, Byblos, and Beirut (fig. I.1) seized a new set of opportunities, trading cedar from Mount Lebanon, along with exquisite items crafted from metal, ivory, and glass, for raw metals from the west. In the process they refined the art of navigation and—so it was said—taught the Greeks another of their inventions, the alphabet.[5] They traveled the length of the Mediterranean and beyond (fig. I.2), and from at least the ninth century BCE established new settlements from Cyprus on their doorstep to the Atlantic coast of Spain, long before the Greeks began to migrate west. The most famous of these western Phoenician settlements was Carthage, founded according to legend by the Tyrian princess Dido. Carthage became a major power in its own right, vying with Rome for supremacy in the west, and under Hannibal Barca almost winning it. The Greek historian Polybius, who witnessed Carthage's final destruction by the Romans in 146 BCE, said that it seemed at the time to be the richest city in the world.[6]

Despite all this, Phoenician history and culture have traditionally been underappreciated by classical historians and archaeologists, who are more interested in the glory that was Greece and the grandeur that was Rome. The language is taught, when it is taught at all, in Near Eastern or Oriental studies departments; the material remains are often studied as biblical or prehistoric archaeology; and the lack of surviving literature means that the Phoenicians seem simply irrelevant to most classicists brought up on Greek and Latin texts. One of the rare exceptions in the English-speaking world was Miriam Balmuth, whose work on archaeology and numismatics regularly analyzed the Phoenician contribution to the history of Sardinia, Spain, and the Near East, as well as blazing a trail for later women scholars to walk in her wake; it was a great honor to give lectures at Tufts University on this topic in her name.

However, my intention here is not simply to rescue the Phoenicians from their undeserved obscurity. Quite the opposite, in fact: I'm going to

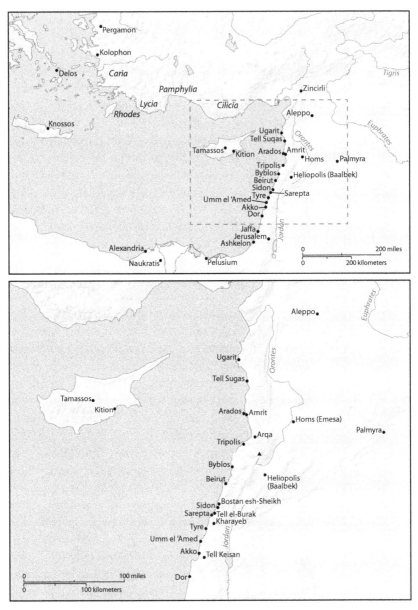

I.1 The Levant and neighboring regions, with places mentioned in the text. The inset depicts the northwestern Levant and Cyprus in greater detail.

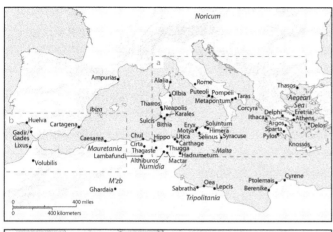

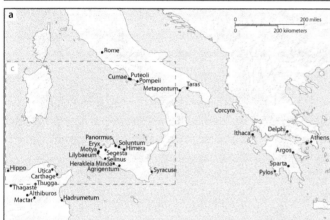

I.2 The western Mediterranean and neighboring regions, with places mentioned in the text. Inset a depicts the central Mediterranean; inset b the far west, and inset c Sicily and Sardinia.

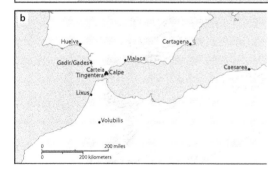

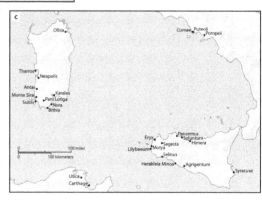

start by making the case that they did not in fact exist as a self-conscious collective or "people." The term "Phoenician" itself is a Greek invention, and there is no good evidence in our surviving ancient sources that these Phoenicians saw themselves, or acted, in collective terms above the level of the city or in many cases simply the family. The first and so far the only person known to have called himself a Phoenician in the ancient world was the Greek novelist Heliodorus of Emesa (modern Homs in Syria) in the third or fourth century CE, a claim made well outside the traditional chronological and geographical boundaries of Phoenician history, and one that I will in any case call into question later in this book.

Instead, then, this book explores the communities and identities that were important to the ancient people we have learned to call Phoenicians, and asks why the idea of being Phoenician has been so enthusiastically adopted by other people and peoples—from ancient Greece and Rome, to the emerging nations of early modern Europe, to contemporary Mediterranean nation-states. It is these afterlives, I will argue, that provide the key to the modern conception of the Phoenicians as a "people." As Ernest Gellner put it, "Nationalism is not the awakening of nations to self-consciousness: it invents nations where they do not exist".[7] In the case of the Phoenicians, I will suggest, modern nationalism invented and then sustained an ancient nation.

Identities have attracted a great deal of scholarly attention in recent years, serving as the academic marginalia to a series of crucially important political battles for equality and freedom.[8] We have learned from these investigations that identities are not simple and essential truths into which we are born, but that they are constructed by the social and cultural contexts in which we live, by other people, and by ourselves—which is not to say that they are necessarily freely chosen, or that they are not genuinely and often fiercely felt: to describe something as imagined is not to dismiss it as imaginary.[9] Our identities are also multiple: we identify and are identified by gender, class, age, religion, and many other things, and we can be more than one of any of those things at once, whether those identities are compatible or contradictory.[10] Furthermore, identities are variable across both time and space: we play—and we are assigned—different roles with different people and in different contexts, and they have differing levels of importance to us in different situations.[11]

In particular, the common assumption that we all define ourselves as a member of a specific people or "ethnic group," a collective linked by shared origins, ancestry, and often ancestral territory, rather than simply by contemporary political, social, or cultural ties, remains just that—an assumption.[12] It is also a notion that has been linked to distinctive nineteenth-century

European perspectives on nationalism and identity,[13] and one that sits uncomfortably with counterexamples from other times and places.[14]

The now-discredited categorization and labeling of African "tribes" by colonial administrators, missionaries, and anthropologists of the nineteenth and twentieth centuries provides many well-known examples, illustrating the way in which the "ethnic assumption" can distort interpretations of other people's affiliations and self-understanding.[15] The Banande of Zaire, for instance, used to refer to themselves simply as *bayira* ("cultivators" or "workers"), and it was not until the creation of a border between the British Protectorate of Uganda and the Belgian Congo in 1885 that they came to be clearly delineated from another group of *bayira* now called Bakonzo.[16] Even more strikingly, the Tonga of Zambia, as they were named by outsiders, did not regard themselves as a unified group differentiated from their neighbors, with the consequence that they tended to disperse and reassimilate among other groups.[17] Where such groups do have self-declared ethnic identities, they were often first imposed from without, by more powerful regional actors. The subsequent local adoption of those labels, and of the very concepts of ethnicity and tribe in some African contexts, illustrates the effects that external identifications can have on internal affiliations and self-understandings.[18] Such external labeling is not of course a phenomenon limited to Africa or to Western colonialism: other examples include the ethnic categorization of the Miao and the Yao in Han China, and similar processes carried out by the state in the Soviet Union.[19]

Such processes can be dangerous. When Belgian colonial authorities encountered the central African kingdom of Rwanda, they redeployed labels used locally at the time to identify two closely related groups occupying different positions in the social and political hierarchy to categorize the population instead into two distinct "races" of Hutus (identified as the indigenous farmers) and Tutsis (thought to be a more civilized immigrant population).[20] This was not easy to do, and in 1930 a Belgian census attempting to establish which classification should be recorded on the identity cards of their subjects resorted in some cases to counting cows: possession of ten or more made you a Tutsi.[21] Between April and July 1994, more than half a million Tutsis were killed by Hutus, sometimes using their identity cards to verify the "race" of their victims.

The ethnic assumption also raises methodological problems for historians. The fundamental difficulty with labels like "Phoenician" is that they offer answers to questions about historical explanation before they have even been asked. They assume an underlying commonality between the people they designate that cannot easily be demonstrated; they produce new identities where they did not to our knowledge exist; and they freeze in time particular identities that were in fact in a constant process of construction, from inside and out. As Paul Gilroy has argued, "ethnic absolutism" can homogenize what are in reality significant differences.[22] These labels also encourage historical explanation on a very large and abstract scale, focusing attention on the role of the putative generic identity at the expense of more concrete, conscious, and interesting communities and their stories, obscuring in this case the importance of the family, the city, and the region, not to mention the marking of other social identities such as gender, class, and status. In sum, they provide too easy a way out of actually reading the historical evidence.

As a result, recent scholarship tends to see ethnicity not as a timeless fact about a region or group, but as an ideology that emerges at certain times, in particular social and historical circumstances, and, especially at moments of change or crisis: at the origins of a state, for instance, or after conquest, or in the context of migration, and not always even then.[23] In some cases, we can even trace this development over time: James C. Scott cites the example of the Cossacks on Russia's frontiers, people used as cavalry by the tsars, Ottomans, and Poles, who "were, at the outset, nothing more and nothing less than runaway serfs from all over European Russia, who accumulated at the frontier. They became, depending on their locations, different Cossack "hosts": the Don (for the Don River basin) Cossacks, the Azov (Sea) Cossacks, and so on."[24]

Ancient historians and archaeologists have been at the forefront of these new ethnicity studies, emphasizing the historicity, flexibility, and varying importance of ethnic identity in the ancient Mediterranean.[25] They have described, for instance, the emergence of new ethnic groups such as the Moabites and Israelites in the Near East in the aftermath of the collapse of the Bronze Age empires and the "crystallisation of commonalities" among Greeks in the Archaic period.[26] They have also traced subsequent changes in the ethnic content and formulation of these identifications: in relation to "Hellenicity," for example, scholars have delineated a shift in the fifth century BCE from an "aggregative" conception of Greek identity founded largely on shared history and traditions to a somewhat more oppositional approach based on distinction from non-Greeks, especially Persians, and then another in the fourth century BCE, when Greek intellectuals themselves debated whether Greekness should be based on a shared past or on shared culture and values in the contemporary world.[27] By the Hellenistic period, at least in Egypt, the term "Hellene" (Greek) was in official documents simply an indication of a privileged tax status, and those so labeled could be Jews, Thracians—or, indeed, Egyptians.[28]

Despite all this fascinating work, there is a danger that the considerable recent interest in the production, mechanisms, and even decline of ancient ethnicity has obscured its relative rarity. Striking examples of the construction of ethnic groups in the ancient world do not mean that such phenomena became the norm.[29] There are good reasons to suppose in principle that without modern levels of literacy, education, communication, mobility, and exchange, ancient communal identities would have tended to form on much smaller scales than those at stake in most modern discussions of ethnicity, and that without written histories and genealogies people might have placed less emphasis on the concepts of ancestry and blood-ties that at some level underlie most identifications of ethnic groups.[30] And in practice, the evidence suggests that collective identities throughout the ancient Mediterranean were indeed largely articulated at the level of city-states and that notions of common descent or historical association were rarely the relevant criterion for constructing "groupness" in these communities: in Greek cities, for instance, mutual identification tended to be based on political, legal, and, to a limited extent, cultural criteria,[31] while the Romans famously emphasized their mixed origins in their foundation legends and regularly manumitted their foreign slaves, whose descendants then became full Roman citizens.[32]

This means that some of the best-known "peoples" of antiquity may not actually have been peoples at all. Recent studies have shown that such familiar groups as the Celts of ancient Britain and Ireland and the Minoans of ancient Crete were essentially invented in the modern period by the archaeologists who first studied or "discovered" them,[33] and even the collective identity of the Greeks can be called into question. As S. Rebecca Martin has recently pointed out, "there is no clear recipe for the archetypal Hellene," and despite our evidence for elite intellectual discussion of the nature of Greekness, it is questionable how much "being Greek" meant to most Greeks: less, no doubt, than to modern scholars.[34] The Phoenicians, I will suggest in what follows, fall somewhere in the middle—unlike the Minoans or the Atlantic Celts, there is ancient evidence for a conception of them as a group, but unlike the Greeks, this evidence is entirely external—and they provide another good case study of the extent to which an assumption of a collective identity in the ancient Mediterranean can mislead.[35]

The book falls into three parts, expanded versions of the three Balmuth lectures I gave at Tufts. The first contrasts the familiar picture of the Phoenicians as a coherent people or culture with the very different story told by our ancient sources. Chapter 1 situates the modern image of the Phoenician people in the rhetoric and politics of the modern era. I begin in twentieth century Lebanon and Tunisia, where new nation-states found it helpful to invoke the Phoenicians as literal and spiritual ancestors, and argue that such modern uses of the ancient Phoenicians rely on an underlying conceptualization of the Phoenicians themselves as a "nation," which was in itself a relatively new idea, a product of nationalist interpretations of antiquity in nineteenth-century Europe.

In chapter 2, I show that the ancient evidence for self-identification as what we would call an ethnic group is by contrast very weak. Although we have more than ten thousand inscriptions in Phoenician, almost all of which are votive or funerary, and so identify a dedicant or defunct, they identify that person according to their family relationships, or, occasionally, their cities or islands of origin. We have no evidence before late antiquity of people referring to themselves as Phoenician, or using any other collective self-description, or for a sense of shared ancestry, origins, or native land. In chapter 3, I turn from internal to external perceptions, and in particular to the literature of the Greeks and Romans to show that even when they defined "Phoenicians" as a collective, they used the term as a rather vague label invoking a variety of social and cultural distinctions, including linguistic differences, rather than to denote a distinct ethnic group linked by history, territory, or descent.

In the second part, I move on from texts to objects and practice, looking at how Phoenician-speaking people acted and interacted, at home and abroad, without starting from the assumption that they were acting as a "people." My argument in chapter 4 is that there is no evidence from material culture for a larger Phoenician civilization or identity until Carthage began to mint coinage at the end of the fifth century BCE depicting a palm tree (in Greek, *phoinix*). Even this, however, was not so much an embrace of collective identity as the exploitation of an external notion of Phoenicity to consolidate Carthage's growing regional power. I look particularly at the effects of settlement overseas, since it is sometimes suggested that distance strengthens identities based on a common homeland, but although Levantine communities throughout the Mediterranean engaged in a great deal of cultural and technological exchange with each other, these ties were partial and ambivalent, and they also cultivated associations with many other peoples and places.

At the same time, the dynamics of migration did produce new sets of cultural and political links between subsets of Phoenician-speakers that transcended familial, professional, and civic ties. In the rest of part 2, I explore two examples of group-making in the religious sphere: the cult of Baal Hammon (chapter 5), which from the eighth century BCE separated a relatively small group of migrants from the Levant and tied them closely to each other through the practice of child sacrifice, and the cult of Melqart (chapter 6), which from at least the fourth century BCE linked a much larger number of migrant communities throughout the west back to the homeland. Carthage was a central player in both these communities, and I will make the case that the new level of political, religious, and cultural interconnection across the Phoenician-speaking Mediterranean in the fourth century coincided conveniently, again, with that city's rise to imperial power.

The final part of this book is about the vivid afterlives of these phantom Phoenicians. I will argue that despite the view taken in most textbooks that Phoenician history comes to an end with the conquests of Alexander in the east and the destruction of Carthage in the west, interest in Phoenician culture and the Phoenician past actually increased in the Hellenistic and Roman periods. This interest was however driven by outsiders' perceptions in the east (chapter 7) and the west (chapter 8), and it was premised on cultural identification rather than ethnic identity. While the original Levantine cities and settlements remained focused on their own local past and local disputes, "Phoenicianisms" were used both to contest and to promote the imperial power of larger states.

This was a pattern that continued in later European history, when identifications with the Phoenicians featured regularly in the construction of national identities from the early modern period. My final chapter traces another set of examples that takes us back to the beginning: the intertwined identifications with the Phoenicians by English and Irish intellectuals from the sixteenth to the twentieth century. English intellectual fantasies established historical roots and authority for the Kingdom of Great Britain in a Phoenician past, while as we have seen, Irish scholars used imagined Phoenician settlement on their island to oppose British imperial ambitions there. Long before the era of nation-states—and the modern scholarly accounts of the Phoenicians themselves as a "nation" with which I begin—the Phoenicians were contributing to nationalist ideologies and being constructed by them.

There is one very obvious objection to my basic approach here, which is that in arguing that ancient Phoenician-speakers rarely if ever identified themselves as such, I am arguing from silence. A lack of evidence for collective identity is not evidence for its absence, especially when we have no surviving Phoenician literature and relatively little material evidence at all. Some would argue that the loss of the kind of literary sources in which Phoenicians would have more naturally expressed and explored larger communal identities gives us a false impression of their self-understandings, although there is no positive indication that such literature ever in fact existed in Phoenician, and I suggest in this book that a lack of shared identity may even explain why it never developed. Others would make the even stronger point that the major coastal cities of the Levant were built around good ports that mostly survive to this day, obscuring the ancient levels, and even where they have been exposed—as at the sites of ancient Tyre—excavation has understandably tended to stop at the spectacular Roman levels. And although the material evidence from the western Mediterranean is more abundant, it is poorly published and understood, and even the extensive epigraphic record is almost entirely composed of formulaic dedications from sanctuaries. A chance find of a new inscription could produce a self-identified ancient Phoenician tomorrow.

Mine is not, however, so much an argument from silence as an argument *for* silence: a silence that can open up other spaces of investigation. I cannot demonstrate that no one in the ancient Mediterranean ever thought of her- or himself as Phoenician, nor will I try to do so. But without positive evidence for such a collective identification, I will insist that we cannot arbitrarily adopt one as our working assumption. We don't have to plaster over this gap in our knowledge by applying an arbitrary label according to our own taste: we can choose instead to attend to the evidence that we do have and to the stories it tells. This book is not about the lack of evidence for Phoenician identity; it is about what we can do with that fact.

I should also emphasize right from the start that the suggestion that the Phoenicians were not a self-conscious collective, or even a clearly delineated historical civilization, is not new: this point has been made in a variety of ways in recent years by a large number of scholars, including Claude Baurain, Corinne Bonnet, Eduardo Ferrer Albelda, Giuseppe Garbati, Helena Pastor Borgoñon, Tatiana Pedrazzi, Jonathan Prag, Michael Sommer, Erik van Dongen, Nicholas Vella and Paolo Xella.[36] My work is deeply indebted to theirs, as it attempts to extend it in space, across the whole of the Mediterranean, in time, from the Bronze Age to late antiquity, and in scope, to suggest a series of alternative modes of identification and association among Phoenician-speakers in the ancient world, as well as by contextualizing the modern idea of the Phoenicians in nationalist discourse.

It is a pleasure to acknowledge the numerous debts I have accumulated over the course of this project. First and foremost, I want to thank Bruce and Becky Hitchner, Noah Barrientos, and everyone else at Tufts for making me so welcome when I delivered the Balmuth Lectures there in 2012. I owe particular thanks to Bruce for the invitation, for the interest he has taken in the project before and after the lectures, and for his helpful comments on the first draft of this book.

As I have explored a wide range of topics within and beyond "Phoenician studies" in relation to this project, I have also benefited greatly from the advice, ideas, questions, and unpublished papers of many generous friends and colleagues, including (in addition to those mentioned below) Maria Giulia Amadasi Guzzo, Ana Arancibia Román, Stefan Ardeleanu, Piero Bartoloni, Imed Ben Jerbania, Lisa Bendall, Sven Betjes, Amelie Beyhum, Corinne Bonnet, Annelies Cazemier, Angelos Chaniotis, Moheddine Chaouali, Bruno D'Andrea, Helen Dixon, Roald Docter, Avraham Faust, Lisa Fentress, Ahmed Ferjaoui, Eduardo Ferrer Albelda, Peta Fowler, Suzanne Frey-Kupper, Giuseppe Garbati, Brien Garnand, Carlos Gómez Bellard, Joseph Greene, Jonathan Hall, Stephen Heyworth, Susan Hitch, Katherine Ibbett, Alicia Jiménez, Kostis Kourelis, Robin Lane Fox, José Luis López Castro, John Ma, Emanuele Madrigali, Patchen Markell, Andrew Meadows, Richard Miles, Barack Monnickendam-Givon, Teresa Morgan, Bärbel Morstadt, Ana María Niveau de Villedary y Mariñas, Matthew Nicholls, Ida Oggiano, Adriano Orsingher, Emanuele Papi, Raj Patel, Nicholas Purcell, Yousif Qasmiyeh, Eugene Rogan, Andrea Roppa, Philipp von Rummel, Hélène Sader, Brian Schmidt, Lucia Sheikho, Bert Smith, Rosalind Thomas, Claire Weeda, Tim Whitmarsh, Andrew Wilson, Greg Woolf, Liv Yarrow, and José Ángel Zamora López. I am especially grateful to Irad Malkin, whose generous commentary and friendly skepticism have fostered this project from beginning to end, and to my longtime collaborator Jonathan Prag, for his advice, ideas, photography, and encyclopedic memory for bibliography.

I have also received a great deal of practical help along the way from my Oxford colleagues at Worcester College, in the Faculty of Classics, and in the Humanities Division, as well as from that other great Oxford institution, Combibos Coffee House. I finished a first draft of this book during a period of leave funded by a Zvi Meitar/Vice-Chancellor Oxford University Research Prize in the Humanities, and I am very grateful to Mr Meitar and to the university for that opportunity. I also owe particular thanks to Lorne Thyssen for support in various Phoenician endeavors, and to Fiona Thyssen for giving me a quiet and beautiful place to write at a crucial stage in the development of the argument I present. And at a greater distance now, I am still thankful for the broad training and wide horizons provided by the Ancient History and Mediterranean Archaeology doctoral program at the University of California, Berkeley, and to my PhD supervisor Erich Gruen and the other members of my committee, Andrew Stewart and Mia Fuller, who all remain personal and intellectual inspirations.

I have tried out some of my ideas in talks at a number of universities—Bristol, Brown, Cambridge, Malaga, Oxford, and Princeton—as well as at a colloquium at El Khroub (Constantine) organized by the Algerian Haut-Commissariat à l'amazighité, and I am very grateful for those invitations, and for the comments and questions I received on those occasions. I have also benefited from participation in the Spanish research project "La construcción de la identidad fenicia en el Imperio romano" (HAR2010-14893), financed by the Ministerio de Economía y Competitividad, Spain, and directed by Manuel Álvarez Martí-Aguilar.

A significant number of the arguments proposed in this book have also been discussed in essays and articles along the way, most of which were collaborative publications.[37] I owe a huge debt of gratitude to my coauthors, Daniel Hadas, Bob Kerr, Matthew McCarty, Neil McLynn, Valentina Melchiorri, Peter van Dommelen, Nick Vella, and Paolo Xella, not only for the expertise that they brought to those publications, but for the lengthy and illuminating discussions that went into producing them and the many other ways in which they have all helped me with this project.

As this book reached a conclusion, Ilya Afanasyev, Manuel Álvarez Martí-Aguilar, Olivier Hekster, Alfred Hirt, Tamar Hodos, Wissam Khalil, Katy Mullin, Miri Rubin, Scott Scullion, and Mark Woolmer read final chapter drafts, sometimes two or three; and Denis Feeney, Henry Hurst, Carolina López-Ruiz, Becky Martin, and Peter van Dommelen read the whole text. I can't thank them and the readers for Princeton University Press enough for the improvements their comments have made; I can only apologize that I have not taken all of their excellent advice. Alex Wilson helped me put together the final manuscript, saving me from a number of mistakes at the last minute; he and Aneurin Ellis-Evans helped me acquire the images and permission to publish them; and Tzveta Manolova made sketches for several of the maps. I am very grateful to them all, as I am to my editor Rob Tempio for his help, encouragement, and excellent company, to Ellen Foos, Matt Rohal, and Ryan Mulligan for shepherding the manuscript through the press with great patience and cordiality, to Beth Giantagna for unflappable copyediting, and to Jan Williams for compiling the index.

My final thanks must, however, go to my family, and in particular to my parents, Richard and Christine; to my stepfather, Jim; to my parents-in-law Biddy and Henry; and to my husband Christopher, who read endless drafts as I worked on this book, and made me a lot of tea. I couldn't have written it without him, Ptolemy, and Andromache. Naturally none of those listed here should be taken to endorse my arguments and interpretations, especially the cats, and I remain responsible for the remaining errors.

I have tried as far as I can in what follows to retain the tone of the Balmuth lectures, which were delivered to a refreshingly mixed group of students, graduates, and faculty from a range of disciplines across the humanities and social sciences. This is not therefore primarily a book for specialists—who will already know the evidence presented here and will have their own views on my interpretation of it—nor is it a textbook; instead, what I present is a set of hypotheses, inviting debate and dissent. This means that the book necessarily gives only a very partial perspective on Phoenician history and geography, relying on examples and case studies rather than exhaustive description and catalogue. Two of the bigger and more regrettable geographical gaps are Cyprus and the far western Mediterranean: for the latter, see now Celestino and López-Ruiz (2016). For those who would like to know more about the people and places discussed in this book, the most up-to-date syntheses of research on Phoenician history and archaeology are Bondì et al. (2009), Elayi (2013), and Morstadt (2015). English language overviews include Markoe (2000), Aubet (2001), Woolmer (2011), and, with a particular emphasis on Carthage and the west, Lancel (1995), van Dommelen and Gómez Bellard (2008b), Hoyos (2010), and Miles (2010). Recent essay collections give a glimpse of current scholarly preoccupations: Jiménez (2010), Xella (2013b), Quinn and Vella (2014b), and Garbati and Pedrazzi (2015). Translations are my own unless otherwise indicated; names in English of places and people are those that seem to me most familiar, and therefore least distracting.

PART I

Phantom Phoenicians

CHAPTER 1

There Are No Camels in Lebanon

We start again, this time in 1946, and this time in Phoenicia itself. Three years after Lebanon gained its independence from France, the young Druze socialist politician Kamal Joumblatt gave a lecture in Arabic at the Cénacle libanais, a newly established forum for writers and politicians in Beirut, on "My Mission as a Member of Parliament." His speech ended in an appeal to "hope and confidence," as he reminded his listeners that their new state's glorious history dated back to the ancient Phoenicians:

> On this beautiful golden coast, which thousands of years ago witnessed the emergence of the first civic state, and the growth and diffusion of the first national idea, and the establishment of the first maritime empire, and the emergence of the first form of representative democratic government . . . in this rare spot in the world, where the sea and the mountain meet, embrace, and communicate . . . and in an internal national consciousness, as if Lebanon was self-conscious . . . in this country that has always been open to all the global intellectual currents of human civilization . . . in this ancient young country . . . which gave the world values, ideas, men, institutions, and glory, it is right for us to be optimistic."[1]

Joumblatt's approach to that crucial question for any young country— "Who are we?"—would have been very familiar to his listeners. "New Phoenicianism," or the idea that the modern Lebanese were the inheritors of an ancient Phoenician legacy, had been a significant political and cultural movement in Lebanon since the breakup of the Ottoman Empire, and it is one that has lasted in some quarters to the present day. Its fundamental claim is that the nation of Lebanon is a timeless entity, with a distinctive character and culture determined by its distinctive geography, and a history going back to the city-states of the ancient Phoenicians, long before the arrival of the Arabs in the seventh century CE.

The movement was originally championed by Christians, and in particular Maronite Catholics, but Joumblatt's words capture some of its most important aspects: on the one hand the glorification of the Phoenicians themselves, with an emphasis on their maritime achievements and their contributions to world civilization, and on the other the connections and parallels between them and the modern Lebanese, with an emphasis on the unique geography they shared. But Joumblatt does not just connect the Phoenicians with his new nation through history and geography; he makes them responsible for the idea of the nation itself, reflecting the underlying premise of this modern Phoenician rhetoric that the ancient Phoenicians too formed a coherent "people" or national community.

This chapter argues that the modern notion of the Phoenicians as a people with a shared history, culture, and identity—found in modern textbooks and scholarship as well as in postcolonial political rhetoric about Phoenician forebears—is the product of relatively recent European nationalist ideologies. I then turn in the rest of part 1 to the difficulties of reconciling this modern picture with the fragmentary ancient evidence. Lebanese Phoenicianism is a good place to start, a striking case study in the way in which we moderns can bend the ancient world to our own experiences, and to our nationalist assumptions and ideologies, including the notions that ethnic identities are natural, timeless facts and that ancient "nations" can and even should map onto nation-states.

THE YOUNG PHOENICIANS

The idea that the modern Lebanese were the inheritors of a Phoenician legacy was originally suggested by Lebanese scholars in the nineteenth century.[2] The Maronite Catholic historian Tannus al-Shidyaq made the first explicit association between Phoenicia and Lebanon, and between the mountain and the sea, in his *History of the Notables of Mount Lebanon* (1859): his first chapter, on the borders and populations of Lebanon, discusses the location and population of Mount Lebanon and then those of the "Phoenician cities of Lebanon" (*mudun lubnan al-finiqiyya*).[3] The idea that the Lebanese were in some sense Phoenician quickly gained traction in the early twentieth century among emigrant Lebanese communities in Egypt and the United States, aided by US government documents published in 1911 defining new immigrants from the Syrian coast not as Arabs, but as Christian descendants of the Phoenicians.[4]

It only became popular in Lebanon itself, however, in the aftermath of the First World War. In the context of the collapse of the Ottoman Empire, which had held the region since the sixteenth century, and as the European powers carved up the Middle East, a loose collection of entrepreneurs, intellectuals, and political activists became fascinated by the idea of a link with their celebrated ancient predecessors. It was a largely urban, bourgeois, francophone grouping—one that saw the Phoenicians as natural merchants and champions of protocapitalist free enterprise.[5] These "young Phoenicians" were not for the most part churchgoers, but they tended to have a Catholic education and perspective—most of them were themselves Maronites, and almost all, including Kamal Joumblatt, had attended the Jesuit Université Saint-Joseph in Beirut, where French missionaries had long encouraged the study of local pre-Islamic history and languages.[6] They also relied to a significant degree on the work of French and francophone scholars, including those at the Université Saint-Joseph itself.[7]

Central to the ideology of the young Phoenicians was the conviction that Lebanon and the Lebanese were not Arab. They emphasized instead their metaphorical, spiritual, and sometimes even literal descent from much earlier inhabitants of their distinctive geographical space, where Mount Lebanon cuts off the coastal strip from the rest of Syria, a region they always characterized as peculiarly western or Mediterranean by contrast with the Arabs farther east: "there are no camels in Lebanon," as the slogan goes.[8] They argued among other things that the language spoken in Lebanon was influenced as much by the local ancient languages of Phoenician, Aramaic, and Syriac as by colloquial Arabic, and the poet Said Akl, who died in November 2014 at the age of 103, even invented an alphabet based on Latin rather than Arabic letters in which to write this "Lebanese" language.[9] This rejection of Arab heritage was a long-lived phenomenon: as late as the 1950s, the widely respected Maronite historian Philip Hitti, who taught at Princeton and Harvard, noted that "according to anthropological researches, the prevailing type among the Lebanese—Maronites and Druzes—is the short-headed brachycephalic one . . . in striking contrast to the long-headed type prevailing among the Bedouins of the Syrian Desert and the North Arabians."[10]

New Phoenicianism was closely connected with the broader, and also largely Maronite, struggle for a Lebanese state separate from Syria and the wider Arab world.[11] The Phoenicians provided an attractive prototype and parallel for the new state as well as a convenient alternative to Arab origins, but they also played another very specific role in this Lebanist rhetoric. Within the Ottoman Empire, the area of Mount Lebanon itself had formed a majority Maronite *Mutasarrifate* or privileged administrative region since 1861, alongside a series of other Levantine provinces and sub-provinces that included the coastal cities (fig. 1.1). With the whole of that empire on the negotiating table at Versailles in 1919, most "Lebanists" were arguing for the extension of the old *Mutasarrifate* to form a new state of

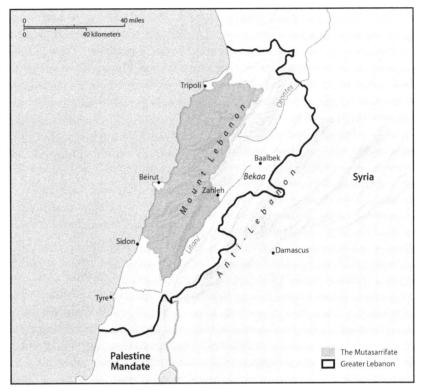

1.1 The Ottoman Mutasarrifate of Mount Lebanon (1861), and Greater Lebanon under French Mandate (1920).

"Greater Lebanon" under a French mandate, which would also include the traditionally Muslim areas of the Bekaa Valley to the east and the cities of Tripoli, Tyre, Sidon, and Beirut to the west. But to make the case for Greater Lebanon as the natural answer to the national question, the Lebanists had to tie together Mount Lebanon, the traditional home in modern times of both the Maronites and the Druze, and the Mediterranean coast, where the ancient Phoenicians built their cities. They did so by positing on the one hand a natural economic relationship between the mountain and the sea, and on the other a long-standing historical connection between the Phoenicians and Maronites that preceded and then by-passed the Arabs: the Maronites had assimilated with the Phoenician coastal population on Mount Lebanon in the sixth century CE, converting them to Christianity along the way.[12]

The neo-Phoenician movement coalesced around the short-lived journal *La revue phénicienne,* published for just four issues in 1919, and strongly

Lebanist in its politics. The first issue appeared in July, immediately after the signing of the Treaty of Versailles on June 28, and at a stage when the future of Lebanon itself and its future relationship to both Syria and France were still quite unclear. The contributors were for the most part Beiruti businessmen,[13] and much of the issue was devoted to the economy: the financial case for Greater or "natural" Lebanon, the country's resources, the hotel and tobacco industries, the problems of small businesses, and the re-provisioning of Beirut. Plenty of space was given to political issues as well: the advantages of a French mandate, the disadvantages of the American King-Crane Commission sent to investigate local attitudes to the partitioning of the Ottoman Empire, and the proper basis of a state. There was also local history, literature, literary commentary, and a diatribe by a medical professor against the corset.

Naturally, the Phoenicians were also present. The issue begins with an introductory page attributed to "L'histoire," presumably written by the editor, Charles Corm, outlining the Phoenicians' history, character, and achievements. They were above all men of the sea, sailing as far as Great Britain; liberal, peaceful; bringing the world civilization, commerce, and industry. Although the author understands that the city-states of the "land" (*contrée*) of Phoenicia were politically autonomous, he presents them as united not only by a common culture but by a common proto-monotheism and unusual rituals: "they all worshipped a higher Divinity to whom they sacrificed human victims."[14] In another article, Jacques Tabet goes further, describing *la Phénicie* as a "country" (*pays*) and suggesting that in the tenth century the rest of "the Phoenician people" (*le peuple phénicien*) had recognized the supremacy of King Abibaal of Tyre—about whom we in fact know barely anything beyond his name—whereby he "brought about the political unification of Phoenicia."[15] The historical importance of this entirely speculative point becomes clear in the essay on the King-Crane Commission signed by "Caf Remime" (that is, the letters KRM, or "Corm" in Phoenician script): "we want this nation [of Lebanon] because it has always come first in all the pages of our history."[16]

A PHOENICIAN NATION

Phoenicianism was by no means the only nationalist movement in the early-twentieth-century Middle East to identify with the great civilizations of the past, and through them with the Mediterranean and the West. Other examples include Pharaonism in Egypt, Assyrianism and Arameanism in Syria, and Canaanism in Palestine, whose adherents looked back to a "Phoenician-Hebrew" Mediterranean civilization dating to the time of King David and King Solomon that colonized the west, a model that was used both for and against Zionism.[17] Furthermore, in Lebanon itself supporters of a "Greater Syria" rather than an independent Lebanon could also appeal to the Canaanites as forebears, and even as the inventors of national sentiments,[18] and there were also Christian as well as Muslim supporters of an even larger Arab nationalism who argued, with the Greek historian Herodotus, that the Phoenicians were immigrants from the Arabian peninsula, and therefore that they actually provided Lebanon with an Arab heritage.[19]

Why was ancient history so important to these modern political movements? In all these cases, not only nation-states but national identities of any kind were a recent import from Europe in a region where polities had previously taken quite different forms and where "identity realms were more local and limited: the family, village, church and so forth."[20] Much recent scholarship has emphasized that nations are not a "natural" form of social organization, but a constructed one; in the words of Caspar Hirschi, they are "not formed by 'objective' criteria like common territory, language, habits, ancestry, fate, etc. but by the common belief in such criteria."[21] Even when geographical, linguistic, or biological links between people do persist over time, it is the communal choice to recognize and value them (or some of them) that creates a national identity. And to justify a new and unfamiliar collective identity, national movements had to create new, shared myths of origin and historical memories for all their citizens. As Eric Hobsbawm puts it, "Nations are historically novel entities pretending to have existed for a very long time."[22] As Asher Kaufman has noted, appeals to ancient ancestors served to distinguish aspiring nations from their neighbors (especially their Arab neighbors), "to highlight their own cultural uniqueness, and emphasize the historical kinship of their own community."[23] And as James C. Scott has remarked of another historical context, the result "is a historical fable that projects the nation and its dominant people backward, obscuring discontinuity, contingency, and fluid identities. Such accounts serve, as Walter Benjamin reminded us, to naturalize the progression and necessity of the state in general and the nation-state in particular."[24]

The reliance of successful nationalism in the present on the perception of a shared past was emphasized at the time by the French orientalist Ernest Renan, in one of the first descriptions of the "nation" as a construct rather than a natural fact. In a lecture in Paris in 1882, Renan asked, "Qu'est-ce qu'une nation?" (What is a nation?) and found his answer not in blood or descent, but in a collective will and collective memories: "A nation is a soul, a spiritual principle. Two things, which to tell the truth are but one, constitute this soul, this spiritual principle. One is in the past, the other in the present. One is the possession in common of a rich legacy of memories; the other is consent in the here and now, the desire to live together, the will to preserve the value of the heritage that has been collectively received."[25]

For Renan, these "memories" were not necessarily real, and he also emphasized the importance of forgetfulness in the creation of a national consciousness: "The essence of a nation is that all its members have a great amount in common, and also that they have all forgotten a great deal."[26] This nostalgic combination of present consent and creative memories is exactly what the neo-Phoenicians in Lebanon cultivated as they saw their new nation into being, and for some of them at least, this tactic was self-conscious and explicit: in 1935, the banker and politician Michel Chiha noted with approval "the conception of Renan . . . who sees the formation of a nation as nothing but the will of the inhabitants of that nation" and that "the principle of Lebanism rests in the exaltation of a glorious past [and] in that of an entirely abstract desire for cohesion."[27]

THE FRENCH MANDATE

In April 1920, the Treaty of Sèvres handed control of Syria, including Lebanon, to France, and from September 1920 "Greater Lebanon" was administered as a separate state within the French "Mandate for Syria and the Lebanon."[28] The French adoption of the Lebanist program is understandable: the desire to distinguish between Lebanon and Syria played into the hands of their colonial policy to encourage local identities such as Phoenician and Lebanese at the expense of the larger and potentially more troublesome contemporary regional identities of Syrian and Arab. Like the Ottomans, the French found it useful to divide the region under their mandate into a number of mini-states, which also included entities for the Alawites, the Druze, and for the areas around Alexandretta, Aleppo, and Damascus (fig. 1.2).[29]

The New Phoenicians flourished in politics, administration, business, and banking during the Mandate years, when it was thought that Lebanon could become the "Switzerland of the East," with its multiple languages, alpine tourism, and attractive financial services.[30] French nationalist scholarship continued to be central to their worldview: in 1934, for instance, Charles Corm dedicated his epic nationalist poem *La montagne inspirée*

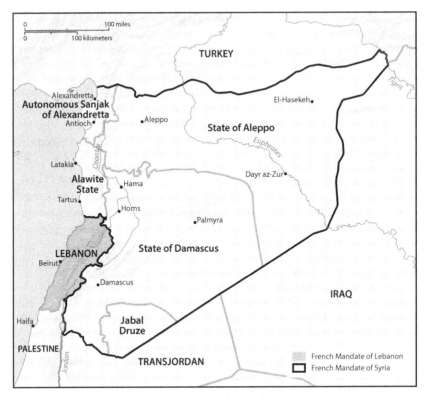

1.2 Lebanon and Syria under the new French Mandate in 1920.

to Maurice Barrès, who had popularized the notion that "soil, geography, and climate constituted the physical anchors of the nation," and to Victor Bérard, whose *Les phéniciens et l'Odyssée* (1902) portrayed the ancient Phoenicians as the source of Hellenic culture and presented the *Odyssey* as a work written from a Phoenician ship.[31] At the same time, the French authorities in Lebanon actively encouraged associations with the Phoenicians. They issued coinage with images of a Phoenician ship, as featured on the ancient civic coinage of the region, and a cedar of Mount Lebanon (fig. 1.3), and planned two very different national museums, a Lebanese one focused on the Phoenicians, and a Syrian one showcasing the Islamic and Arab past.[32] When the former was inaugurated in Beirut in 1937, the front cover of the first issue of its journal boasted another Phoenician ship.[33]

It is perhaps not surprising that at the beginning of the Mandate period there was an "effective boycott of the state by all but a handful of the Sunnite Muslims," but this faded over time,[34] and the New Phoenicians for their part gradually retreated from their strategy of privileging the French

1.3 Five-piastre coin minted in Lebanon under the French Mandate in 1940, depicting a ship and a cedar tree.

language, Catholic faith, and Phoenician past above all else. Michel Chiha in particular, himself a Chaldean Catholic with a Melkite mother from an Iraqi family, argued that Lebanon was a land of many minorities, with many languages, and that the Phoenicians were just one of its past glories—though at times he still emphasized the great differences between Lebanon and the Arab world.[35]

This downgrading of the importance of religion also helped explain away the obvious local problem with Lebanon's timeless "national" past, that Lebanon had not operated as a nation in more recent centuries: with the coming of the Arabs, it was explained, a national sentiment had been transformed—temporarily and regrettably—into a religious one. As Chiha explained, "the principle of individual identity that, under Byzantine domination, had been national (one was or was not a citizen of the Empire), became confessional."[36] Or as Charles Corm put it slightly more poetically in *La montagne inspirée*: "At the beginnings of our history, before becoming Muslims or Christians, we were simply a single people united in a single glory."[37]

When independence from France was finally achieved in 1943 with the support of almost all Lebanese scholars and politicians whatever their declared race or religion, Lebanon was defined in its new National Pact as a country with an "Arab face,"[38] and in 1944, it became one of the founding members of the Arab League. Nonetheless, neo-Phoenicianism remained a useful ideology for the new Lebanese state: the Phoenician origins of Lebanon were now what made it unique, and uniquely pluralistic, within the larger community of Arab nations.[39] Phoenician stories and symbols were adopted by urban elites of various confessional and political persuasions; coins issued by the Lebanese Republic once again featured a Phoenician ship and the famous cedar of Lebanon (fig. 1.4); and from 1956, the annual International Festival of Baalbek became a major showcase for the country's Phoenician past.[40]

Lebanon was not alone in this postcolonial turn to an ancient Phoenician past, and the appeal of the comparison in states with a claim to Phoenician

1.4 Ten-piastre coin minted by the Lebanese Republic in 1955, depicting a cedar tree and a ship.

heritage continues to the present day: in the spring of 2012, just before I delivered the Balmuth lectures, it emerged that two years earlier the aptly named Hannibal Qadhafi, fifth son of the Colonel and head of Libya's General National Maritime Transport Corporation, had commissioned a personal cruise liner named the *Phoenicia*, with design features including marble columns, gold-framed mirrors and a 120-ton tank containing six sharks, along with a team of biologists to look after them.[41] A more interesting comparison can, however, be made with Tunisia, where a form of Phoenicianism centered on the great western colony of Carthage also became popular after independence from France.

NEW CARTHAGINIANS

Under Ottoman hegemony from the sixteenth to nineteenth centuries, Tunisia's history had been presented as purely Arabic, whereas from 1881, the French Protectorate emphasized instead the era of the Roman occupation of North Africa, presenting the Romans as their imperial predecessors in the region—a confrontational approach very different from the one the French adopted in Lebanon.[42] By contrast, Tunisia's two presidents in the era between independence in 1956 and revolution in 2011, Habib Bourguiba and Zine El-Abedine Ben Ali, who took office in a rather literal sense in 1987, made use of all of the region's past, including its indigenous, Phoenician, Roman, and Islamic history, to characterize their own preferred version of its present.[43]

The new state's coat of arms featured a Phoenician ship (identified by the sign associated with the Carthaginian goddess Tinnit on its sail) as well as a pair of scales and a lion holding a sword, with the legend "freedom—order—justice," represented by the ship, lion, and scales, respectively.[44] Bourguiba built his presidential palace at Carthage, now a seaside suburb of Tunis, and encouraged regular arts festivals there, as well as the UNESCO "Save Carthage" archaeological campaigns of the 1970s. State celebrations for the ancient city's twenty-eighth centenary in 1986 happily coincided with thirty years of Tunisian independence.

Under Ben Ali, and encouraged by the World Bank, Carthage was further developed for tourism and commercial purposes, and a "Carthageland" theme park was constructed an hour's drive down the coast.[45] Ben Ali's government also provided sponsorship for foreign exhibitions about Carthage, and in 1994–95, the traveling exhibit *Les routes d'Hannibal* recreated Hannibal's march on Rome, using buses rather than elephants, and presenting fancy-dress episodes from Carthaginian history at stops in Tunis, Madrid, Cannes, and Rome.[46] Though largely promoted by government propaganda and economic elites—the first commercial television channel in the country was Hannibal TV, launched in 2005—the association with Carthage still has wider social resonance in Tunisia, where the national football team is nicknamed "the Eagles of Carthage."

Tunisian Phoenicianism started from an explicitly anticolonial standpoint. Bourguiba was particularly fond of Hannibal as a symbol of resistance to Roman, and therefore European, colonialism, and schoolbooks taught (not unreasonably) that Rome was the aggressor in the Punic Wars, forced Carthage to resist, and prevailed only with the help of another local hero, the Numidian king, Massinissa. As in Lebanon, this was part of a careful negotiation with European ideologies: French continued to be taught in schools, and Bourguiba was in cultural terms a liberal and cosmopolitan figure who promoted considerable social change, in particular in relation to women's rights—a development reflected in a new focus on the role of Queen Elissa, also known as Dido, as the founder of Carthage.

This interest in Elissa, as well as a more general identification with the Phoenician past, went well beyond state propaganda: the distance between Rome and Carthage is embraced in two novels by the francophone writer Fawzi Mellah, *Le conclave des pleureuses* (1987) and *Elissa, la reine vagabonde* (1988), which treat Elissa's story from a variety of local perspectives, including the suggestion that she has been misrepresented in the European tradition and in particular in the work of Virgil, who according to one of Mellah's characters "disfigures" the queen by calling her Dido and ascribing to her a love affair with a Greek sailor, "a vagabond unworthy of our Elissa."[47]

Under Ben Ali, the focus on Hannibal as a "national mascot" continued, but there was also a reconciliation with the Roman past, for pragmatic as well as ideological reasons.[48] The great Roman sites and monuments appealed to tourists, and as in Lebanon, the notion of Tunisia as a crossroads or bridge between Eastern and Western cultures was a useful one, making the country a core participant in a Mediterranean culture. Associations with both the Phoenician and the Roman pre-Islamic past became part of a wider display of openness to the Mediterranean: in this model, the Phoenicians were just one of many roots of Tunisian society and ethnicity.

Furthermore, from at least the 1990s the Carthage connection operated alongside the country's Roman past as a single pole in a very different opposition, a weapon in the hands of the secular government against the increasing popularity of political Islam,[49] "in part as a means of countering efforts by Islamists to encourage Tunisians to identify exclusively with Islam and the Arab world."[50] This strategy downplayed (though it certainly did not deny) the importance of Islam in the history of Tunisia in favor of a more multicultural presentation of the national past "from Carthage to Kairouan." The approach has survived the popular revolution and subsequent negotiations over the new constitution largely intact. A new monument to Hannibal is planned for the Punic Port at Carthage,[51] and in the summer of 2014, postrevolutionary Tunisia celebrated the anniversary of Hannibal Barca's victory over Rome at the Battle of Cannae on August 2, 216 BCE as well as the 2,828th year since Dido's foundation of Carthage in 814 BCE, with a parade and carnival in the ancient Phoenician colony.[52]

LEBANON FIRST

Back in Lebanon, however, the religious associations of Phoenicianist ideology reasserted themselves in the civil war that tore the country apart from 1975 to 1990, and the cosmopolitan ideals of the Lebanese elite gave way to boundary-building.[53] Phoenicianism particularly suited the Lebanese Forces, a coalition of far-right Christian militia groups, including most notoriously the Phalange (*Kataeb*). These groups, strongly encouraged by Said Akl and his journal *Lebnaan*, adopted an inflammatory, anti-Arab rhetoric of Phoenician descent against both Lebanese Arabs and the country's large population of Palestinian refugees.[54] Neo-Phoenicianism was severely tainted by its associations during this period, and when the war ended in 1989, the Ta'if peace accord emphasized again that Lebanon was an Arab state. When the National Museum in Beirut was partially reopened in 1999 after suffering immense damage during the war, the image on the poster was not Phoenician but Greek: Hygieia, the goddess of healing.[55]

Ongoing political tensions between Syria and Lebanon in the generation after the end of the war, and in particular the assassination of the former prime minister of Lebanon Rafik Hariri in 2005, consolidated the political demise of the New Phoenicians. Lebanese separatism became a widespread principle among Arabs as well as Maronites: "Lebanon First" is the slogan of Hariri's son Saad's Sunni-aligned Future Movement party, as well as of the unexpected "March 14" political alliance he made with the Lebanese Forces and the Phalange in 2005.[56] Phoenicianism has remained however a popular cultural ideology: in a series of interviews with Lebanese students in 2005–6, Craig Larkin found that especially among Maronites, "the myth of Phoenicianism . . . remains very much alive and rooted to an ancestral past . . . an intuitive reaction to and rejection of Arabism and Islamic identity . . . [and] very often during interviews this myth was raised as a justification of cultural uniqueness; an explanation of characteristic traits; or a defence of Lebanon's inimitable position in the Arab world."[57]

At the same time, however, the connection between the Phoenicians and the Lebanese can now be evoked once again as part of a shared national past, as in the remarkable research project on the genetic makeup of the Lebanese population led by Pierre Zalloua of the Lebanese American University. In addition to demonstrating particular links to Europe in the DNA of Lebanese Christians (thought to relate to the Crusades), and to the Arabian Peninsula among Lebanese Arabs (presumably a result of the Arab migrations in late antiquity), Zalloua's team showed that about 30 percent of Lebanese men carry what the study identifies as Phoenician genetic traces in their DNA, as opposed to 6 percent of men from all Mediterranean countries put together. The results mean, Zalloua told an interviewer, that "Phoenician is a heritage for all. . . . There is no distinct pattern that shows that one community carries significantly more Phoenician than another."[58]

Zalloua's investigation is part of the broader *National Geographic*-funded "Genographic Project" led by Spencer Wells, who himself went rather further in an interview with *National Geographic*, concluding from the study's apparent finding that "modern Lebanese people share a genetic identity going back thousands of years" that "[t]he Phoenicians were . . . the ancestors of today's Lebanese."[59] But there's a real problem with such a statement: Wells moves from the observation that a certain proportion of the ancient and modern populations of the region have similar DNA to the conclusion that both constitute specific named peoples, without noting the difference between these propositions. In fact, an assumption that "people" always belong to "peoples" potentially distorts the investigation as a whole: the initial decision to seek to identify ancient DNA markers at the level of "the Phoenicians" rests on the assumption that genetic connections at that particular level are, or rather were, more meaningful than those of larger or smaller population groups whose shared DNA markers the team could have investigated instead. In other words, it *assumes* that people in the past who shared this particular set of genetic connections can and should be identified with each other, and *investigates* only which people in the present they should also be identified with.[60]

The difficulty here is that even if some genetic similarities can be demonstrated between an ancient sailor from Tyre and another from Byblos, that doesn't mean that either had any concept of himself as anything other than a Tyrian or a Byblian (if that), that anyone else saw them that way, or that they had or did anything in common beyond that particular genetic likeness. And that is the real problem with co-opting the ancient Phoenicians for any modern nationalist project, sectarian or pluralist: whether or not it relies on the idea of a literal connection through descent or genetic resemblance (both of which all humans at some level share), it assumes that the Phoenicians were a coherent ethnic group themselves, an ancient nation that could form the basis of a modern nation-state. This assumption, as we have seen, has bolstered varieties of nationalist politics and rhetoric in Lebanon for almost a century, but its origins are in nineteenth-century European scholarship, when ideas about the Phoenicians slowly became saturated with the ideas and assumptions of modern nationalism.

INVENTING THE PHOENICIANS

The Phoenicians were a shadowy presence in European scholarly literature from the Renaissance period onward, part of a broader early modern interest in the diverse peoples of the ancient world, prompted by the wider availability of the Greek and Latin texts that discussed them.[61] European interest in the Phoenicians only really began, however, in 1646, when the French Protestant minister and orientalist Samuel Bochart (1599–1667) published a popular book in Latin called *Geographia sacra, seu Phaleg et Canaan* (Sacred Geography, or Phaleg and Canaan), which went through a series of reprints into the eighteenth century.[62] In it, Bochart traced the dispersal of Noah's descendants across the globe after the confusion of the languages at the tower of Babel, with a particular focus on the migrations and settlements of the Phoenicians, describing the enormous influence they had on the world's languages and cultures. He was one of the first scholars to point out and investigate the close relationship between Phoenician and the much better-known Hebrew language, and using this insight, he "roamed the map of the classical world and detected names that might lend themselves to etymological reduction back into Phoenician and Hebrew."[63]

In this manner, he found evidence for Phoenician presence from Thule in the far north to India in the far south.[64]

Scholars in this period did not portray the Phoenicians as a full-fledged ethnocultural group: as Timothy Champion puts it, they were still "a somewhat mystical part of the Mediterranean world, available to be invoked as exotic outsiders and as the origin of cultural traditions."[65] Bochart, for instance, calls them a *gens* (people), but presents them throughout his work simply as merchants and colonists from the same region. This "thin" depiction of the Phoenicians also comes out very clearly in the hit didactic novel *Les aventures de Télémaque* by Archbishop Fénelon, which was published in 1699, translated into every European language, and became the most popular book in France in the eighteenth century.[66] The work was written as a guide to kingship for Fénelon's pupil, the Duc de Bourgogne, who was second in line to the throne, but who was outlived by his grandfather Louis XIV, with the throne passing eventually to his son. Supposedly a continuation of the fourth book of the *Odyssey*, the book imagines the travels of Odysseus's son Telemachus in the company of his tutor, Mentor, who is given many opportunities to share his opinions on politics and political morality. Naturally, the pair run into the newly fashionable Phoenicians on their travels, and in book 3 they are carried to Tyre by Narbal, the commander of the Tyrian fleet, who passes the time explaining Phoenician seamanship and commerce: "You see, Telemachus, the power of the Phoenicians: they are formidable to all the neighbouring nations by their numerous vessels; from the trade they carry on as far as the Pillars of Hercules they derive such wealth as surpasses that of the most flourishing peoples."[67] Although Phoenicia has "neighbouring nations" in this passage, elsewhere only Tyre is given the label "nation" itself, while the Phoenicians are simply "so famous in all the known nations."[68]

In 1758, interest in the Phoenicians spiked again when the distinguished numismatist Jean-Jacques Barthélémy deciphered the Phoenician alphabet from a pair of bilingual dedications found in Malta in the late seventeenth century, one of which had been sent to Louis XVI as a present. This era of European scholarship culminated in the German manuals of Wilhelm Gesenius, who published the first full-scale manual of the Phoenician language with a collection of all the Phoenician inscriptions then available in 1837, and Franz Carl Movers, who collected the classical and biblical sources for Phoenician history and religion (1841–56). As Mario Liverani notes, "No wonder we don't find any reference there to a complex image or characterization of the Phoenicians, nor any value judgment (beyond the implicit, artless admiration that many scholars have for the objects of their studies). The search for 'origins' was already under way, that is to say for the provenance of the Phoenician people (on the basis of notices in classical sources), but attention did not yet focus on the delineation of 'character,' a largely ethnographic and colonial project, involving (and deriving from) reports of activities, specialisms, cultural idiosyncrasies and behaviors in contact with others and in daily life."[69] Things were changing though: Movers does present the Phoenician "people" (*Völkerschaft*) as an entity, one member of a larger group of Semites tied together by ancestry, language, and religion.[70]

The later decades of the nineteenth century saw a shift to a perception of the Phoenicians as a distinct and separate ethnocultural collective. This can in part be explained by the expansion of European colonialism and colonial archaeology in the Levant and North Africa,[71] but it also mapped onto the development in European ideologies of what Paul Gilroy has called "the nation as an ethnically homogenous object," and the "fatal junction of the concept of nationality with the concept of culture."[72] It relied heavily on the newly perceived importance of both race and environment, and the distinctive cultures and mentalities they created:[73] around the year 1850, as Fernand Braudel put it, "*civilization* (and *culture*) moved from the singular to the plural."[74]

One early example is John Kenrick's *Phoenicia* (1855), which builds onto the work of Bochart and Movers a cultural element, with chapters devoted to the Phoenicians' alphabet and language, to commerce, to navigation, to mining and metallurgy, and to manufacturing and the arts—although the arts receive only four pages, about the same as a "Note on the Natural History of the Buccinum and Murex."[75] On the basis of the works at Jerusalem attributed to King Hiram of Tyre—little else was available at the time—Kenrick declares that the "aesthetic character of Phoenician art" was "national and local," these words apparently being used as synonyms, and neither as a compliment.[76] He also devotes a long chapter on the "Origin of the Nation" to an attempt to make coherent sense of the different origins and genealogies of the Canaanites and Phoenicians suggested in the biblical tradition, the classical sources, and modern linguistic scholarship.

Ernest Renan himself then played a major part in the consolidation of the modern image of the Phoenicians when he traveled to the Levant in 1860–61 at Napoleon III's command. Although he accompanied a French expeditionary force sent to support Mount Lebanon's community of Catholic Maronites in their conflict with the British-backed Druze, his own mission was to study what he called "the ancient Phoenician civilization" (*la vieille civilization phénicienne*), a smaller scale follow-up to Napoleon Bonaparte's great Egyptian expedition of 1798–1801 that had brought the glories of ancient Egypt to the attention of the French public.[77] Renan pressed the French soldiers into service in a series of excavations at Byblos (Phoenician Gebel), Tyre (Sur), Sidon, and Arados (Arwad), explaining that he took care not to be distracted from the important historical questions by the allure of potential museum pieces "while remaining of course attentive to the interests of our collections."[78] Although the project did not in the end produce a great deal of Phoenician material, the results were published between 1864 and 1874 in beautiful drawings and trenchant prose as the *Mission de Phénicie,* a work that did much to promote the study of the Phoenicians in Europe.[79]

For Renan, the Phoenicians were a "people"[80] and a "nation,"[81] with a distinct art and architecture, if not a very impressive one: "In general, in their buildings, the Phoenicians seem to have had little force of character."[82] Nonetheless, he took a rather narrow view of the extent and nature of ancient Phoenicia: "Phoenicia was not a country; it was a series of ports, with a rather narrow hinterland. These towns, situated at intervals of ten or twelve kilometers, were at the center of an entirely civic life, as in the Greek towns. Phoenician civilization did not reach the mountain, and had little effect on the people of Syria."[83] However, and conveniently for those who would later see Lebanon as distinct from (or even within) the Arab world, Renan reflected at length on the atypicality of the Phoenician character within the larger category of "Semitic" peoples to which contemporary linguistics and racial science had assigned them: their famous practicality and business acumen, not to mention their political institutions and polytheistic religion, were quite at odds with the general image of the Semitic race at the time.[84]

Renan did not make a clear connection between the modern Maronites and the ancient Phoenicians, although he noted that "the inferiority of the Phoenicians as artists seems, furthermore, to have persisted to the present day in the country they inhabited,"[85] and that "the Lebanese race, whether Christian or Muslim, is, if I may say so, iconoclastic and ignorant of art. . . . The Maronite churches are very severe and forbid statues."[86] However, he did describe the Maronites themselves as a "nation,"[87] dismissing the Muslims by contrast as "half-savage or dull-witted . . . inferior races,"[88] and the map of the region explored by his expedition that accompanied Renan's publication, which covered a large area including Mount Lebanon, the cities of the coast, and the Beqaa valley (fig. 1.5), was revived by Lebanists in 1920 to support the case for Greater Lebanon.[89]

Back in the nineteenth century, Renan's expedition to Phoenicia increased the material available to scholars interested in the Phoenicians, and the launch in 1867 of his *Corpus Inscriptionum Semiticarum*, still the definitive collection

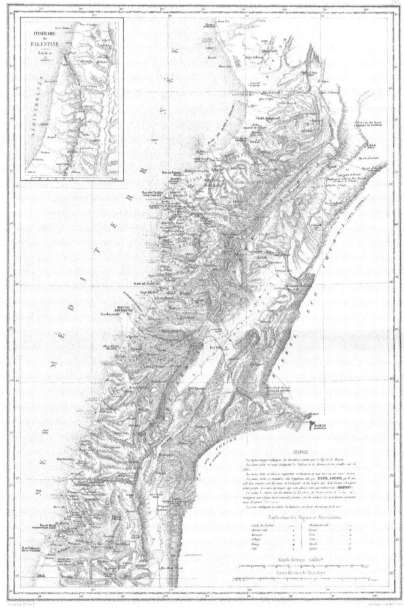

1.5 Ernest Renan's map of the area explored by his mission to Phoenicia in 1860–61.

of Phoenician inscriptions, provided another enormous boost to the field. This may help to explain why the notion of a discreet national, ethnic, and cultural identity of the Phoenicians became more explicit in later studies.[90] At the same time, Phoenicia became an object of study in itself: compare the title of the hugely popular work published from 1730 to 1738 by Charles Rollin, *Histoire ancienne des égyptiens, des carthaginois, des assyriens, des babyloniens, des medes et des perses, des macédoniens, des grecs*, with George Rawlinson's 1869 *Manual of Ancient History, from the Earliest Times to the Fall of the Western Empire, Comprising the History of Chaldaea, Assyria, Media, Babylonia, Lydia, Phoenicia, Syria, Judaea, Egypt, Carthage, Persia, Greece, Macedonia, Rome, and Parthia*, or Ernest Babelon's 1888 *Manuel d'archéologie orientale: Chaldée, Assyrie, Perse, Syrie, Judée, Phénicie, Carthage*.

In 1885, Georges Perrot and Michel Chipiez dedicated a volume of the popular French *Histoire de l'art dans l'antiquité* to Phoenicia and Cyprus. At the beginning they define the Phoenicians with some circumspection as "the peoples [*tribus*] who settled on the coast at the foot of Mt. Lebanon," assigning them on the basis of the similarity of Phoenician and Hebrew, and after considerable discussion of the contemporary debate on this point, to the "grande race sémitique" (broader Semitic race).[91] By the end of the work, however, after noting that despite the poverty and unoriginality of their art, the Phoenicians were masters of industry and commerce, they are less hesitant about defining the Phoenicians as a racial group in themselves: "it has been very well said that the Phoenician had some characteristics of the medieval Jew, but he was powerful, and he belonged to a race whose strength and superiority in certain respects should be recognized."[92]

In 1889, George Rawlinson's *History of Phoenicia* calls the Phoenicians a "nation," and assigns them on similar linguistic grounds to a larger Semitic "group."[93] In the third edition, published in the 1890s, the language is stronger: Rawlinson begins the work with a declaration that the Levantine coast is "inhabited by three nations, politically and ethnographically distinct," Syria, Phoenicia, and Palestine, and he devotes a chapter to "The People—Their Origin and Ethnic Character."[94] The book now concludes with a "General Estimate of the Nation" in which, after the traditional observation that the skills of the Phoenician "race" were in exploration and commerce rather than literature or art, Rawlinson awards them a "rank among the chief of the secondary powers of the earth."[95]

Also in 1889, Richard Pietschmann published a *History of the Phoenicians (Geschichte der Phönizier)* in which he too describes the Phoenicians as a "nation," though he notes that in their case this was a rather vague concept, and he treats their own national self-consciousness as an open question.[96] Concern for internal or "emic" definitions of ethnicity or nationhood was, however, unusual by this period; peoples, nations, and races were usually discussed as if they were simply natural facts, even if the precise categorization of specific examples was open to debate. And these natural nations had equally natural cultures: as Nicholas Vella has noted, all the popular nineteenth-century works on the Phoenicians from Renan's *Mission* onward, "included an immense corpus of objects, integrating inscriptions, coins and seals," and "common language and script, religion and burial practices, dress and personal ornaments, and other attributes were taken as material markers for an ethnic group with undisputed roots." In describing and isolating so-called Phoenician culture, Vella suggests, such books and exhibitions in a sense invented it.[97]

The popularity of the Phoenicians in the nineteenth century should not however be overestimated: the celebration of Phoenician achievements in this period competed with a more popular European scholarly model that privileged the Greeks, then a newly independent nation, and denied them close links with their "oriental" neighbors. And in the strongly anti-Semitic academic atmosphere of the early twentieth century, the Phoenicians became considerably less fashionable, at least in Europe.[98]

MOSCATI'S PHOENICIANS

In 1963, Sabatino Moscati, professor of Semitic philology at the University of Rome, effectively refounded the field of Phoenician studies in a lecture that put the question of Phoenician identity center stage, asking his audience, "Who were the Phoenicians, really? What were the distinguishing features and characteristics of their civilization, what were the historical, political, religious and artistic events and qualities that defined and shaped it? Because so far it seems that the unity, the autonomy, the homogeneity of the people and culture have merely been assumed rather than investigated."[99] The answer, Moscati reassured his listeners, was to study all the documentation carefully so that "Phoenician civilization can emerge as a historical object. . . . At the end of the day, it seems clear that the divisions between the Phoenician cities and their dominant civic consciousness were compatible with a relative homogeneity intrinsic to the population of the region and distinct from that of their neighbors."[100]

Moscati's re-visioning of the Phoenicians stripped them, for the most part, of the negative stereotype and racial science of earlier scholarship and was much less interested than those studies in their origins and national character.[101] Nonetheless, the Phoenicians were still a "people," "civilization," or "nation,"[102] with distinct limits in space (from Tell Suqas in the north to Akko in the south), and in time (from the end of the Bronze Age kingdoms to the conquest of their cities by Alexander the Great, c. 1200– 332 BCE),[103] made up of individuals not necessarily of the same race (*razza*) or from the same place (*provenienza*) "but who take on a homogenous character though having in common a geographical area, a language and a historical-cultural process."[104] Whether or not they appreciated that themselves was of little interest or importance. In 1988, this approach was still at the heart of Moscati's Phoenician studies—"I was interested in the reality of a people"[105]—and although in 1992 he admitted that "national consciousness was rather ephemeral among the Phoenician cities, where citizenship was a more important reference point,"[106] in 1993 he continued to defend the "incontestable" notion of an "ethnic reality," and a "Phoenician civilization" defined by "a series of intrinsically valid characteristics." Any further debate on the subject he declared "otiose."[107]

It should come as no surprise then that the spectacular exhibition *I Fenici* (*The Phoenicians*) at the Palazzo Grassi in Venice in 1988, organized by Moscati and sponsored by Fiat, was curated in the same way as the antiquarian corpora of the nineteenth century, with artifacts of "Phoenician" culture displayed according to their genre and geographical provenance. The joke at the time went that that "Sabatino Moscati invented the Phoenicians, Gianni Agnelli manufactured them."[108] And this could still be said of the exhibition *La Méditerranée des Phéniciens* (*The Mediterranean of the Phoenicians*) held at the Institut du monde arabe in Paris in 2007, where the various skills, crafts, and characteristics of the Phoenicians were once again sumptuously presented in splendid isolation from each other and from similar artifacts from other places.[109] Furthermore, this notion of the Phoenicians as a collective with a shared chronology, geography, language, history, and culture is still alive and well in the specialist literature: in the most important recent textbooks in Spanish, Italian, and English they are referred to as a "people," a "civilization," and a "distinct ethnic group."[110]

This interpretation of the Phoenicians as a people has also informed recent literature on nationalism. One of most influential recent studies of communal identity in the ancient world is Anthony D. Smith's magisterial *Ethnic Origins of Nations* (1986). Smith is no "primordialist," arguing for the timeless existence of natural nations, nor does he accept the "modernist" position that sees the construction of ethnic identity as inextricably bound up with the rise of the modern nation-states. Instead, he argues that since antiquity people have been constructing themselves as what we would now call ethnic communities, "collective cultural units and sentiments" that "form the models and groundwork for the construction of nations."[111]

Smith explicitly sees the Phoenicians as one example of this phenomenon: "In ancient Sumer, Phoenicia and Greece, we find two kinds of sentiment side by side, a political loyalty to the individual city-state, and a cultural and emotional solidarity with one's cultural kinsmen, as this is interpreted by current myths of origin and descent."[112] While there were "deep-seated rivalries" between individual Phoenician states, these "co-existed with strong . . . pan-Phoenician . . . sentiments based on a common heritage of religion, language, art and literature, political institutions, dress and forms of recreation."[113] Furthermore, in Phoenicia "a common Canaanite fertility religion, common language and alphabet, seafaring activities and colonies, temple construction and geographical location on peninsulas, all provided the basis for common sentiments among different strata and city-states in defence of their life-style."[114]

We don't need to worry too much about the specific historical claims here: Smith did not claim to be a specialist on the Phoenicians. Instead, my argument in this book is that Smith's notion of the Phoenicians as an ethnocultural group isn't just wrong, but the wrong way round: in the case of the Phoenicians at least we are not dealing with the ancient ethnic origins of modern nations, but the modern nationalist origins of an ancient ethnicity.[115] My answer to the question Moscati posed in 1963 is that nothing did in fact unite the Phoenicians in their own eyes or those of their neighbors, and that his Phoenician people, or civilization, or nation, is not actually a real historical object, but rather a product of the scholarly and political ideologies I have discussed in this chapter. Such modern ideas about the ancient Phoenicians are thoroughly interwoven with ideas about the modern nation-state. That does not in itself, of course, mean that they cannot also be true. But the picture presented by our ancient sources is very different.

CHAPTER 2

Sons of Tyre

What makes people see themselves, or others, as a "people"? Or to put it another way, how can we define a particular sociocultural group as "ethnic"? There is general agreement that the notion of shared ancestry is a core aspect, often associated with an idea of shared territory: "blood and soil."[1] In addition, shared attributes, including language, religion, or particular physical characteristics, may accompany and bolster the sense or impression of groupness attached to any particular ethnic identity, although they are not by themselves enough to diagnose it: the focus of ethnic claims is on historical connections between people as opposed to their contemporary links.

Although the academic study of ethnicity only began in the twentieth century,[2] most scholars accept that what we would now categorize as ethnic groups—or, as they are often still called, "nations"—can be found in earlier periods as well.[3] But how can we detect such groups, especially at great historical distance and when we have very little direct evidence of how the people concerned thought and talked about themselves? Anthony Smith takes perhaps the broadest and most helpful view on this question, suggesting that there are six different criteria by which we can recognize an ancient ethnic group—a collective name, a common myth of descent, a shared history, a sense of solidarity, an association with a specific territory, and a distinctive shared culture— and that such groups should fulfill all of these criteria at least to some degree.[4] I would argue that on the available evidence the Phoenicians fulfilled none of them.

I will focus in this chapter, however, on the most obvious criterion for identifying a people, and one that puts the emphasis on self-identification rather than the views of others: their possession of a collective name. This is how, as Smith says, "they distinguish themselves and summarize their 'essence' to themselves."[5] It is well known that no one ever called her- or himself "Phoenician" in Phoenician, and this is hardly surprising, since *phoinix* (φοῖνιξ) is a Greek word. More surprising, perhaps, is how few people called themselves Phoenician even in other languages (including Greek), and what I will also show in this chapter is that there is no evidence for the use of any other communal self-designation either, despite the common claim that our Phoenicians described themselves as "Canaanites." Instead, a survey of the limited available evidence suggests that Phoenician-speakers defined themselves, at least in their inscriptions, in terms of their cities and, even more, their families.

PHANTOM PHOENICIANS

First, what evidence is there for self-declared Phoenicians? One of the most famous candidates scratched his name in Etruscan on a *tessera hospitalis* or hospitality token in the second half of the sixth century BCE.[6] This small ivory plaquette, found in a grave in the Santa Monica necropolis at Carthage, would have been one of a matching pair that could be reunited to prove the existence of a relationship of mutual friendship and hospitality between two individuals and their descendants. It has a wild boar carved on one side and an inscription on the other that begins *mi puinel karθazie*. The word *mi* means "I am"; *karθazie* means "belonging to Carthage"; and some scholars have interpreted *puinel* as a second ethnic designation related to *phoinix* and/or its Latin equivalent *poenus*. However, as Jonathan Prag has pointed out, it would be odd—indeed unique—to identify oneself with two "ethnics" but no personal name.[7] It is much more likely that "Puinel" here is simply the man's own name: Etruscan epigraphy reveals plenty of names beginning *Pui-* or even *Puin-*.[8] Puinel may be the dead person himself, and so a man of Etruscan origin or descent living in Carthage, or more likely (since it would be strange to keep one's own half of a hospitality token) the name of an associate with origins in Carthage who has at some point acquired a local name in Etruria. The high level of contact and exchange between Carthage and Etruria in this early period renders both possibilities quite plausible.[9]

Given that *phoinix* is a Greek term and was regularly used by Greeks to describe people from the Levant, we might expect to find more people calling themselves Phoenicians in Greek contexts abroad. More generally, a French person talking to other French people in France would probably describe herself in terms of her city rather than as "French," unless she wanted to clarify or emphasize the point. But that same person being introduced to an American in New York City might well call herself "French"—and we might again expect the same principle to hold true for "Phoenicians" living and working overseas.

This isn't just about being polite: increasing distance from home can lead to increasing identification with it. Indeed, some Greek historians have argued that collective identities above the level of the city-state, such as Rhodian, Ionian, or indeed Greek itself, emerged in the context of large-scale migration around the Mediterranean by Greek-speakers in the first half of the first millennium BCE.[10] It would not be surprising if people from the Levant also found their commonalities in foreign contexts, where the extent to which they shared a language, gods, ritual practices, and a regional origin would become more obvious to themselves as well as to others.[11]

In fact, however, a recent survey by Jonathan Prag found just five Greek-language inscriptions that mention people called Phoinix. One is a lead curse tablet from fifth-century BCE Selinus in Sicily, which gives several examples of Phoinix used simply as a personal name, like that of Phoinix the (Greek) Myrmidon in the *Iliad*. In four later texts from the Aegean, however, it does appear to be an epithet, since it appears alongside a personal name, and sometimes alongside a patronymic as well: a fourth- or third-century gravestone from Eretria for one Ergasion Phoinix, two third- and second-century inscriptions from Delos mentioning a Herakleides Phoinix and an Apollonius Phoinix, and a contemporary inscription from its neighboring funerary island of Rheneia erected by Megas Phoinix, son of Dionysius.[12]

The first thing of note here is that all of these texts are from the Hellenistic period, after traditional textbooks would put an end to Phoenician history, although this may simply reflect a more general pattern by which epigraphic evidence becomes more abundant in this period. The second is that we do not know if the people thus named were actually from the Levant; indeed, if the man called Apollonius Phoinix really was a Phoenician, he "would be the only known foreigner standing surety for contracts on Delos."[13] The third is that it is quite possible that the name Phoinix carried no ethnic connotations at all in these contexts: the word *phoinix* had a wide range of other possible meanings in Greek, including the color purple or crimson, the date palm, and the immortal bird,[14] and it is surely not a coincidence that three of these five examples are from Delos, an island sacred to Apollo, and therefore closely connected with the emblem of the palm tree (*phoinix*) under which he was said to have been born there.[15]

Two other Hellenistic-period inscriptions discussed by Prag record the manumission at Naupactus in central Greece of a slave "of Phoenician stock"[16] and the burial on Rheneia of a "woman from somewhere in Phoenicia, since she was from Ashkelon,"[17] but the latter is a reference to geographical origin rather than descent, and both seem in any case to be descriptions of these individuals by other people: there is no question that "Phoenicians" were a category in *Greek* thought, as we will explore in more detail in the next chapter.

It is worth pausing longer over an unusual funerary monument from Athens, erected for a man called Antipatros from Ashkelon by one Domsalos from Sidon sometime in the third century BCE (fig. 2.1). A bilingual Greek and Phoenician epitaph sits above a sculpted relief of a corpse on a bier fought over by a lion and a man in front of the prow of a ship, followed by a six-line Greek epigram, in a different hand, which rather awkwardly explains the unusual imagery.[18]

2.1 The funerary stele erected at Athens for Antipatros of Ashkelon by Domsalos of Sidon in the third century BCE.

Epitaph:

Ἀντίπατρος Ἀφροδισίου Ἀσκαλ[ωνίτης]
Δομσαλὼς Δομανὼ Σιδώνιος ἀνέθηκε

Antipatros son of Aphrodisias, an
    Ashkelonite.
Domsalos, son of Domano, a Sidonian,
    dedicated (this).

ʾNK ŠM[.] BN ʿBDʿŠTRT ʾŠQLNY
ʾŠ YṬNʾT ʾNK DʿMṢLḤ BN DʿMḤNʾ
ṢDNY

I (am) Shem[.], son of Abdashtart, an
    Ashkelonite.
(This is the stele) which I Domseleh, son
    of Domhano, a Sidonian, erected.

Epigram:

μηθεὶς ἀνθρώπων θαυμαζέτω εἰκόνα
    τήνδε
ὡς περὶ μέν με λέων, περὶ δὲγ
    πρῶιρ᾽ἰγκτετάνυσται.
ἦλθε γὰρ εἰχθρολέων τἀμὰ θέλων
    σποράσαι.
ἀλλὰ φίλοι τ᾽ἤμυναν καί μου κτέρισαν
    τάφον οὕτηι
οὓς ἔθελον φιλέων, ἱερᾶς ἀπὸ νηὸς
    ἰόντες.
Φοινίκην δ᾽ἔλιπον, τεῖδε χθονὶ σῶμα
    κέκρυνμαι.

Let no one wonder at this image,
that extends around me on the one side
    a lion, on the other a prow.
For an enemy lion came wanting to de-
    stroy me,
but friends came to my aid and buried
    me in this tomb,
whom I loved and in whom I delighted,
    coming from a sacred ship.
I left Phoenicia; my body is hidden in
    this earth.

The wording of the epitaph in both languages is very similar, and both versions identify both the dedicator and the deceased by their cities of origin.[19] Nonetheless, Antipatros's imagined claim in the epigram that he has "left Phoenicia" has been seen as providing evidence for an overarching Phoenician identity in this diasporic context: Jennifer Stager, for instance, suggests that the "label transforms the deceased and, by extension, his comrades from members of a subculture determined by city-state boundaries (e.g., Sidon, Ashkelon) to members of a unified cultural group. . . . For the people of these city-states residing as a cultural minority in Athens, individual city-state identity gave way, at times, to an externally determined collective identity, 'Phoenician.' "[20] However, Stager herself notes that the use of the word "Phoenicia" in the epigram (which does not seem to have been composed by a native Greek-speaker[21]) "facilitated epigrammatic (scansion) and cultural legibility to the Greek-speaking audience,"[22] and I would argue that the phrase is better read as an attempt by a Phoenician-speaker to communicate in the local Greek "language." "I left

Phoenicia" is not an identity claim by or on behalf of the dead man, but a simple fact about Antipatros's geographical origin. The writer presumably intends to draw attention to the sadness of dying far from home in terms that would make sense to a Athenian audience, themselves familiar with the idea of "Phoenicia" as much as or perhaps more than they were with individual Levantine cities.[23] This probably also explains the single reference to a Phoenician in Latin epigraphy, an imperial-period tombstone from Noricum that commemorates a "Phoenician girl" (*punica virgo*)—and again, this wording is unlikely to have been the girl's own choice.[24]

PHANTOM CANAANITES

This lack of evidence for the use by Phoenicians themselves of that Greek label is not usually seen as a problem; the standard claim in modern scholarship is that the Phoenicians described themselves with a word from their own language, "Canaanite."[25] There is, however, very little evidence for this usage either, and I want to suggest that the examples that are usually given have been misconstrued.

The only explicit claim ever made in Levantine cities to be part of the region of Canaan, indeed the only time that the word Canaan (KNʿN) is found written in Phoenician, is on bronze coins minted by the city of Beirut in 168 BCE and for the rest of the second century, which give the city's name as "Laodikeia mother in Canaan" (LʾDK ʾM BKNʿN).[26] This phrase is sometimes taken as evidence itself for a self-identification by Phoenician-speakers as Canaanite, but it describes the city rather than its inhabitants, and its political context means that it should not be taken as a neutral label, drawing on long-term local usage, but rather interpreted as a carefully fashioned intervention in regional rhetorics of power. It is a version of the name "Laodikeia in Phoenicia" imposed on Beirut by the Greco-Macedonian Seleucid kings, where "in Phoenicia" distinguishes this city from the Laodikea on the Sea farther north. It is not, however, a straightforward translation, but a local rewriting in political and cultural as well as linguistic terms: as well as adding to the Seleucid name the notion of being a "mother [city]," which, as I shall discuss further in chapter 7, speaks to competition with neighboring coastal cities, the Phoenician legend transliterates "Laodikeia" but then replaces the Seleucid name for the larger region with a local toponym. There is nothing here to suggest a long-standing local equivalence, or that this is anything other than a one-off experiment in reaction to a specific political context.

The only direct claim to personal "Canaanite" identity that is regularly cited by scholars is found in a third- or second-century BCE inscription marking an offering made at the tophet sanctuary at Cirta (modern Constantine) in Algeria. The inscription in its published form reads as follows: "To Baal Hammon, this is what Abdeshmun ['BD'ŠMN] son of M'DR, a Canaanite man from Carmel ['Š KN'N MQRML], citizen of 'Y'RM, vowed. He heard his voice, he blessed him."

Here I translate the relevant phrase 'Š KN'N as "Canaanite man," following the text and translations given in the French publication of the inscriptions from the sanctuary (*Cananéen*) and in the standard German collection of noteworthy Phoenician inscriptions (*Kanaanäer*).[27] One point emerges immediately: there would be no point in mentioning Canaan in this inscription unless it was to draw attention to something unusual—and so its use here would suggest that it was *not* common to make a connection with Canaan in a diasporic Levantine community like this one. If being "of Canaan" (or indeed "Canaanite") was considered true of everyone making dedications in Phoenician at this sanctuary, there would be no reason to point it out in this particular case—or alternatively we would expect to see it mentioned more often.

However, the text as published is not what is written on the stone: the final letter of the word concerned is not a nun but a lamed, giving not KN'N (Canaan) but KN'L. This was pointed out almost fifty years ago by Roland de Vaux, and is quite clear on the published photograph of the stone (fig. 2.2), but his observation has largely been ignored in the subsequent scholarly literature.[28] If KN'L is a place name, we do not know where it is. And it is not even clear where we should be looking: the apparent reference to Mount Carmel immediately afterward is one of the things that has made the reading "Canaan" appealing, except that Carmel should be spelled with an initial kaf not a qof in Phoenician: KRML. Furthermore, Abdeshmun says that either he or his father is also a citizen of 'Y'RM—another unknown place, although the aleph at the beginning of word would usually suggest that it refers to an island. Given where Phoenician-speaking settlements on islands are located, this would probably be a reference to somewhere in the western Mediterranean.[29]

Furthermore, if KN'L is an error on the part of the stonecutter, and the correction of his text to KN'N is in fact correct, the phrase could simply mean that he is "a merchant": KN'N is found with this sense several times in the Hebrew Bible and early Christian sources.[30] And even if the word was supposed to be KN'N and did refer to the place "Canaan," it is unlikely that it was a straightforward adjective meaning "Canaanite." Semitic languages

2.2 The second-century BCE marker from the El Hofra sanctuary at Cirta recording a dedication by Abdeshmun, in which he describes himself as a man from KNˤL, and not as is usually claimed KNˤN (Canaan). The lamed (L) is circled.

construct *nisba* adjectives that identify people with places by adding a suffix to the name of the place concerned, giving masculine forms like "Israeli" or "Yemeni." Since vowels are not traditionally marked in Phoenician and Punic script, it might then seem that KNˤN in the inscription could be read as an adjective of this kind, pronounced *kanaanī*, making ʾŠ KNˤN an ethnic phrase: "a Canaanite man." However, Maria Giulia Amadasi Guzzo has recently demonstrated that where ethnic adjectives occur in Phoenician, the final -ī sound is in fact usually spelled out, with a yod (Y).[31] So the more obvious way of reading ʾŠ KNʿN would be in a weaker sense, as a "construct" phrase, another standard Semitic usage in which two nouns are juxtaposed to indicate an association of some kind between them. This is sometimes, but not necessarily, one of belonging or possession: the construct phrase "cat-Tom," for instance, would mean Tom's cat, but "factory-widget" would mean a widget factory, not a factory that belongs to a particular widget. In this case, the most straightforward way of reading the text would be as a simple claim about geographical origins rather than a declaration of personal identity: the man or his father was from Canaan.

Coincidentally, the one piece of indirect evidence commonly cited for people calling themselves "Canaanite" is also from Algeria, although it was written more than five hundred years later. According to the standard published text of Saint Augustine's *Unfinished Commentary on Paul's Letter to the Romans* (394/5 CE), "if you ask our local peasants what they are, they reply, in Phoenician, 'Chanani.'"[32] This claim has been almost universally accepted as evidence of the existence of self-identified Canaanites in Africa in late antiquity,[33] but again there are serious grounds for hesitation.

The first problem is that this is not a direct self-identification, or even a firsthand ethnographic report of real-life encounters, but a hypothetical answer to a hypothetical question given by hypothetical peasants, and one that helps to illustrate the rather obscure theological point being made in this chapter of Augustine's treatise. It is almost certainly also secondhand, part of an argument made not by Augustine himself, but by Valerius, his predecessor as bishop of Hippo. As Augustine explores in his commentary the connections between the Holy Trinity and the Latin word *salus* (which means both "greetings" and "salvation"), he recalls an anecdote told by Valerius about meeting some Phoenician-speaking peasants who explain to him that this Latin word *salus* sounds like the Phoenician word for "three" (ŠLŠ) (13.1–2). Valerius was particularly excited by this coincidence because he could relate it to the story in Matthew's gospel of the "Canaanite woman" (*Chananaea*), "that is to say the Phoenician woman [*punica mulier*] who came from the area of Tyre and Sidon, who in the gospel plays the role of the gentile" (13.3) who came to ask Jesus for help (*salus*) because her daughter was tormented by a demon (Mt 15:21–28). The new information from the peasants, also described as *punici*, helps to explain the Trinitarian point of the gospel story: by asking for *salus*, she was really asking for the Trinity:

> Tria enim mulieris lingua salus vocantur, erat enim Chananaea. Unde interrogati rustici nostri, quid sint, punice respondent: Chanani, corrupta scilicet sicut in talibus solet una littera, quid aliud respondent quam: Chananaei?[34]

> For in the woman's language *tria* is said as *salus*. For she/it was Canaanite,
> for which reason our rustics, when asked what they are (*quid sint*), reply in
> Phoenician "Chanani"; with one letter corrupted of course, as is usual in such
> cases, what else are they replying but "Chananaei"?

This second conversation with the peasants is imaginary and seems intended to establish that they speak the same language as the woman, because (on their own account) they are originally from the same place, and so their observation about the meaning of *salus* would apply to her as well.

There seems little doubt that the full argument, including the real-life and the hypothetical encounters with peasants, should be attributed to Valerius. Indeed, the whole chapter ends with the comment that "whether this consonance of words came about by accident or by providence should not be pursued aggressively so that everyone agrees, but enough for the enjoyment of the listener to admit the elegance of the expounder," suggesting that Augustine is picking up the reins again from his colleague, with a politely raised eyebrow.[35] And the sentence at issue certainly does not fit comfortably with Augustine's wider writings: although he often mentions Canaanites, this is the only passage in any of his works that locates them in North Africa rather than the Levant.

However, as with the much earlier inscription from Cirta, there is also a textual problem. A survey of the extant manuscripts of the *Unfinished Commentary* suggests that the standard published text of the crucial sentence cannot in fact have been the reading of the archetype, the manuscript to which all extant copies relate back.[36] In all but three of the eighteen relevant surviving manuscripts (*T*, *V*, and *B*) the peasants were asked not *quid sint*—"what they are"—but *quid sit*: "what it is."

In itself the fact that many of the manuscripts reproduce one particular reading wouldn't mean much—the nature of the copying process meant that mistakes could spread easily through a manuscript tradition—but a new *stemma* or family tree of the manuscript tradition compiled by Daniel Hadas has revealed that *T* and *V* have a single common ancestor, and that *B* was in effect an early scholarly edition of the text, based on several manuscripts, and prone to correcting them by conjecture. This makes it much more likely that the plural reading is not a preservation of the archetype reading, but a correction of it by two individual scribes. The correction can be explained in both cases by their reading of *chanani* as a Latin plural and therefore as requiring a plural verb, and would also have been encouraged by the plurals of *interrogati rustici nostri* immediately beforehand. It seems that when the first modern edition of the text was published in 1506, it took the *sint* reading from a manuscript of the type represented by *B*, and that this reading has survived as part of the standard text simply by force of tradition.[37]

That the archetype had *sit* does not necessarily mean that this is what Augustine originally wrote, and it is entirely possible that the corrections to *sint* were in fact correct. On the other hand, the singular reading *sit* has its merits. Augustine does not elsewhere use the phrase *quid sint*, "what they are," for indirect questions about people in the plural, but rather *qui sint*, "who they are."[38] Furthermore, the text specifies that the answer the peasants give is "in Phoenician," but in Phoenician *Chanani* (KNʿNY) would be a singular *nisba* adjective of the type discussed above, not a plural. And finally, the singular "what it is" would most obviously relate to the language of the Canaanite woman, rather than the identity of the Algerian peasants, which would make good sense in this context. The whole passage is, after all, about language, and the implication of Augustine's description of both the woman and the peasants as *punici*, Phoenician, may also be a linguistic one: it is a striking fact that the standard reference of the term *punicus* in Augustine's writing is not to an ethnic group but to the Phoenician language and its speakers.[39]

This alternative reading would not, however, make sense of the second part of the sentence, where *Chanani* is glossed as *Chananaei*—although there is a considerable variety in the readings of that word too in the different manuscripts.[40] The truth is that the passage is hard to understand on either reading, but it should by now be clear that this poorly transmitted report of a hypothetical conversation cannot be used as proof of a self-conscious identification as "Canaanite" on the part of Algerian peasants in late antiquity. If not a misunderstanding of a corrupt text, is it at best Augustine's, or more likely Valerius's, own suggestion that the peasants they call *punici* would self-identify as Canaanite.

And even if Augustine—or Valerius—did mean to say that local Phoenician-speaking peasants would if asked describe themselves as Canaanite, this impression did not necessarily come from the peasants themselves. There was a coherent and long-standing literary tradition postulating an emigration of biblical Canaanites to Africa.[41] This first emerges in a second century BCE Jewish work called the Book of Jubilees, where we are told that one of the revelations received by Moses on Mount Sinai was that when the four sons of Noah's son Ham were assigned their own lands to populate after the Flood and the subsequent destruction of the Tower of Babel, Canaan was given the coastal region of northwest Africa, west of Egypt and Libya (the domains of his brothers Mizraim and Put).[42] This story offered an alternative explanation for the presence of Phoenician speakers in the Maghreb to the classical narrative of Tyrian colonization and gave the Phoenician-speaking inhabitants of Africa a place in the sacred geography of Noachic descent. A first-century CE reference by Josephus to Ham's offspring inhabiting the Mediterranean coast of Africa must pick up on the same tradition.[43]

Much later again, in the sixth century CE, Procopius of Caesarea gives one of the more elaborate versions of this story, explaining that the peoples of ancient Phoenicia fled to Libya as refugees from the Israelite invasion of their country and founded many cities there, retaining their language to his present day.[44] To illustrate his point, he calls as witnesses two white stone stelai in a fortress in Numidia inscribed in "Phoenician letters" and in the "Phoenician language" saying: "We are they who fled from the face of Joshua, the robber, the son of Nun."[45] As Philip Schmitz has demonstrated, Procopius's claim depends not on his local knowledge but on lost passages of early Christian chronographers such as Sextus Julius Africanus, and ultimately on the Septuagint translation of the Book of Joshua: "Whatever Procopius may have seen or been told, his 'translation' of the inscriptions he reported is borrowed from early Christian chroniclers' attempts to populate the west with Canaanites displaced by Joshua. The link with Jubilees . . . could indicate that the earliest Christian chroniclers depended on earlier Hellenistic Jewish speculation about Hamite migrations."[46] We might say much the same about Valerius and Augustine.[47]

PHOENICIANS AND CANAANITES

This raises a broader problem with the notion that the people the Greeks called Phoenician traditionally called themselves Canaanite: it depends on the assumption that the two words mean the same thing—or at least something fairly similar.[48] But for a long time these terms were used about different places and people. While the Greeks' "Phoenicia" was always a coastal strip, the "Canaan" of the Near Eastern sources, including the Hebrew Bible, was considerably larger, including the coastal cities but often extending as far inland as the River Jordan if not beyond.[49] These regions were also of course seen from different perspectives: Canaan from inland, where a whole series of interconnected cities and states housed people speaking very similar languages; and Phoenicia from the sea, where the coastal cities were all that most Greek-speakers saw. And as has often been pointed out, the Canaan and Canaanites of the Hebrew Bible were largely ideological constructs representing the enemies of Israel, rather than historical references to a real social group.[50]

The first sign of actual equivalence between the two terms comes in the intermittent association of the "Canaanites" more specifically with the Levantine coast in biblical texts of the middle of the first millennium BCE.[51] This may relate instead, however, to the secondary meaning of the term "Canaanite" found in these later books of the Hebrew Bible and already mentioned above, in which it refers to merchants. It is only in the third to second century BCE that the Septuagint translation of the Hebrew Bible into Greek, made in Alexandria, renders "the land of Canaan" on five occasions as "Phoenicia" or "the land of the Phoenicians"—although it also translates it with variations on *Chanaan* more than 150 times.[52] Apart from the more or less contemporary legend on the coins from Beirut discussed above, the correspondence is only found again in the Roman period. In the second century CE, Philo of Byblos displaces the equation from places to people, mentioning a "Chna" whose name was changed to "Phoinix"—by, he seems to imply, Greek historians who have distorted the local myths he now records.[53] It is not until the third century CE that Herodian says straightforwardly that Phoenicia's original name was Chna.[54]

CITIZENS AND KIN

If there is no evidence for anyone self-identifying as Phoenician before late antiquity, and the evidence that some called themselves Canaanite is highly suspect, how did people we call "Phoenician" actually describe themselves? In the Phoenician-language texts from the Levant itself, people tend to define themselves by reference to their city or, rather more often, their family: it is common for Phoenician inscriptions to list several generations of ancestors.[55] Identification by one's father or city goes back at least as far as the eleventh century BCE, when a group of more than sixty arrowheads gives the names of their owners along with patronymics or, more rarely, other identifying phrases, including "Sidonian" or "Akkian."[56]

Explicit identity claims made by Phoenician-speakers abroad mostly date from the fourth century BCE and later, but they are still focused on family and, to some extent, the city-state.[57] Civic identities are sometimes expressed in Phoenician-language inscriptions, usually as simple adjectives: "Aradites" at Carthage, for example.[58] From the Hellenistic period, some of these civic identities are couched in more political language: a "man of the people of ('Š B'M) Cossura," "citizen of (B'L) Hammon."[59] However, inscriptions also regularly record professions, political and religious offices, and, especially, family relationships, going back as many as seventeen generations in two extreme cases from Olbia on Sardinia and from Carthage.[60] In both these examples, however, the claim about descent may well have been bound up with a civic one: it seems likely that the dedicators intended to list a genealogy (real or invented) going back to the foundation of their colony.[61]

Conversely, a form of identification that on the face of it looks "civic" may in fact have more to do with family and ancestral origins. "Sons of" particular cities are found in Phoenician inscriptions throughout the Mediterranean, including sons of Tyre at Carthage and Sabratha in North Africa, sons of Carthage in Lebanon, and a son of Arqa, north of Byblos, at Tamessos on Cyprus.[62] The phrase itself is exported from the Levantine homeland: we find sons of Ugarit and sons of the land of Canaan in the thirteenth century BCE, and there are many other examples in Near Eastern texts from the Bronze Age.[63] The label "Son of Tyre" or "Son of Carthage" usually comes at the end of a genealogy of two or more generations, meaning that it is unclear whether it describes the author of the inscription or an ancestor. But an unusual example from Carthage dedicated by a woman, one "GDN'M daughter of Baalyaton son of Tyre," reveals that the phrase must refer in that case (and therefore very likely in the others) not to the person who erected the stone, and so to that person's own city, but to the home of the most distant ancestor listed.[64]

In the western Mediterranean, regional identities are also visible, with about fifteen people identifying in Punic inscriptions at Carthage as "Sardinians."[65] This suggests a primary link neither to their Levantine origins, nor the larger Levantine diaspora in the west, but specifically to the island on which they resided, and which they shared with others. Furthermore, although the dating of this evidence for a Sardinian identity to the fourth century and later may reflect the loss of earlier examples, it echoes other patterns of evidence for the construction of regional identities among Greek-speakers in the same period: "Sicilian," for example, became a standard identity claim in Greek inscriptions in Sicily from the fourth century, when the generic identity of *Sikelos* seems to have replaced an earlier practice of referring to Greeks (alone) in Sicily as *Sikeliotes*.[66]

More detailed evidence for attitudes to identity in Levantine migrant communities comes from Greek and bilingual inscriptions, with some of the best examples found in the Aegean.[67] These suggest that even overseas Phoenician-speakers identified according to their towns of origin, maintained links with them, and congregated in communities on the basis of those ties. The fourth- and third- century epigraphic evidence from Athens tells us most about self-described Sidonians, who were also identified as such in official contexts by the Athenian authorities.[68] An Athenian decree from the mid-fourth century BCE honored "Strato, king of the Sidonians" (Abdashtart I) with proxeny (public guest-friendship) rights and exempted visiting merchants who lived in Sidon and had civic rights there from the metic tax and other civic obligations.[69] Another, dated to 323/2 BCE, gave honors including proxeny to Apollonides, son of Demetrius of Sidon,[70] while in a third-century bilingual inscription from the Piraeus area, an association (*koinon*) of Sidonians connected with a temple crowned a religious official in "year 14 of the people of Sidon."[71]

Tyrians also received proxeny honors, undermining a theory that "Sidonian" was in fact a metonym for "Phoenician" in these contexts.[72] And in an Athenian decree of 333/2 BCE found in the Piraeus, merchants of Kition on Cyprus were allowed to acquire land to build a temple to Aphrodite, "like the Egyptians have built the sanctuary of Isis."[73] Several bilingual Phoenician and Greek inscriptions erected by Kitians that have been found in the Piraeus area suggest that these merchants were largely if not entirely native Phoenician-speakers, and it is striking that the Athenians identify this group of people by their city, although they identify the Egyptians by their land as a whole. And this practice seems to reflect the identities of the people who used the shrine, not just the Athenians' perception of them: one Greek dedication to "Heavenly Aphrodite" (Aphrodite Ourania) found in the Piraeus region was composed by a woman called Aristoklea who describes herself as a "Kitian."[74]

This sanctuary is also interesting in itself, since it was not used only by Kitians but also by people from Salamis, about twenty-five miles away from Kition in eastern Cyprus. Alongside the funerary monument erected by Domsalos of Sidon for Antipatros of Ashkelon, this suggests that small-scale regionalism among Phoenician-speakers in the Hellenistic period could relate to their places of origin as well as the places that they settled, although Phoenician-speakers in Athens may well have had rather different and less permanent migration patterns than the "Sardinians" found in the west.[75]

Inscriptions from the Aegean island of Delos provide another particularly interesting case study of diasporic organization and solidarity in another context where Levantine merchants were in a minority, albeit a wealthy and powerful one. Delos was a major banking and trading center, so sacred to Apollo that birth and death were prohibited on the island. Levantines first appear in the epigraphic record in the fourth century, when Tyrian "sacred sailors" (*hieronautai*) dedicated images of Tyre and Sidon there.[76] Philokles, "King of the Sidonians," then dedicated golden crowns at Delian sanctuaries and had a Soteria festival held on the island in his honor about

280 BCE,[77] and another embassy came from Byblos in 276.[78] Most of our evidence for Phoenician-speakers is, however, for people who actually lived on the island, at least temporarily, after 166, when the Romans made it a free port under Athenian control, ushering in a brief era of great prosperity.[79] Greek-language inscriptions record the presence in this period of people from cities including Arados, Beirut, Sidon, Tyre, Ashkelon, and Carthage.[80]

As at Athens, the people from these different cities not only identified primarily with each other but also organized themselves in civic groups. There were separate shrines and dedications on Delos for the gods of different Levantine cities;[81] there is evidence for sustained endogamy or intermarriage among the Aradites;[82] and people from the different cities took different sides during the Mithridatic Wars.[83] There were also professional associations attached to particular cities: in 178 BCE, businessmen of "Laodikeia in Phoenicia" (the Seleucid kings' name for Beirut, as noted above), who were involved in warehouses and shipping, voted honors to one Heliodorus, a minister of Seleucus IV;[84] a *synodos* (assembly) of Aradites may have erected an honorary statue in 162;[85] and in 153, the "*synodos* of the Herakleists [i.e., Melqartians] of Tyre, merchants and shippers" commemorated establishing a physical base in the city.[86] At about the same time, "the *koinon* (association) of the Poseidoniasts of Beirut, merchants and shippers and *endocheis*" honored Marcus Minatius, a Roman banker, for enabling them to set up a similar establishment,[87] and around 90 BCE, the same *koinon* honored another Roman benefactor, Gaius Octavius.[88]

Although links between individuals from different Levantine cities on Delos appear comparatively weak, Phoenician-speakers did have substantial interactions with the Greek and Italian populations. They frequented the gymnasium; participated in politics, the Greek ephebate, and the Delian Games; intermarried with Italians; and dedicated at Greek sanctuaries— though apparently not at each other's.[89] The honors awarded by the Beiruti Poseidoniasts to their Roman benefactor included the right to participation in the social activities of their *koinon*, and their large and impressive establishment includes shrines to Ashtart, "Poseidon of Beirut," and the goddess Roma, as well as a dedication of the famous image of Aphrodite beating off a satyr with her slipper, which could be read as a distinctly Greek joke. Perhaps the best example of a well-connected Levantine man living on Delos in this period is Philostratos, a citizen of Naples, originally from Ashkelon, who honored the "Italians" (*Italikoi*) on the island and was honored by them, who funded part of the "Agora of the Italians" as well as the sanctuary of the gods of Ashkelon, and whose son was an ephebe at Athens in the late 90s BCE.[90]

IDENTIFYING DIFFERENCE

The practices of the "Italians" on Delos make a striking contrast with those of Phoenician-speaking merchants. They not only identified as "Italians," but operated professionally in four corporate associations dedicated to different gods with no reference to civic attachments,[91] and they came together in the second century to build the enormous "Agora of the Italians."[92] Inscriptions by "Israelites" are also found on Delos,[93] and in 166 BCE, a group of "Syrians" organized themselves as a *koinon* to celebrate the festival of the Syrian goddess.[94] Interestingly, however, Greeks on Delos sometimes seem to have shared the Levantine lack of enthusiasm for regional ethnic identities. It is unsurprising that there are honorific decrees by the "Athenians established at Delos" from the period when the Athenians were officially responsible for the governance of the island,[95] but a subscription for repairs to the Agora of the Italians lists a variety of Greeks and Levantines by giving their names, patronymics, and the names of their cities, mentioning two Delians, three Athenians, a Salaminian, a Chiot, a Knidian, a Tyrian, and a Sidonian, although it lists thirty-six Italians by name and patronymic only.[96]

A similar picture emerges in other contexts. By the Hellenistic period, people from the Levantine cities were winning prizes at several of the great Greek festivals, including the Delian and Nemean games, the Theseia and the Panathenaia.[97] Like Greeks, of course, "Phoenician" winners at these games are always recorded as coming from particular city-states, but in other Hellenistic-period inscriptions, too, they are labeled by their cities, even when others are given larger group identities. One Greek inscription of about 200 BCE on a public tomb for mercenaries who fought for Iasos in Caria identifies the dead in a surprising variety of ways: some solely by patronymics; some, including Phoenician- and Greek-speakers, also according to their city (Aradite, Sidonian, Synopean, Tyrasian, Byzantian, of the Antiochenes); and others with patronymics and larger place-based identities—of the Galatoi, Mede, Cilician, Scythian. This is a nice illustration of the range of possibilities available, and of the place of Phoenician-speakers on one Greek language spectrum.[98]

Evidence from elsewhere, however, also suggests that Greek and Phoenician speakers could see things differently. It is, as already noted, relatively common to find several generations of ancestors listed in Phoenician-language inscriptions, while it never became normal in Greek epigraphy to give more than one, and Greeks tended to focus on the immediate family or on legendary ancestors, gods and city-founders, rather than on the intervening generations.[99] More strikingly, although both groups identified primarily in relation to their cities rather than larger ethnic constructs, the Greek norm was to call both citizens and their cities by ethnonyms ("Athenian, the Athenians"), reserving toponyms ("Athens") for specific references to the physical urban center,[100] while in Phoenician, use of the toponym for cities is standard. Kings, for instance, are always kings of a particular city rather than of a group of citizens: MLK GBL (king of Byblos), MLK KTY (king of Kition), MLK SDNM (king of Sidon—which was literally called in Phoenician "the Sidons").[101] For Phoenician-speakers, it seems, cities were places more than communities. This may relate to different political cultures: the fourth-century inscription recording the diplomatic relations between Athens and Sidon names the partners in the agreement as on the one hand the "Athenians," and on the other the "king of Sidon" and his descendants.[102] Fifth- and fourth-century coinage from the "Phoenician" cities also suggests that civic identity was seen and valued rather differently there than among their Greek neighbors: unlike contemporary Greek examples, almost all these coins name the king rather than his city.[103]

For the most part, Greek-Phoenician bilingual inscriptions found in Greek contexts simply follow the Greek norm and give civic identities as adjectives in both languages, but some exceptions suggest that the identity of the same person could be conceptualized differently in Greek and Phoenician, and that Phoenician-language inscriptions were more focused on family and ancestry than Greek ones. The third-century inscription from the Piraeus mentioned above that honors a religious official of the Sidonian community, for instance, calls him "Shamabaal son of Magon" in Phoenician, but "Diopeithes the Sidonian" in Greek.[104] Another interesting example occurs in the third- or second-century bilingual dedication whose discovery on Malta in the eighteenth century led to the decipherment of the Phoenician script. This reads in Phoenician, "To our lord, to Melqart, Baal of Tyre, [the thing] that your servant Abdosir and his brother Osirshamar, sons of Osirshamar, son of Abdosir, have dedicated, because he [i.e. Melqart] heard their voice, may he bless them," and in Greek, more simply, "Dionysos and Serapion the sons of Serapion, Tyrians, to Herakles Archegetes."[105] The two men describe themselves in Greek as Tyrians, but the Phoenician text simply names the brothers and their father, with no direct mention of a civic identity.[106] Their city of origin is still evoked in the dedication to "Melqart, Baal of Tyre"; even then, however, it is the brothers' religious rather than civic connection with Tyre that is emphasized.

Finally, there is literary evidence that Phoenician-speakers were less inclined than Greeks were at times to subsume civic identifications under

larger regional ones. We have no evidence for communal Phoenician institutions of the kind that evolved among Greeks abroad in the Archaic period
like the "Helleneion" sanctuary in sixth-century Naukratis in Egypt, where
Herodotus says that Greeks from several cities, Ionian, Dorian, and Aeo-
lian, worshipped, or the altar to Apollo Archegetes at Naxos described by
Thucydides as "used by all Greeks."[107] There is no reason to think that such institutions would not be reported in the literary sources we do have: Herodotus does in fact record a fifth-century "Camp of the Tyrians" at Memphis,
another Egyptian city further to the south, where "Phoenician Tyrians" live
around the temples of Proteus and foreign Aphrodite (Ashtart).[108] Although
Herodotus glosses these Tyrians abroad as "Phoenician," on his own account
this is something they themselves (or perhaps their Egyptian hosts) don't
feel the need to do. In the case of the Hellenion, by contrast, it seems that the
name was chosen by the migrants rather than their hosts (or Herodotus):
more than twenty dedications from Naukratis have been plausibly restored
as offerings "to the Gods of the Greeks," a phrase that find no parallels in
Phoenician.[109] This suggests that these Greek-speakers abroad chose (like
the Italians later did on Delos) to identify with other Greeks, emphasizing
at least in this context their collective Hellenicity, rather than to assemble
in civic groups, like contemporary Tyrians. Can external commentators like
Herodotus take us further in the search for Phoenician identities than the
evidence that survives from the Phoenicians themselves? That is the question that I will explore in the next chapter.

CHAPTER 3

Sea People

One of the most striking developments in studies of ethnicity over the past few decades, as in studies of identity in general, is a much greater emphasis on how people, and peoples, define themselves—"emic" perspectives—over how they are defined by others ("etic" perspectives).[1] But even if the emphasis here too is on how the people we call Phoenicians saw themselves, we don't need to discount the views of others. For one thing, external commentators might reveal collective identifications on the part of Phoenicians that are not apparent from our limited Phoenician-language sources. And furthermore, self-identification does not happen in a vacuum: not only does a sense of "us" need some "them" from which to differentiate itself, but other peoples' opinions often affect the delineation of self.[2] Internal and external perceptions can be difficult to disentangle: as we have already seen, for example, when local intellectuals and politicians label the Lebanese population "Phoenician," this looks like an emic claim, but it involves an etic perspective on the ancient Phoenicians and relies in part on the doubly external perspective of European scholarship.[3]

I will argue in this chapter, however, that external sources fail to reveal a sense of common identity, history, or origins on the part of the ancient Phoenicians themselves, but suggest instead that they were not seen even by their neighbors as a homogenous ethnic group or nation. Instead, the label picks out social characteristics, designating a group united by contemporary culture and practice rather than by historical links, and it tells us more about the authors who use it than about their "Phoenician" subjects.

Near Eastern sources are unhelpful here, as they do not have a concept of Phoenicia.[4] Usually they simply identify people as belonging to one of the coastal cities, even in contexts where others are given larger regional designations: the *Ahiqar*, for instance, a fifth-century BCE Aramaic document from Elephantine in Egypt, contrasts the "Sidonian" who is familiar with the sea with the "Arabian" who is more comfortable inland.[5] If a larger geographical region is identified, it is much larger than our "Phoenicia." In addition to the broad and vague concept of "Canaan" found in the Hebrew Bible that I discussed briefly in the previous chapter, the Assyrians, whose rise to power began in the tenth century BCE, labeled the whole of the Levant "Amorite" or "Hittite" (the former a geographical term, the latter a cultural one). In the later eighth century, Sargon could call a region stretching from Cyprus to the Euphrates "the wide land of Amurru, the Hittite-land in its entirety,"[6] and by the late seventh century, "Hittite" seems to have become the standard regional description for an area much larger than Phoenicia.[7]

It is only Greek and then Roman authors who delineate a smaller region called Phoenicia, describe as Phoenicians those who come from that area, and constitute the sole source of our own concept of the "Phoenicians." In this chapter, I will look first for clues preserved in these sources about the identities held by the people they discuss, and then at how the Greeks and Romans themselves conceptualized their "Phoenicians."

MYTHICAL COMMUNITIES

One obvious place to look for communal identity is in accounts of common historical memories, which, as Ernest Renan reminded us above, need not be real memories of events that actually happened. Promisingly, Herodotus tells us in his seventh book that "the Phoenicians, as they say themselves, used to live in the Erythrean Sea [our Indian Ocean], but migrated to Syria, where they now live on the coast."[8] This could be interpreted not simply as a communal memory but as a constitutive event for the Phoenicians, like the stories of the joint Achaean expedition to Troy, or the Israelite Exodus: "[s]tories of migration, movement and settlement are important for notions of origin and identity."[9]

All may not be as it seems, however: when the same story about Phoenician migration from the Indian Ocean is reported in passing in Herodotus's opening series of claims and counterclaims in relation to the Persian Wars, it is assigned to Persian rather than Phoenician sources.[10] Furthermore, Herodotus's reliability when it comes to ascribing the stories he tells to particular peoples has been called into serious question, not least since the tales allegedly told by the Persians at the beginning of his work are largely in fact taken from Greek myth.[11] Even if his story of Phoenician migration was based on a real conversation with "Phoenicians" and is elsewhere attributed to the Persians in error, who was Herodotus actually talking to, and was the label "Phoenician" their own or his? The only specific encounter that Herodotus mentions in Phoenicia is with priests of the temple of Melqart at Tyre, from whom he learns about the foundation of that city (and temple) 2,300 years earlier: this story of migration from the Indian Ocean would fit nicely into that conversation, and it would not be surprising if Herodotus generalized Tyrian views of their civic origins to the larger group of "Phoenicians" of which he himself certainly considered the Tyrians to be members.[12] Different considerations apply to his story that in 525 BCE the "Phoenicians" who served in the Persian fleet refused to fight for the Persian king Cambyses against the Carthaginians on the grounds that they could not make war on their "children," to whom they were bound by "great oaths."[13] If true, then this was a sensible as well as sentimental move in the face of the rising power in the west. But even if this was a claim made by all three Phoenician contingents fighting for Cambyses, that does not mean they saw themselves as a collective, only that Tyrians, Sidonians, and Aradites all migrated to the west.[14]

If accounts of historical events are problematic, what evidence do we have from Greek sources for Phoenician myths of common descent? Greek authors of the Classical period supply an eponymous founder-figure for Phoenicia, Phoinix, but the tales of his adventures do not seem to be based on local sources, and Phoinix and his family, including Agenor, Kadmos, and Europa, are only explicitly associated with Phoenicia in Greek myth from the sixth or even fifth centuries BCE, rather later than they make their first appearances in Greek literature.[15] Furthermore, Phoinix in these Greek tales is the founder of Phoenicia, rather than of the Phoenicians, an important distinction: these stories do not perform a political function, demarcating (for locals) a territory or polity belonging to Phoenicians, but simply an explanatory one, accounting (to Greeks) for the country called Phoenicia.[16]

Even the Greek stories told about Phoinix as a founder are strangely incoherent, suggesting some ambivalence about their meaning.[17] The fullest account is supplied by Apollodorus in the second century BCE: Agenor, who was born in Egypt, "left for Phoenicia and became a king,"[18] and after his daughter Europa was abducted by Zeus in the guise of a bull, he sent his sons Phoinix, Kilix, and Kadmos with one Thasos to search for her, telling them not to return without her. When they failed in their mission "Phoinix settled in Phoenicia, Kilix settled near Phoenicia and all the country subject to himself he called Cilicia, Kadmos . . . settled in Thrace and Thasos founded a city Thasos."[19] The implication is that Phoinix gave his name to the place he settled, just as his brothers did, but this is awkward, since Phoenicia is explicitly said to have been his starting point.

Similar problems arise in the earliest surviving reference to Phoinix as a founder, a fragment from a play by Euripides. The passage begins: "Kadmos the son of Agenor, leaving the city of Sidon, came to the land of Thebes; born

Phoenician [*phoinix*], he changed his stock [*genos*] to Hellenic once he set-tled on Dirce's plain." The anonymous speaker then promises to explain why Kadmos had to come to Thebes, "having left Phoenicia's land," and begins by saying that Agenor had three sons, who also included Kilix "from whom Cilicia is named" and "Phoinix, from whom that land takes its name." At this point, however, the text breaks off.[20] We do not know if Euripides went on to explain how Phoenicia got its name from Phoinix, but it seems unlikely that it was supposed to have happened before his brother Kadmos was "born Phoenician" in Sidon and subsequently "left Phoenicia's land."[21] The Sidonian context also seems awkward, making the eponymous founder of Phoenicia as a whole a descendent of the king of one of its constituent cities.[22]

A later story about the same family, in which a notion of kinship sug-gests a shared descent myth, at least between Tyre and Sidon, is explicitly said to come from local sources. Curtius Rufus, writing in the first cen-tury CE, claims that when Alexander the Great stormed Tyre in 332, the Sidonians fighting in his army "mindful of their kinship [*cognatio*] with the Tyrians—for they believed that Agenor founded both cities—secretly protected many of the Tyrians and took them to their ships, in which they were hidden and conveyed to Sidon. By this deception 15,000 were saved from the victor's cruelty."[23] However, although the facts that Curtius relays are reasonably plausible, the explanation given for them need not be part of the original story—and even if we do accept that it owes something to Sidonian beliefs, these may have emerged closer to Curtius's own time than the events he recounts.

The best hope for getting to a local origin myth through Greek-language sources comes from the second-century CE *Phoenician Enquiry* of Philo of Byblos, now preserved only in fragments recorded by later authors.[24] Claims that Philo worked from local sources go back to at least the third century CE, when Porphyry of Tyre described the *Phoenician Enquiry* as a transla-tion of the work of one Sanchuniathon who lived in Tyre before the Trojan War,[25] and who Philo himself tells us was drawing on the commentaries of the Egyptian god Thoth.[26] Perhaps unsurprisingly, Philo's work was largely dismissed as Greek storytelling until a treasure trove of Bronze Age mythi-cal texts discovered at the port of Ugarit in 1929 and fragments of the Hit-tite Kumarbi myths found in Turkey a few years later revealed surprisingly close parallels with parts of his text. As a result, Philo is now usually seen as exploiting Near Eastern legends as well as Greek ones, although it is very difficult to tell exactly when this is happening, and to what extent.[27]

There are, however, good reasons to read Philo's story of the origins of Phoenicia as one that had emerged relatively recently, and in a Greek cultural context. He tells us that Kolpia and his wife Baau begot mortal sons whose children in their turn "settled Phoenicia," gave their names to its mountain ranges, founded Tyre, and discovered useful things like fire and fishing, salt and the alphabet.[28] The clue to the "Hellenicity" of this tale is that several of the humans listed, including Pollux, Misor, Sydyk, and Chousor, who is identified in the text with Hephaistos, are better known in both Greek and Near Eastern myths as gods: the whole passage is indebted to euhemerism, the atheist fashion of the Hellenistic period in which supposed gods were rationalized as historical persons.[29]

Elsewhere in his work, Philo recounts a different myth of regional foundations, which positively undermines the notion of a collective and exclusive Phoenician identity based on common descent: the god "Kronos," whom Philo identifies with El, founds Byblos as the first city in Phoenicia and later gives it to the goddess Baaltis, shortly after he has given Attica to his daughter Athena and at the same time as he gives Beirut to Poseidon, the Kabeiroi, the Agrotai, and the Halieis.[30] This is a story about cities rather than regions, where gods and not humans are the founders, it mixes Greek and Near Eastern gods and places, and it makes no specific link between these gods and the later human populations of the places they are given.

There is then no solid evidence in the Greek sources for an identity as Phoenician among their "Phoenicians." They can, however, tell us a lot about how these Phoenicians were perceived by their neighbors—and how these perceptions helped those neighbors construct their own identity. Things change over time, of course, and I will look here first at the Archaic and Classical periods, then later at Greek authors, and finally at the picture of the Phoenicians painted in the Roman period.

GREEK PHOENICIANS

The Phoenicians' debut in Greek literature is in Homer's *Iliad*, so it dates to the eighth or seventh century BCE. The Greek word *phoinix* must in fact relate to the word *po-ni-ki-jo* found in second millennium BCE Linear B tablets from the palaces at Pylos and Knossos, which already seems to have a similar range of meanings, including "crimson" and "palm tree," but the term is not used as a description of a group of people in these texts.[31] Once they do appear, however, these Phoenicians are fundamentally a people of—and on—the sea.[32] This is an idea that Homer may well have inherited from a Near Eastern tradition: the kings of Arados, Tyre, Sidon, Byblos, and others are called "kings of the seacoast" in ninth-century Assyrian texts.[33]

However that may be, very little is said about the Phoenicians as a group by any Greek author in the Archaic and Classical periods other than that, as Homer put it, they are "famous for their ships" (*nausiklutoi*); there is no sense of a shared Phoenician character, culture, or society, and the focus is instead on their parallels and relationships with Greeks.[34]

Homer's Phoenicians are already firmly associated with the sea. At the funeral games for Patroklos in the *Iliad*, the first prize in the footrace is the most beautiful silver mixing bowl in the world, made by "Sidonians [*Sidones*], well skilled in handicrafts," but brought across the "murky sea" by Phoenician men (*phoinikes andres*).[35] The people making bowls on land are identified according to their city, but the people transporting and trading the same bowls are generic "Phoenicians."[36] This point is reiterated in a later *scholium* or marginal comment on a manuscript copy of this passage, which declares that "to a supreme degree the Phoenicians were the first to plow the seas."[37] A similar notion is found in the *Odyssey*; when Odysseus pretends to Athena that he is a fugitive from Crete, he tells her that he was carried to Ithaca as a paying passenger by "lordly Phoenicians" who have allegedly now returned to "well-peopled Sidonia": here Phoenicians at sea are again associated with the city of Sidon on land.[38]

And that is about all there is to them: Susan Frankenstein has already argued that Homer does not present the Phoenicians in ethnic terms at all: in the Archaic period "Phoenician . . . refers to a category of people involved in certain recognisable activities rather than to a single ethnic group, e.g. in the Homeric poems, all traders are 'Phoenicians'."[39] Erich Gruen notes, furthermore, that Homer's Phoenicians are "without a monolithic character": while some individuals are presented as greedy, other tales reflect well on Phoenician characters.[40] Perhaps unsurprisingly, "Phoenicia" itself is a vague concept in Homer, described only as being on a route between Cyprus and Egypt.[41]

Two or three hundred years later, Herodotus is clearer on the geography: Phoenicia is the northern part of the seacoast of Syria, including the cities of Tyre and Sidon, with Palestine to the south separating it from Egypt.[42] However, he never directly locates "Phoenicians" in "Phoenicia."[43] Furthermore, although their maritime and mercantile associations continue to be emphasized, Theodore Mavrogiannis has pointed out that despite more than forty references to Phoenicians, Herodotus gives "no organised description of the Phoenicians with their customs and traditions, as we have in the case of the Egyptians, Ethiopians, Persians, and Scythians."[44]

Herodotus's Phoenicians are people of the sea from their first appearance in the first chapter of the first book, where we are told that learned

Persians blame the Phoenicians for the dispute between the Greeks and the barbarians that led to the Persian Wars: "For these, they say, having come to this sea from the sea called Erythrean [our Indian Ocean], and settled in the country where they still now live, at once began to make long sailing voyages. Among other places to which they carried Egyptian and Assyrian merchandise, they came to Argos . . . and set out their cargo."[45] A few days later, these Phoenicians kidnap the Argive king's daughter, Io, and make off for Egypt. But trade and abduction are not the only reasons that Herodotus's Phoenicians take to the sea: the Phoenicians also make up the core of the Persian fleet.[46] It is worth noting in this context that although Herodotus repeatedly refers to this naval force as simply "Phoenician," its leaders are identified according to his own account by their individual cities of Tyre, Sidon, and Arados, suggesting that they in fact commanded separate contingents, while other distinguished captains in the Persian navy are described in larger regional terms as "Cilician," "Lycian," "Cypriot," and "Carian."[47] As well as military operations, Phoenician ships undertook peaceful expeditions, such as a circumnavigation of Africa on behalf of the king of Egypt, and they founded settlements, temples, and gold mines abroad.[48] Again, the way these events are described can be noteworthy: Herodotus follows his discussion of the foundation of the temples of "Herakles" at Tyre with a comment that "Phoenicians" established another temple of Herakles at Thasos on their voyage in search of Europa: as in Homer, the move here from the activities of the people of Tyre at home to those of Phoenicians overseas is striking.[49] Indeed, Herodotus's persistent association of the sea with the Phoenicians as a whole, rather than with particular civic communities, makes it all the more likely that he would have extended a story of Tyrian origins in the Indian Ocean to the Phoenicians as a whole, as suggested above.

The few episodes Herodotus recounts involving Phoenicians that are not actually set at sea are still almost all connected with overseas contact of one kind or another. Kadmos and his fellow-migrants taught the alphabet and the worship of Dionysus to the Greeks,[50] and in turn the Phoenicians acknowledged that they learned circumcision from the Egyptians—although Herodotus notes that they tended to give it up through contact with the Greeks:[51] by his account, they just are not very good at practicing distinctive collective behavior. At the same time, Herodotus draws attention to the connections between Greeks and Phoenicians, including the existence of Phoenician elements at the heart of Athens: the tyrant-slayers Harmodius and Aristogeiton, he reports, were members of the Gephyraian clan who (despite their own claims to the contrary) were Phoenicians who had come with their leader Kadmos to Greek Thebes.[52]

As we have seen, Herodotus is by no means the only author in this period interested in the Phoenician background of Kadmos and in the fictive kinship relations between Greeks and Phoenicians his adventures created. Euripides's Phoenician Women, the chorus of his tragedy by that name, have stopped in Thebes on their way to become temple slaves at Delphi because of the kinship between Tyre and Thebes. And in this case again, Phoenicians are found away from home, and they have arrived by sea.[53] Thucydides conforms to the same pattern: he mentions Phoenicians only in passing, but they are on the seas and overseas. He describes their piratical settlements on islands in the very distant past,[54] and also lists them among the "barbarians" who later lived in Sicily, the first author to our knowledge to describe them as such, explaining that: "The Phoenicians too lived round all of Sicily, occupying both coastal promontories and adjacent islands for the sake of trade with the Sikels. But when many Greeks sailed in by sea after them, the Phoenicians left most of these places and settling together lived in Motya, Soluntum and Panormus . . . partly because the voyage from Sicily to Carthage was shortest from there."[55]

It should be no surprise that intellectuals writing at a time of unprecedented maritime travel and migration by Greek-speakers quickly associated Phoenicians with the sea: that was where they encountered them, both close to home and farther away. And this was not only a phenomenon of the far west, where Levantines and Greeks settled in proximity: Herodotus and other authors emphasize the extent of cohabitation by Greeks and Phoenicians in the Aegean, and the material evidence also supports literary accounts of Levantine activities, settlements, and cults there.[56] Still, why did Greek authors recognize some sailors from other Mediterranean city-states as fellow-Greeks and others as something else?

One thing that would have clearly distinguished "Phoenicians" from Greeks for Greeks was their language. The role of the Greek language as a criterion for Greekness itself is disputed: Jonathan Hall has argued that despite a great deal of evidence for mutual comprehension across dialects, there is little for the "awareness of a common Hellenic language" before the fifth century, and that even then the relative linguistic homogeneity of the epigraphical evidence from the Classical period might conceal a great "diversity of oral idioms."[57] Nonetheless, it would not be necessary for a Greek to be able to understand every other form of spoken Greek to note that Phoenician is very different from all of them: one can imagine a Londoner baffled by a Glaswegian, but still readily able to distinguish the language being spoken from Arabic. The importance of language in Greek perceptions of "Phoenicians" seems to be confirmed in a fourth-century letter supposedly written by Plato, which warns that a time may come when "in the whole of Sicily, overthrown by the Phoenicians or Opici and brought under their dominion, there will hardly be a trace of the Greek tongue."[58]

Nonetheless, these new neighbors must have seemed rather familiar to the Greeks: also from city-states and often ports, the Phoenicians were traders and migrants much like themselves, who went about siting their settlements in a very similar way, on straits, in pairs, and where possible offshore.[59] Some have gone so far as to suggest that the Greeks took the idea of the *polis* from the Levantine city-states.[60] Such early contact, cohabitation, and familiarity helps explain why Greek authors tended to give the Phoenicians a less distinctive treatment than other peoples.

There is, however, another important factor in the Greek construction of the Phoenicians: developing identities among Greek speakers themselves. These meetings were taking place at a time when, as Irad Malkin has put it, "Greeks, as Greeks, came to recognize specific commonalities among themselves, articulating them in terms of common narratives, ethnic geneaologies, awareness of a common language, and access to Panhellenic cults."[61] Sub-Greek identities also coalesced in this period, constructing supposed kinship groups such as Dorian and Ionian as well as regional identities like Rhodian.[62] As noted in my introduction, these processes of identity construction were initially aggregative rather than oppositional, emphasizing similarities between the same people more than their differences from other peoples, but the treatment of the Phoenicians in Greek literature illustrates the way in which the Greek-speakers could also constitute themselves in terms of identifications with non-Greeks. Similarities and interactions can be as important as binary oppositions for the constitution of collective identity, and identification *with* can somethimes do more than identification *as* or *against*.[63] By highlighting their similarities with the Phoenicians, Greek-speakers identified themselves too as people of the sea; through kinship connections with Kadmos and his family, as well as through the "translation" of Phoenician gods into Greek equivalents to be discussed in chapter 6, they tied themselves into the story of Phoenician colonization, and through that, into longer, grander, and more exotic narratives.

CHARACTER DEVELOPMENT

Signs of a hardening of the boundaries between Greek and Phoenician were already emerging at the end of the fifth century, when Thucydides could call the Phoenicians barbarians in the passage mentioned above. His report of the arrival of the Phoenicians in Sicily also seems to generalize contemporary frictions, in that it "implies resistance and conflict right from the start between two ethnicities, Phoenicians and Greeks, whereas in fact the initial situation in Sicily had been more fluid, reciprocal, and transitory."[64]

This interest in firmer boundary-marking continues in later Greek authors. For Pseudo-Skylax, who wrote a *periplus*, or sailing gazetteer, of the Mediterranean in the fourth century, the Phoenicians were again "barbarians," a subgroup of the Syrians who lived on the coast of Syria from the Thapsakos River (probably the Orontes) down to Ashkelon, as well as in colonies elsewhere.[65] Unusually for him, Pseudo-Skylax does not name Phoenicia itself, a choice that continued the tradition of disassociation between the people and the place: "And past Caria is Lycia, an *ethnos*. . . . And past Lycia is Pamphylia, an *ethnos*. . . . And after Pamphylia is Cilicia, an *ethnos*. . . . There is after Cilicia the *ethnos* of the Syrians. And in Syria there live, on the coast, the Phoenicians, an *ethnos*."

This passage also fits in with a hardening sense of Phoenician "groupness": Pseudo-Skylax is the first surviving Greek author to describe the Phoenicians as an *ethnos*. To call a group an *ethnos* in ancient Greek was not, to be sure, to describe it as an ethnic group in modern terms. If Greek-speakers wanted to specify a group of people who were understood to share descent, or at least to be "enlisted automatically by birth"— something closer to a modern definition of ethnicity, whether objective or subjective—they could use the term *genos*, from the root *gignesthai*, "to be born."[66] *Ethnos* by contrast simply meant a group of individuals—sometimes animals—who had something in common, from descent to class to gender. It was often used with a meaning similar to the vague English term "people," whether at the level of the city-state or in larger regional groupings. It is important to note, however, that both terms could be used very vaguely and often interchangeably, and this new development is still significant.[67]

The Greek stereotype of the Phoenicians also develops new aspects in the fourth century, suggesting a thicker conception of them as a coherent group with a particular character. But although some authors seem to describe them as wily or even mendacious, the examples we have may implicate Greeks as well. In his *Republic*, for instance, Plato has Socrates call his imagined community's origins myth a "Phoenician thing" (*Phoinikikon ti*), but then he explains this as the kind of story about the past that (Greek) poets tell; here the association of Greek myth with a "Phoenician" practice may in fact undermine notions of Greek virtue and superiority. The same could be true of a fragment of a comic play hesitantly attributed to Aristophanes, in which a character says, "I am becoming a true Phoenician:

with one hand I give and with the other I take away," but we do not know whether the character speaking is a Greek or a Phoenician.[68]

Although these examples are not necessarily criticisms,[69] an association with deceitfulness seems to have stuck: two centuries later, Posidonius of Apameia called a story told by the people of Gadir (Latin Gades, modern Cádiz) about the foundation of their city a "Phoenician lie."[70] And another story suggests that deceitfulness was not the only negative association with the Phoenicians, at least in regions where Greeks and Phoenicians lived in close proximity: around the year 300 BCE, the poet Hermesianax of Kolophon recounts the tale of Arkeophon, a prosperous man from Salamis in Cyprus whose parents were "undistinguished" Phoenicians, and whose efforts to woo the daughter of King Nikokreon (r. c. 332–310) failed because the king, himself descended from Teucer, a comrade of Agamemnon in the Trojan War, "was ashamed of Arkeophon's ancestry, since his parents were Phoenicians." Arkeophon's subsequent attempts to persuade the girl to sleep with him without telling her parents are also a failure, and he starves himself to death; justice is served, however, when the princess's hauteur as she watches Arkeophon being cremated annoys Aphrodite, who turns her to stone.[71]

Could a stronger and more negative sense of the Phoenicians from the late fifth century map onto changes in Greek constructions of their own identities? As noted above, the fifth century did see a distinct hardening of the boundaries between Greeks and non-Greeks in Greek literature, and the development of a more (though by no means entirely) oppositional and hierarchical sense of Greekness.[72] The new characterization of the Phoenicians as "barbarians" fits into this trend, as does evidence for the assimilation of the Phoenicians with other barbarians in opposition to Greeks: in a speech that Plato puts into the mouth of Aspasia in his *Menexenos*, for instance, she praises the Athenians "because we are purely Hellenes and not mixed with barbarians. You will not find the descendants of Pelops, Kadmos, Aigyptos or Danaos or the many others who are barbarian by nature but Hellenes by convention living among us."[73]

This is, however, a difficult example: the author seems to satirize Aspasia's views, a point that emerges from the simple fact that Aspasia herself is not an Athenian but a Milesian.[74] And it is easy to overemphasize the Greek, or Athenian, "invention of the barbarian" even in the fifth century, when "Hellenic" identity was already increasingly defined in terms of culture and education rather than kinship and descent, a change commented on by the fourth-century orator Isocrates when he says that Athens brought it about that "the name of 'Hellenes' no longer evokes a descent-group [*genos*] but a way of thinking [*dianoia*] and that people are called 'Hellenes' who share in our education [*paideia*] rather than our origin [*phusis*]."[75]

One reason for the more distinctive and critical presentation of the Phoenicians in Greek sources in this period may have been the role played by Sidonians, Tyrians, and Aradites in the Persian navy. This force was so closely identified with its Phoenician members that both Herodotus and Thucydides could simply refer to the whole of the Persian fleet as Phoenician, and Herodotus tells us that three Phoenician triremes were displayed at three Greek sanctuaries after their victory over the Persians at Salamis in 480 BCE.[76] The reaction though, if that is what this is, seems to start rather late,[77] and it is likely that the increasingly negative presentation of the Phoenicians as a whole was encouraged just as much, if not more, by the decidedly negative stereotype of the Carthaginians and their allies that began to develop in the fifth century in reaction to contemporary hostilities in the central Mediterranean between Greek-speaking communities and Carthage.

There seems to have been a sense among Greeks of a signficant connection between their Carthaginian and Phoenician enemies in different parts of the Mediterranean. Herodotus tells us that after the battle of Lade in 494, the Phokaian general Dionysus fled Ionia to operate as a pirate, targeting Phoenician and then Carthaginian and Etruscan merchant shipping for punishment.[78] The same mentality may explain Herodotus's report that the Sicilians placed the Athenian battle against the Persian fleet at Salamis and the Syracusan battle against the Carthaginian army at Himera on the same day in 480 BCE.[79] Although untrue, this notion persisted in Greek literature, and even became more elaborate, with the fourth-century historian Ephorus of Kyme claiming that the Persians and Phoenicians had approached Carthage before Himera, asking for its aid against Greece, just as the Greeks were supposed to have approached Syracuse for support against Persia.[80] Jonathan Prag has shown that this synchronism between Himera and Salamis worked in Sicily as part of a new form of propaganda that conflict with Carthage from the fifth century onward suggested to the island's Greek tyrants: just like Athens and Sparta in their wars against the Persians, they could now pose as the liberators of Greeks from barbarians.[81]

The connection between Phoenicians and Carthaginians is emphasized in literary reports of the latter's western wars, where they are sometimes simply called "Phoenician." Examples include Pindar's celebration of Hieron the king of Syracuse, in which he expresses the hope that after his city's victories at Himera and then at Cumae (in 474 BCE) the Phoenician and Etruscan battle cry will remain quiet (perhaps another hint that the fundamental reference of the term was linguistic); the fourth-century BCE letter by "Plato" quoted above; and a third-century BCE mention by Theocritus of Phoenicians on "the outer edge of Libya." Two hundred years later, Diodorus Siculus reports a fleet attacking Syracuse in 396 BCE in what he calls both a war with the Carthaginians and a "Phoenician war"; he also regularly refers to Syracuse's Carthaginian opponents as "Phoenicians."[82]

Nonetheless, most Greek discussions even of western Phoenicians continue to treat them in a relatively neutral way, with little sign of strong differentiation between Greeks and Phoenicians: Aristotle's account of the constitution of Carthage, for instance, treats it in the same way as his Greek *poleis*, comparing and contrasting it in particular with the constitution of Sparta; Eratosthenes praises the good qualities of the governments of Carthage and Rome despite the fact that they are barbarians; and Polybius compares the Carthaginian and Roman constitutions to that of Sparta, and once again closely associates Phoenicians with the sea: maritime pursuits are their "ancestral craft," and something they are much better at than all other people.[83]

ROMAN PHOENICIANS

The picture in Latin sources is not so different. Even in the Roman period there was still a pretty vague idea of what, and where, Phoenicia actually was: for Strabo in the early first century CE, it was the coastal part of Coele Syria, extending from Orthosias south of the Eleutheros River all the way down to Pelusium, while for Pomponius Mela, writing just a little later in c. 45 CE, the Syrian coast is divided into Palestine, Phoenicia, and Antiochia. A decade or two later again, Pliny the Elder says that Phoenicia is an earlier name for part of what he simply calls Syria; those who insist on dividing the region further, he says, would call the middle part of the coast Phoenicia, with Syria to both the north and south; elsewhere however he traces Phoenicia from a former town called Crocodilion, south of Dor, up to Arados.[84]

The Latin vocabulary used in reference to the Phoenicians embodies this rather vague and even contradictory picture. The original Latin word for Phoenician was *poenus*, a simple transliteration of the Greek *phoinix* without the initial aspiration—a feature that Latin lacked until the second century BCE.[85] With its alternative adjectival form *punicus*, this term was applied indiscriminately to Phoenicians in the east and west.[86] Although toward the end of the Republic a new, aspirated word *phoenix* appeared, it was not commonly used, and the precise difference between the two Latin words *poenus* and *phoenix* was never fully clarified. Cicero makes a relatively rare distinction between eastern *Phoenices* and western *Poeni* in his speech for Scaurus delivered in 54 BCE: "All the records and histories of the past have demonstrated to us that the Phoenician people [*genus . . . Phoenicum*] is the most deceptive [*fallacissimum*]; the *Poeni* who arose from them have taught us through the many rebellions of the Carthaginians that they have not degenerated from their ancestors."[87] In the same year, however, he uses the term *Poeni* in *De republica* to mean Phoenicians of all kinds.[88] Furthermore, it may not be as certain as translators have traditionally assumed that when, in a speech to the senate in 56 BCE, he includes the *Poeni* among the "peoples and nations" (*gentes nationesque*) that the Romans surpass in piety (though not in cunning), he is thinking specifically of the Carthaginians.[89]

Confusion continues in the Imperial period, although *poenus* remains the standard term for "Phoenician" in Latin. *Phoenix* is occasionally used to distinguish the eastern Phoenicians as a separate group—the opposite of the modern practice of distinguishing the western Phoenicians from the main category—but in the mid-first century CE, Pomponius Mela refers to the "Phoenicians [*Phoenices*] who crossed from Africa to Tingentera" in Spain; it is unclear whether he is using *Phoinices* here of western Phoenicians or deliberately evoking an idea of an archaic eastern migration.[90] At times, the two are simply treated as synonyms: in the third or fourth century CE, the Latin prologue to the work of Dictys of Knossos refers (fantastically) to the text as being written originally in Phoenician letters (*phoenices litterae*), which a few lines are later called *punicae litterae*.[91]

Poenus and *punicus* are still used of eastern as well as western contexts in late antiquity. Augustine uses the term *phoenix* only once, as opposed to more than thirty-five instances of *punicus*; as we saw in the preceding chapter, for instance, he calls the Bible's Canaanite woman "a Canaanite, that is, a Phoenician woman who came from the region of Tyre and Sidon" (*Chananaea . . . hoc est punica mulier de finibus Tyri et Sidonis egressa*).[92] As noted above, this is more likely to be a reference to the language she speaks than an ethnic identification, and Augustine's general usage of the word *punicus* seems to relate to a shared language rather than to kinship, raising the distinct possibility that in the Latin as well as the Greek tradition the term continued to have a primarily linguistic meaning.

In one especially interesting passage, however, Augustine calls that language "Phoenician [*punica*], that is, African [*afra*]."[93] This picks up on another tradition whereby Latin authors from the late Republic onward deployed *poenus* and *punicus* to refer to things related to North Africa as a whole, both within and beyond the Levantine settlements there—perhaps at least in part because of the widespread use of the Punic language in the region, a topic to which I will return in chapter 8.[94]

The most famous example comes in the first ever use of the phrase usually rendered in English as "Punic faith," which is of course to say lack of faith, in Sallust's *Jugurthine War*, written in the 40s BCE. Here *punica fides* is ascribed not to a Phoenician of any kind, but the Mauretanian king Bocchus: "But I find that Bocchus more from *punica fides* than for the reasons he claimed lured both the Romans and the Numidian (i.e., Jugurtha) with the hope of peace."[95] More prosaically, in the second century BCE, Cato describes the pomegranate as a "Phoenician apple" (*malum punicum*).[96] Furthermore, the association between "African" and "Phoenician" works in both directions: Servius's late antique commentary on Virgil's *Aeneid* explains his maritime "rocks which the Italians call the altars" as the place where the "Afri et Romani" made a treaty.[97]

Despite the vaguenss of the language they used, Roman period authors did inherit from western Greeks the stereotype of the Carthaginians as deceptive, encouraged of course by the Punic Wars.[98] For Plautus in the third century, a "true Carthaginian" knows every language but cunningly pretends not to, and the late republican rhetorical handbook dedicated to Gaius Herennius quotes a speech of presumably mid-second century date claiming that the Carthaginians were confirmed treaty-breakers.[99] And again, this stereotype of Carthaginians was sometimes extended to Phoenicians as a whole in Roman contexts: according to Diodorus, a false treaty made by a Roman embassy with King Perseus of Macedon in 172 BCE led some of the older Roman senators to reflect that "it was not fitting for Romans to imitate Phoenicians, so as to overcome their enemies through deception and not through virtue."[100] We have already seen views about Phoenician deception expressed by Cicero, and a little later we have Livy's famous description of Hannibal's *perfidia plus quam punica* or "more than Phoenician perfidy."[101]

At the same time, deception is not the only Phoenician stereotype that later Roman commentators inherited from the earlier Greek sources. Cicero in particular repeatedly raises their maritime associations: in his speech about the Agrarian law of 63 BCE, he explains the Carthaginian tendency to fraud and mendacity not by their *genus*, as in the speech for Scaurus, but by the fact that their harbors brought them into contact with merchants and strangers,[102] and in *De republica*, written in 54 BCE, the same year as the speech for Scaurus, he describes the Phoenicians (along with the Etruscans) as a people of the sea: "[N]one of the barbarians were themselves originally sailors except the Etruscans and the Phoenicians [*Poeni*], the latter for commerce and the former as pirates."[103] Shortly afterward, the grammarian Verrius Flaccus tells us that "Tyrian waters" (*Tyria maria*) have become proverbial because the *Poeni,* originally from Tyre, have become so powerful on the sea that navigation is dangerous for everyone,[104] and a few decades later Pomponius Mela says that the *Phoinices* "discovered how to set sail on the sea by ship, how to conduct naval conflict, and how to rule over other peoples."[105]

"Phoenician," then, was not deployed in Greek and Roman literary sources to designate an ethnic group in and from Phoenicia. In its earliest usage, it was simply a vague term for Levantine sailors who spoke a distinctive language, and Greek authors tended to emphasize a wide range of similarities, geographical connections, and family relationships between these people and their own. The fact that the toponym and ethnonym do not map onto each other in several Greek sources—the wrinkles in the intellectual logic—suggests that the Phoenicians were not identified by their neighbors as a specific people attached to a specific place, culture, or history. The Phoenicians were first perceived as having a more distinct character in the late fifth century BCE, in the context of tensions between Carthage and Greek-speaking cities in Sicily. In the Roman period a stronger and sometimes more negative stereotype emerged, but there was still confusion over the appropriate vocabulary: *phoenix, poenus,* and *punicus* were used to designate a variety of Phoenician-speaking groups, and there was in particular a distinct tendency to use the adjective *punicus* in relation to North Africa as a whole, not just its Levantine inhabitants or settlements, and to the Phoenician language.

LITERATURE AND IDENTITY

I hope it is now clear that attempts to identify the Phoenicians as a single ethnic group, related by history, territory, or descent, do no justice to our ancient sources on this topic, internal and external. There is, however, an obvious objection to the story I have been telling so far, which is that it disregards the limitations of this evidence. Although our sources for Phoenician self-presentation are substantial—more than ten thousand inscriptions—the simple fact that they are inscriptions renders them suspect on this point: Greek and, for the most part, Hebrew epigraphy also lacks such large-scale "ethnics," despite the fact that the terms "Hellene" and "Israelite" do appear in their literatures, and we would hardly expect inscriptions to render foundation myths or historical stories of the sort we find, for instance, in Greek myth and the Hebrew Bible. We simply do not have Phoenician literary evidence of the kind that historians have used to reconstruct developing Greek and Israelite identities in the ancient Mediterranean.

Nonetheless, our lack of "appropriate" sources for ethnic identity in the case of the Phoenicians may not be a real loss for this particular project. For one thing, as we saw at the end of the previous chapter, different attitudes about identity between Phoenicians and others still emerge even from evidence in the same genre. For another, internal descriptions are usually smaller and more localized than external ones.[106] And finally, there is a real question mark over whether the kind of literature in which ancient intellectuals explored being Greek or Israelite ever actually existed in Phoenician.[107]

Despite earlier epic and mythical texts found in the archives from Ugarit, a near neighbor of the cities we traditionally classify as Phoenician, there is as yet no direct evidence for myth, epic, or poetry being written in the "Phoenician" cities of the first millennium BCE: the romantic idea that there is a lost world of Phoenician prose and poetry written on papyrus does not come from the ancient sources. Denis Feeney has pointed out that Greek and Latin literature is in fact an unusual phenomenon in the ancient Mediterranean: "It may appear natural for literate societies to have a literature, but this is a modernizing assumption against which we must be on our guard."[108]

It is perhaps telling that Herodotus gets his story of "Phoenician origins" from conversations with Tyrian priests, not from written documents. And although Pomponius Mela says rather vaguely in the first century CE that the Phoenicians invented "letters and literary works as well as other arts,"[109] when it comes to specifics, we hear only of technical writings of various kinds: Josephus says that Tyre kept archives going back to the time of Hiram and Solomon,[110] and Strabo sings the praises of the philosophers of his own period from Tyre and Sidon, associating the latter in particular with arithmetic and astronomy (both invented, as he points out, to aid trade and navigation).[111] At the same time, there were, of course, literary authors from the cities of the northern Levant who wrote in *Greek*, including Antipater of Sidon and Meleager of Gadara, who was educated at Tyre, and most famously Philo of Byblos, and I will return to them in chapter 7.[112]

Evidence for literature in Punic, the western dialect of Phoenician, is also missing, at least for the first millennium BCE. An agricultural treatise written by one Mago is the only item picked out for mention by Pliny (and indeed translation by the Roman senate) from the Carthaginian library that was donated to the "petty kings" of Africa after the destruction of that city; we do not know what the rest of the books in this library were about. Nor do we know in what language(s) they were written.[113] As Feeney has recently pointed out, it is very likely that Greek was a well-known language at Carthage, and there is no particular reason to think that the Carthaginians would have used a different one to participate in literary, philosophical, and theatrical pursuits: departure from the Mediterranean's Greek norm in this respect was, he argues, a development peculiar to Rome.[114] Punic was, however, a literary language by late antiquity: Augustine tells us that many things have been saved from oblivion in books written in Punic.[115]

If Phoenician literature itself did not exist, that would in itself be a real and interesting difference in cultural practices between Phoenician-speakers and Greek- and Hebrew-speakers in the Mediterranean of the first millennium BCE, which might relate to the apparent differences in their attitudes toward identity. Among the Greeks and Israelites, the invention of communal literatures involved not only the fabrication of literary languages that could be understood horizontally across a variety of regional subdialects, but also the contemplation and consolidation of group identity: from the massed Achaean army of the *Iliad* to the wanderings of the children of Israel to the athletes and spectators that Pindar celebrates traveling together between Greek competitions.[116] The existence of such identities among an intellectual elite then meant that they were also available to a wider group of people at times of pressure, such as the Persian invasion of Greece or the Babylonian exile of the Israelites, as one way of dealing with a difficult situation: this is, after all, the traditional catalyst for the emergence of ethnic identity. We have no evidence that the same was true of the Phoenicians.

It is relatively easy then to show that on the evidence available to us the ancient Phoenicians do not live up to standard modern scholarly definitions of an "ethnic group." We have no evidence that they used a common name, or shared notions of territory, history, or descent, or that others saw them as a clearly delineated "people." Ethnicity in this narrow sense is not, however, all there is to identity, and in this book I am interested in groupness and group-making as a whole. What did Phoenician-speakers have and hold in common; how did they differentiate themselves from others; and what sort of group or groups were created in this process? In the next part, I turn from text and theory to cultural practice, to investigate what patterns of interaction and identification emerge in the period up to the siege of Alexander in the east and the destruction of Carthage in the west. I begin in the next chapter by asking whether our "Phoenicians" act as a group in any contexts, concluding that the evidence for this is weak, and then focus in the rest of part 2 on smaller and more specific groups that Phoenician-speakers did form with each other.

PART II

Many Worlds

CHAPTER 4

Cultural Politics

The most vivid stories of collaboration, diplomacy, and cultural exchange in the Iron Age Levant are the tales told in the Hebrew Bible of the dealings between Tyre and the Israelite kingdoms to its south, first during the tenth century BCE, when Tyre and the United Monarchy supposedly operated a joint trading fleet and collaborated on the building of the temple in Jerusalem, and then in the ninth century when Ahab, ruler of the Northern Kingdom, married Jezebel, daughter of Ittobaal of Tyre.[1] However unreliable the details of these stories may be, there is also epigraphic evidence for linguistic similarities throughout the Levant in this period, as well as archaeological evidence for shared architectural tastes, including a striking mutual interest in volute (so-called Aeolic) capitals. Fergus Millar has pointed out that in Jerusalem "to the very end Tyrian shekels were the standard currency in which the Temple dues were to be paid."[2]

This illustrates the main point I want to make in this chapter: although Phoenician-speaking communities in the Mediterranean naturally had a great deal in common and a lot to do with one another, they made contacts and identifications at least as easily with other neighboring places and people. There is very little in their cultural artifacts or behavior to suggest self-conscious community-building at the level of "Phoenician" until Carthage began to promote that identity to and for its imperial subjects at the end of the fifth century. I will start by looking at the evidence for joint political activity among "Phoenicians" in the Levant, before turning to cultural interaction in that region, and then moving on to the west, where the modern notion of a "Punic world" can obscure the extent of collaboration between different groups of migrants. I will then go on in the next two chapters to examine specific case studies of political, social, and cultural networks that Phoenician speakers did construct with each other and others.

POLITICS BEYOND THE RIVER

The great Near Eastern imperial powers that dominated the Levantine coast from the tenth to fourth centuries BCE never treated Phoenicia as a single political region or province. There were at least two Assyrian administrative units in the coastal region, one (Ṣimarra) stretching north of Tripolis from the eighth century, and another (Ṣidunu), which from the seventh century reached north from Sidon past Beirut and Byblos, although it did not include Tyre, which was not directly governed.[3] The Persians, who controlled the region from 539 to 332, treated the cities as relatively autonomous units within their fifth satrapy, known as Eber-Nari or "beyond the river" (Euphrates), which also included Palestine and Cyprus.[4]

This approach reflects the facts on the ground: it is well known that the "Phoenician" cities never formed a political unit and rarely even cooperated with each other. As Maria Eugenia Aubet has pointed out, the very topography of the coastal plain, "made up of compartmentalized regions separated from each other by river valleys and mountain spurs, [which] formed a kind of internal patchwork which favoured the development of individual political units organized into city states" encouraged separation.[5] The cities back almost straight onto Mount Lebanon, with little agricultural hinterland north of Sidon. Along with their natural harbors, this physical geography encouraged the inhabitants to look out toward the Mediterranean—a shore-to-ship perspective—rather than toward their meager hinterlands or to each other.[6]

Although occasional alliances arose across the whole of Syro-Palestine, as against the Assyrian monarch Shalmaneser III in 853–845 BCE, the cities usually acted independently, and sometimes against each other's interests. Not only did they operate separate fleets, but they had a tendency to leave each other exposed: Tyre, for instance, held out alone against a Babylonian siege from 585 to 572 and then against Alexander's siege in 332. They were also prone to making hostile takeovers, especially across the southern agricultural plain dominated by Sidon and Tyre, which is relatively easy to traverse. The annals of the Assyrian king Sennacherib record a King Luli of Sidon ruling over a large part of southern Phoenicia in the early seventh century, for instance, including Tyre's mainland settlement (Ushu), though the island of Tyre itself is not mentioned;[7] in the early fifth century, Eshmunazar II of Sidon records in an inscription on his sarcophagus that he took Dor and Jaffa, even farther south, into Sidonian control;[8] and in the fourth century, Pseudo-Skylax lists a number of cities under either Tyrian or Sidonian control.[9]

Suggestions that Tyre and Sidon made up a joint kingdom or confederation in the ninth to eighth centuries are, however, highly suspect.
Josephus calls the ninth-century monarch Ittobaal king of the Tyrians
and the Sidonians, but he also calls him simply king of the Tyrians, and
Philip Boyes has pointed out that the former nomenclature is most obviously interpreted as an attempt by Josephus to reconcile his own information from Tyrian sources, that Ittobaal was the king of Tyre, with the
account in the biblical Book of Kings, composed six centuries earlier, that
he was the king of Sidon.[10] The only contemporary evidence that might
suggest joint kingship is an inscription from Cyprus that reads, "[Ahi]
tub, governor of Qarthadasht ('New City'), servant of Hiram, king of the
Sidons." But although this is often taken as a reference to Hiram II of Tyre
(c. 739–730), we cannot assume that: we know nothing of Sidonian kings
or colonization in this period, and there is no reason to dismiss the possibility that the Sidonians too had a king called Hiram or that they founded
a settlement on Cyprus.[11]

Similarly, a suggestion that in the mid-fourth century Abdashtart I of
Sidon also served as Abdashtart II of Tyre depends on a highly speculative
connection between the inscription mentioned in chapter 2 recording the
honors given by Athens to "Strato, king of the Sidonians" (Abdashtart I), who
died around 352 BCE, where there is no mention of Tyre;[12] a Roman-period
reference to the appointment of a king called Strato at Tyre by Alexander
after his conquest of the coastal cities in the 330s, where there is no mention of Sidon;[13] and a fourth-century bilingual Greek/Phoenician dedication
set up at Delos by Tyrian "sacred sailors" (*hieronautai*) bringing offerings
from Tyre and Sidon, which mentions in the very fragmentary Phoenician
section a king whose name begins with the letters 'BD.[14] If this king's name
should indeed be completed as Abdashtart (and there are plenty of other
possibilities), the origin of the sailors suggests that this would have been
the later, Tyrian, king enthroned by Alexander.[15]

That the ship carried gifts from neighboring Sidon as well does suggest a relationship of some kind between the two cities, although the
hieronautai are identified solely with Tyre, so it was not at that time a formal confederation. Tyre and Sidon were also both involved in the foundation of Tripolis, a "triple city" they were said to have established jointly
with Arados.[16] This new settlement was, however, made up of three quite
separate communities on different sites,[17] and according to Strabo, Arados
had itself been founded by people who had "fled" from Sidon, so the foundation of another new city to its north could be seen in terms of an ongoing association between the neighboring cities of Tyre and Sidon, and of

evolving Sidonian migration patterns, rather than as an example of intra-city solidarity between three originally separate communities.[18]

Diodorus makes another, more striking claim about Tripolis, however: "This city has the highest reputation among the cities of Phoenicia, for it so happened that the Phoenicians held a common council there and deliberated on the greatest matters."[19] Unfortunately, he does not specify which Phoenicians held common councils, when this happened, or for how long. The passage introduces the story of a revolt by the Sidonian king Tennes against the Persians around 350 BCE, in which Diodorus also tells us that a Phoenician alliance was formed (presumably in Tripolis), and we might suspect that he is generalizing from information on coordination during this particular episode to more permanent arrangements, perhaps drawing on the Greek model of the Panionion and its common councils.[20] If his account does preserve a real wartime coalition, or even a more permanent common council, that might suggest increasing political cohesion in the fourth century under greater pressure from the Persian king; under more pressure from Alexander, of course, this breaks apart. Indeed, as we saw in chapter 3, the Sidonians joined Alexander's assault on the city of Tyre—a factual report that is more reliable than their own claim to have secretly rescued many of their Tyrian neighbors during the episode.

The "Phoenician" cities of the Levant operated largely as autonomous political units, coming together at times in larger regional groups, but only as a whole, it seems, for what may well have been a brief period in the fourth century BCE. Do their cultural practices tell a different story? Looking for a collection of shared cultural traits is after all a tried and tested method for identifying a coherent group of "Phoenicians" going back to the works of the nineteenth-century scholars discussed in chapter 1, who carefully collected and catalogued a "Phoenician civilization" craft by craft. The trouble is that it doesn't work.

POTS AND PEOPLE

Understanding the ancient world as divided into a series of "peoples," each with what Anthony Smith called "a distinctive shared culture," depends on an implausible idea of how culture works. As Sian Jones has explained, this "culture-history" model developed in the context of emerging nationalisms in nineteenth-century Europe and made an important contribution to "the political manipulation of the past in Nazi Germany."[21] The best-known advocate of this kind of thinking in Mediterranean history is Fernand

Braudel, who described a "civilization" as "a collection of cultural characteristics and phenomena" found within "a space, a 'cultural area,'" and attributed to these civilizations or cultures "characters" and a "collective psychology, awareness, mentality or mental equipment" that make their reactions to events "an unexpressed and often inexpressible compulsion arising from the collective unconscious."[22]

The culture-history model is still widely used to justify the claims of self-identified ethnic groups to territory on the basis of a continuous cultural heritage: a curious recent example is the dispute over the name of the former Yugoslavian Republic of Macedonia and its attendant claim to Alexander the Great as a national hero, including the renaming of Skopje Airport in 2007 as Skopje Alexander the Great Airport; the 2009 petition against these appropriations, which was signed by 372 international classics scholars, made the equally dubious argument that the Macedonians, including Alexander, were "thoroughly and indisputably Greek."[23]

In recent decades, however, the idea that distinctive cultures can be mapped onto particular groups of people has become increasingly unpopular among scholars. One difficulty is simply the fact that it ignores how people saw themselves, or even how they were seen. Instead, this approach delineates cultural blocks and then associates them with specific peoples, whether or not they or their contemporaries did so. In principle, one could argue that ancient or "vernacular" conceptions of collective identity, whether perceived from the inside or the outside, shouldn't matter all that much to an ancient historian. There's no obvious reason, after all, to privilege the notions held in the worlds we study—they were conceived and used to manage living in those worlds, not to aid the interpretation of them in an exhaustive scholarly fashion. That said, there is very good reason to resist applying modern ethnic labels that carry a preexisting assumption of a communal identity before it has actually been demonstrated—especially when the material evidence also contradicts an idea of narrow and homogenous identity.

A bigger problem is that the culture-history model suffers from what Paul Gilroy has called "an overintegrated sense of cultural and ethnic particularity," or to put it slightly differently, that pots are not people.[24] And, indeed, it is never possible in practice to classify the archaeological record into geographical blocks. As Stephen Shennan puts it, "if we examine the distribution of individual types of archaeological material, especially if we use quantitative rather than mere presence-absence information, we find not neatly bounded entities but an enormous variety of cross-cutting patterns."[25] It is hardly surprising, then, that when ancient texts disclose the boundaries of ancient "peoples," these tend not to align with distributions of material culture.[26] This is certainly the case with the Phoenicians, where instead of revealing a single shared "culture," different artifacts and practices turn out to be characteristic of smaller or larger regions, or in some cases, simply different ones.

Despite the fame of Phoenician craftsmanship, and in particular of their "high arts," many of the most famously "Phoenician" cultural artifacts have on closer inspection very tenuous links with Phoenicia itself.[27] Instead, these luxurious artifacts are a continuation of the "international style" of the Late Bronze Age, produced and purchased in an area much larger than ancient Phoenicia, and sometimes not actually found there at all.[28] It is well known, for instance, that the beautiful metal bowls with mythological and hunting scenes discovered in Italy, Cyprus, Iraq, and Iran, which are regularly labeled "Phoenician" in museums and textbooks, have never actually been found in "Phoenicia" or in Levantine settlements abroad, and that only a single one—out of about ninety—has a Phoenician inscription.[29] The real reason that these objects have been associated with Phoenicia is that Homer mentions exquisite metal bowls from Sidon in the *Iliad*, but even if he is talking there about artifacts like these, that is no reason to associate them with all the Phoenician cities, rather than, as he says, Sidon.[30] Similarly, Glenn Markoe has admitted of "Phoenician" ivories that "very few examples have been recovered from the Phoenician homeland. . . . In truth, there is little hard evidence to associate them with any of the major Phoenician production centres; such attributions are based entirely on stylistic supposition."[31] There is equally little evidence for either metal or ivory working in "Phoenicia" itself, nor can a lack of excavation fully account for the lack of evidence for use of these luxury objects in Phoenicia itself, since they are very rare even at thoroughly excavated sites.[32]

Might more everyday practices and objects reveal a shared Phoenician culture? Even Erik van Dongen, one of the most skeptical of the scholars now reevaluating the evidence for "Phoenician" ethnicity and culture, has suggested that "Phoenicia may be defined linguistically," and that it is possible to define a Phoenician "archaeological character," a "fuzzy set" of certain pottery styles and a particular genre of domestic architecture, which "has more to do with social, ecological and geographical factors . . . than that this material culture somehow 'belongs' to the inhabitants of these regions."[33] Although van Dongen must be right that prosaic and functional explanations to do with cost, available materials, workshop and apprenticeship practices and so on probably account for distinctive types of housing or pottery in particular areas, the case for distinctive "Phoenicity" in all three phenomena he identifies may be optimistic.

   Language is especially interesting, since it can be a powerful signifier of identity, but it does not have to be: Gaelic, for instance, has floundered in postcolonial Ireland, where the economic pressures to shift to English have had more impact than local "pride and prestige."[34] And in northern New Guinea, a relatively unified region in terms of social relations and material culture, more than sixty languages in several different families are spoken.[35]

   In this case, however, there is a question mark over whether the Phoenicians shared a language at all.[36] Phoenician, Hebrew, Moabite, Ammonite, and Edomite are usually grouped together as "Canaanite languages," which, with Aramaic and Ugaritic, make up the "northwest Semitic" language family.[37] All these Canaanite languages were almost certainly mutually intelligible (the standard distinction between a dialect and a language),[38] and the language spoken in the Iron Age Israelite (Northern) Kingdom was particularly close to that spoken in the neighboring "Phoenician" cities to its north.[39] At the same time, there were distinct dialects within Phoenician itself, most famously Punic, the version of Phoenician used in the western colonies.[40]

   Similarly, it is difficult to pinpoint a single "Phoenician" model for domestic architecture. Because there has been very little excavation of domestic contexts in the north of Phoenicia, almost all the evidence we have comes from a few sites fairly close to each other in the south, and even this suggests a great deal of variety. Hélène Sader summarizes the results of the excavations of Persian period housing in Beirut in the 1990s as follows: "Nine house plans were identified: these Phoenician houses had three to ten rooms of different shape and size, which were variously organized"; a house of similar date at her own site of Tell el-Burak, a coastal settlement between Sidon and Tyre, is different again.[41] There are also parallels between southern Phoenician sites and those of neighboring parts of Israel, both in terms of the layout of the houses and the pier and rubble wall construction technique, which seems to appear first in Israel.[42] It is worth noting that temple typologies also share certain features right down the Levantine coast, but they differ within "Phoenicia" itself in terms of construction techniques and cultic equipment.[43]

   So-called Phoenician ceramic forms with bichrome and later red slip decoration are also found all along the Levantine coast, in both Palestine and Phoenicia, as well as on Cyprus, with shapes becoming more standard across the whole of Syro-Palestine from the sixth century onward.[44] Again, the "Phoenician" identification is based largely on excavations in the south of Phoenicia, especially at Sarepta, Tyre, Tell Keisan, Tel Dor, and more recently Beirut, and again these reveal considerable local variation, with occasional signs of a regional circulation in the area of Tyre, Sidon, and Dor.[45] It is telling that some specialists prefer to use the broader term "Cypro-Phoenician pottery," while others study this material in the much smaller contexts of individual production sites and local regions.[46] Similarly, the use of striking terracotta masks in funerary and ritual contexts actually originated in Bronze Age Syria and the southern Levant. Evidence of this practice is found in Cyprus by c. 1150 BCE, but only appears in the northern Levant in the Iron Age, when it continues to be popular further south and in Cyprus as well.[47]

If we reject this culture-history approach, then, and the objective identification of "civilizations," are there other ways to detect collective identity from culture? Of course, it is rarely the primary function of cultural artifacts and practices to mark or generate a corporate identity, or indeed any other mentality: there are usually much more practical or simply contingent reasons for particular choices.[48] This does not mean, however, that those choices cannot also carry symbolic meaning, and it is obvious that material culture and cultural behavior is at times used to construct collective identities of various kinds.[49]

Here the "relational" understanding of identity most famously articulated by Fredrik Barth can be useful. This approach focuses not so much on the experiences and characteristics that "we" share, but on the things that keep people apart, the differences between "us" and "them," and the importance of marking boundaries *between* groups.[50] This approach is based on the plausible conviction that identity of any kind, personal or corporate, needs an "other" to make any sense, and that it is contact between groups—friendly or unfriendly—that leads to the formation of self-identity within groups. According to this model, identity is defined not by "the sum of cultural traits contained by it but by the idiosyncratic use of specific material and behavioural symbols as compared with other groups."[51] The markers that define that identity can change with changing circumstances, and they can emphasize what might seem to outsiders quite small differences from quite similar people.

This relational approach has the major advantage that it tries to diagnose people's own choices rather than assessing them entirely from the outside and in retrospect. It is still, however, problematic. For one thing, even where identity is being marked in and with material culture, it is hard without textual help—and hard often even with it—to distinguish between the different kinds of identities that can be marked. Jonathan Hall has argued, for instance, that ethnic identity "cannot, in the absence of confirmatory literary evidence, be assumed from the mere detection of cultural signaling in the archaeological record," giving the example of hippies, whose distinctiveness "in terms of dress, coiffure, music, diet, vehicular transport and even to a certain extent nomenclature . . . will be archaeologically identifiable in the material record of the future" and might therefore be mistaken for an ethnic group.[52] And Naoíse Mac Sweeney has noted that having established a case for the marking of group identity in archaeological evidence, scholars too often then simply assume that this is an ethnic identity, whereas "the two processes should be separated, and the social meaning of a group identity should only be interpreted after its presence has been properly established."[53] Furthermore, the most important thing is rarely the artifact itself, but rather how it is used: as Edward Bispham has pointed out, people's cultural lives have a grammar as well as a vocabulary, and we cannot deduce much about grammar from traces of individual nouns and verbs.[54]

The bigger problem for those seeking a Phoenician identity, however, is that this approach, again, just doesn't work: people simply do not seem to mark boundaries as "Phoenician." Funerary practice provides an example of how a relational approach might take us further than culture-history, yet difficult questions remain when we can identify an outgroup but not who counts as "in." This is another area in which the evidence presents a distinctly mixed picture.[55] Inhumation is the usual form of burial in the larger Syro-Palestinian area, but cremation burials are found at a number of sites from the tenth century, and they become particularly common south of Beirut until inhumation becomes standard practice again across the whole region in the Persian period. There is also great variation even within individual cities: both inhumation and cremation can be found in the same cemeteries in the north and south of the region, sometimes even in the same graves.[56] It is striking, however, that cremation was most popular in the part of Phoenicia nearest Israel, and it could have marked for those who practiced it one distinct and meaningful difference from their neighbors to the south.[57] Even so, the group constructing this exclusive identity by cremating its dead would not be "Phoenicians" in general, but some southern Phoenicians.

In general, however, the people we call Phoenician seem to mark similarity more than difference, and not only with each other. A brief exploration of civic culture suggests that cosmopolitan identifications with people and places farther afield jostled with very localized phenomena, and although there is plenty of evidence for cultural interaction between "Phoenician" cities as well as with "foreign" ones, as on the political stage this only achieves some level of regional density toward the very end of the period under examination here.

COSMOPOLITAN CITIES

The basic urban model found at Iron Age Tyre, Sidon, Byblos, and Arados, with upper towns and their public buildings separate from lower towns, is repeated throughout the Syro-Palestinian area,[58] but these ports also looked rather different from each other. The visual culture of Arados, for instance, made particular use of Syrian models,[59] and Byblos of Egyptian ones.[60] Indeed, the most striking feature of civic art and architecture in the periods of Assyrian and Persian domination is its eclectic cosmopolitanism. The richest evidence is from Persian-period Sidon, at the time the largest and most important city on the coast, and now through the accidents of archaeology the best known to us, so I will take it here as a case study.

The Sidonians drew on a range of originally Persian, Egyptian, Cypriot, and Greek motifs for their art and architecture, from a series of small Egyptianizing shrines (*naiskoi*) of fifth-century or earlier date carved with sun disks and *uraeus* (cobra head) friezes (fig. 4.1) to the sculpture found at the sanctuary of Eshmoun outside the town at Bostan esh-Sheikh, which includes Assyrian-style column bases (fig. 4.2), Ionic column capitals, "temple boy" statues with Cypriot prototypes, bearded sphinxes and Egyptian gola or "throat" cornices, an elaborate Greek-style "tribune," and the bull capitals also found in Persian royal palaces.[61] Another rich collection of "foreign" cultural references is found in the city's sixth- to fourth-century BCE royal necropolis, now the star exhibit at the Istanbul Archaeological Museum. The monumental sarcophagi collected there, from the famous "Alexander Sarcophagus" to remarkable one-of-a-kind artifacts like the Lycian tomb (fig. 4.3), present an extraordinary range of artistic borrowings from the art of Egypt, Greece, Anatolia, and the Near East, often on the same object, but again with very little sign of any "local" element.[62] The variety of form as well as content gives the whole ensemble the sense of a developing collection: the search, it seems, was always for the next exotic, complex technique or artifact.[63] This is a form of cultural hybridity in which all the ingredients came originally from elsewhere. It is also of course evidence for the practices of the very wealthy, but that in itself reminds us again that economic and political connectivity is often more important to the ruling class than ethnic difference.

The Sidonian evidence also reminds us that the modern scholarly focus on differentiation from others can obscure the importance of identification with others in the production of one's own identity. The cultural quotations involved are not straightforward identity claims: references to art from Persia do not of course constitute claims to be Persian.[64] And in this

4.2 A fourth-century BCE marble Assyrian-style column base decorated with abstract vegetal ornament at the Bostan esh-Sheikh sanctuary near Sidon.

4.1 An "Egyptianizing" *naiskos* from Persian-period Sidon depicting a throne flanked by sphinxes, a frieze of cobra heads (*uraei*), and a winged solar disk.

4.3 The fifth-century BCE "Lycian sarcophagus" from the Royal Necropolis at Sidon, excavated under the Ottomans and now on display at the Istanbul Archaeological Museum.

particular case, the commissioners of this architecture and sculpture were not trying to make a point about an affiliation with any particular people or culture, but quite the opposite: by making identifications with external traditions that were popular expressions of urban sophistication across a much larger region, they were emphasizing above all the cosmopolitan nature of their own cities and cultural practices.[65]

The production of another kind of sarcophagus, the "anthropoid" type, seems to have been limited to Sidon and its reputed daughter-city of

Arados.[66] This appears to be a local adaptation of Egyptian anthropoid sarcophagi brought back by Sidonian troops for (re)use at the Sidonian royal necropolis in the sixth century, from where it was adopted for wider use and remained popular into the fourth century, if not longer (fig. 4.4). As usual, one of the most striking aspects of these artifacts is their variety and cosmopolitanism. In particular, the basic Egyptian model was modified over time by techniques, and probably technicians, from a variety of Greek-speaking regions, and the marble used is almost always Greek (Parian, Thasian, or Pentelic). Finds of these sarcophagi have been limited in the Levant to Sidon and Arados, and it is not clear that they were made or even used outside

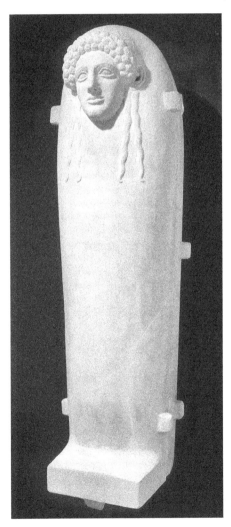

4.4 A fifth-century BCE anthropoid sarcophagus from Sidon using a variety of Egyptian and Greek techniques to commemorate a woman.

these cities, which were responsible, respectively, for fifty-nine and twenty-seven of the eighty-six sarcophagi from the area with a secure provenance.[67] Although there are several other examples from the region whose precise findspots are unknown, it is particularly striking that no certain examples have yet been found at Tyre. This may change with further excavation, but as things stand, the anthropoid sarcophagi only reveal a strong cultural connection across two specific Phoenician cites that maps onto a particular political connection between them.

As S. Rebecca Martin has shown, however, interaction between the Phoenician cities does seem to intensify in the Persian period, a phenomenon that she very plausibly associates with the cities' shared experience of serving in the Persian navy.[68] One example comes from the funerary world. Although many different grave types are found in "Phoenicia," including fossa, shaft, cist, hypogeum, and rectangular forms, and different vessels (or none) are used for the dead body or ashes, the fifth and fourth centuries see a hint of an emerging set of identifications across "Phoenician" elites: in a recent survey of burial practice in the Levant, Helen Dixon has pointed out that "in the Persian period elites from Arados southward all seem to signal their status through the use of marble, stone, and clay sarcophagi placed in rock-cut tombs."[69] Sarcophagus burials are not unique to the Phoenician region in the eastern Mediterranean in this period, and so they do not seem to be marking strong group differentiation from other people in other places, as opposed to the status differentiation within communities that Dixon points out, but this increasingly common choice may well reflect increasing contact and interaction among these civic elites.

The Persian period also saw a distinct intensification of cultural exchange and borrowings between the Levant and Levantine migrant communities in the west, especially among the upper classes. Western findspots of anthropoid sarcophagi, for instance, include Malta, Sicily, Gadir, and Carthage: most or all of these are imports from Sidon or Arados.[70] And it is easy to find eastern quotations in western monumental architecture: a fragment of a small shrine found at Nora on Sardinia, for instance, recalls the larger and better preserved monument at the so-called *maabed* sanctuary at Amrit on the coast of Syria.[71] And the borrowings went in both directions: examples of green jasper seals found at Tharros on Sardinia, probably made there using the products of the local jasper mines, have also been found at Byblos in this era.[72] People traveled as well as goods and ideas: a late fourth-century inscription from Athens honors Apses the Tyrian and his father Hieron, awarding them crowns and grants of proxeny for bringing grain to the city on a journey that also took them to Carthage.[73] This voyage from Tyre to Carthage was no doubt typical; it is telling, however, that father and son operated in Athens as well.

At the same time, we need to be careful not to assume that there was a permanent and universally respected "special relationship" between the cities of the Levantine coast and the colonies in the west. Despite the tale preserved by Herodotus and discussed in chapter 3 that the Phoenicians refused to attack their Carthaginian "children" for Cambyses in the sixth century, later Carthaginian attitudes to Tyrians at least could be rather different. Livy records a suggestive episode in which Hannibal, in exile with the Seleucid king in the early second century BCE, meets a Tyrian called Aristo at Ephesus and sends him to Carthage with secret messages for his allies. Aristo's scheme was discovered, and he was denounced in the senate by Hannibal's enemies as a "Tyrian stranger" (*advena*): "A fierce debate ensued, with some arguing that he should be seized and imprisoned as a spy, and others countered that there were no grounds for such extreme measures, and that it would set a bad example to arrest visitors [*hospites*] without good reason: the same thing would then happen to the Carthaginians at Tyre and the other markets in which they frequently traded."[74] Although Aristo the Tyrian is an obvious person to send to Carthage, he is not received there as a compatriot, but as a foreign visitor, to be treated at best as visitors from other trading centers should be. Of course, Livy was not a firsthand witness to these events, but if he is following Polybius here—as he probably is—then the impression of likely Carthaginian attitudes is contemporary.[75]

One way to understand cultural relations between ancient Mediterranean city-states is in terms of "peer polity interaction." This is the idea that in an environment in which significant power differences between communities do not exist, change within them can often be explained by contact, collaboration, and competition rather than by purely internal developments or active external imposition.[76] Religious choices provide an interesting case-study.[77] The different "Phoenician" cities worshipped different groups of deities, but in similar patterns, in which one is usually recognizable as the primary or civic deity, often accompanied by a consort: the Lady and Lord of Byblos, Melqart and Ashtart at Tyre, Ashtart and Eshmun at Sidon.[78] Sometimes the gods themselves are shared: Reshef is found at Byblos, Sidon, and Kition, and there are references to Eshmun's cult at Tyre and Arados as well as Sidon. These gods can at the same time mark cosmopolitan cultural identifications with places further afield: Ashtart is not only shared, but borrowed, since she is found rather earlier in Egypt and Syria than in Phoenicia.[79]

At most, however, these civic pantheons made up a "polythetic set," with similar but varying attributes, as opposed to a "diagnostic set," whose attributes are universal within the set but not beyond it.[80] And other aspects of religious practice seem likely to be confined to individual cities. One of the most famous "Phoenician" rituals is the spring resurrection ceremony that took place to celebrate the "reawakening" (*egersis*) of Melqart at Tyre, when an effigy of the god was burned on a pyre,[81] but although death and resurrection rituals were common throughout the Near East, the evidence that this also happened in Sidon for Eshmun and in Byblos for Adonis is from well into the Roman period and of dubious reliability.[82] Nor is there positive evidence that the *egersis* of the god was also celebrated at the great Iberian Melqart temple at Gadir.[83] Furthermore, other ritual practices now commonly considered "Phoenician," including child sacrifice, sacred prostitution, and necromancy, are also attested over a larger region.[84]

The coinage of the Persian period provides a vivid illustration at a civic rather than personal level of "Phoenician" coastal cities learning from each other but also from others, and differentiating themselves at a civic level in this period. Arados, Byblos, Tyre, and Sidon, the four Levantine cities that fielded substantial naval fleets, began to mint their own silver and bronze coinage in the mid-fifth century.[85] There is considerable variation in when and how they did this, but also evidence for increasing standardization between them.[86] So Arados always used the Persian weight standard; Byblos and Tyre experimented with the Attic one; but over time, and somewhat inconsistently, Byblos, Tyre, and Sidon adopted a new standard that was based on a silver shekel and is now known as "Phoenician." The designs used on the coins are for the most part rather different, but the cities did share certain motifs, such as the hippocamp found on coins at Arados, Tyre, and Byblos, and the galley that is featured on the coinage of Arados, Sidon, and Byblos (fig. 4.5). The coins also, however, betray a great deal of interest in design of coinage elsewhere. The bearded head on the fifth- to fourth-century Aradite coinage mimics Athena coinage at Athens, to the extent that when her eye moved from frontal to profile at the end of the fifth century, so did that of the deity at Arados. Tyrian coinage by contrast portrays the famous Athenian owl, though it renders the bird in a distinctly Egyptian style, while Sidonian reverses feature Achaemenid royal imagery—the lion hunt, the man in a chariot, the standing archer—throughout the Persian period.[87]

What we find then in the cosmopolitan Levant is that while there is nothing to suggest a Phoenician "civilization", or indeed an identity as Phoenician, there is a lot of evidence for cultural interaction both with other "Phoenician" cities and with "foreign" ones. The identifications and

4.5 Examples of Persian period silver coinage from the Levantine coastal cities. (a) Byblos: galley above hippocamp (obv.) and lion attacking bull (rev.); (b) Sidon: galley (obv.) and chariot scene (rev.); (c) Tyre: deity riding a hippocamp (obv.) and owl (rev.); (d) Arados: bearded male head (obv.) and galley (rev.).

references made in the material culture of these cities are interesting precisely because they can tell us about things *other* than ethnic identity, revealing in particular the quotation of "foreign" material culture as a marker of, among other things, one's own class, status, and cosmopolitanism.[88] How does this fit in with practice in the migrant communities to the west?

DIASPORIC NETWORKS

There is no question that a variety of aspects of material culture differentiated Phoenician-speaking communities in the western Mediterranean from their neighbors, from distinctive cisterns and cooking vessels to shared tastes in ornaments and architecture. Certain artifacts, techniques, and motifs occur more often, sometimes much more often, in the visual and material culture of these cities than elsewhere, and they sometimes differentiate their inhabitants from their Levantine past as well: decorated razors, for instance, are found in Levantine settlements in Africa, Sardinia, and Spain, but not in the Levant.[89]

Nonetheless, the widespread scholarly concept of a "Punic world" in the western Mediterranean can be problematic. Like the Latin word on which it is based, the term "Punic" is used with several different meanings in modern scholarship, from "western Phoenician," to "Carthaginian," to the mixed populations and cultures resulting from Phoenician colonization of a region, to (as in this book) the western dialect of the Phoenician language, and this is potentially confusing.[90] Furthermore, despite the undoubted existence of a polythetic set of overlapping tastes and mutual borrowings, strong arguments have been made against the notion of a single, homogenous "Punic" culture. As in the east, there is also great diversity within individual regions and islands,[91] and there are complex connections with other populations and practices. Particular difficulties are associated with a very specific model championed by Sabatino Moscati in the mid-twentieth century that then became standard in much European scholarship, according to which the "Punic world" dates only from the sixth century BCE, replacing a "Phoenician" phase in the west, and was a direct result of increasing Carthaginian hegemony in the region.[92] Sandro Filippo Bondì has recently emphasized the extent to which the different regions of the Phoenician-speaking western Mediterranean in fact grew further apart from each other from the sixth century in terms of their artistic and artisanal production, with local influences becoming much more important; he labels these "Punicities."[93]

More important from my point of view is that there is no indication that the quotidian usages and borrowings noted above carried strong meaning for group-formation: similarity in material culture is the predictable consequence of the proximity of migrant communities sharing a mutually intelligible language, and, no doubt, often origins in the same city or region: in a world of peer polity interaction, other Phoenician-speaking communities would have been the most obvious peers. This would have made these cities seem familiar to people coming from other Phoenician-speaking places, and relatively unfamiliar to visitors from elsewhere, but as Peter van Dommelen and Carlos Gómez Bellard have said, it "appears highly unlikely that there was ever a comprehensive Punic identity."[94] Furthermore, although sharing a language and no doubt other ties of family and friendship naturally encouraged relationships between Phoenician speakers, these were by no means exclusive.

The evidence from the Aegean discussed in chapter 2 suggested that "Phoenicians" living in communities there not only identified firmly, and sometimes to an unusual degree, with their original city-states, but that they also built up political, economic, social, and cultural networks with their new neighbors as well as with other "Phoenicians" from their own cities and regions. I want to suggest in the remainder of this chapter that such complex interrelationships were also the norm at Carthage and the other more permanent settler communities in the west, where there is a great deal of evidence for Phoenician-speakers fighting, trading, visiting, and even living with people of other languages and origins. I will concentrate on the evidence for the central Mediterranean, which has attracted particular recent attention for the extensive connections between Greek, Levantine, North African, Sicilian, and Italian merchants, rulers, and elites attested there in the mid-first millennium BCE.[95]

One example of this is the regularity with which military alliances were made between "Phoenician" and "foreign" cities. The ones we hear of in the sixth century tend to be joint expeditions with the local population against attempts by Greek-speakers to found colonies in the region: Pausanias tells us that around 580 BCE, "Phoenicians and Elymians" prevented Pentathlos founding a colony in western Sicily,[96] and that Carthage allied with the Etruscans to defeat Greek colonists at Alalia in 535,[97] as well as with the Libyans and the Macae to defeat the Spartan Dorieus's attempt to found a colony in Tripolitania c. 515.[98] According to Herodotus, Dorieus's attempt to found another colony in western Sicily about five years later was foiled by the "Phoenicians and Segestans."[99]

In the fifth century, even Greek cities joined forces with the Carthaginians against other Greeks. Herodotus reports that at Himera in 480 Carthage fought with other Phoenicians, Libyans, Iberians, Ligyes, Elisyci, Sardinians, and Cyrnians, who had all been invited by the local Greek despot to help him regain his city from Theron of Agrigentum; Diodorus claims that the Selinuntian Greeks were also allied with Carthage during this campaign.[100] Thucydides tells us that during the Sicilian Expedition of 415–413, the Athenian generals sent to Carthage for aid against Syracuse, and that the Syracusans considered doing the same against Athens.[101] And such notices continue in the fourth century: Diodorus says that in 397, Greeks were ready to support Motya against Dionysius I of Syracuse and that Cyrene allied with Carthage in 322.[102] Less convincingly, the Roman poet Silius Italicus lists the Greek communities of Cyrene, Berenike, and Barke among Carthage's African allies in the third-century BCE Hannibalic War.[103] The accuracy of these individual notices matters less here than the overall impression we get that military alliances across what would seem to be ethnic lines were considered plausible, indeed normal.[104]

Like war, commerce was a unifying force. Carthage traded with cities in the Levant, the Aegean, Cyrenaica, mainland and eastern Greece, Etruria,

Sicily, southern Spain, and, from the end of the third century BCE, Italy.[105] Even at the relatively small North African port of Sabratha, a quarter of the amphorae found that date from the fifth to the third centuries BCE come from the Greek island of Corcyra, and almost a quarter of the finewares are Attic imports, before a dramatic if unsurprising reorientation toward trade with Italy and the northern Mediterranean from the third century BCE.[106] Trade led to cohabitation: there were Carthaginian merchant enclaves in fifth-century Sicilian Greek cities,[107] just like the ones set up by Levantine cities in Athens and Delos, and by the middle of the first millennium, Carthage itself had a Greek community.[108] The mixed population of that city also included Italians, and intermarriage seems to have been common among elites: the Hamilcar who led the Carthaginian troops at Himera in 480, for instance, was said to have a Carthaginian father and a Syracusan mother; in the later third century, the noblewoman Sophonisba married two Numidian kings; and Hannibal himself married an Iberian woman, as did Hasdrubal, his predecessor in the Iberian command.[109]

As in the Levant, openness to external models and cultural ideologies was in itself a distinguishing feature of western Phoenician-speaking settlements.[110] At Carthage, significant numbers of foreign imports and locally made reproductions were incorporated into eating, drinking, and funerary practices from the city's earliest history. Egyptian artifacts were very popular grave goods in the city, especially sphinxes, scarabs, and figurines of gods such as Anubis and Bes,[111] and in the fifth and fourth centuries, "Greek fine-wares and wines dominated the Carthaginian tables."[112] Dining customs too seem to have come more into line with those of Greek-speakers: the study of animal bones shows that the consumption of pork increased dramatically from the fifth to second centuries, although we are told by ancient authors that contact with pigs was forbidden by Phoenician tradition.[113] If it is true that the Carthaginian senate banned the teaching of Greek in the early fourth century to prevent treasonous communication with enemies, this did not last long: Hannibal himself was supposed to have had a Spartan tutor who taught him Greek language, philosophy, and history.[114] By the Hellenistic period, architectural elements more usually associated with Greek-speaking cities were also common, such as the Ionic capitals at the new port built in the early second century.[115]

Furthermore, "foreign" references regularly occur in what would seem symbolic contexts at Carthage, suggesting that marking the boundaries of identity in material culture was not a central concern. Greek and Egyptian deities and mythological scenes are often featured on the jewelry and the razors found in burials, for instance, and there are Egyptian and

Greco-Egyptian elements in theophoric Carthaginian names such as Abd-is (Servant of Isis) and Abd-osir (Servant of Osiris), suggesting more than merely aesthetic engagement with other traditions.[116]

Furthermore, there were cults to Egyptian, Greek, Anatolian, and Mesopotamian gods in western Phoenician cities.[117] Diodorus tells us that there were "temples revered by the Greeks" at the Levantine settlement of Motya on Sicily,[118] and the goddess worshipped at nearby Eryx could be interpreted as Aphrodite, Ashtart, Venus, or an indigenous mother goddess, according to visitors' tastes.[119] In 396, in one famous example, Carthage established an official state sanctuary of Demeter and Kore, staffed by members of the city's Greek community, in an attempt to appease these gods after the Carthaginian general Himilco and his army pillaged their shrine in Syracuse.[120] This shows that there was no prohibition on establishing foreign religious shrines, although as Corinne Bonnet has underlined, it is not in itself an instance of cultural "Hellenization," but the appropriate solution to a specific problem the Carthaginians faced at the time.[121] That does not, however, explain the considerable number of informal, rural sanctuaries in North Africa and on the Mediterranean islands that adapted the imagery associated with the worship of Demeter and Kore in Greek contexts, and perhaps even adopted those goddesses themselves—no names have been found—for their own local purposes.[122]

There is also considerable evidence for technological and cultural exchange alongside economic interaction between "Greek" and "Phoenician" cities in Sicily in the Persian period.[123] This phenomenon is vividly illustrated in the civic coinages minted by Levantine settlements in western Sicily from the later fifth century BCE, first at Motya and then at Panormus, which continued to mint its own coins throughout the fourth century. They borrow their standards, techniques, and iconography from other cities in Sicily, both Greek colonies like Himera and Syracuse and indigenous cities such as Segesta (fig. 4.6), to the extent that Panormus, Motya, and Segesta even shared dies for coins.[124] Furthermore, the earliest legends at Panormus and Motya are in Greek, and are almost always expressed as Greek-style ethnics: "of the Motyans" and "of the Panormitans"; these are replaced in time by the Punic toponyms MṬW' and ṢYṢ.[125] The same is true of Sardinian architecture: at Tharros, where domestic *opus signinum* floors demonstrate the transmission of pavement technology and expertise between Phoenician-speaking centers, a rock-cut temple looks both to Greek and Levantine traditions in a distinctively central Mediterranean combination, featuring Doric pilasters, volute capitals, and an Egyptian gola cornice that closely resembles examples found at Amrit, Sidon, and now Tyre.[126]

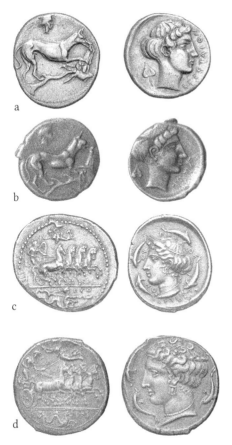

4.6 Late fifth- and early fourth-century BCE silver coinage from Sicily. (a) A didrachm from Segesta with a dog standing over a stag's head below a small female head on the obverse, and on the reverse the head of the nymph Aegesta, an ivy leaf, and the legend "of the Egestans." Both sides are reproduced very closely in (b), a didrachm from Motya: although the earliest Motyan imitations of this coin had a Greek legend "of the Motyans," this one simply names "Motya" in Punic. (c) A tetradrachm from Syracuse, with a quadriga on the obverse driven by Eros, who is being crowned by a winged Nike, and below this scene Skylla reaching for a fish; on the reverse the head of the nymph Arethusa is surrounded by four dolphins and the Greek legend "of the Syracusans." (d) A tetradrachm from Panormus that closely imitates the Syracusan coin, though Skylla becomes a hippocamp, and the city is named in Punic.

Borrowings went in both directions: Pompeii provides particularly significant evidence for identifications with Carthage and other Phoenician-speaking cities of the central Mediterranean;[127] volute capitals are found in central Italy;[128] items of jewelry made from the decorative glass beads popular at Carthage were prestige items in Italian cemeteries and circulated widely in Sicily;[129] during the Hannibalic War, both Taras and Metapontum minted silver half- and quarter-shekels;[130] and the Romans imported "small and humble" beds from Carthage as part of their funerary ritual.[131] This phenomenon is not confined to Italy: the Greek settlements of Emporion in Spain, for instance, borrowed imagery from Carthaginian coinage in the third century BCE.[132]

To the extent that such choices reflect identity at all, it is—again—the identity of civic elites as part of a wider Mediterranean aristocracy. Interaction between colonists and indigenous populations in the Mediterranean is often discussed; what is striking in the evidence that I have looked at in this chapter is the extent of interaction between different colonial populations: migration encouraged interaction and competition in contexts where being from elsewhere created a connection in itself.[133] There is, however, one western instance of an appeal to Phoenician identity in this period, and it is with this that I will finish.

CARTHAGE'S PHOENICIAN COINAGE

The first coins minted by Carthage were silver tetradrachms that appeared around 410 BCE. They often bore the Punic legends QRTHDŠT (Carthage, literally "New City") and MHNT ("Camp," presumably a reference to the army), but they circulated only in Sicily, suggesting that they were needed to pay Carthage's mercenaries in the city's campaigns against southern Sicilian cities in 409–405 BCE.[134] Like the earlier coins minted in western Sicilian cities, the technology, the Attic weight standard, and some of the iconography of this "Siculo-Punic" coinage was borrowed from Greek cities,[135] but the very first series introduces something new. The obverse features a horse, usually just its front half, being crowned by a flying figure: this animal has been connected somewhat speculatively with a sun god, or more attractively with the account given in Justin's summary of Pompeius Trogus of the discovery of a horse's head during the digging of the foundations of the new city.[136] On the reverse, however, is a palm tree, or, in Greek, a *phoenix*, "Phoenician" (fig. 4.7a).[137] Unlike other imagery on these Siculo-Punic coins, such as the female head based on the head of Arethusa on the second series of this coinage (fig. 4.7b) that is borrowed from Syracuse and also appears on contemporary coins from Panormus, this palm tree draws on no obvious

a

b

4.7 "Siculo-Punic" silver tetradrachms minted by Carthage for circulation in Sicily in the late fifth century BCE. (a) The obverse depicts the front part of a horse being crowned by a winged Nike, with the legend "Carthage" (QRTHDŠT), and the reverse features a palm tree with the legend "the camp" (MHNT). (b) On the obverse is a female head surrounded by dolphins that (like the coins from Panormus in fig. 4.6d) imitates the head of Arethusa on the coinage of Syracuse (fig. 4.6c); on the reverse, a horse stands before a palm tree.

models—palm trees are rarely found on earlier coins of any origin, and not at all in Sicily—and the pun on "Phoenician" is very unlikely to be a coincidence in the coinage of a "Phoenician" city.

The fact that this is a Greek term is hardly an objection among the cosmopolitan, multilingual Carthaginians, especially given that their own language did not provide an alternative.[138] "Phoenician" would furthermore have been an appropriate Greek label for the great western maritime power to adopt, given its connotations of trade, migration, and the sea in Greek discourse. And in any case, if the usual explanation that these coins were originally minted to pay mercenaries in Sicily is correct, the initial recipients of this coinage were more likely to know Greek than Punic, and the *phoinix* would remind Greek-speakers of the side by which they were being paid. There is more to this image than pure pragmatism, however, as shown by its longevity: the horse, the palm tree, and the divine head "are the basic types found on Carthaginian issues in all metals,"[139] and the palm was still used on the silver and bronze shekel-based coinage Hannibal minted in southern Italy during the Second Punic War.[140] It reveals a deliberate choice to use a new image to convey a new message: as Suzanne Frey-Kupper has put it, "the punning type of the palm tree . . . stands for the large community of Phoenicians spread all over the Mediterranean."[141]

This maps onto a change in the nature of Carthaginian imperialism, especially in Sicily. C. R. Whittaker argued in a classic article published in 1978 that until the fourth or even third century BCE, Carthage's expansionary strategies primarily involved the control of ports of trade rather than "direct territorial conquest and annexation, a system of provincial administration, the levying of tribute, a method of exploiting land, unequal alliances and . . . trade monopolies and controls."[142] Scholars now quibble about some of the details, but no one has succeeded in disproving Whittaker's basic hypothesis for the sixth and most of the fifth centuries.[143] Counterexamples do not convince. Stories of a Carthaginian general called Malchus who subjugated the western part of Sicily in the mid-sixth century, including the settlements of Motya, Panormus, and Soluntum, and a decade or two later campaigned unsuccessfully in Sardinia, if reliable at all probably record brief local disputes.[144] Polybius's account of a treaty between Rome and Carthage in 509 BCE mentions an area controlled by Carthage in Sicily and provides rules for the conduct of Roman trade in Sardinia and Libya as well as the banning of Roman ships from sailing down the African coast east of a "Fair Promontory" (probably Cap Bon), but although this suggests some form of local hegemony and a desire to protect the city's local interests, it does not demonstrate direct territorial control—and since

Rome could not realistically have claimed territorial control over the Latins listed as "subject" to them in this treaty in 509, either Polybius's date is wrong, or some exaggeration was acceptable in these matters.[145]

There is even less evidence for Carthaginian imperial activity in Sicily, Sardinia, or Spain for much of the fifth century,[146] but by the end of it, the evidence begins to fail Whittaker: Diodorus Siculus, who has an unsurprisingly detailed knowledge of Sicilian affairs, tells us that in a treaty between Carthage and Dionyius, the tyrant of Syracuse, in 405 BCE, the Carthaginians received Gela, Camarina, and perhaps other Greek-speaking towns on the island as tributary, in addition to recognition of their rule (*arche*) in the west of the island, encompassing the indigenous Elymians and Sicanians as well as the Phoenician colonies there.[147] While the precise arrangements on the island changed often over the fourth century, Carthaginian hegemony in the west of the island was regularly recognized by treaty.[148] Carthaginian coinage entirely replaced local issues in Phoenician-speaking cities by around 300 BCE, and the legends on that coinage included MHSBM (Treasurers), and B‘RṢT (in the territories), both of which have plausibly been taken as indications of greater institutionalized control.[149] There are also indications that Carthage maintained relatively strong control over Sardinia in the fourth century,[150] held a significant territory and a significant number of the coastal cities in North Africa,[151] and had extensive interests in Spain as well.[152] By the third century, we have no real reason to doubt the substance of Rome's claim, as reported by Polybius, that just before the First Punic War started in 264 BCE, "Carthaginian aggrandisement was not confined to Libya, but had embraced many districts in Iberia as well; and that Carthage was, besides, mistress of all the islands in the Sardinian and Tyrrhenian seas [and] lords of nearly the whole of the rest of Sicily."[153]

This significant expansion in state-building activities from the late fifth century coincides with the adoption of the *phoinix* or palm tree on Carthage's coinage, and imperial ambition also explains the reappearance of that palm tree on the smaller bronze coinage that Carthage started to produce for circulation throughout the western Mediterranean in the mid-fourth century, "making deliberate use of a limited range of generic types across a wide area of Carthaginian control."[154] The iconography on this so-called supra-regional bronze coinage had a practical purpose: since there were no numbers stamped on the coins, their images denoted the value. As Paolo Visonà explains, "we can assume that a Punic merchant at Tharros or Lilybaion would have known how many bronze units with a prancing horse . . . were equivalent to a gold or electrum denomination with a standing horse."[155] But as Suzanne Frey-Kupper has pointed out, it also had an ideological purpose: "the limited concentration on a small number of anepigraphic supra-regional types also appears to suggest the relative cultural and political unity of the Punic world."[156] These coins put the *phoinix* into purses throughout the area that Carthage controlled, a good choice for a burgeoning imperial power looking to draw together a broad group of its own subjects around an idea bigger than the imperial city itself: the bronze type with a horse standing before a palm tree, produced from around 300 BCE, outnumbered all other coin types in western Sicily in the third century (fig. 4.8).[157] Just as Carthage borrowed Greek technology for this coinage, and without a preexisting corporate identity in their own language to exploit, they also borrowed a Greek label to construct a new corporate identity that emphasized links between their Phoenician-speaking subjects, whatever their origins may really have been.

4.8 "Supra-regional" bronze coin minted by Carthage in the late fourth to early third century BCE, with a female head on the obverse and a horse standing before a palm tree on the reverse.

This appeal to common Phoenician identity made by a rising imperial power in and about its new domains is a striking example of the way that identity claims, and in particular ethnic identity claims, can be a tool of control rather than self-empowerment. Creating new identities, emphasizing existing ones, or adopting them from external sources has always been a useful way for political leaders to define and, where necessary, motivate their subjects, whether or not they subscribe to them themselves: the classic example from the ancient world is of course Alexander the Great's appeal to Panhellenic sentiment in his crusade against Persia, despite the weakness of his own claims to Hellenic identity. At the same time, a group identity would have become increasingly attractive to Carthage's allies with the increasing level of military hostility between Phoenician and Greek speakers in the central Mediterranean. It is unsurprising, then, that the image of the palm tree was picked up by Carthage's closest Sicilian dependents in the fifth and fourth centuries: some late fifth-century civic coinage from Motya has a palm on the reverse (fig. 4.9),[158] and coins from the second half of the fourth century at Rosh Melqart copy the Carthaginian type of the horse standing in front of the palm tree.[159]

4.9 Late fifth-century silver litra from Motya with a gorgon on the obverse and a palm tree on the reverse.

This is the only clear evidence for Phoenician identity that emerges from the many contacts, connections, and identifications made by and between Phoenician-speaking cities in the ancient Mediterranean. It opens up the question of what other kinds of communities they did construct, which will be the subject of the rest of part 2. I want to concentrate on phenomena that tend to be particularly significant for self-representation and meaningful expressions of group identity, so I am going to focus on ritual and religion; as David Mattingly has emphasized, this "is a key area of life in which communities define their identities—at times in ways that associate them with others and at other times creating social distance between them and others."[160]

CHAPTER 5

The Circle of the Tophet

According to Diodorus of Sicily, when the Carthaginians were suffering greatly under siege from the Syracusan general Agathokles in 310 BCE, they thought they knew why: they had displeased their two most important and supportive gods.

> Because they thought that Herakles, the god responsible for those who settle abroad, was especially angry with them, they sent a large sum of money and many very costly votive offerings to Tyre. For having come as settlers from that city, it had been their custom in earlier times to send to the god a tenth of all that accrued to the public revenue; but later, when they had acquired great riches, and were bringing in remarkable levels of revenue, they sent very little indeed, esteeming but little the deity. . . . They also accused Kronos of turning against them inasmuch as in earlier times it had been their custom to sacrifice to this god the noblest of their sons, but later, buying children in secret and rearing them, they sent these to the sacrifice. . . . Hastening to put their error right, they chose two hundred of the noblest children and sacrificed them publicly; and others who were accused sacrificed themselves voluntarily, being no fewer than three hundred. There was in that city a bronze statue of Kronos, extending its hands, palms up and sloping towards the ground, so that the child placed in its arms would roll down and fall into a kind of gaping pit filled with fire.[1]

The rest of part 2 will focus on the cults of these two gods, Melqart (called Herakles in Greek), and Baal Hammon (Kronos), as examples of community building within the Levantine diaspora that illustrate the advantages of looking beyond a "people," to people themselves. This chapter looks at the way in which the infant-sacrifice cult of Baal Hammon created distance for a small group of Levantine migrants in the central Mediterranean—both from their homeland and from other diasporic communities, including other Phoenician-speaking settlements in the west. I then turn in chapter 6 to the more widespread cult of the Tyrian god Melqart, which tied together Phoenician-speaking settlements throughout the Mediterranean, but also linked them with wider diasporic networks, including Greek ones.

The phenomenon of child sacrifice at Carthage and its neighboring colonial settlements has generated much scholarly discussion, but that has
largely focused on the nature of the rituals, and in particular on whether
the infants were actually killed or had already died of natural causes.[2] By
contrast, what I want to investigate here is what the cult can tell us about
the construction of colonial communities. After a brief discussion of the
evidence for the sites and rituals involved, I will ask what brought this
group of settlements together in the first place, what sort of community
developed between them, and how it eventually broke down.[3]

TOPHET CULT

Diodorus is just one of more than thirty Greek and Roman writers who
say that the Phoenicians, and especially the Carthaginians, sacrificed their
children. When a god is specified, he is called Kronos in Greek, and in Latin
Saturn; when the ritual is described, it involves burning in fire.[4] In the early
twentieth century, these literary accounts began to be associated with a distinctive type of sanctuary identified in some of the Levantine settlements in
the western Mediterranean: open-air enclosures containing the urn burials
of cremated infants and animals (usually sheep). These individual burials
are often signaled with stone markers, sometimes with inscriptions that
describe votive offerings to Baal Hammon (BʿL ḤMN) and his consort, Tinnit (TNT).[5] Some of these sites have also yielded evidence for cremation on
pyres, as well as altars, shrines, and other cultic installations.[6] The first such
sanctuary was recognized at Motya in 1919;[7] in 1921, an enormous site at
Carthage came to light;[8] and about ten have now been identified altogether,
dating from the eighth to the second century BCE (fig. 5.1).

The connection between these sites and the ritual phenomenon described
in the literary texts has been a matter of some controversy since they were
first excavated, and by the 1990s, it was standard to dismiss the accounts
of child sacrifice as hostile Greco-Roman propaganda, and to interpret the
sanctuaries instead as special and especially sacred burial places for still-
born children and infants, with sacrifices an exception if they happened at
all. This view has now, however, been abandoned by many scholars because
it is contradicted by all the available literary, archaeological, and epigraphic
evidence. This includes the coherent and unequivocal claims in contemporary Greek sources that the practice existed—and which, as it happens,
present this custom more as curious than repulsive—and the osteological
evidence from the cremated remains that the ages of the children at death

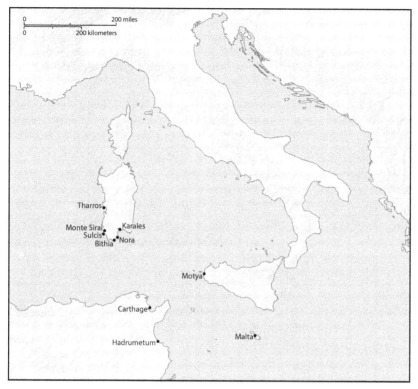

5.1 The circle of the tophet: sanctuaries established in the eighth to the second centuries BCE, including both certain and very likely sites.

are incompatible with normal patterns of infant mortality. Most important, though, is the dedication formula on the inscriptions, reproduced thousands of times in different places and periods with hardly any variation, that describes the children as thanks-offerings, proffered because a request made by the sacrificer had been granted. In a typical example, for instance, the text reads, "To Lady Tinnit, face of Baal, and Lord Baal Hammon, (that thing) that Arish, son of Bodashtart, son of Baalshillem, maker of strigils, vowed, because he [Baal Hammon] heard his [Arish's] voice."[9]

We do not know what (if anything) these sanctuaries were called by contemporaries, but modern scholars quickly labeled them "tophets" after the name given in the Hebrew Bible to the place in the Valley of Ben Hinnom in Jerusalem where people were said to have killed their children and "made them pass through the fire."[10] I will use the familiar term here for convenience, though it is not ideal: there is no reference to burial in the biblical passages, and the archaeological evidence from these sites—lamps, masks, incense burners, and images of dancing figures and women with drums[11]—suggests that a rich variety of ritual activities took place there beyond the sacrifice and cremation of infants.[12]

Tophet sanctuaries and the practices that went on there make an ideal case study of contemporary conceptions of community and identity, enabling us to go far beyond the evidence for shared fashions discussed in the previous chapter. Even if we set aside dramatic later descriptions of mass civic rites like the one with which I began, the evidence for performative rituals suggests that tophets were collective, communal institutions. Indeed, these sanctuaries seem to have served as a focus for civic identity: they were almost always established at the same time as the settlements themselves, and they were often carefully respected by later city walls.[13] They were also large—the sanctuary at Carthage was at least three thousand square meters in size, with at least ten thousand markers and perhaps twenty thousand funerary urns deposited there over the course of its existence from the eighth to second centuries BCE.[14] There is also evidence for "public works" at the Carthage tophet, suggesting that it was actively administered, whether or not it was a formal state establishment: the sanctuary was periodically resurfaced, service roads were preserved, a *favissa* (sacred refuse pit) was created to free up space for more burials, and at some point there was a large-scale extension to the west.[15]

The individual depositions and inscriptions support this impression. The very repetitive nature of the formulae used to describe the act of dedication suggests that a shared social and religious ideology was at stake, and although the inscriptions on the tophet markers simply record offerings made by individuals (presumably the parents), urns containing the remains of more than one infant separated by less than nine months in age suggest that these rituals were not limited to the nuclear family.[16] And Greek literary accounts, for what they are worth, suggest that at least at times the rite was conducted for the good of the whole city: in addition to the account of the mass sacrifice under siege from Agathocles in 310 BCE, Diodorus says that an epidemic in the Carthaginian army during the siege of Agrigentum in 407/6 led the Carthaginian general Himilcar to supplicate the gods by sacrificing a child to Kronos "according to his people's custom" as well as drowning a herd of cattle in the sea as an offering to Poseidon.[17]

Tophets, then, were sites where gods, family, civic society, ritual, sacrifice, and death all came together, and that gave them a peculiar power to represent the people who used them both as a civic community, and a larger diasporic network. Not much larger, however: although Sabatino Moscati suggested that the tophet was a distinctive component of "Punic" settlements in the Mediterranean,[18] it is obvious from a glance at the distribution map that they are not found west of Sardinia at all. Child sacrifice, or at least its monumental commemoration, was not characteristic of the "Phoenician" diaspora as a whole, nor was it a marker of Phoenician or Punic identity. The group of central Mediterranean settlements with tophets constituted only a small subset of the wider Levantine diaspora in the west. The relative scarcity of this cult means that the users of the tophets must have formed a self-conscious group: this was a rare and highly distinctive ritual choice, and we see evidence for the same basic practices at all the surviving sites, practices that identified the worshippers with each other in a way that also served to differentiate them from their neighbors—including other Levantine migrants in the western Mediterranean. How might such a phenomenon have come about?

COMMUNITY AND DIFFERENCE

The first tophets for which we have good evidence were established at Carthage, Motya, and Sulcis on Sardinia in the mid-eighth century, all at—or possibly very soon after—the founding of the settlements themselves.[19] The earliest evidence for Levantine settlement on Malta also goes back to the middle of the eighth century,[20] and although the evidence for a tophet there—an early-nineteenth-century excavation near Mdina found sixty vases filled with very small bones, assumed by the excavators to come from children or animals, along with two inscriptions that refer to a *molk*, or offering, to Baal Hammon—can only be dated to the seventh century by the letter-forms of the dedications,[21] we might reasonably suspect that this sanctuary also dated to the original foundation.[22]

More tophets were later established in Africa at Hadrumetum (modern Sousse) along the coast from Carthage (seventh or sixth century), and in Sardinia at Tharros (seventh century), at Nora (sixth century), and at Monte Sirai (fourth century).[23] Other potential tophet sites in Sardinia have also been identified: in addition to an as yet unexcavated site with signs of combustion identified at Pani Loriga, a settlement founded in the late seventh century, a tophet may well have existed for a relatively brief period in the seventh to sixth centuries on the island of Su Cardulinu at Bithia on the south coast, where there is an area of urns containing bones and votive objects and a small Archaic altar; and there was a cremation cemetery with urns and fragmentary markers at Karales (modern Cagliari) dating from the fifth or fourth century.[24] Finally, a second tophet may have been established in Sicily at Lilybaeum, the successor-settlement to Motya set up by Carthage in the fourth century, where eight Hellenistic-period stelai have been found that resemble tophet markers elsewhere.[25] With the exception of Monte Sirai, all these would have been established at the same time as the urban settlement in which they are found.

These settlements seem to have formed a distinct community from the start. The close relationship between the four earliest western sanctuaries is underlined by the similarities in their seventh- and sixth-century epigraphy: all the sanctuaries use very standard formulations, declaring that they are a monument of an offering—sometimes, in examples from all four early sanctuaries, a *molk baal*, "the offering of a person/citizen"—that a named person has given to Baal Hammon.[26] This reflects broader cultural connections between these settlements: the housing found at early Sulcis and early Carthage, for instance, is very similar.[27]

There are also clear continuities with Near Eastern ritual practices such as the use of the *favissa*, as well as particular kinds of cremation rites and burials, and child sacrifice itself is well attested in the Levant in Iron Age literary sources, including the Hebrew Bible.[28] While the relevant biblical passages concentrate on the tophet at Jerusalem and do not explicitly refer to such activities in the "Phoenician" cities of the central Levantine coast, Curtius Rufus in the first century CE describes an intriguing attempt during Alexander's siege of Tyre in 332 BCE to revive the custom of sacrificing a free-born boy to "Saturn." This evidence problematizes attempts to explain the function of child sacrifice purely in terms of the western colonial context, in relation, for instance, to the demographic requirements of a new settlement.[29]

At the same time, the tophets marked difference from the homeland. No equivalent sites have yet been found on the Levantine coast, or anywhere else in the Near East.[30] It seems likely, then, that it was only in the colonial world that the practice became fully institutionalized and ritualized with special sanctuaries.[31] The establishment of tophets broke with the traditions of the homeland at the same time as it preserved them, both reiterating the relationship with home and moving toward cultural independence.

This should come as no surprise; as the cultural theorist Stuart Hall put it, in colonial situations "our relation to [the past], like the child's relation to the mother, is always-already 'after the break,'" with cultural identities framed simultaneously by "the vector of similarity and continuity, and the vector of difference and rupture. . . . The one gives us some grounding in, some continuity with, the past. The second reminds us that what we share is precisely the experience of a profound discontinuity."[32] And Corinne

Bonnet has already suggested a parallel for the development of the tophet rites in the cultural practices of African slaves in Portuguese Brazil, including the *candomblé* or "ecstatic rites . . . which involved several gods related to natural elements . . . or to African tribes" and recalled but did not replicate this involuntary diaspora's African origins.[33]

Like the rites themselves, the gods involved were magnified in the west. Baal Hammon seems to have been a prominent civic deity throughout Carthage's history. But no rites to Baal Hammon are recorded in the Levant, and although the name by which he was known in the west does occur as an element in Levantine personal names from the eleventh to sixth centuries, it appears in its own right only in a late-ninth-century inscription from Zinjirli in southern Anatolia and on a sixth-century amulet from Tyre.[34] In the late fifth century, a new name appears on the tophet inscriptions at Carthage, that of a goddess whose name, TNT, was for a long time vocalized by scholars as "Tanit," until Greek inscriptions excavated at the later tophet at Cirta revealed that there at least she was called "Tinnit."[35] Like Baal Hammon, however, Tinnit makes only rare earlier appearances in the epigraphic evidence from the Levant, where she seems to be particularly associated with the area of Sidon: she is invoked as "Tinnit [of] Ashtart" in a seventh- to sixth-century inscription from Sarepta,[36] and appears as a component of fifth-century Sidonian proper names.[37] At Carthage, by contrast, she became extremely popular over the course of the fourth century, with dedications regularly made to both "Lady Tinnit" and "Lord Baal Hammon." Tinnit is usually named first, but then described as "Face of Baal."[38]

The tophet inscriptions are not the only evidence that despite their humble origins, these gods became very important in Carthage itself: the ninth-century Byzantine manuscript of the *periplus* of Hanno says that this account of a voyage along the coast of West Africa, probably to be dated to the fifth century BCE, was set up in the *temenos*, or sanctuary, of "Kronos," and Servius's late antique commentary on Virgil's *Aeneid* calls "Saturn" and "Juno" the "parent gods" (*dei patrii*) of the city.[39] Furthermore, their Levantine origins still seem to have mattered: an inscription from Carthage (though not from the tophet) describes Tinnit as BLBNN, which probably means "of Lebanon."[40] These gods looked both backward and forward, identifying with the homeland, but at the same time making a new and better life in the west, just as the colonists themselves were trying to do.

Beyond differentiating the "circle of the tophet" from the culture of the Levant, the rituals and gods that tied these communities to each other also differentiated them from earlier Levantine migrants who had established themselves further west from at least the ninth century BCE, at Huelva and

Gadir on the Atlantic coast of Spain, at Utica on the Mediterranean coast of Africa, and no doubt elsewhere as well.[41] No evidence for child sacrifice or tophet-style sanctuaries has been found at these earlier sites, although there are literary attestations of a *Kronion* or Kronos sanctuary that was established with the settlement at Gadir.[42]

Furthermore, the tophets underlined the difference in cultural and cultic practices between the settlers and the local populations in the places they chose to live. There are no known western precedents or parallels for this kind of sanctuary, and at Tharros, the new sanctuary was established on top of the still-visible ruins of an abandoned Nuragic village, a move that called attention to the earlier settlement at the same time as it obliterated it, reaffirming the foreign identity of the ritual practitioners.[43]

Finally, and over time, these sanctuaries created moral distance from other Mediterranean powers. Although Greek literary sources tended to report the custom relatively neutrally, foreign politicians picked the custom out for particular disapproval: Justin records an edict of the Persian king Darius c. 491 BCE that banned the Carthaginians from sacrificing humans and eating dog meat; Plutarch tells us that Gelon, the tyrant of Syracuse who defeated the Carthaginians in 480 at Himera, inserted a clause in the peace treaty that the Carthaginians should stop sacrificing their children; and Porphyry has one Iphikrates forbidding human sacrifice to the Carthaginians at an unknown date.[44] The reliability of these specific reports is less important than their plausibility to their readers. In this context, it is particularly striking that a study of an admittedly rather small sample of 130 urns from the Carthage tophet has suggested that child sacrifice became more rather than less popular at Carthage as the city increasingly came into conflict with Greek-speaking states of Sicily: the proportion of urns containing human bones to those with only animal remains increased from 70 percent in the seventh to sixth centuries to 90 percent in the fourth.[45] If this finding is reliable, the tophet was not only something that made the Carthaginians and their allies different in their enemies' eyes, and often wrong, but it seems that the Carthaginians may have embraced that.

A THEORY OF ORIGINS

What created this very particular way of relating to the homeland, to other Mediterranean powers, to other migrants, to locals, and to each other? Explanations for the limited diffusion of tophet cult in the western Mediterranean have traditionally been based on other differences identified between the colonies with tophets and those without them, such as varying levels of urbanization and divergent funerary practices. One widespread theory interprets the settlements with tophets in the central Mediterranean as larger agricultural settler colonies, while those farther west were smaller, focused more on metal extraction and trade, and therefore less in need of "civic" sanctuaries like tophets.[46] This model fits in neatly with the distinction sometimes hypothesized by scholars of ancient Greek history between the *apoikia* (settlement) and the *emporion* (commercial) colony-types, but not with the archaeological evidence from the Levantine settlements in the west: there is in fact much more evidence for developed urbanism in the far western colonies than from the central Mediterranean sites with tophets, where extensive agricultural exploitation of a rural territory began for the most part only in the fifth or even fourth century.[47]

Furthermore, the supposed noncommercial nature of these central Mediterranean settlements is called into serious question by their co-location at short and easy sailing distances from each other in strategic locations around the Straits of Sicily, through which ancient literary sources tell us almost all east-west shipping had to go: journeys between the earliest settlements with tophets would normally have taken no more than two days.[48] Exclusive control of the straits would have provided this group of communities with a wealth of economic opportunities, from the simple provision of ports and facilities, to taxing transit, to taking an active role in trade itself—all activities that would also have represented a challenge to established trading practices and networks in the western Mediterranean, including those of earlier Levantine migrants. The later foundations would then have reinforced the original settlements in a variety of practical ways, both commercial and agricultural. Hadrumetum in particular could have exploited or controlled coastal access via Cap Bon to the Sicilian strait—while Bithia, Nora, and Monte Sirai were agricultural centers that supplied the earlier coastal colonies, with Monte Sirai providing especially useful points of contact with the hinterland.[49]

Did this tightly knit group of settlements only come together overseas, or was it based on an existing community in the Levant? Bruno D'Andrea and Sara Giardino have recently explored the possibility that the distinctive groups of Levantine migrants in the diaspora could have originated in different political factions, different classes, or different cities in the homeland.[50] But what if the connection between this group of settlements that conducted child sacrifice was, quite simply, child sacrifice?

This practice may well have been unusual in the east as well the west. Discussions in the Hebrew Bible claim that it aroused anger and disgust among some at least of the Israelites, and that it was banned in Jerusalem by

King Josiah in the late seventh century;[51] it seems reasonable to suppose that it might also have been controversial among the Israelites' northern neighbors on the Levantine coast. There is no more evidence for the practice in the east after the sixth century, and it is described as something that used to happen in Phoenicia in the past by Philo of Byblos, or his Hellenistic sources.[52] According to Curtius Rufus, the attempt at Tyre in 332 BCE to revive the tradition was successfully opposed by the city elders, suggesting that there were reservations about the custom there by that date: one wonders about the circumstances in which it had originally died out—or was, as in Jerusalem, banned. It seems a plausible hypothesis, then, that the western settlers who practiced this particular and unusual form of cult came not from a different place or political faction in the homeland from other Levantine migrants, but from a different religious tradition, and so had a preexisting connection with each other that led them to settle in close proximity in the west.

Perhaps the central Mediterranean settlers even left, at least in part, because of local disapproval of their religious customs. We have no evidence that Carthage was an official colony of Tyre, and the foundation myth preserved by Roman authors, which I will argue in the next chapter has a core going back to Carthaginian sources, suggests quite the opposite: the story involves personal betrayal, religious irregularity, and finally the flight from Tyre of refugees under the command of Princess Elissa.[53] Like the exodus of the Puritans to the New World, the formation of the "circle of the tophet" could have been a reaction both to new opportunities in the west and new religious restrictions in the east.[54]

Informal or even involuntary migration would make sense of these migrants' ambivalent treatment of Levantine traditions. In Gillian Shepherd's classic essay on Archaic Sicilian funerary architecture, she points out that the innovative choices made by Greek migrants to Sicily find closer parallels in the informal colonial cultures of North America established by migrants fleeing religious persecution and economic hardship at home than in the formal, governmental British foundations in Australia, where "British" cultural models were more closely followed.[55] My suggestion here is that western tophet culture follows a similar pattern, perhaps for similar reasons.

This notion of a trading network of religious extremists may seem counterintuitive, but social and religious connections are standard facilitators of commercial trust and cooperation, and there would be interesting parallels with later and better-documented groups with both religious and commercial interconnections. The M'zabites are a case in point. This isolated group of Ibadite Muslims have traded since the Middle Ages from the M'zab valley in Algeria, 350 miles south of Algiers, and today still run a widespread network of small shops throughout the Maghreb as well as in France.[56] Religion is literally at the center of the seven towns that make up the M'zabite community, of which the best known is Ghardaia. They are all constructed around a hilltop mosque, with the houses arranged around it in concentric circles or semicircles, although the roads converge on the market outside the ramparts. The ten thousand or so inhabitants of the valley are famous for their deeply conservative religious practices, emphasizing "disassociation": marriage with non-M'zabites is strongly discouraged; women, who wear head coverings that reveal just one eye, do not leave the valley; non-Ibadites are not allowed to spend the night in their holiest town, Beni Isguen, and strangers are not allowed into certain parts of the town at all. At the same time, M'zabite men are traditionally expected to travel outside the valley for years at a time to serve the commercial interests of their families and wider communities. The economic dynamism and success of the cities has always been based in great part on their religious principles, including sobriety and a strong work ethic, as well as their close links of kinship and religious practice.

It is impossible to know how close a parallel the M'zab valley provides for the circle of the tophet, though it is tempting to note that a principle of dissociation might explain the obscure provision in the treaty struck between Rome and Carthage in 509 BCE that if a ship belonging to the Romans or their allies is driven by weather or hostile forces beyond the "Fair Promontory" (probably Cap Bon) in the vicinity of Carthage, they must depart within five days, having taken only what they need for repairs and offerings, as well as, perhaps, the requirement in the same treaty that traders have to operate in the presence of a local public official.[57] However that may be, these new sanctuaries served to distinguish this group of colonists from others who spoke the same language and perhaps even emigrated from the same city, and religious, social, and commercial links emerge from this investigation as more important in the making of the circle of the tophet than kinship or civic origins.

A SMALL WORLD

So much for its origins. How did this community actually work? Many scholars have placed Carthage at the center of the tophet network from the very start, whether actively imposing the sanctuary form on its subcolonies and subjects, or simply providing neighboring settlements with an example they couldn't safely refuse.[58] However, although Carthage was always the largest Phoenician-speaking settlement in the central Mediterranean,[59] and as such it must always have been a major player in the events that unfolded there,[60] the evidence from the tophets themselves suggests that these ritual communities developed and worked together as peers rather than operating under Carthaginian control.

In some senses, the Carthaginian tophet was actually the odd one out from the start, located to the south of the town on a low plain, while other tophets tended to be founded to the north on rocky hills and heights.[61] Furthermore, most of the settlements and sanctuaries involved were in Sardinia—indeed, unlike in Sicily and Africa, every significant early Levantine settlement on Sardinia had a tophet. And Carthaginian religious "influence" is not much in evidence in the sanctuaries outside North Africa: although the earliest dedications at Motya, Sulcis, and Malta record offerings to Baal Hammon, he and Tinnit rarely appear in later inscriptions at tophets other than Carthage and Hadrumetum, though the fact that there are relatively few inscriptions on the Sardinian and Sicilian markers at all may obscure the roles these divinities played there.[62] Taken as a whole, the material culture of the earliest tophets gives little sense of central direction or coordination: there is a great deal of variety, fluidity, and experimentation in the eighth and seventh centuries in relation not only to the types of pottery used, but also the nature and treatment of the dedications (from infants to cows and sheep, to birds and tortoises), and the kinds of objects buried with them.[63]

One example of this experimentation is the seventh-century initiative taken at Carthage to use stone monuments to mark deposits. These markers reinforced the ambivalence of the connections the sanctuary made with the Levantine past. Most of the basic marker-forms are also found earlier in the east, including the *naiskoi* (small shrines) that became the standard monument type at the Carthage tophet in the sixth to fourth centuries (fig. 5.2).[64] Like the little Levantine shrines of the same period mentioned in the preceding chapter, these adopted Egyptianizing decorative techniques, and the motifs carved on them often also find their models or inspiration in the Levant.[65] As with other aspects of the western tophet cult, however, this is a matter more of inspiration than imitation: female figures occur in the east only in three-dimensional form, for instance, especially as small votive figurines, while at the Carthage tophet they are depicted in relief.[66]

Furthermore, some popular Carthaginian motifs such as the lozenge are entirely absent in the east, while others, like the bottle idol, can be found in the Levant but become much more important in the west.[67] Another interesting example of the latter phenomenon is the so-called sign of Tanit (fig. 5.3), which appears on markers at Carthage from the sixth century

5.2 *Naiskos*-type tophet markers at Carthage with borders framing, *from front to back*, a baetyl, a lozenge, and blank spaces.

5.3 *Naiskos*-type tophet markers at Carthage with borders framing, *from left to right*, a bottle idol, and a lozenge alongside a sign of Tanit.

but is found occasionally in the Levant from the ninth century to at least the third.[68] Despite the traditional name given to this symbol, there is no positive evidence for a connection with the goddess Tinnit, a point I try to highlight by preserving in this particular phrase the more traditional transliteration of this goddess's name: the "sign of Tanit" is not necessarily a symbol of Tinnit. There is, nonetheless, a striking similarity in the way that both the goddess and the symbol arrive in the west in the Persian period from relatively obscure eastern origins.

In their earliest phase, these markers also disassociated Carthage from all the contemporary western sanctuaries, and meant that for a considerable period, the other tophets looked more like each other than like the Carthage sanctuary. From the sixth century, however, a significant number of the other tophets started to use markers too, often adopting the *naiskos* form that was then becoming popular at Carthage.[69] The phenomenon of the markers brings the sanctuaries closer together as a visual group, at least for a while—at Motya markers are only found in sixth-century levels[70]—but a comparative survey does not suggest slavish imitation of Carthage by the others. Instead, it provides a case study of the complexity with which these communities marked their relationships with each other, with the homeland, and with other people in the Mediterranean in this period. There are, of course, differences of a purely practical nature: the type of stone available locally has consequences for the techniques applied to it, and the details of the decorative moldings are probably due to local workshops and apprenticeship networks. Other choices, however, suggest ambivalence toward and even differentiation from each other.

The most dramatic distinction is between the iconography on the markers from Carthage and Sulcis, very likely the two earliest tophets.[71] Since the markers catalogued from the Sardinian site lack stratified excavation data, only broad comparisons between these two sites over a period from the sixth to second centuries can be made, but the differences are clear: human figures appear on 71 percent of the catalogued markers from Sulcis but only on about 6 percent of those catalogued from Carthage, where the depiction of geometric figures, and in particular baetyls (pillars), is much preferred.[72] Furthermore, at Sulcis men and women are featured in a variety of poses, clothed and nude (fig. 5.4); at Carthage, by contrast, the range of human types is much more restricted.

A broader comparison of the catalogued markers from Carthage, Motya, Tharros, and Nora that can be dated more closely to the sixth to fourth centuries BCE suggests that while baetyls and, to a lesser extent, bottle idols are fairly popular everywhere, these tophets have very different

5.4 A marker from the tophet at Sulcis depicting a woman with a drum, framed by elaborate architecture below a winged sun-disk and a frieze of upright cobras.

proportions of human figures: high at Nora and Motya, as they were at Sulcis, but much less so at Tharros. At the same time, the iconographic differences between Carthage and its maritime near-neighbor Motya are almost as great as those between Carthage and Sulcis: this is particularly obvious in the distribution of the lozenge/hexagon symbol, which is quite popular at Carthage, but much less so at Tharros and Nora, and very rare at Motya. It was completely absent at Sulcis and Carthage's African neighbor of Hadrumetum.[73] Hadrumetum does not in fact follow Carthage's model at all closely in this period. Markers only started to appear there in the late fifth century or even later, and the few published from Level II (c. 400–250 BCE) are very eclectic.[74] In addition to a scene of an enthroned deity that finds extensive parallels in the east, but not at Carthage, two depict triple baetyls, putting them closer to markers from some of the Sardinia sites than to Carthage, where single baetyls were the norm.[75]

Different tophets also signal different relations with the Levant on their markers. Clear iconographic identifications with the "homeland" are in fact more common in the other tophets than at Carthage.[76] Motya seems to make particularly close and direct identifications with the subjects and techniques of Levantine art:[77] only there, for instance, do we find representations of thrones of the type depicted on *naiskoi* from Sidon, and which are also found in three-dimensional form in the east, with the western in-novation that one of the Motyan examples actually has a figure sitting on the throne. Moscati puts this Sicilian-Sardinian phenomenon down to a sea route from the east that "presumably excluded Carthage," with Sicily as the stepping-stone (*punto di passaggio*) to Sardinia.[78] This may have something to it, but ideas do not travel on their own: choice was involved here as well, and Sicilian and Sardinian traders and travelers would hardly have been unaware of fashions at Carthage.

So Carthage is by no means always the central reference point for the tophets in this period, but the iconographic evidence does not point to straightforward regional or island patterns either: instead, it suggests that the tophets made a variety of identifications across the whole network, and that within the circle of the tophet different sites carried out different forms of cultural negotiation with the homeland. Concepts from social network theory can be helpful here. The normal experience in networks of all kinds, from friendship circles to the Internet, is that in choosing which connec-tions to make, "nodes" (in this case the people attached to the individual sanctuaries or settlements) prefer to link with other nodes that already have a lot of links, which would explain the significant role played by Carthage as a visual model without requiring either imperial imposition or craven imitation. At the same time, the varied and cross-cutting visual identifica-tions within the circle of the tophet suggest a continuing proliferation of what social network theorists call "weak links" within and across the group as a whole, adding up to a coherent, dynamic, and noncentralized system, or "small world." In this system, peer polity interaction and competition, as well as sociocultural links, prove stronger than imperialism or political relationships.[79] This state of affairs, however, was not to last.

FRAGMENTATION AND EMPIRE

The wars between Carthage, Syracuse, and Rome in the central Mediterranean seem in themselves to have made little difference to the overall shape of the circle of the tophet. Motya's sanctuary survived that city's destruction at the hands of Dionysius I of Syracuse in 397 BCE, perhaps even into the third century,[80] and the Sardinian tophets were not affected by the Roman annexation of the island in the mid-third century, operating until the third or second century at Nora and Tharros, the second century at Monte Sirai, and the second or first century at Sulcis. At Monte Sirai there is even evidence that major works took place in the tophet toward the end of the third century, when the island was already under Roman control.[81] There were, however, profound changes in the visual relationships between the sanctuaries in this period: from the fourth century, the appearance of the tophets conforms to regional patterns rather than making links across the whole network and beyond, and Carthage looms larger, both as an example to follow and one to reject—a direct result, I will suggest, of increasing Carthaginian imperialism in the central Mediterranean in this period.

The appearance of the Carthage sanctuary itself altered dramatically in this period, with the markers now for the most part flat limestone slabs or *stelai* with gables and often acroteria in the Greek style. At the same time, a new core set of symbols emerged: the sign of Tanit, which appears on 48 percent of catalogued markers from this period (as opposed to only 5 percent of those from the fourth century and earlier), the caduceus on 35 percent, the hand on 31 percent, and the combined crescent-disk on 25 percent (fig. 5.5). Interestingly, these motifs are all found on flat stone monuments in the Near East as well.[82] This standard symbolic set appears with particular frequency on the thinner and smaller—and therefore cheaper—markers, while larger, thicker, and presumably more expensive markers tend to depict a wider range of motifs, making identifications with Egypt, Greece, and Etruria, as well as the Levant.[83] These motifs include on occasion palm trees, which feature on 5 percent of the fourth-century and later markers, and almost all (twenty-eight out of thirty) appear on the thicker and apparently more expensive markers (fig. 5.6): if this is a symbol of identity, it was an identity more popular among the wealthier users of the sanctuary.[84]

The different choices people made about the style and expense of the markers they commissioned fits in with epigraphic evidence suggesting that by the fourth century, a broad social range of people were using the sanctuary at Carthage, from priests and politicians to butchers and metal workers, as well as freedpeople and even slaves.[85] It also fits in with a significant decrease in the variety, quality, and size of the urns in this period, which suggests that the sanctuary was being used by a broader range of people than before.[86] These developments might relate politically to what Serge Lancel labeled the "democratic evolution" of the city in the late fourth and third centuries,[87] and economically to the shift from extensive to intensive agricultural production on the part of small-scale producers suggested by the dramatic rise in sites in the hinterland of Carthage, where a rural survey found only nine in the fourth century but fifty in the third and second.[88]

5.5 A relatively late flat marker with acroteria from the Carthage tophet, depicting a hand, a sign of Tanit, and a caduceus above a large fish, and an inscription below a crescent-disk.

5.6 An elaborate flat marker with acroteria from the Carthage tophet with a human figure flanked by two palm trees and two caducei, above an inscription framed by volute ("Aeolic") capitals. There is a sign of Tanit in the gable above a winged solar disk.

The tophets geographically closest to Carthage fell into visual line with it in this period.[89] This is especially obvious at Hadrumetum, a military ally of Carthage from at least the late fourth century until it submitted to Rome in 149 BCE.[90] By contrast with the earliest markers discussed above, those from Level III (c. 250–150 BCE) make multiple identifications with contemporary examples from Carthage, featuring gables and acroteria, "Hellenizing" features, inscriptions to Tinnit as well as Baal Hammon, and depictions of signs of Tanit and caducei. There is a striking bias at Hadrumetum toward the motifs found on the higher-quality markers from Carthage, including Egyptian and Greek architectural elements, and a significant number of more old-fashioned bottle idols (which still appear on 6 percent of the "thicker" markers from Carthage that have been catalogued, but only 1 percent of the "thinner" ones) and baetyls, which have more or less completely disappeared at Carthage by this time. By contrast, there is just one example of the hand that is particularly popular on lower-quality markers from Carthage.[91] The conscious appropriation of the iconographic range of only the higher-quality stelai at contemporary Carthage, as well as the somewhat archaizing set of motifs, might suggest a smaller and more conservative community in which sacrifice was still restricted to the wealthier citizens. It certainly suggests that what we are seeing here is not simply "influence" or mindless imitation, but choice and active adaptation, with class and status being relevant factors in those decisions.

Another African community approaches Carthage from a different perspective in this period, but just as closely. Cirta (modern Constantine) was a cosmopolitan Numidian royal city situated about one hundred kilometers inland from the Algerian coast. The markers found in the sanctuary there can be dated from the late third to mid-first centuries BCE on stylistic grounds, although all the precise dates given in the inscriptions are from the second century.[92] It is usually thought that an expatriate community established the tophet at Cirta, perhaps people from Carthage itself: 94 percent of the names of the dedicants are Semitic, although there are also Libyan, Greek, and Latin ones.[93]

As at contemporary Carthage and Hadrumetum, the offerings at Cirta are dedicated to both Baal Hammon and, on 17 percent of the markers, Tinnit.[94] Human figures are very uncommon, and the form of the markers draws inspiration from contemporary Carthaginian ones, though acroteria are rare (fig. 5.7).[95] The repertoire of motifs is relatively small, and similar to that found on the thinner, less expensive markers at Carthage in the corresponding phase. The most common symbols are the crescent-disk, caduceus, hand, and in particular, the sign of Tanit, which occurs on well over half the markers—242 out of 448—and is often presented, as in figure 5.7, in a strikingly anthropomorphized fashion.[96] Furthermore, the dedicants at Cirta seem at pains to stress the unusual nature of their offering, with several mentions of a *molk adam*, "the offering of a human," the first direct reference to human sacrifice since the mentions in the very early dedications to *molk baal*, "the offering of a person/citizen."[97] This explicit naming of a practice linked both in reality and the popular imagination to Carthage itself seems to emphasize the Cirtan community's connections with that city.

At the same time there are, as everywhere, local peculiarities: depictions of weapons, for instance, are unusually popular at Cirta. And while the sanctuary presumably distinguished its users from the rest of the civic community in a religious sense, the dedicants used the local Numidian regal era for dating, and there are indications of new mentalities behind the language used: the inscriptions, for instance, tend to give just one generation of ancestors rather than the two or more standard at Carthage.[98]

Much bigger differences are however found in Sardinia, where Carthage no longer exercised much attraction as a visual model in the Hellenistic period, and the forms and iconography of the markers become more distinctive. Although the Sardinians remained aware of Carthaginian fashions, it seems that in the fourth century the small visual world of the tophet broke into two distinct regional fragments. Signs of Tanit do appear on some of the late markers at Tharros and Nora, but *naiskos*-style markers continued to be used there rather than the flat *stelai* fashionable at contemporary Carthage; no hands are found, and just one or two caducei. There is little reference to the iconography of the wider Mediterranean, and the markers seem to have been discontinued altogether at both sanctuaries sometime in the fourth or early third century.[99] At Sulcis, the markers do become flatter and thinner, acquiring gables and acroteria, and both Greek and Egyptian architectural elements frame the main motif, but the principal motifs remain for the most part human figures, as they are at the new and nearby site of Monte Sirai.[100]

How can we explain this new pattern of smaller regional networks of identification? It can't be due to Roman intervention: the markers on Tharros and Nora disappear long before Roman victory in the First Punic War and Rome's subsequent annexation of the island in 237 BCE. It seems more likely that it relates to a political shift within the circle of the tophet, and in particular to the increasing power of Carthage, especially on Sardinia. Diodorus mentions that after a revolt in 379, the Carthaginians

5.7 A marker from the tophet at Cirta, depicting a crescent-disk, a star, a sign of Tanit, and a caduceus above an inscription and a horse's head.

quickly recovered the island, and a fourth-century treaty that Polybius records between the Carthaginians and Romans no longer subjects the latter to commercial regulation there, as in 509, but forbids them from trading or founding cities on the island (or in Africa) at all.[101] More important, only significant and relatively formal Carthaginian hegemony over the island by the third century would make sense of the treaty of 237 transferring it to Rome after that city's victory in the First Punic War.

We have seen here that tophet sanctuaries are not a "Phoenician" or even "Punic" phenomenon. Instead, ritualized child sacrifice and tophet cult was a geographically and culturally restricted phenomenon, practiced among a small group of Phoenician-speaking migrant communities in the central Mediterranean, a community based on a potent combination of commerce and religion that marked itself off from other Levantine settlers in the west, as well as from the homeland in the east. The cultural identifications marked visually between the sanctuaries, and their cities, reached their height in the sixth to fourth centuries BCE, not as a series of cultural alliances with Carthage, but as an interconnected crisscrossing network of sites in which the different sanctuaries could also underline their difference and distance from each other in their visual cultures—distances that then increased with increasing Carthaginian power. By this time, however, a bigger religious network of larger Mediterranean centers had eclipsed the collective identification with the circle of the tophet, and it too was closely associated with Carthaginian imperialism.

CHAPTER 6

Melqart's Mediterranean

Baal Hammon was not the only god to whom the Carthaginians turned under siege in 310 BCE, according to the passage of Diodorus that introduced chapter 5. The other was Melqart, "King (MLK) of the City (QRT)," whose cult was said to have been introduced at Tyre alongside that of Astarte in the tenth century by King Hiram, who was also the first to celebrate his annual Awakening or *egersis*.[1] In this chapter, I look at the connections Melqart made between the Levant and the western settlements, those he encouraged within the Phoenician-speaking world of the west, and the ways he reached beyond it, especially through his identification with Greek Herakles. Melqart's temple cult, unlike that of Baal Hammon, created a broad and open network that linked its adherents not only to each other, but also to other migrants as well as local populations across the Mediterranean. I will also suggest that this was a relatively new phenomenon in the fourth century BCE, knitting together what had until then been rather separate western regions, and perhaps even connecting Tyre's central Mediterranean "colonies" to their mother city for the first time.

CHILDREN OF TYRE

Our Greco-Roman sources agree that Tyre kept its children close, and that ties between these colonies and their mother city were focused on its principal god. As usual, we know most about Carthage, where Diodorus's claim that the Carthaginians were accustomed to sending a tithe of their revenues back to Melqart fits in with other glimpses we get of an ongoing relationship.[2] Justin's second-century CE epitome of the lost universal history written by Pompeius Trogus in the Augustan period informs us that in the sixth century BCE the Carthaginians were sending a proportion of their war profits to Melqart, and Curtius Rufus, writing in the first century CE, adds that they also adorned Tyre with the spoils of the cities they captured.[3] And although Diodorus suggests that the tithe payments had been neglected in the years leading up to the events of 310 BCE, other authors say that when Alexander besieged Tyre in 332, he found sacred ambassadors (*theoroi*) from Carthage there to celebrate an annual festival of "Herakles," probably the *egersis*. This visit to their "mother-city" was "according to an ancient custom [*nomimon*]", says Arrian, whose principal sources on Alexander's campaigns were contemporary; Curtius Rufus amplifies the point in his discussion of the same episode, noting that the Tyrians had founded Carthage, and so were always honored as their ancestors.[4] The evidence for the period of the Punic Wars includes the suspicious treatment at Carthage of the Tyrian Aristo described in chapter 4, but there are also indications of regular diplomatic relations between the cities—when Hannibal fled Carthage in 195, and was recognized on the nearby island of Kerkennah, he gave word that he had been sent on an embassy to Tyre[5]—and in the mid-second century, Carthage was still sending a boat to Tyre with the first fruits.[6]

The connections between Carthage and Tyre are also emphasized in the two foundation myths associated with the African city. The first we hear of is reported by Philistos, a Sicilian historian writing in the first half of the fourth century, who says that the city was founded by Azoros and Carchedon before the Trojan War.[7] These names are based on those of "Tyre" and "Carthage" themselves, and they show that a connection between those two cities was already being made by this time. At the beginning of the third century, another Sicilian historian, Timaeus of Tauromenium, recorded a different tradition, according to which the city was founded in 814 BCE.[8] Everything else we know about the story Timaeus told comes from fragments preserved in an anonymous ancient work, *On Women*: King Pygmalion of Tyre killed his sister Elissa's husband, and she fled the city with a number of other citizens, and traveled to Africa—travels that according to Timaeus later acquired her the epithet D(e)ido, the wanderer. Once she arrived in Africa, she founded the city of Carthage but then refused to marry the local king, Hiarbas, instead throwing herself from her palace onto a flaming pyre.[9]

According to the later writer Appian, this second story was the one told at Carthage itself: "The Phoenicians founded Carthage in Africa fifty years before the capture of Troy. Its founders were either Zorus and Carchedon, or, as the Romans and the Carthaginians themselves think, Dido, a Tyrian woman, whose husband Pygmalion, the ruler of Tyre, had murdered and then hidden the deed."[10] Other evidence also suggests that the story of Dido originated among Phoenician-speakers: Timaeus claims elsewhere to have consulted "Tyrian records" (τὰ παρὰ Τυρίων ὑπομνήματα),[11] and Josephus says that the same story was told by the second-century BCE author Menander of Ephesos, who he also says translated the ancient documents of the Tyrians from Phoenician into Greek.[12]

Carthage may even have promoted this legend on its coinage. Some intriguing silver tetradrachms it issued in Sicily around 320 BCE or a little later depict on their obverse an elegant woman wearing a pleated Phrygian tiara (fig. 6.1). Nothing names the woman, and neither the reverse—a lion walking in front of a palm tree—nor the legend Š'MMḤNT (of the people of the camp) provide any clue. Kenneth Jenkins, however, points out that it was common for Greek colonies to depict founders on their coinage, "which makes it perfectly possible and plausible for the same usage to be envisaged in the case of the Carthaginian coins in question."[13]

More elaborate versions of this Carthaginian foundation legend are preserved in Augustan period sources: Virgil's *Aeneid* brings together the story of Dido with that of the Trojan hero Aeneas, while Justin's epitome of Trogus preserves the basic outline of the story told in *On Women* as we have it, but adds a wealth of colorful detail.[14] Some of this may go back to Timaeus's original account: personal names such as Pygmalion, Elissa, and Acherbas (Pumayyaton, Elishat, and Zakerbaal), and the institutions of sacred prostitution, the hereditary priesthood, and the practice of immolation seem likely to come from Levantine sources. Other aspects seem to have been added in the Greek tradition, in particular the famous story that Dido, so that her crew could rest, acquired land for her new city by tricking the locals into selling her as much territory as could be covered with an ox hide, and then cutting the hide into such thin strips that it could surround the whole of the hill on which she then founded her city, and which was called as a result the "Byrsa." This anecdote must derive from a Greek source since *bursa* is the Greek word for "hide," and it also plays into the developing Greco-Roman stereotype of Phoenician deceitfulness and treachery. Its presence in Justin's account is nonetheless no reason to call into question the local origins of the earlier version of the story transmitted by Timaeus.[15]

These foundation legends connect Tyre and Carthage from at least the fourth century, even if Melqart himself appears in the story only in Justin's

6.1 Silver tetradrachm issued by Carthage in Sicily c. 320 BCE, depicting a woman in an elaborate headdress on the obverse, and on the reverse, a lion in front of a palm.

late account, and in a minor role: Dido's husband Acherbas was the high priest of Melqart, and after his death, Dido fled Tyre with the god's *sacra*, the symbols or objects associated with his cult.[16] It is impossible to say for certain whether this element of the story also goes back to the original version, but it does seem to involve local knowledge—the best candidates for these mysterious *sacra* are the dual pillars and perhaps also the olive that famously adorned Melqart's sanctuaries at both Tyre and Gadir.[17]

There is no doubt however that Carthaginian coinage promoted a connection with Melqart in the Hellenistic period: a series of silver tetradrachms minted in Sicily for about a decade around 300 BCE depict on their obverse a head of "Herakles" that must under the circumstances have been understood as Melqart (fig. 6.2a).[18] Two Hellenistic period inscriptions also mention a "House" or "Temple" (BT) of Melqart at Carthage, and although there are few direct invocations of Melqart in the extant epigraphic record from the city, the title "Resuscitator of the God" (MQM 'LM), which is found in more than twenty-five inscriptions of Hellenistic date, is presumably connected with the concept, if not the actual practice, of the *egersis*.[19] Furthermore, "Melqart" forms part of more than 1,500 attested Carthaginian names, such as Hamilcar and Bodmilcart.[20]

All these connections suggest that by the fourth century Carthage had a relatively strong civic identity as a Tyrian colony under the protection and power of Melqart, and as Irad Malkin has noted, its relationship with Tyre seems more "expressive, continuous and formal" than we hear of in the case of Greek colonies and their mother cities.[21] Carthage was not, however, the only Levantine settlement that Tyre was supposed to have founded abroad, and others had stronger claims to early ties with Melqart.

A WESTERN NETWORK

Stories of the foundation of Gadir in particular involve both the Tyrian authorities and Melqart in a more central role. Velleius Paterculus reports that the city was established by the fleet of Tyre around 1100 BCE,[22] dating the event with reference to the Trojan War, but apparently repeating a story told at Gadir itself: according to Strabo, the Gaditani said that the Tyrians founded their city on the orders of an oracle from Herakles, but Posidonius dismissed this as a "Phoenician lie," suggesting that both Posidonius in the early first century BCE and Strabo a couple of generations later considered this story to come from local sources.[23] The scholia to Dionysius's *Periegesis* even suggest that Herakles was himself the founder of the city, though it is impossible to know where that idea came from.[24] Certainly the city had an ancient, famous, and wealthy temple of Melqart, which was said to contain the pillars and the olive tree that symbolized the god, as well as his bones. We also have it on the not entirely reliable authority of Silius Italicus that the temple contained no statues or images of the gods, its timber never decayed, the priests were celibate, and women and swine were prohibited.[25]

Two other western settlements were traditionally held to have similarly early origins, and similar connections: Velleius Paterculus says that Utica, on the Mediterranean coast of Tunisia, was founded by the Tyrian fleet a few years after Gadir, and Pliny the Elder says its temple of "Apollo," founded at the same time as the city, had timber that never decayed, recalling Silius Italicus's description of the temple at Gadir. Across the Strait, Pliny mentions another shrine (*delubrum*) of Herakles at the settlement of Lixus on the Atlantic coast of Morocco, which was said to be older even than the one at Gadir.[26]

A new reading of a colonial foundation discussed in Justin's epitome of Trogus now reveals the extent to which these mutual identifications with Melqart and Tyre created a web of relationships between these powerful western Levantine settlements, as well as a set of mutual identifications and obligations. In a passage recounting the succession of imperial powers in Spain, Justin explains how the foundation of a colony led to the imposition of Carthaginian rule on local kingdoms:

> Then after the reigns of the kings, the Carthaginians were the first to take Hispania under imperial control. For when the Gaditani, on the orders of a dream, transferred the *sacra* of Melqart from Tyre, from where the Carthaginians also had their origin, to Spain, and founded a city there, and the peoples of Spain, jealous of the growth of the new city, as a result made war on the Gaditani, the Carthaginians sent help to their kinsmen [*consanguinei*]. In a successful campaign there they both saved the Gaditani from injury and to their greater injury added part of the province to their own empire. Afterwards, since the first expedition went so well, they sent Hamilcar as general with a great force to occupy the province.[27]

The reference to the new colony in this passage has traditionally been related to the foundation of Gadir itself, after which there would be a tacit chronological leap to a rather later dispute between that city and local peoples, which prompts the intervention of Carthage—an episode that should be placed in the sixth or fourth centuries, according to one's views on the chronology of Carthaginian imperialism in Iberia—and then finally a reference to Hamilcar's occupation of part of Spain in 237 BCE. But in his recent reinterpretation of this passage, Manuel Álvarez Martí-Aguilar has pointed out that the reference cannot be to the foundation of Gadir, since the founders of the new city are already "Gaditani."[28] Furthermore, he argues, the phrasing of the passage precludes a lengthy gap between the colonial foundation and the dispute with the neighboring peoples. Justin's method of epitomizing Trogus is to omit excess material rather than to summarize, and he signals such omissions with words that express transitions; here he signals in his standard fashion two significant chronological gaps, between the reigns of the Iberian kings and the foundation of the colony (*deinde*, "then"), and between the first and second Carthaginian expeditions (*postea*, "afterward"), but there is no sign of a break between the foundation of the colony and the disputes with the locals that lead to Carthaginian intervention.[29]

Álvarez Martí-Aguilar goes on to suggest that Trogus was actually referring here to the foundation of Carteia, on the Spanish coast, near the Rock of Gibraltar, which can be dated archaeologically to the mid-fourth century. This is a period when Gadir was increasingly active within Iberia, and when Carthaginian imperial intervention in Spain is realistic. It is comfortably earlier than Hamilcar's expedition of 237 to which Justin refers at the end of the passage—in which, according to Polybius' near-contemporary account, Hamilcar was in fact recuperating lost territory.[30] There certainly was a Roman-period cult of Herakles at Carteia,[31] and Strabo preserves a report by the third-century BCE author Timosthenes that Carteia's neighbor Calpe (Gibraltar), which is often run together with Carteia in ancient sources, was founded by Herakles and in ancient times called Herakleia.[32]

Whether or not Justin's colony was in fact Carteia, this reinterpretation of Justin's anecdote tells us a great deal about the functions of the Melqart cult. For one thing, it creates further vertical sets of ties between Tyre, its colonies, and those colonies' own colonies: according to Justin, the Tyrians allow the Gaditani to take sacred objects (again, *sacra*) from the metropolitan sanctuary of Melqart for the foundation of their new colony, just as—in his story of Elissa—he claims had happened more informally in the case of Carthage. For another, it creates a new set of horizontal connections: the relationships that Gadir and Carthage both have with Tyre create a bond between them, which was conceptualized at least by Trogus as based on blood. This bond obliged Carthage to send military support to Gadir, just as the Tyrians expected Carthaginian help in 332 BCE. The notion of kinship between these cities is also known to Silius Italicus in the first century CE, who calls the Carthaginians "Tyrians" and describes Gadir as "cognate" with them.[33] And in his account of the foundation of Carthage, Justin brings

Utica into this network as well, saying that when Carthage was founded, ambassadors arrived from Utica to bring gifts to their kinsmen (*consanguinei*) and encourage them to found a city.[34] Álvarez Martí-Aguilar describes this community as "a network of cities whose inhabitants recognised Tyre as their motherland and the source of the political and religious legitimacy of their own communities, tied together by kinship through the figure of Melqart . . . a kinship that implies inherent obligations of help and support."[35]

Carthage, Gadir, Utica, Lixus, and another city that I shall call here for the sake of simplicity Carteia all then shared an interest in Tyre and its principal god, expressed in terms of kinship. They also shared a related group of foundation stories—the only foundation legends attached to Phoenician-speaking settlements, in contrast to standard Greek practice—all of which directly involve Tyrians, one way or another; in the cases of Gadir, Carteia, and Carthage, they also record the transfer of cult objects from the Tyrian temple of Melqart. For Gadir and Lixus, these accounts claim that a temple of Melqart was established in the new settlement, and for Gadir and Carteia, they involve an oracle from Melqart, which in itself recalls the strange story found in the late antique author Nonnus of the foundation of Tyre itself on two wandering "ambrosial" rocks on the instructions of the same god.[36] These myths align these cities with each other.[37]

Melqart's cultic network, however, spread well beyond the self-proclaimed ancient colonies of Tyre. The best evidence for this is from Sardinia, where an inscription found at Tharros, dated from the third- to second-century BCE, records the construction of a temple, described in some detail, and dedicates it "to the lord, to the holy god Melqart on [or "over" or "above"] the rock . . .". This is a reference to the rock on which the city of Tyre was built, and that gave the city its name.[38] The words "to the lord, to Melqart on the rock ['L ḤṢR]," also appear on two other fourth- or third-century inscriptions from Sardinia, a stone column found at Karales, and a bronze plaquette commemorating building activity at the great sanctuary of Sardos at Antas, as well as on a third-century statue base from Ibiza.[39] The phrase emphasizes the connection between the god and his city, and therefore a connection through the god to Tyre, suggesting that being Tyrian was an important part of these western identities, even outside a formal colonial context.[40] A very similar phrase is found on the third- or second-century BCE dedications by two brothers to Melqart B'L ṢR (Lord of Tyre) found on Malta and discussed above.[41]

Elsewhere, Strabo tells us that in Iberia there was an island "sacred to Herakles" near Huelva, and another island "of Herakles" near Cartagena.[42] There is also evidence from sixth- or fifth-century western Sicily for the name Abdmelqart (slave or servant of Melqart), and a city called Rosh Melqart (RŠ MLQRT, Cape Melqart) issued coinage in the later fourth century BCE.[43] This seems very likely to be the south coast city of Herakleia Minoa, which was originally, according to Herodotus, a colony of Greek Selinus. Carthage had taken the city by 357 BCE and seems to have controlled it for much of the following century: it would have made sense for the Carthaginians to rename it, at least for minting purposes, for their own equivalent god to Herakles.[44] Finally, Ptolemy the Geographer says in the second century CE that Melqart had a temple on Malta.[45]

Across the western Mediterranean, the cult of Melqart of Tyre actively connected Tyrian colonies back to their mother city in the east; it is no surprise then that Diodorus describes him as the god responsible for those who settle abroad (παρὰ τοῖς ἀποίκοις).[46] This involved not only bilateral ties between Tyre and its colonies, but encouraged a network of connections between these overseas settlements based on the figure and cult of Melqart, and over time the cult was adopted in a variety of other Phoenician-speaking contexts in the west. But Melqart did not simply bind Levantine migrants to each other: his cult also tied them to Greek colonial populations and traditions, and in particular to the Greek god Herakles.

FELLOW TRAVELERS

Herodotus knew as early as the fifth century BCE that Melqart "was" Herakles: when he tells of his visit to the famous sanctuary of Herakles at Tyre, he is describing the temple of Melqart.[47] Such syncretism was of course common in the polytheistic ancient Mediterranean: "Religion was a universal *langue*; the local names of the deities the distinctive *parole*."[48] Herodotus also knew that Herakles could stand in for other gods as well: when he went to Melqart's Tyrian temple, he was on a mission to explore the origins of "Egyptian Herakles," but he also visited a shrine at Tyre to "Herakles of Thasos."[49] Similarly, although other Greek authors always refer to Melqart as "Herakles," they sometimes specify that they mean the "Tyrian Herakles" to distinguish him not only from the Greek or "Argive" hero of the same name, understood to be considerably younger, but also from a considerable number of other foreign gods.[50]

Nonetheless, it must have been particularly easy to make a connection between Melqart and Herakles. As Richard Miles has pointed out, they were both figures who straddle the divide between god and human: "Herakles, the son of Zeus and a human mother, had to earn the right to become a god himself through his heroic feats; Melqart, although a god, was also the first mythical king of Tyre and ancestor of its royal lineage."[51] Both were said to have been reborn through fire.[52] And both were closely associated with colonization: as we have seen, Melqart is at the heart of several of the Phoenician foundation stories preserved in Greco-Latin texts—these are in fact the only myths associated with him—while Herakles prepares the way for Greek settlement by conquering large territories and founding the dynasties that found colonies, guaranteeing in both cases the new arrivals' right to the land they seize.[53] Indeed, it seems that the relationship between these two figures in the Greek imagination might have evolved in relation to the geography of migration west: Colette Jourdain-Annequin has argued very plausibly that some of Greek Herakles's exploits, in particular stealing the cattle of Geryon and the apples from the Gardens of the Hesperides, acquired a more specific geography for Archaic and Classical Greek authors from centers of Melqart worship—Geryon was localized at Gadir, for instance, and the Gardens of the Hesperides at Lixus.[54] Irad Malkin suggests furthermore that the particular association of Melqart with Tyrian colonies such as Carthage and Gadir "probably heightened Greek awareness of Herakles, whom they identified with Melqart, as a hero associated with, or even justifying, colonisation."[55]

That the connection between Melqart and Herakles was well known to Greeks is illustrated by an episode a century after Herodotus's visit to the Tyrian temple, when another and less welcome visitor announced himself. In 332 BCE, Alexander the Great accepted the submission of Tyre in the face of his advancing troops but demanded, in the words of Curtius Rufus, "to sacrifice to Herakles, whom the Tyrians especially worshipped, on the grounds that the kings of Macedon believed themselves to be descended from the same god, and that he had also been advised by an oracle to do so."[56] Whether or not Alexander really gave the reasons Curtius reports, his supposed descent from Herakles was an important aspect of his self-presentation, witnessed not least by the large amount of coinage he issued depicting himself in the guise, and lion skin, of the god. This would explain his particular desire to publicly associate himself with Melqart, although as Brian Bosworth has noted, this unusual request at the time of the annual rite of the *egersis* "must have looked like an attempt to control or interfere with the celebration of the national festival," underlining Tyre's status as his vassal. The Tyrians' polite refusal prompted Alexander to besiege the city for seven months, ending with its total defeat.[57]

This may in fact have been the episode that interested Phoenician-speakers themselves in the Greek syncretism between the two gods.[58] There is certainly plenty of evidence that the same association was made on their side as well: perhaps most famously, Silius Italicus tells us that the doors of the temple of Melqart at Gadir were decorated with the twelve labors of Herakles, although Philostratus makes the more modest claim that they were depicted on a stone altar there dedicated specifically to the "Theban" rather than the "Egyptian" Herakles, whose own bronze altars were bare.[59] It is less clear, however, when this association began to be made by Phoenician-speakers, for although there are a considerable number of representations of Herakles found in Phoenician-speaking contexts that may in those contexts refer to Melqart,[60] the first clear example of "a purely Greek Herakles serving as equivalent for Melqart" comes in the tetradrachms minted by Carthage around 300 BCE discussed above, which were modeled closely on a popular type produced by Alexander and his immediate successors at mints across the eastern Mediterranean (fig. 6.2).[61] As with their earlier appropriation of the *phoinix*, it seems likely that the Carthaginians took a Greek idea here and made it their own.[62]

It has nonetheless been suggested that a connection between the two gods among Phoenician-speakers can, on the contrary, be traced back as far as the sixth century, on the evidence of the limestone statuettes of a male figure, often now labeled in museums and catalogues as Herakles and/ or Melqart, that was very popular in Cypriot sanctuaries from the sixth to fourth centuries. The figure combined the Greek attributes of Herakles—the club and the skin of the Nemean lion worn as a headdress, with the paws tied together at the chest—with the long-standing Near Eastern tropes of the Smiting God and the Master of Animals: the figure holds the club aloft

6.2 Herakles coinage. (a) Carthaginian tetradrachm of c. 305–295 BCE, depicting on the obverse an image of Herakles—or Melqart—wearing a lion skin headdress, and on the reverse, a horse's head and palm. The head draws openly on the head of Herakles depicted on coinage issued by Alexander and his successors in the eastern Mediterranean, such as (b), a silver tetradrachm issued by Ptolemy I in the years 323–316 BCE with a portrait of Herakles on the obverse, and on the reverse, Zeus on a throne with an eagle and scepter.

6.3 "Master of the Lion" limestone figurines from sixth-century Cyprus, often identified with Herakles.

in his right hand, behind his head, and in his left hand grasps an undersized lion (fig. 6.3).[63] However, there are no dedications to Herakles on Cyprus in this period, and as Derek Counts has pointed out, there is something distinctly odd, according the logic of the Greek tales, about Herakles wearing the skin of the lion he is about to defeat and flay.[64] There is furthermore no direct evidence for an association with Melqart at all, and the sanctuaries involved are dedicated to a variety of other gods, including Reshef and Apollo.[65] Counts notes that the hybrid figure speaks more obviously to the notion of mastery over animals in this agricultural landscape than of any particular Greek or Phoenician god: the same sanctuaries often have "Masters of Rams" of similar date, and the neutral label "Master of the Lion" captures well the nature of the image as well as the extent of our ignorance about its meaning in its local context.[66]

Attempts to date the adoption of the image of Herakles into the cult of Melqart are complicated by the fact that we have no certain idea of what Melqart was supposed to look like before his image was "replaced" by that of Herakles in western contexts. Literary descriptions of the Melqart sanctuary at Gadir suggest that the cult image was aniconic,[67] and there is only one representation in the east that is actually labeled as Melqart, in an Aramaic inscription on a stele of about 800 BCE from Breidj in northern Syria, near Aleppo (fig. 6.4). Here we see a bearded, bare-chested god wearing a short Egyptian-style kilt and a conical hat striding forward in profile with a bow on his back, what seems to be a lotus flower in his right hand, and a fenestrated axe in his left. As Bonnet notes, this "is clearly a composite image with Egyptian and Syro-Hittite affiliations," and so it is difficult to tell whether this one example from well outside "Phoenicia" represents a canonical image of the god.[68]

Some coin issues may provide portraits of the god before his Herakleian makeover. Silver coinage issued at Tyre from about 425 to 333/2 BCE features a bearded god holding out a bow and quiver and riding a winged sea horse or hippocamp (see fig. 4.5c).[69] This image is based on the Persian running archer type, and there are no attributes or echoes of Herakles.[70] Nothing explicitly identifies the rider as Melqart, but as Jessica Nitschke has pointed out, it is hard to see which other god he could be, at least at Tyre, and the maritime symbolism suits a god so associated with overseas migration.[71] The Sicilian city of Rosh Melqart provides another very likely portrait of Melqart among its later fourth-century issues (fig. 6.5): given the city's name, the god is the obvious identification for this rather generic bearded male head with an earring.[72]

From the late fourth century, however, there is a great deal of Herakleian imagery in Phoenician-speaking contexts where the reference seems very likely or even certain to be Melqart: in particular, depictions of Herakles and his attributes became very popular on coinage throughout the Phoenician-speaking regions of Iberia and North Africa, minted at real or supposed Levantine settlements, but also considerably beyond.[73] The third-century examples of the head of Herakles in his lion skin from the great Melqart cult center of Gadir must be understood as representing Melqart, and this seems very likely to be true as well for later coins from Spain that adopt the same type; some of the African examples are more ambiguous. Melqart is only explicitly associated with Herakles in a written Phoenician source for the first time to our knowledge in the third- or second-century bilingual inscriptions from Malta, where the two brothers from Tyre map the phrase "To our lord, to Melqart, Baal of Tyre" in Phoenician onto the Greek text "To Herakles Archegetes."[74]

6.4 A stele from Breidj, near Aleppo, depicting the god Melqart. Now in the Aleppo Museum.

6.5 Obverse of a silver tetradrachm with the Punic legend "Rosh Melqart," depicting a bearded man who may represent the god Melqart.

Whenever it became standard, this representation of Melqart as Herakles would have made the connection between these gods even more obvious and immediate to adherents of Melqart than to those of Herakles, who was not after all depicted as Melqart. And if when Phoenician-speakers looked at Melqart, they saw Herakles, it would have been hard for them to conceive of Melqart's cult in exclusive terms. In their use of Herakleian iconography for their Tyrian god, then, western migrants from the Levant connected themselves to Tyre and to each other at the same time as to the Greek colonies in the western Mediterranean protected by Herakles.

This is not, however, just a story about links within and between migrant populations in the Mediterranean: unlike Baal Hammon, Melqart was an easily translatable god, and he could also make connections with local precolonial populations, who on occasion adopted him as part of their own stories.[75] On Sardinia, for instance, the second-century CE Greek author Pausanias records a story associating "Herakles" with one "Makeris," surely an attempt to render Melqart into Greek, as well as with a local hero: "The first sailors to cross to the island are said to have been Libyans. Their leader was Sardos, son of Makeris, the Makeris named Herakles by the Egyptians and the Libyans."[76] Sardos is the Greek name for the god known in Latin as Sardus Pater (Sardus the Father), who was worshipped at a sanctuary founded at Antas in southwestern Sardinia in the late fifth or fourth century BCE. Pre-Roman inscriptions there call him Sid Babi: Sid is an import, the name of a minor deity in the Levant; Babi seems to be the local name for the god.[77] Like the relationship between Herakles and Melqart, the identification between Levantine Sid and this Sardinian god was forged between new neighbors, but in this case between settlers and settled.[78] And the further association between this dual god and Melqart was not simply a Greek conceit: a fourth- or third-century inscription at Carthage refers to "SidMelqart."[79]

This foundation myth for Sardinia does not involve Melqart directly, only his son. It nonetheless brings Melqart into the heart of local history: just as the Sardinian Babi-Sid-Sardos is descended from the African Makaris-Melqart-Herakles, so the Sardinians are politically dependent on Melqart's African city of Carthage. Corinne Bonnet sees the story as an example of "the legitimization of the colonial dominion exercised by Carthage over Sardinia."[80] Furthermore, as noted above, the Antas sanctuary has also yielded a fourth- or third-century dedication to Melqart of Tyre recording building activity in the sacred area, which might suggest that the god had a significant presence at the site,[81] and this is by no means the only evidence for Melqart on Sardinia.

It may even be that Carthage actively encouraged his cult on the island: there is a reference in the building inscription for the Melqart temple at Tharros to officials of QRTḤDŠT, although that is as likely to be the town known in Greek as "Neapolis," across the bay from Tharros, or perhaps even Tharros itself, as to the African "new city."[82] But even if Carthage was not formally involved, the adoption of Melqart as the father of an important local god could still have been a response to the increasing hegemony of "Tyrian" Carthage in the fourth and third centuries, a way of making sense of it, and of integrating it into the particular mixed indigenous and colonial culture of the island. Both the indigenous and immigrant population would have benefited from such a strategy, and as noted in chapter 2, this is the period in which a "Sardinian" identity becomes visible for the first time.

Myths are one of our few keys to the way that the colonial world saw itself, and colonists and their new neighbors seem to have seen their shared gods in terms that made ethnic differentiation between Phoenicians, Greeks, and Sardinians irrelevant. Given his strong identification with Herakles, at least among Greeks, from a relatively early date, Melqart would have been a peculiarly poor choice as a focus for a bounded and oppositional Phoenician identity, and as we have seen Herakles, Melqart, and Makeris did not in practice consolidate exclusive collective identities at all: they were too easily and inclusively shared, and in colonial contexts they performed a mediating rather than a distinguishing role. The way that both Greek and Phoenician-speaking migrants as well as local populations in the western Mediterranean could construct settlement myths involving the same legendary figure underlines again the extent to which migration created a common Mediterranean world. The adoption of Melqart opened the door to the Mediterranean as a mythical whole and allowed his adherents to construct themselves and their relationships in Mediterranean-wide terms. All in all, it is not surprising that the imagery of Herakles/Melqart was adopted more widely outside Carthage than the narrowly ethnic symbolism of the palm tree, which after the fifth- and fourth-century examples from Motya and Rosh Melqart mentioned in chapter 4 is found only on the second- to first-century BCE coinage of Thagaste in Algeria.[83]

AN IMAGINED COMMUNITY?

Popular and open as it may have been, was the network of Melqart the continuation and expansion of an interconnected Tyrian colonial system dating back to foundations in the Archaic period, or was it a later invention? All the documentary evidence relating to Melqart in the western Mediterranean is, after all, from the fourth century and later. And this is not simply a result of a lack of evidence from earlier periods: as we saw in the previous chapter, there are a significant number of formal and institutional references to Baal Hammon in seventh- and sixth-century contexts from several western sites. There is one earlier reference to a god who may be related to Melqart, but is not the civic god of Tyre: in 2003, an inscription was discovered on Ibiza, incised on a tablet made of animal bone and dating to the first half or middle of the seventh century BCE, recording a dedication to "EshmunMelqart," a double name otherwise attested only at the sanctuary of Batsalos-Kition on Cyprus in the fourth century.[84] This may be an otherwise unknown Cypriot deity, but whatever cult or circumstance lies beneath his brief appearance in the western Mediterranean, the reference to Eshmun, a god of Sidon, means that this must be part of a different story from that of Tyre and its foundations abroad and suggests that a different relationship between the western migrants and their homeland could be envisaged in the seventh century, involving the gods of multiple mother cities.[85]

It is also only in the fourth century that a privileged set of relationships between Tyre, Carthage, Utica, and Gadir are first described in a treaty concluded between Carthage and Rome, probably in 348 BCE. The earlier treaty between the cities, plausibly dated by Polybius to 509, had mentioned only "Carthage and its allies," but in its fourth-century renewal, the Uticans and the Tyrians with their "allies" are listed alongside Carthage.[86] Furthermore, while the first treaty forbade travel beyond a "Fair Promontory" (probably Cap Bon), in the second, travel beyond a "Mastia Tarseion" to "maraud, trade or found a city" is also forbidden. While there has been much debate over the identity of Mastia (and?) Tarseion, the most plausible approach associates the latter at least with the Greek name "Tartessos," which usually describes a region in southwestern Spain, but is also frequently used as a name for Gadir and Carteia themselves (alone among Iberian cities, providing another link between the pair).[87] The inclusive wording of the Carthaginian alliance in the treaty fits in neatly with the probable dating of Carteia's foundation by Gadir with Carthaginian involvement, and it is worth noting that if the treaty is specifying a particular town here, Carteia, located right on the Strait of Gibraltar, would have been a sensible strategic choice.

It may be that the bilateral colonial connection between Tyre and Carthage itself was also reimagined or even invented in this period. It is in the fourth century, after all, that we have the first evidence for foundation myths that link Tyre with the origins of Carthage, in one case through the names of "Azoros" (Tyre) and "Carchedon" (Carthage), and find the first detailed illustration in our sources of the purportedly long-standing relationship between these cities, when Carthaginians are found celebrating the *egersis* at Tyre under attack from Alexander. These ambassadors are said to have initially encouraged the Tyrians to expect aid from their city, and although Carthage in the end proved unable or unwilling to provide military support, Tyre did send some noncombatants to safety there.[88] And, during the siege, the Tyrians themselves are said to have drawn courage from their colonial relationship with Carthage: Justin reports that "Tyrian spirits were lifted by the example of Dido, who, having founded Carthage, conquered a third of the world,"[89] at the same time as, according to Curtius Rufus, they considered reviving their ancient habits of child sacrifice, a practice by then firmly associated with the western city.[90] This was successfully opposed by the city elders, as noted above, but if the story is reliable, it would seem that by the fourth century the Tyrians accepted a link between the contemporary rites of Carthage and their own past practice in this respect. Nonetheless, almost all the positive initiatives in the relationship seem to come from Carthage rather than Tyre. A generation later, it was the Carthaginians who turned to the Tyrian god—along with their own Baal Hammon—for aid under siege from Agathokles, suggesting that they had not been paying him sufficient honor in the past, and a few years later again, as we have seen, they were issuing coinage with his image, and perhaps also with that of their founder Dido. This is in addition, the period in which we find a new interest at the Carthage tophet in symbols that make direct reference to the Levant.

Although Tyre is traditionally seen as the driving force behind the "Phoenician" colonization of the western Mediterranean in the Archaic period, we actually have very little evidence for that model. It is striking that while historians are often suspicious of later traditions about Greek colonial foundations, supposed Phoenician colonies are rarely given the same level of scrutiny, even though the sources are often much scantier.[91] The evidence that a temple of Melqart was an important feature of the settlements of Gadir and Lixus from an early date makes a genuine, formal connection between those cities and Tyre an attractive hypothesis, but there is less evidence to support the notion that Carthage was originally a formal or even informal Tyrian colony.[92] There is certainly no indication that Tyre retained, or indeed ever had, political control or representation in Carthage or any other western city, and many of its supposed daughter-cities could originally have been more informal foundations with settlers from multiple cities in the homeland, as proposed for the "circle of the tophet" in the previous chapter, and perhaps also suggested by the EshmunMelqart inscription found on Ibiza.[93] However that may be, by the fourth century it had become convenient at both Carthage and Tyre to emphasize long-standing links between them, in the context of the broader network of Melqart described in this chapter.

It may also have become convenient in this period for other cities to align themselves with the new network of western Levantine power. This might explain a curious story told about the Sicilian city originally founded as Minoa, which acquired the Greek name Herakleia in the sixth century, fell under Carthaginian control for much of the fourth century and is probably the city that issued coinage in that period as "Rosh Melqart." Herakleides of Lembos's second-century BCE epitome of Aristotle's fourth-century *Constitutions* says that before it was settled by Minos of Crete, Sicilian Minoa used to be called Makara, which is very likely to be a reference to Melqart, at least as heard by Greek ears.[94] As we have seen, however, there is no direct evidence for Melqart cult on Sicily before the fourth century. It may be that the earlier Greek name for the city, the prominence of the Greek syncretism between Herakles and Melqart in the later fourth century, and the city's new connection with Carthage, together prompted a new tale of its origins that reached Aristotle's researchers, creating an earlier phase of the city's history that gave it long-standing ties to Melqart and, through him, to Carthage.[95]

There is no particular reason to doubt that Tyrians founded settlements overseas in the Archaic period, and that they promoted their civic cult of Melqart abroad, but my argument here is that there is reasonable grounds to suspect that the articulated "network of Melqart" described in this chapter, interrelated by colonization, kinship, and myth, was a later development, and one that should be associated with political shifts at Carthage. A fourth-century date for its emergence would map neatly onto to the growth of Carthaginian power across the western Mediterranean, in particular over the other western Levantine settlements involved, and the central position of Carthage within this network is striking. They make treaties with third parties on behalf of the other cities while picking and choosing between their own obligations to them: unavailable to aid Tyre under siege, for instance, they do manage to send help to Gadir—perhaps unasked, and, it seems, to their own much greater benefit. Whenever the various colonial connections between Tyre, Carthage, Gadir, Utica, and Lixus really began, the fourth century was when they started to play a major political role in Carthaginian state-building, a moment that coincided with the fragmentation of the older, smaller, and denser central Mediterranean circle of the tophet.

Furthermore, the expansion of the network of Melqart beyond the core Levantine settlements in this period also reflects Carthage's expanding regional ambitions. With the help of Dido, another great Tyrian, Melqart allowed the Carthaginians to present their growing power not as hostile encroachment on the lands of other states but as a rediscovery of ancient brotherhood in a shared Tyrian community, links that also consolidated Carthage's promotion of a brand new "Phoenician" identity on the coinage it issued across the regions it controlled.

My purpose here in part 2 has been to show that the experience of migration changed Phoenician-speaking people and their cultural practices, and in some ways brought them closer together. They created a variety of interlocking worlds based on a range of connections, which also interacted to varying degrees with the ideas and identities of others, and challenged traditional connections between religion, commerce, culture, and imperialism. Networks of mutual identification grew up among subgroups of colonies, whether from the bottom up and from the beginning, as in the circle of the tophet, or later among established powers, as with the network of Melqart. While the gods, rites, and visual culture of the tophet kept the homeland, the new home, and other colonial populations at a distance, Melqart embodied by contrast a strong relationship between self and mother, involved a much larger network of Phoenician-speakers than did the tophet cult, and at the same time reached out to other migrants and even to local populations. Carthage played an important role, however, in both these groups, and the Greek notion of the "Phoenicians" was exploited primarily in an imperial context in the palm tree coinage issued by the state of Carthage. These are stories that would be lost if we looked only for Phoenician identity and considered the Phoenicians themselves a group that always already existed.

In the next part, I am going to show how the evidence for Phoenician identifications increases after the conquests of Alexander and the destruction of Carthage through a series of case studies spanning more than two millennia. I will start with the new interest in the Phoenician past that developed in the Hellenistic and Roman Levant, move on to the phenomenon of "Punic persistence" in Roman Africa, and finish with the invention of a Phoenician past in Britain and Ireland from the sixteenth to nineteenth centuries, which will take us back to where we began. My argument will be that this increasing interest in the Phoenicians does not reflect the increasing visibility of an existing ethnic community, but reveals instead, and again, the deployment of "Phoenicianism" in the service of autonomy, power, and honor.

PART III

Imperial Identities

CHAPTER 7

The First Phoenician

In the third or fourth century CE, a writer called Heliodorus from the Syrian town of Emesa (modern Homs) wrote a novel in Greek. *Aethiopika* tells the story of the romance between a Greek nobleman and an Ethiopian princess who was born white by an accident of "maternal impression"—an ancient literary phenomenon by which the mere sight of a person of another color by a pregnant woman could change the color of the unborn child—then abandoned by her mother, and must now make her way back home to reclaim her ancestral throne.[1] The final line of the work is an authorial *sphragis* or "seal": "So concludes the composition of the Ethiopian story about Theagenes and Charikleia. It was composed by a Phoenician [*phoinix*] from Emesa, of the stock [*genos*] of the descendants of the Sun, son of Theodosius, Heliodorus."[2] This is the first time in the currently surviving evidence that anyone calls himself a Phoenician, and the circumstances place him a considerable distance inland from the Levantine coast and many hundreds of years after the history of the Phoenicians is traditionally taken to have ended, with Alexander's conquest of the coastal cities in 332 BCE.

I will try to make sense of Heliodorus's self-description in this chapter by contextualizing it within the increasing popularity of the Phoenicians, and of the idea of being Phoenician, in the Hellenistic and then Roman periods. This did not, however, involve the widespread embrace of a Phoenician ethnic identity: the coastal cities focused on their competing claims to the newly renowned Phoenician colonies and heroes, while the authors of Phoenician histories, often seen by modern scholars as patriotic champions of their people, were writing not so much *as*, but rather *about* the Phoenicians. In fact, one of the greatest enthusiasts for Phoenician culture and identity to be found in ancient sources was a Roman emperor from Emesa, and it is this, I will finally suggest, that can explain Heliodorus's unprecedented claim.

THE PHOINIX IS A TREE

After Alexander's death, the Levantine coast initially came under the control of the Ptolemaic dynasty in Egypt, who disputed hegemony over the region with the Seleucid kings of Syria for more than a century, and eventually ceded it to Antiochus III in 198 BCE. Seleucid rule in the Levant was already in decline in the face of increasing Roman aggression by the reign of Antiochus IV (r. 175–163 BCE), and the area was politically unstable until Pompey arrived in 65 BCE, deposed Antiochus XIII, made Syria a Roman province, and added to this province the coastal cities. The administrative arrangements for the region under the Ptolemies and then the Seleucids are unclear, but there are occasional references in formal contexts to a larger region known as "Syria and Phoenicia" or "Koile Syria and Phoenicia," which, at least in the Seleucid period, seems to have had a single governor.[3]

The rule of the Hellenistic kings over these cities was comparatively light—they imposed no colonies, for instance, as they often did elsewhere—and although Greek cultural institutions and artifacts are found in the region in the Hellenistic period, the transition from monarchies to popular sovereignty of some kind should not be seen as evidence for "Hellenization," invited or imposed; as Fergus Millar has pointed out, these cities were "rather like Greek *poleis* anyway."[4] Nonetheless, traditional models for domestic and religious architecture persisted, as did local customs, priesthoods, and magistracies, as well as the language: at the sanctuaries of Umm el-'Amed and Kharayeb, for instance, amid sculptural and architectural models taken from Greece and Egypt, all the Hellenistic-period inscriptions are in Phoenician.[5] At the same time, continuing local rivalries sometimes erupted into violence, as between Arados and Amrit in the 140s BCE.[6]

The juxtaposition of external hegemony and local autonomy in the Hellenistic period is vividly illustrated in the cities' second-century BCE coinage. From 198, when its Ptolemaic governor finally surrendered the city to Antiochus III, Tyre minted a very unusual series of bronze coins. The four denominations had a portrait of the Seleucid king Antiochus III on the obverse, as was standard on coins across the Seleucid Empire, but on the reverse, they featured local imagery: in descending order of value, a stern, a prow, a palm tree, and a club.[7] Three of these motifs obviously refer to core civic attributes of Tyre: the stern and prow emphasized the city's maritime focus and activities, and the club was an attribute of Herakles, and so could represent Tyre's own god. But what about the palm tree, or *phoinix* (fig. 7.1)? A palm tree *tout court* would not make much sense in this context, where it has no known local associations.[8]

7.1 Early-second-century BCE Tyrian bronze coin with Antiochus III (obv.) and palm tree (rev.).

One obvious parallel is the palm on the Carthaginian coinage discussed in chapter 4, a widespread, long-lasting, and well-known image in the western Mediterranean that must have been familiar to Tyrians traveling in that region. The obvious conclusion would be that it carries the same basic punning meaning: "Phoenician."[9] Furthermore, this association between the palm, the city, and the group-designation seems to be confirmed by the first-century BCE poet Meleager of Gadara, himself educated at Tyre. In an epitaph written for his fellow-poet Antipater, Meleager describes the iconography on the latter's tomb: a cock with a scepter, holding in his claws a palm branch. Does this represent a victory in battle or the games, wonders Meleager? No, he says, "the *phoinix* means not victory, but his fatherland, Tyre of many children, proud mother of the Phoenicians [*Phoinikes*]."[10] Similarly, in the second-century CE *Leukippe and Klitophon* by the Alexandrian author Achilles Tatius, when an oracle advises sending an offering to Herakles at a place that is "both island and city," whose people are "named for a tree," the mystery is solved when one Sostratos explains that Tyre is meant because it is an island and "the *phoinix* is a tree."[11]

But if Carthage's coins promoted a common Phoenician identity across the broad regions it controlled in the west, this later civic coinage puts Tyre itself back in the driver's seat after Carthage's humiliation in the Second Punic War at the hands of Rome, emphasizing Tyre's primary role in the networks of Phoenician-speaking settlements both at home and overseas discussed in the previous section. And these coins do not simply declare a Phoenician identity on the part of the Tyrians: the *phoinix* also makes a Tyrian claim to Phoinix himself, the founder of Phoenicia according to Greek myth.

This emerges clearly from a comparison with the types that neighboring cities began to issue thirty years later, when seventeen cities in Syria, Palestine, and Asia Minor adopted similar systems of what is often now called "quasi-municipal" bronze coinage.[12] As with the earlier Tyrian issues, these had the Seleucid monarch (now Antiochus IV) on the obverse, and local types on the reverse. The fact that this major shift in the nature of regional coinage seems to have happened for the most part in a single year (169/8 BCE) suggests that it was an initiative of the Seleucid authorities—the maintenance of local differences is, after all, a traditional tool of imperial hegemony—but it is unlikely that they chose the specific local types.[13] Not all the "Phoenician" cities participated enthusiastically, or indeed at all: Tripolis only produced occasional issues of a single denomination of quasi-municipal coinage, five in all between 166/5 and about 140 BCE, and Arados continued to mint entirely autonomous coinage in this period.[14] Sidon, Byblos, and Beirut, however, all began to mint the same four bronze denominations as Tyre (fig. 7.2).[15]

It is clear from a comparison of these coins that the four cities used their new coinage to speak to each other. The two higher denominations at Byblos and Beirut match two pairs of civic gods, six-winged El and Isis Pharia (the Egyptian lighthouse goddess) at Byblos with Baal Berit (the Lord of Beirut) and Ashtart at Beirut; this Ashtart at Beirut is on a prow, and a prow is also found on the same denomination at Tyre; the Tyrian coins with a stern and with a prow map Sidonian ones of the same

| Tyre | Sidon | Beirut | Byblos |

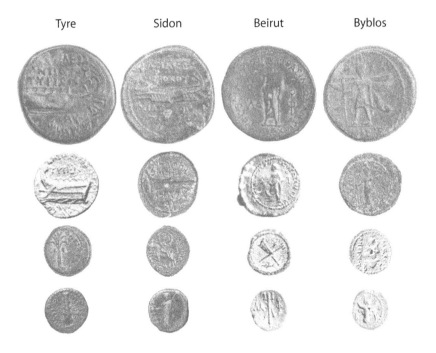

7.2 Reverses of the "quasi-municipal" bronze coins from Tyre, Sidon, Beirut, and Byblos, minted from 169/8. At Tyre these depict, in descending order of size, a stern, a prow, a palm tree, and a club. Sidon: a galley, a rudder, Europa on the bull, Dionysus. Beirut: Baal-Berit, Ashtart on a prow, a rudder and trident, a lone trident. Byblos: El, Isis Pharia, Harpocrates, an Apis bull. The smallest denomination at Sidon sometimes depicts Apollo or a maenad instead of Dionysus.

denominations with a galley and a rudder; and Shadrapa (Greek Dionysus) on Sidon's smallest coins makes a pair with Melqart (Greek Herakles) on the same denomination at Tyre, both great traveling gods of the Mediterranean. Even without these other denominational pairings, however, it would be hard to resist the temptation to read Tyre's palm tree alongside Sidon's Europa on the same denomination as a punning reference to her kinsman Phoinix.

Through its claim to Phoinix, the founder of Phoenicia, Tyre could also assert a claim to be the mother city of the other "Phoenician" cities in the Levant. That this was controversial is shown by competing Phoenician legends on the Sidonian and Tyrian municipal coinage under Antiochus IV: Sidon describes itself on one of its denominations as the mother city of Cambe, Hippo, Kition, and Tyre (LṢDN ʾM KMB ʾPʾ KT ṢR), while Tyre describes itself on all but one of its denominations as "mother of the Sidons" (LṢR ʾM ṢDNM).[16] Similarly, the appearance of Europa on the coins of Sidon in 169/8 BCE to match Tyre's existing Phoinix coinage must be read as a counterclaim to the house of Agenor, including Phoinix himself, and Kadmos, founder of Thebes, supported by the appearance on the smallest Sidonian denomination of Dionysus, a common Theban type. This fits in with the wording of a Sidonian inscription of around 200 BCE that commemorates the victory of Diotimus of Sidon in the chariot race at Nemea, which calls Sidon the mother city (*metropolis*) of Kadmean Thebes, and the "house of the descendants of Agenor."[17] Competition between the cities for the house of Agenor would also explain one Tyrian emission toward the end of Antiochus IV's reign that "borrows" an image of Europa on a bull to replace its usual prow on its second-largest coins.[18]

Phoinix could also, however, help emphasize Tyre's role as a colonial metropolis abroad, a point underlined on the other denominations by the maritime imagery and the image of Melqart himself, the god responsible for migrants. Like Melqart, Phoinix was sometimes said to be the father of colonial founders overseas: a scholion to Apollonios says that in one version of the story of Kadmos the founder of Thebes he was the son of Phoinix rather than Agenor,[19] and according to Klaudios Iolaos, writing around the first century CE, Phoinix's son Archelaos founded a "Gadeira": either Iberian Gadir or Gadara in modern Jordan.[20] If attempts to read Archelaos here as a deformed reference to Herakles are correct, there was even an ancient version of Tyre's story in which Melqart was the son of Phoinix.[21]

This conversation was not limited to Tyre and Sidon: although the quasi-municipal coinage of Byblos makes no obvious colonial claims at all, preferring to emphasize cultural identifications with Egypt, that of

Beirut uses maritime imagery similar to the Tyrian and Sidonian issues, depicting a prow and a rudder, and, as discussed in chapter 2, the legends name the city as "Laodikeia mother in Canaan" (L'DK 'M BKN'N), a partial transliteration of the Seleucid name imposed on the city of Laodikea in Canaan, which not only substitutes a convenient local name for the Greek "Phoenicia," but introduces an entirely new element, that of being a mother city. Here, however, the claim is not to be a mother of other cities but simply "in Canaan".[22]

The local symbols and personalities on the coinage issued by these cities fueled local political rivalries, but they should not be interpreted as a form of resistance to Greek rule or culture in the region.[23] As with the network of Melqart, the "Phoenician" label invoked by the Tyrian palm tree coinage was not an exclusive one, since the Tyrians borrowed, or reclaimed, the language, the hero, and the identity itself from the Greeks. The broader rival claims of Tyre and Sidon to members of the house of Agenor also continued to associate them with the Greeks who originally told these tales; as Fergus Millar has pointed out in relation to the Sidonians, by adopting these Greek stories they "acquired both an extra past and a reinforcement of their historical identity; and they also simultaneously gained acceptance as in some sense Greeks."[24] And these were not the only basis for claims they made to blood relationships with Greeks: in the second century BCE, an embassy from Tyre to Delphi asserted that there was kinship between the two cities.[25]

At the same time, the Phoenician-language legends on the coinage of all four cities demonstrate a continuing disinclination to claim collective identity even at a civic level, and the bilingual ones at Tyre and Sidon maintain the traditional distinction discussed in chapter 2 whereby city names in Phoenician were normally toponyms, and in Greek, ethnonyms. So we have "of Gebel" (or "of Holy Gebel") at Byblos and "of Laodicea" at Beirut, while Tyre has both (Ph.) "of Tyre" and (Gk.) "of the Tyrians," and Sidon has (Ph.) "of the Sidons" and (Gk.) "of the Sidonians." The coinage of other cities in the region also follows this pattern: the single denomination of quasi-municipal coinage issued by Tripolis has the Greek legend "of the Tripolitans,"[26] and the fully autonomous coinage of Arados has, also in Greek, "of the Aradites."[27] This consistent relationship between choice of language and form of reference suggests that the minters were well aware of the different norms, which makes later "interference" between the languages all the more interesting, especially when they perpetuate local norms: from the first century BCE, the fully autonomous silver coinage of Tyre has a Greek legend that reads "of Tyre."[28]

MOTHER OF THE PHOENICIANS

It was only under Roman rule that Phoenicia became a true political entity. By the early second century CE, "Phoenicia" was the name of one of the three administrative districts or eparchies that made up the province of Syria, along with "Syria" and "Commagene."[29] A corresponding regional league, or *koinon*, of Phoenicia had also been formed to administer the imperial cult by the time reference appears to it on the second-century CE coinage of Tyre, associated with an image of a temple.[30] This designation of Phoenicia as a subdistrict of Syria may not be new: as noted above, the region is occasionally referred to as "Syria and Phoenicia" in the Hellenistic period, and in the Augustan period, a senator was sent to "Syria and Phoenicia,"[31] though we have no positive indication in either case of two entities separately administered at any level.

In the late second century, Phoenicia finally became a province in its own right, when Septimius Severus split the province of Syria into Syria Coele and Syria Phoenice, both of which, however, extended east from the coast to the desert (fig. 7.3).[32] It was not until around 400 CE that a Roman province called Phoenicia mapped onto the original Greek geographical conception of Phoenicia: in this period, the province of Syria Phoenice was split again, this time from north to south, with its western half becoming "Phoenice prima" or "Paralia" ("old" Phoenicia, with its administrative center at Tyre) and the eastern region "Phoenice secunda" or "Libanum," which included Palmyra and Heliopolis, and had Emesa as its capital.[33]

Local traditions continued under Roman rule. Semitic names remained common, for instance, and although the last surviving, datable Levantine inscription in Phoenician is from 25/4 BCE, there is a second-century CE potsherd with a Phoenician inscription from the sanctuary of Kharayeb, and in the third century CE, Ulpian of Tyre could still refer to contracts made in languages including *assyrius sermo* (Aramaic) and *poenus sermo* (Phoenician).[34] Beirut, where a colony of Roman military veterans was imposed in the Augustan period, and where there is a great deal of evidence for Latin and for Roman cultural practices, was an exception rather than the rule.[35]

There is also evidence for continued rivalries and occasional hostilities between "Phoenician" cities in this period, with Herodian reporting frictions between Beirut and Tyre in the mid-190s CE.[36] Civic competition between Tyre and Sidon continued to involve claims to the family of Agenor: Sidon's autonomous bronze coinage featured Europa on a bull through to the end of the Julio-Claudian period, and she appeared again

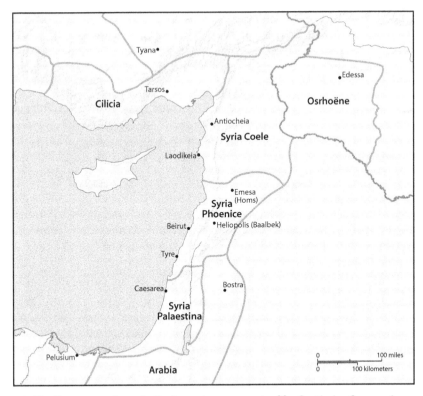

7.3 The Roman provinces in the Levant as reorganized by Septimius Severus in the late second century CE.

under Trajan and Hadrian, while Tyre continued to mint bronze coins with a palm tree on the reverse well into the third century CE.[37] But new aspects of contention also emerged in the Roman period, when rival Tyrian and Sidonian claims to Levantine colonies overseas are for the first time explicitly expressed in the language of "Phoenicity." We have already seen Meleager's first-century BCE description of Tyre as "proud mother of the Phoenicians," and this is echoed in the opening passage of Achilles Tatius's second-century CE *Leukippe and Klitophon*, where the narrator describes Sidon as "the mother city of the Phoenicians" and the Sidonian *demos* as "the father of the Thebans."[38] And the geographer Strabo tells us in the early first century CE that the claim was one made by the cities themselves, in conscious competition: "After Sidon is Tyre, the largest and oldest city of the Phoenicians, and a rival to the former in size and in the fame and antiquity transmitted in many myths. So although the poets have prattled more about Sidon than Tyre (Homer makes no mention of Tyre), the colonies sent to Libya and Iberia, and even outside the Pillars, sing rather the praises of Tyre. In any case, both cities have been glorious and illustrious, both in olden times and the present day: there is a dispute in both cities as to which of them one might call the mother city [*metropolis*] of the Phoenicians."[39] This new phrase suggests that "Phoenician" was considered more a colonial than an ethnic identity, one that the Tyrians and Sidonians so did not so much participate in as generate. As at Carthage, but by slightly different means, the Tyrians and Sidonians imposed Phoenician identity on others more than they claimed it for themselves.

Yet another axis of regional rivalry for the title of "mother city" opened up in the late first century CE, when Domitian awarded Tyre the Roman status of *metropolis*, meaning in that context not a colonial mother city, but the leading city in a particular area.[40] We get a sense of how the Tyrians used this new title to reinforce their older claims to metropolitan status of other kinds from an honorific inscription they erected at Didyma between 100 and 104 CE for one Julius Quadratus of Pergamon, where they call themselves "the council and the people of the Tyrians, of the sacred, inviolate, autonomous metropolis of Phoenicia and the cities of Koile Syria and other cities, and mistress of a fleet."[41] A very similar formulation was used in a letter sent to Tyre by the Tyrians based in Puteoli in Italy in 174 CE that begins, "Letter written to the *polis*. To the magistrates, council, and people of the supreme motherland, the sacred, inviolate, autonomous *metropolis* of Phoenicia and other cities, mistress of a fleet, those of the Tyrians living in Puteoli send greetings."[42] This was not, however, the city's formal title awarded by Rome—other inscriptions simply call it "Metropolis of Phoenicia and Koile Syria"[43]—but rather the city's own interpretation of its full status in the light of that award, and the awkward reference to "other cities" must reflect Tyre's own claim to the "Phoenician" colonies overseas.

The status of colonial founder continued to be important in the self-presentation of these cities as they made their way up the Roman civic hierarchy. In or shortly after 198 CE, Septimius Severus promoted Tyre to the honorary status of Roman *colonia*, a title that again denoted high imperial favor rather than literal colonial settlement.[44] Yet it was not until the reign of the emperor Elagabalus (218–22) that Sidon was finally awarded both these Roman honors—probably at the temporary expense of Tyre, whose coins stopped giving the city's full colonial title just as those of Sidon began to do so.[45]

At this point, both cities began to issue new coin types featuring legendary local history and heroes, with a particular focus on colonial founder figures. Under Elagabalus and then Severus Alexander (222–35), Sidon produced reverses of Europa sitting on a bull (fig. 7.4a), Kadmos standing on a ship's prow (fig. 7.4b), and Dido seated on a throne,[46] while from the reign of Elagabalus to that of Gallienus (260–68), Tyre produced coins with reverses of Dido building Carthage (fig. 7.4c) and Kadmos teaching the alphabet to the Greeks.[47] Alfred Hirt has suggested very plausibly that the appearance of the famous founder figures Dido and Kadmos at Tyre was a silent riposte to the Roman shift of the honorary title of *metropolis* to Sidon: whatever the label, it implies, Tyre is the real mother city.[48] Furthermore, it was also the real home of the house of Agenor, and just as in the 160s BCE, Tyre poached Europa's image again in the 250s CE, this time associating her (and therefore her whole family) firmly with the ambrosial rocks of the city of Tyre (fig. 7.4d).[49]

Far from asserting a collective identity, this coinage continued to reinforce the historical distance between the cities and assert their own claims to Greek legends, to Roman status, and to the Phoenician colonies overseas. As Kevin Butcher has pointed out, the stories depicted not famous "Phoenicians," but famous citizens of individual cities, and perhaps even to the descent claims of specific local families.[50] Such localizing readings are supported by the fact that Tyrian coins not only depict the ambrosial rocks on which the city was supposed to have been founded (fig. 7.4e), but also the Tyrian dog who bit a murex shell and thereby discovered the secret of the famous murex dye.[51] At the same time, it undoubtedly played to an increasing interest in Phoenicia and Phoenician history among outsiders in the Roman Imperial period, many of whom would have been handling this civic coinage.[52] I turn now to historical accounts, and other examples of how people from the Levantine cities made good use of Phoenicia's new fame and reputation in this period.

a   b   c   d

e

7.4 Bronze coinage issued by Sidon and Tyre in the third century CE, reverses only: (a) Sidon: Europa and the bull, issued under Elagabalus; (b) Sidon: Kadmos on a ship's prow, issued under Elagabalus; (c) Tyre: Dido building Carthage, issued under Elagabalus; (d) Tyre: depicting Europa, the bull, and the ambrosial rocks, issued under Valerian I; (e) Tyre: ambrosial rocks, issued under Gordian III.

THE INVENTION OF PHOENICIA

Pomponius Mela's *Chorography*—a work of popular geography written in the mid-first century CE—says that the *Phoenices* "have made Phoenicia famous. They are a clever stock of men and they excel in the duties of war and peace."[53] More generally, Mela gives pride of place to Phoenician places and achievements, both east and west, to the extent that his has been labeled a Phoenician perspective, and the work interpreted as patriotic.[54] However, although Mela does says that Phoenicians from Africa live in his Iberian hometown of Tingentera, he does not claim to be one himself, and Phoenician identity was certainly not a prerequisite for interest in our topic in his period: Mela was writing in the time of Emperor Claudius, who had himself written eight books of Carthaginian history.[55] Around the same time, the Jewish historian Josephus mentions one Dios, who was well thought of for the accuracy of his inquiries concerning the Phoenicians, claiming to use his work in the Tyrian archives, along with that of a Menander of Ephesus.[56] Josephus also tells us about "Mochos, Hestiaios, and the Egyptian Hieronymos," who all wrote *Phoinikika* (Phoenician matters),[57] and later authors add to this list the names of Theodotos, Hypsikrates, Sanchuniathon, and Klaudios Iolaos.[58]

Mochus and Sanchuniathon are the only members of this group for whom dates are ever given, although they are not terribly helpful, as they put these characters before the Trojan War.[59] All the same, at least some of these works are likely to date back to the Hellenistic period. Do they belong to the genre of laudatory "national history" that became popular in that era?[60] The most famous examples are from the third century BCE, when a Chaldean astronomer-priest named Berossus wrote a "History of Babylonia," and Manetho, a priest at Egyptian Heliopolis, wrote a "History of Egypt." In both cases, these authors sought to impress on their new Macedonian overlords the particular achievements of their own people and polities by writing accounts of their glorious past.[61] Mark Edwards summarizes the phenomenon in national terms: "Nation was thus induced to compete with nation. . . . On the one hand, these cultures sought the esteem of foreign masters, correcting the disingenuous representations by which they had hitherto been deceived; on the other hand, peoples who had been rivals for a millennium could be expected to strive as earnestly for literary pre-eminence as once for dominion over lands and men."[62]

For Edwards, however, Hellenistic-period Phoenicia "had no part in this royal theatre," and it is indeed hard to make the case that the authors of *Phoinikika* were creating patriotic histories in the same sense.[63] This is, it seems, a different phenomenon, and one that reflects outsiders' interest in the subject rather than local knowledge or self-identification. The Greek authors concerned never call themselves Phoenician in the surviving fragments, and it is not until the second century CE that other writers call any of them Phoenician.[64] Furthermore, it is striking that these authors do not seem to have much access to privileged information about the Phoenicians: what we know of the stories and information they conveyed would for the most part have been familiar from Greek literature and the Hebrew Bible, including the kidnap of Europa, Menelaus's travels, the age of Noah, and the relationship between the kings of Tyre and Jerusalem.

In fact, the only surviving example of something that might bear comparison with the work of authors like Berossus and Manetho is the celebrated work of Philo of Byblos, written in Greek in the second century CE, around the time of Emperor Hadrian, and preserved in fourth-century CE excerpts by Eusebius of third-century extracts by Porphyry. As discussed in chapter 3, this text draws on both Greek and Near Eastern sources and traditions, and is presented (at least by Porphry) as a translation of the work of the much earlier writer Sanchuniathon. The basic text may in fact have been Philo's own, or he may have exploited an existing work, but the structure, themes, and rationalizing euhemerism of the work mean that any "original" could not have been written earlier than the Hellenistic period.[65]

Philo's work is certainly often read in the Hellenistic-period tradition of Berossus and Manetho. Aaron Johnson, for instance, explains Philo's strategy like this: "By providing Phoenician names and slight alterations to otherwise well-known episodes of Greek mythology, Philo effectively claims the stories for the Phoenicians. In effect, Philo is saying: 'What you Greeks thought was yours, is really ours.'"[66] Is this quite right? Like other writers in Greek, Philo certainly does recognize a people called the Phoenicians, whose ancestry he attempts to trace, although he does not present them as strongly culturally differentiated from others: by his account, they share religious practices and perceptions with the Egyptians.[67] He is also interested in what he calls Phoenician sources on theology and myth, and highly critical of other Greek authors on these subjects, dismissing them as derivative and misguided. However, despite the traditional scholarly assumption that Philo was, as Mark Edwards has put it, a Phoenician "by origin who had adopted the tongue and culture of the Greeks,"[68] he does not describe himself as a Phoenician in what survives of the text, and he is not described as such by others either. And while Porphyry in the third century CE calls Philo's work the "Phoenician Inquiry" (*Phoinikike historia*), it is not clear whether this is supposed to be the title given to the book by its author or a later description of it.[69]

Rather than reading Philo as a late example of Hellenistic nationalism, it is easier to contextualize him in the world of the Greek novel, a new literary genre in the Imperial period, and one in which Phoenician settings and characters were strikingly popular. The best example is probably Achilles Tatius's second-century CE *Leukippe and Klitophon*, which not only begins in Sidon, but has a hero from Tyre, and contains vivid descriptions of both cities.[70] The author locates the cities in a Phoenician context, returning throughout the text to the different meanings of the word *phoinix*, with lengthy discussions not only of the palm tree, but also of the bird.[71] Another second-century CE romance by Lollianos was simply called *Phoinikika*, although it is not clear from the surviving fragments whether any of the action—which includes human sacrifice, cannibalism, ghosts, and at least two orgies—actually takes place in Phoenicia.[72] And the *Ephemeris belli troiani*, a novel of the third or fourth century that presents itself as the work of a combatant at Troy called Dictys of Knossos, explains in its prologue that the original text, written in Phoenician, was discovered in Dictys's tomb on Crete.[73]

Although interest in the history and traditions of Phoenicia and the Phoenicians blossomed in the Roman Empire, then, there is no clear evidence for Phoenician identification or patriotism in local contexts. There certainly are attestations of pride in Phoenician history and associations on the part of Greek-speakers from the region when they are talking to other Greek-speakers from elsewhere. In addition to Philo's work, for instance, Dorotheos of Sidon refers in his first-century CE text on astronomy to the "God-fashioned Phoenicians," and in the second century, Pausanias claims to have encountered another Sidonian who praised "Phoenician" ideas about the gods, only to be told rather tartly by Pausanias that they were in fact the same as Greek ones.[74] These examples demonstrate the acceptance of a Greek category in Greek contexts, the same phenomenon we find when the second-century CE Tyrian rhetor Adrianus announces his arrival in Athens by appealing to the famous tale of Kadmos bringing the alphabet to Greece: "Once again letters have come from Phoenicia."[75] Abroad, as Adrianus knew, Kadmos was simply a Phoenician hero of the Greek and now Roman mythical world.

And again, this cultural enthusiasm for Phoenicia and Phoenicians in the Roman Mediterranean should not be interpreted as oppositional. In fact, it reflects Roman political encouragement for the concept of Phoenicia itself. Designating Phoenicia as a political region allowed its Roman rulers to administer their imperial territory in an explicitly local framework, at the same time as it cut across existing local power dynamics. It also allowed the Romans to change what Phoenicia meant, and one excellent example of this is the reinvention of Syrian Emesa as a Phoenician city.

PHOENICIAN GAMES

When Septimius Severus finally created a province of Syria Phoenice in the late second century CE, it bore little relation to the traditional historical geography of Phoenicia, but included cities as far away as Emesa, around seventy kilometers inland on the banks of the Orontes. Emesa was the hometown of several members of the emperor's family, including his wife Julia Domna, her sister Julia Maesa, and the latter's grandson, the notorious teenage Emperor Marcus Aurelius Antoninus, or Elagabalus. Even before his elevation to the purple, the young man was the priest of the great Emesan god Elagabal ('LH'GBL), and as emperor installed this deity at Rome itself in the form of his cult statue, a large black stone. The Syrian city found unsurprising political favor as well from the Severan dynasty, given the title of *colonia* by Julia Domna's son Caracalla, and a new status of *metrokolonia* by Elagabalus.[76]

The inclusion of Emesa in Syria Phoenice was not simply a matter of bureaucratic convenience. Roman sources describe the city as being in Phoenicia, and they call its citizens Phoenicians, including members of the imperial family: the contemporary author Herodian, for instance, describes Julia Maesa as a Phoenician by *genos*, or stock, "from the city of Emesa in Phoenicia," and he says that the name of the city's god was Phoenician.[77] He also emphasizes the Phoenician cultural affinities of Elagabalus himself, claiming that he had Roman officials wear long tunics "according to the Phoenician custom [*nomos*]" for the rituals of his new god at Rome, and that he refused to have anything to do with pigs, again "according to the Phoenician custom." More subtly, Cassius Dio, another contemporary, says that Elagabalus secretly slaughtered young boys to offer them to his god.[78] This is not to say that Elagabalus and his family encouraged, or received, an exclusive identification as Phoenician: Fergus Millar has emphasized the "indiscriminately Oriental" associations made in Herodian and Dio's contemporary reports of Elagabalus's public behavior, with Herodian himself remarking that Elagabalus's clothing was a cross between the garb of Phoenician priests and the luxurious clothing of the Medes, and Dio reporting that the young emperor acquired the nickname "the Assyrian."[79]

Nonetheless, some of Elagabalus's actions seem to have been deliberately designed to encourage Phoenician associations. Herodian, for instance, tells the story of how the young emperor imported as a wife for his own deity a great statue of a goddess from Carthage, "Ourania" (Ashtart), supposedly originally set up by "Dido the Phoenician," a move that neatly connected the African and Syrian origins of the Severan dynasty through a Phoenician diasporic relationship.[80]

Furthermore, a new imperial enthusiasm for Phoenicia and even being Phoenician under Elagabalus could explain the appearance of palm branches for the first time since the Julio-Claudian period on the coinage of Sidon, a city that was, as we have seen, especially favored by the Emesan emperor,[81] as well as on the coinage of Emesa itself (fig. 7.5). The Emesan coins are particularly interesting because their legends make it clear that they depict the urns given as prizes at the "Pythian games" that Elagabalus had established in the city, a smaller version of the great festival held for Apollo at Delphi, and on the coins, these urns are flanked by palm shoots rather than by the laurel shoots that would have been usual at Delphi. Whether or not this reflects practice at the games themselves, on its coinage the city is representing those games as "Phoenician."

Emesa's new Phoenician identity under Rome helps to explain, finally, why Heliodorus not only called himself a Phoenician, but drew particular attention to this claim. Although the concluding *sphragis* of the *Aithiopika* has sometimes been seen as a later addition, Ewen Bowie has shown that it picks up on a set of "Phoenician games" in which recurring forms and compounds of *phoinix* (φοῖνιξ) weave in references throughout the text to the different senses of the word: it describes merchants from Tyre, but also the crimson of dye or blood, dates and palm shoots and branches, and the mythical bird, as well as the flamingo (*phoinikopteros*). A particular concentration of these "φοῖνιξ terms" in the final book "prepares us for Heliodorus' last throw, when . . . he signs off as ἀνὴρ Φοῖνιξ Ἐμισηνός, 'a Phoenician

7.5 Bronze coin of Emesa, depicting the emperor Elagabalus (obv.) and prize urns from the local Pythian games flanked by palm branches (rev.).

man from Emesa.' Only now do we realize why the writer has been juggling so persistently with various senses of φοῖνιξ."[82]

It has been suggested both that Heliodorus used his novel to emphasize his own status as an outsider, a figure from the margins of the Greco-Roman world, and by contrast that it represents an embrace of Hellenism.[83] I want to bring Rome into the picture as well, but not to argue that in his *sphragis* Heliodorus was proudly declaring a political identity as an inhabitant of Roman Syria Phoenice, nor that he was laying claim to the cultural capital that "being Phoenician" appears to have brought to Emesa and its Roman politicians. On the contrary, I will show that the sheer variety of meanings that the term *phoinix* is used to convey in the rest of the text calls any fixed identity claim into question, especially a fixed ethnic association. Instead, the *sphragis* is better understood in its historical, political, and cultural context as a comment on Phoenician identity claims rather than a genuine claim to that identity in itself.

Tim Whitmarsh has already made the case that Heliodorus's self-description as a *phoinix* should be seen against the background of this particular novel's interest in the complex relationships between genealogy, origins, culture, and personal identity, and of its delight in the contested, unreliable, and even unreal nature of identity claims.[84] Examples of mistakes, complications, and confusion over identity are almost endless: the heroine alone is presented as having two ethnicities, three fathers, and at least one lucky escape from death through mistaken identity. In fact, identity games are such a central feature of Heliodorus's novel that it promotes, as Whitmarsh has put it, "a conception of identity not as an innate essence but as the product of human culture, forged in the perceptions of others,"[85] to the extent that Heliodorus's "emphasis upon cultural costume is a challenge to a general acceptance of the 'naturalness' of ethnicity."[86]

Whitmarsh's detailed studies of this aspect of Heliodorus's work draw attention to the number of "false Greeks" found in the text: the Egyptian priest Kalasiris is mistaken for a Greek, and he claims that Homer was an Egyptian; the heroine, the Ethiopian Charikleia, is consistently referred to as Greek; her lover Theagenes is reported as making a series of ridiculous claims that his own obscure Ainianian clan had the noblest ancestry in the entire province of Thessaly, and was descended from the heroes Hellen and Achilles.[87] As he notes, Theagenes's claims are "presented ironically, despite frequent references to 'race' [γένος] and the 'truth' of the matter."[88]

I would add that the novel's "Phoenicians" are also hard to pin down in terms of identity: Phoenicians from Tyre are described as dancing in the Assyrian style, for instance, while the phoinix-bird "comes to us from the

Ethiopians or Indians."[89] And at the end, I would suggest, Heliodorus presents himself as another example of this phenomenon: he is both a *phoinix* from Emesa, and "of the *genos* of the descendants of the sun [*Helios*]." As with his claim to be a *phoinix*, the author's assertion that he is a descendant of the sun picks up on a host of references throughout the text to the sun, to the sun god Helios (and his Greek equivalent Apollo), and to his descendants, culminating earlier in book 10 in the heroine's claim to be descended from the sun.[90] It must also play on an association with Emesa's god Elagabal, rendered in Greek as Heliogabalus, and seen, in this period at least, as a sun god.[91] Both claims in the *sphragis* then are part of the novel itself, not just a technical appendix. Furthermore, the juxtaposition of a possible with an impossible claim raises a question over the seriousness with which we are supposed to take either of the identifications: the reinvention of Roman Emesa as Phoenician is as good an example of the meaninglessness of ethnic identity claims as is a claim to be descended from the sun, and the sentence as a whole draws attention to the new and perhaps awkward dual identity imposed on the town by its inclusion in the province of Phoenicia and its new Phoenician cultural reputation.

The *sphragis* may also be a more specific reference to, or parody of, the "Phoenicianization" of Emesa's god, city, and emperor under Elagabalus: the novel was certainly written after his reign, and perhaps not very long after.[92] This would fit in with other plausible references to the emperor and his Phoenician pretensions in the novel: the coins issued with palm shoots to celebrate his Pythian games prefigure an episode in the *Aithiopika* in which Chariklea awards Theagenes a palm shoot rather than a laurel when he wins the hoplite race at Delphi itself,[93] while the closing sequence sees the foreign hero settled in Ethiopia and invested as a priest of the Ethiopian sun god.[94] However that may be, it should by now be clear that the *sphragis* cannot be taken as a straightforward statement of ethnic identity either on the part of the author or his fictional persona: Heliodorus, from a time and place well beyond the bounds of what most earlier authors would have labeled Phoenicia, was using his novel to play literary games with the new and fashionable identity that Roman emperors had imposed on himself and his hometown.

I have argued in this chapter for growing interest in the Phoenicians in the Hellenistic and Roman periods, during which Phoenicia itself became a political entity and expanded well beyond its confines in earlier Greek and Latin literature. Contributions to the literature on Phoenicia even from the region itself were, however, more antiquarian than patriotic, responding to external interest rather than any emerging internal identification. The new enthusiasm for Phoenicia and Phoenicians did not bring the coastal cities of the Levant together in a shared regional identity, but provided them instead with useful new weapons for their continuing cultural and political rivalry, in which claims to found Phoenicia, the Phoenicians, and Levantine settlements overseas, served local political positioning rather than broad ethnic identitifications. At the same time, the idea of being Phoenician supported the Roman imperial project, and more specifically the projects of the Severan dynasty. In the next chapter I turn to that family's other place of origin, North Africa, to suggest that there too the Phoenician past became more popular and visible under Rome, and that there too it was used both to evade power and enforce it, within and beyond ancient Levantine settlements, and that Phoenicity came in the end there to denote an African rather than Levantine identity.

CHAPTER 8

A New Phoenician World

The Libyan port of Lepcis Magna, the best-preserved ancient city in North Africa, was highly favored within the Roman Empire. As early as the Augustan period, its enormous theater, amphitheater, forum, and great temple to Roma and Augustus, adorned with sculptures of the imperial family, reflected the desire of the local politicians and businessmen who built them to demonstrate their loyalty to and involvement in that imperial project.[1] This culminated in the ascent to the imperial throne of the city's native son, Septimius Severus (r. 193–211), whose long and successful reign expanded the empire east as far as the River Tigris, and took him from its southern regions to its most northerly reaches: he died at York, attempting to conquer Scotland for Rome.

A curious anecdote recorded in the account of the lives of the later emperors known as the *Historia Augusta* suggests, however, that there was more to Lepcis than this Roman perspective might suggest: when Septimius Severus's sister came from Lepcis to visit him in Rome, her bad Latin was such an embarrassment to him that he sent her home again.[2] Whether or not this incident really happened, it was apparently plausible to suggest that even the grandest families in Lepcis still spoke Punic at home. The city also continued to take ostentatious pride in its Levantine roots in the Roman period, as illustrated in a pair of inscriptions the city of Lepcis erected at Tyre in the second century CE, recording in Latin and Greek a gift "from the colony of Ulpia Traiana Augusta Fidelis Lepcis Magna to Tyre, which is its own metropolis as well."[3] Like the Tyrian inscriptions from Didyma and Puteoli discussed in the preceding chapter, the wording here plays on double meanings: Lepcis is both an honorary Roman *colonia*, and a colony of Tyre in the literal sense, while Tyre was an honorary Roman *metropolis*, as well as the real mother city of Lepcis. The phrasing also picks up directly on Tyre's own standard claim to be mother city of colonies abroad as well as *metropolis* of Phoenicia—a claim that was in fact repeated at Lepcis itself at the very end of the second century, when Tyre was finally awarded the status of *colonia* by Septimius Severus, and the grateful city erected a statue of the emperor's son Geta in his African hometown from "the colony of Septimia Tyre, metropolis of Phoenicia and of other cities."[4]

Unlike the Lepcitan inscriptions, this Tyrian dedication does not focus on the particular colonial relationship between these two individual cities, but rather on Tyre's more general status as a mother city at home and overseas, and I will suggest in the first part of this chapter that an emphasis on its own Levantine colonial past was actually a new phenomenon at Lepcis itself in the Roman period, a way of underlining and preserving the city's relative political autonomy within the context of Roman power. As in the east, I will argue, this strategy also appealed to the wider Roman interest in Phoenician history, but did not involve the construction of a Phoenician identity: when the city identifies its own origins at Tyre, after all, it is in relation to that single Levantine city. I will then contextualize this case study in a much broader and longer-lasting regional phenomenon, whereby a religious, political, and linguistic package initially established in Levantine settlements was adopted across the whole of Roman North Africa, serving to nuance, exploit, and localize power under Roman rule.

LANGUAGES OF POWER

The settlement of Lepcis had been established on the coast of Tripolitania by the end of the sixth century BCE. By the second century, it was tributary to Carthage and then, after King Massinissa's successful campaign in the region, to Numidia. At the beginning of the Jugurthan War (112–105 BCE), the city sued for friendship and alliance with Rome against the Numidian king, and although it later backed Numidia and the Pompeians in the Roman civil war of the 40s BCE, the city was a Roman ally again in campaigns against local Libyan peoples in the Augustan period. Its precise political and tributary status in relation to Rome in this period is unclear, but it managed to maintain a form of autonomy at least on a local level for centuries, still minting its own coinage under Tiberius, and operating under Phoenician magistracies and maintaining local priesthoods throughout the first century CE. Until the Flavian period, Lepcis is always referred to simply as a *civitas* (town) in its Latin epigraphy, while the local Roman proconsul is regularly described on inscriptions as the *patronus* of the city, with no suggestion that he exercised official authority there. The city only received political recognition as a Roman *municipium* under Vespasian in the 70s CE, and was then promoted to the higher honorary status of *colonia* in 109.[5]

Despite these honors, and despite the Roman-style monumental architecture that defined the city's visual appearance, Sergio Fontana pointed out some time ago that the archaeological evidence reveals the persistence of the Phoenician language in its western Punic dialect, as well as of Phoenician names, and of religious symbols and burial practices familiar from Carthage, well into the third century CE, especially in relation to the less wealthy and to women.[6] Building on Fontana's work, I have suggested myself that a great many Phoenician references can be found alongside the Roman ones in political and civic life as well.[7] Local priesthoods and Levantine civic institutions are found throughout the first century CE, including the existence of a public assembly ('M) of a kind familiar from earlier Phoenician-speaking cities in the western Mediterranean, and the appointment of *shofetim*, or sufetes, as the city's chief magistrates.[8] The city's coinage continued to name Lepcis in Punic into the reign of Tiberius, and featured the portraits and symbols of the two Levantine gods named in a late Hellenistic-period Punic dedication as "Lord Shadrapa and Milkashtart, lords of Lepcis."[9] At least one new temple in the Augustan period was dedicated to Shadrapa (Greek Dionysus, Roman Liber Pater), and monumental Phoenician inscriptions were erected in addition to Latin ones on several prominent buildings of the Julio-Claudian period, including the market, theater, and imperial cult temple.[10]

It would be a mistake, however, to see these phenomena as signs or symbols of resistance to Roman power. These Phoenician references operated in addition rather than in opposition to identifications with Rome. Roman priesthoods and civic institutions were introduced alongside local ones,[11] the city's coinage paired reverses featuring Shadrapa and Milkashtart with obverse portraits of Augustus and later Tiberius,[12] and the temple to Roma and Augustus was built under Tiberius right beside the Augustan-period temple dedicated to Shadrapa, putting the local and imperial gods literally on an equal footing.[13] It is apt that both buildings use the so-called Punic cubit as well as the Roman foot in their construction.[14]

The same can be said of the Punic in the monumental inscriptions. The Latin epigraphy of Lepcis uses Roman dating and nomenclature as standard, and regularly names the Roman emperor, but in bilinguals the Punic sometimes provides an "edited" version, leaving out Roman titles and officials and emphasizing the local contribution: the Punic sections of the bilingual inscriptions inside the theater of 1/2 CE, for instance, simply omit the whole section of the Latin text that relates to the emperor, including the imperial dating (fig. 8.1).[15] The Roman emperor is invoked by the Latin but then put in his place by the Punic, placed alongside but not fully integrated into the local context.

8.1 Bilingual Latin-Punic inscription within a molded *tabella ansata* from the theater at Lepcis (*IRT* 321, 1/2 CE). The Latin inscription reads: "When Imperator Caesar Augustus, son of the deified one, chief priest, was invested with tribunician power for the 24th time, and was consul for the 13th time, father of his country, Annobal Rufus, adorner of his country, lover of concord, priest, sufete, prefect of the rites, son of Himilcho Tapapius, had this made with his own money and dedicated it himself." The Punic inscription reads: "Hannibal, who adorns his country, who loves the complete knowledge, sacrificer, sufete, chief of the 'zrm-sacrifices, son of Himilkart Tapapi Rufus made it according to plan at his own expense and consecrated it."

These bilinguals distinguish the local and the Roman in other ways too, even as they juxtapose them. The Punic version of the inscription commemorating the building of a market in 8 BCE does begin with the same invocation of the Roman emperor as the Latin text, but provides local equivalents for his titles rather than simply transliterating them: instead of being consul, imperator, and invested with tribunician power, he is head of the army and supreme leader, with the authority of the ten rulers.[16] The juxtapositions set up an alliance between local and imperial sources of power at the same time as their proximity emphasizes their fundamental differences. And they lasted a long time: bilingual Punic and Latin inscriptions are found until at least 92 CE,[17] although both the prominence of the Latin sections and the extent to which the Punic ones borrow their phrasing and vocabulary increases over this period, so that by the end of the first century, the Punic inscriptions get closer to true translations.[18]

This linguistic and cultural bilingualism did a lot of practical work for its speakers: as well as accommodating Latin-speaking visitors to the city, the use of Latin in inscriptions established the speaker's superior education, status, and connections by comparison with the majority of the city's Punic-speaking population, at the same time as the Punic versions demonstrated his solidarity with them, and sometimes undermined the imperial institutions that the Latin versions celebrated.[19] The combination of Latin and Punic linguistic traditions, and the cultural phenomena associated with them, created a third set of meanings, inappropriate for the expression of simple Romanization or resistance, and properly local—although on a practical level, the plurality of languages, names, and institutions in daily official and unofficial use at Lepcis would have discouraged Roman attempts fully to comprehend and communicate in this independent city.

At the same time, Roman and Phoenician phenomena were just two elements in a complex cultural multilingualism maintained at Lepcis in the Imperial period, suggesting that asserting a single fixed identity was not a major concern. One significant set of references is to the architectural motifs of the Hellenistic east that provide what Andrew Wallace-Hadrill has called "an alternative language of power" in the Roman period, and especially to the architecture of Alexandria and Cyrenaica.[20] This can be seen in the new temples erected on the Old Forum in the Augustan period, in the treatment of their moldings, in the use of the heart-shaped double pilasters also found at Cyrene and Ptolemais as well as Alexandria in this period, and in the popularity of the Doric order itself, which was obsolete at Rome by this date.[21] There are also associations with other African cities further west: the theater at Lepcis, for instance, was built shortly after and in a similar style to the one built at Caesarea by Rome's Numidian ally Juba II.[22] This cosmopolitan approach to culture continued for a long time, as shown by the table of measures set up in the marketplace at Lepcis in the third century CE that still comprises the Punic cubit, the Egyptian cubit, and the Roman foot.

With its multiple languages and cultural references, Lepcis constructed a web of links with the homeland, with Rome, and with other cultures past and present that avoided clear identification with any of them, evading in particular Roman cultural hegemony at the same time as it benefited from Roman imperial patronage, and emphasized its own autonomy from any single source of imperial power. This construction also involved the reconstruction of the city's past.

REINVENTING LEPCIS

Levantine customs at Lepcis were not simply survivals from the city's colonial history, but instead emphasized that particular past in quite new ways. The use of the Phoenician language provides some examples. Autonomous coinage with Punic legends only appears in the late second or first century BCE in Lepcis and the other Tripolitanian cities, after the destruction of Carthage, when ports in Spain and Mauretania had already been minting it for a century or more.[23] Punic inscriptions began even later—indeed the very idea of writing on stone in either Latin or Punic came relatively late to Tripolitania, sometime in the first century BCE, and largely, it seems, for practical reasons having to do with the quality of the available materials.[24] Elsewhere in North Africa, and especially at Carthage, there was a longstanding Punic "epigraphic habit" in religious, votive, and funerary contexts, but this was not something that had apparently ever been a standard part of civic traditions in the Tripolitanian cities, and building inscriptions in Phoenician were a complete novelty in Africa.[25]

So the use of Punic on coins and inscriptions did not survive the coming of Rome in Tripolitania; it mapped onto it. Nor was it the only available alternative to Latin at Lepcis, as Sallust suggests that Libyan was already known in the city by the time of the Jugurthan War in the late second century BCE: "only the language of this city had been changed by intermarriage with the Numidians; the laws and customs are the most part Sidonian, which they retained the more easily because they passed their lives far from the king's power."[26] Phoenician was a *new* language of public self-presentation in this area, and the choice to use it was not unmarked, not merely an obvious, traditional, and purely practical choice as opposed to an ideologically charged one to use Latin. The positive choice of Latin and Phoenician as the languages of the public epigraphy involved a new, public assertion of both Roman imperial and Phoenician colonial elements in the city.

Even Lepcis's status as a colony of Tyre may have been an invented tradition. There is considerable confusion in our sources over the city's origins: Sallust, who served as a Roman governor in Africa in the triumviral period, and was proud of his local sources, gives by far the most detailed description of the foundation—an entire sentence—specifying that Lepcis was "founded by Sidonians, who are reported to have left their homes because of civil discord, and come to that region in ships."[27] By the first century CE, however, Pliny the Elder and Silius Italicus both call the city a colony of Tyre.[28] It is tempting to conclude that such identifications have more to do with the contemporary dispute between Tyre and Sidon as to their preeminence as a mother city than with events in the sixth century BCE, and that Lepcis was not necessarily established as an official foundation, or even by a Levantine city-state at all. While Sallust's story makes the foundation sound like a private enterprise, rather like the traditional story of the foundation of Carthage itself, scholars have also persistently raised the possibility that Lepcis was in fact founded from Carthage, a city with which it certainly had commercial ties from an early date, perhaps in the aftermath of Dorieus the Spartan's attempt to found a colony in the late sixth century BCE in this strategically and commercially important area between Cyrene and Carthage.[29]

As with Carthage, the civic gods of Lepcis were not well known in the Levant.[30] There are only a couple of mentions of Shadrapa in the eastern Mediterranean, probably from the Persian period, while he is found in the west at Carthage, Sicily, and Sardinia. Milkashtart is not attested in the Levant between thirteenth century Ugarit and the Hellenistic-period temple at Umm el-'Amed, though there are mentions of him in fourth-century Malta, third-century Carthage, and second-century Gadir.[31] Furthermore, while the dual pantheon reproduced on the coinage of Lepcis fits in with the custom in most of the Phoenician-speaking coastal cities of establishing pairs of leading civic deities, this male couple might have looked a little strange in the homeland. And much more than in the case of Carthage, the colonial status of the city seems to have been celebrated more in discourse than practice. There is no evidence in our sources for sending tithes or booty home, for instance, or any other political connections between Lepcis and Tyre before the exchange of dedications with which this chapter began. Furthermore, in its new references to a Levantine past in the Roman period, "Phoenician" Lepcis looks surprisingly like its African neighbors.

PUNIC PERSISTENCE?

Despite the Roman annexation of Sicily and then Sardinia in the mid-third century BCE, the fall of Spain after the Second Punic War, and even the destruction of Carthage in 146 BCE, the phenomenon of "Punic persistence" in the western Mediterranean is well known.[32] Systems of urban and rural settlement, architectural styles, building techniques, weight standards, pottery shapes, artisan methodologies, and measurement systems all showed distinct continuities during a period of great political upheaval. Stability in material culture alone might be explained in practical terms by the availability of resources and expertise, but local customs and institutions were also maintained: languages, magistracies, rituals, and deities.

Peter van Dommelen has argued in a series of discussions of the Sardinian evidence that such practices are not simply evidence for passive "persistence" or "survivals" but instead demonstrate the ongoing vitality of pre-Roman customs under Roman rule, the "new and original achievements of Punic culture."[33] These institutions not only survived, but they continued to develop within what appears to have been a thriving network of direct cultural exchange between different Phoenician-speaking regions even after Roman conquest. Particularly strong connections were maintained between Africa and Sardinia, as Sardinian religious and domestic architecture continued to respond to contemporary North African models, and the Sardinians continued to import pottery from North Africa and to imitate new ceramic forms being produced there.[34] And although he argues that these Sardinian choices need to be understood in their own contexts as based in fundamentally local dynamics of interaction and competition,[35] van Dommelen has also suggested that in some cases they can be interpreted in terms of cultural, or "silent," resistance to Rome, especially among local economic elites, noting how much evidence there is for political and military resistance to Rome in Sardinia in the same period.[36]

I want to show in the rest of this chapter that van Dommelen's arguments can be taken in a new direction in a North African context, where even such late and iconically "Roman" buildings as the amphitheater at the inland city of El Jem in Tunisia were still planned on the Punic cubit.[37] I will focus on the persistence, further development, and continuing interaction of a cultural "package" of religious, political, and linguistic institutions associated with the Levantine coastal settlements over a long period of time and over great distances.[38] In its early stages this can be interpreted, at least in part, in terms of cultural identification with Carthage and cultural resistance to Rome. This would map onto intermittent military resistance to Rome in republican and early imperial North Africa, from the major war in Numidia led by Jugurtha in the late second century BCE, which was said by the late Roman author Orosius to have set off a revolt in the Roman province of Africa itself, to the long struggle against Tacfarinas in the first decade of Tiberius's reign, which involved African populations from Mauretania to the Libyan desert.[39] This cultural package did not, however, involve any clear identification *as* Carthaginian or Phoenician, and over time these practices constructed a distinctive African regional network of their own, and one that made most sense in terms of Roman rather than local rhetoric.[40]

RITUAL REIMAGINED

If there is something more surprising, more disruptive of commonplace assumptions, than the practice of child sacrifice itself, it is the fact that it continued under Roman occupation. Several of the Sardinian sanctuaries survived the Roman annexation of that island in 238; there is evidence for activity at the tophet site at Carthage for at least a generation after the destruction of the city; the sanctuaries at Cirta and Hadrumetum continued to function until the first and second century CE, respectively.[41] And even more surprisingly, about a hundred new sanctuaries were established *after* the fall of Carthage in the distinctive style of the old tophets, with burnt offerings buried in urns in an open-air sacred space, often with markers, in African towns all the way from Tripolitania to Mauretania (fig. 8.2).[42]

The adoption of this initially restricted sanctuary type across a very broad area has been taken as evidence for an essential cultural, and in particular religious, continuity in Africa in the face of Roman imperialism.[43] This sits uncomfortably, however, with the innovative aspects of the Roman-period tophets. The new geography of tophet cult not only involved new sites but also new worshippers: although it might be tempting to associate the phenomenon with refugees from the destruction of Carthage in 146 BCE, or hinterland communities who had previously used the tophet at Carthage itself, the new sanctuaries almost always date from at least a generation later, the names recorded there are a mixture of Libyan, Punic, and, more rarely, Roman, and the extended genealogies of offrands found at Carthage are missing.[44]

Furthermore, as Matthew McCarty has argued, the rites conducted in these new sanctuaries did not simply imitate or idealize earlier practices.[45] Offerings of infants, for instance, seem to have been relatively rare in the Roman period. Although the Christian bishop Tertullian reports that

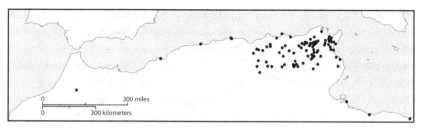

8.2 Tophet-style sanctuaries established in Roman North Africa between the late second century BCE and the second century CE.

children were still sacrificed in areas of Africa in the late second century CE,[46] positive evidence has been found so far at only three of the new sites. At Althiburos, there are multiple references to a *molk adam*, the sacrifice of a human, on inscriptions that can probably be dated from the second century BCE to the first century CE; this is the same phrase found slightly earlier at Cirta. At Henchir el Hami (c. 100 BCE to second century CE), the ashes of sheep and of children of six months or younger were found in more than three-quarters of the 268 urns so far examined from the site. And at the sanctuary at Lambafundi, where the markers at least date to the second to third century CE, two urns contained the remains of infants.[47] It is striking that all three of these sites are well inland, making them particularly unlikely to be survivals of earlier Levantine practice, while tophet-style sanctuaries established on the coast have as yet offered no such evidence for infant sacrifice or burial.

There is evidence for change in other respects as well. One striking example is that whereas before the destruction of Carthage offerings had always been by individuals, Punic inscriptions on markers of the first century BCE and CE throughout central Tunisia record that whole groups of citizens (*baalim*) made communal dedications at the sanctuaries.[48] The offerings themselves change as well, and in particular the burnt remains of birds, barely attested in the "original" tophets at all, became very common: the urns from at least seven of the new sanctuaries contain only bird bones.[49]

The stone markers demonstrate the flexible and changing nature of the cultural identifications involved in the new African sanctuaries. Initially, they tend to be flat, gabled slabs of the kind already found at Carthage in the Hellenistic period, though rarely with acroteria (fig. 8.3). Where there are inscriptions, they are in Phoenician, and they preserve much of the standard formula that is found at Carthage, including the name of the god Baal Hammon, though Tinnit is conspicuous for her near total absence.[50] The iconography in these early phases reproduces the most popular motifs from Carthage, including the so-called sign of Tanit, the caduceus, baetyls, crescents, and disks, and sometimes the human figures more familiar from the Sicilian and Sardinian tophets, as well as a number of entirely new motifs including rosettes, fruit, grain, and vegetal motifs. With or without child sacrifice, it is hard to imagine that these new sanctuaries did not in their early phases suggest cultural identifications with Carthage in the minds of the people who established them and visited them.

Over time, however, these African communities continued to rethink and reframe the rites conducted in these sanctuaries over time to suit their own changing local contexts, and these changes took them a long way from

8.3 A marker from an early Roman North African tophet-style sanctuary (second century BCE–first century CE, perhaps from Algeria). A sign of Tanit is flanked by caducei below a crescent-disk, which is morphing into a sign of Tanit itself, and is flanked by astral symbols. In the pediment is a 12-petaled rosette in a disk. The Punic inscription records a dedication to Baal by Gaius Julius Arish, son of Adonbaal.

the Carthaginian model. The appearance of the markers changed drastically over the Imperial period, often depicting very elaborate multiregistered collations of symbols and images (fig. 8.4).[51] By the end of the first century BCE, Latin inscriptions begin to be found, and they increasingly replaced Punic ones, just as over the first century CE, Roman Saturn was gradually

8.4 A marker from a late Roman North African tophet-style sanctuary (first–second century CE, perhaps from Algeria). In this elaborate scene, a figure wearing a tunic and mantle stands on a pedestal and makes an offering on an altar in a shrine framed by columns and a pediment. On the pedestal, a Latin inscription names Lucius Julius Urbanus; oddly, it is written right to left. Below is a sacrifice scene; above are agricultural scenes and in the pediment an especially smiley crescent-disk.

adopted in place of Baal Hammon. This was not, it seems, a straightforward translation into Latin or a simple syncretism with a Roman god, since it involved not only a new name, but also a new epithet, a new image-type, and new forms of interaction with the god.[52] There were also changes in the ritual itself that appear to have aligned it more closely with standard Roman practice, including a greater explicit emphasis on the moment of sacrifice rather than on the vow or the deposition, with burials entirely abandoned sometime in the second century, and monumental altars or built temples erected in several sanctuaries by the middle of the third. Links with the local past were still often preserved through, for instance, the "curation" of the earlier markers in and around the new temples.[53]

This is not, then, a case of straightforward cultural resistance to Roman norms and customs. The confrontational impression given by the adoption of child sacrifice in new areas is reinforced by the explicit references at

Althiburos and Cirta to "the sacrifice of a human." But there is little evidence for Roman disapproval. Indeed, there is good evidence at Carthage itself, reborn as the flagship Roman colony in Africa, for the cults of both Tinnit, now called Caelestis, and Baal Hammon/Saturn.[54] Furthermore, Matthew McCarty has demonstrated that in the second century CE, the Roman army itself facilitated the spread of what had by then become "Saturn" cult in the area north of the Aurès, with legionaries, now largely recruited from other parts of Africa, establishing sanctuaries in a zone that had previously been distinctive for their absence.[55] The first claim that child sacrifice was banned in Africa is made by Tertullian in the late second century CE, and he seems to be referring to a specific incident in a specific place, in which some priests were crucified on trees at the behest of the local Roman proconsul.[56] He dates the event rather vaguely, but says that his father's military cohort was a witness to it, suggesting that it was fairly recent.

Instead of straightforward resistance, the new tophets symbolized continuing civic power in a very similar way across a wide region. Over time, the widespread adoption of the same novel ritual practices and representations over these large areas suggests that if these communities had Carthage in mind, it was only in a distantly reimagined way: they were responding much more immediately to each other. And since the phenomenon had died out in the rest of the Mediterranean by the end of the Hellenistic period, the associations of the cult both to insiders and outsiders must over time have become less "Carthaginian" or "Phoenician" and more "African."

ROMAN MAGISTRATES

We can tell a similar story about magistracies. Civic leaders known in Punic as *shofetim* (ŠPTM), meaning "judges," and transcribed into Latin as *sufetes*, are attested in a number of Levantine city-states in the eastern and western Mediterranean in the first millennium BCE. In the west we have pre-Roman evidence from Carthage, where hundreds of *shofetim* are attested at the tophet from at least the fourth century, and from Gadir, Karales, Bithia, Sulcis, and Nora for the third century. *Shofetim* are also recorded in Hellenistic-period Sicily at Eryx, a town that is not traditionally considered a Phoenician settlement but hosted an important sanctuary of Ashtart and was often an ally of Carthage.[57] And they continued to be appointed in the Levantine settlements long after the Roman conquest of the territories concerned: at Bithia into the second or third century CE, and at Karales and Sulcis even after the towns became Roman *municipia*.[58]

8.5 Identified towns in Roman North Africa with evidence for sufetes.

Again, however, it is in Africa that the institution really took off in the Roman period, attested in more than forty cities, most well beyond the coastal colonial zone, and with the last dated example from the reign of Commodus (fig. 8.5).[59] The phenomenon is often interpreted as the survival of an older institution that only becomes visible in this period as a result of a more general rise in epigraphic evidence.[60] It has even been suggested that it was imposed on these towns by Carthage before its own destruction, although we have no evidence of such impositions, and they seem distinctly unlikely in the case of cities as far away as Volubilis.[61]

Moreover, the evidence for African sufetes outside Carthage almost all dates from after 146 BCE, with the only possible exception a bilingual Punic/Libyan inscription erected in the city of Thugga in 139 BCE, which refers to the last Numidian king, Massinissa's grandfather Zilalsan, in Punic as a *shofet*.[62] Assuming that this was not simply an honorary title, we do not know where Zilalsan served. There is no reason to think that it was Thugga itself, where the chief civic magistrates are listed in the same Punic document not as ŠPTM but with the title MMLKT, "ruler" or "prince."[63] By the first century CE, however, a Latin inscription does name a *sufes* in the *civitas* of Thugga, demonstrating that there at least this was a new adoption in the Roman period.[64] Absence of evidence is not, of course, evidence of absence, but while it is entirely possible that the origins of the African sufetate lie in Carthaginian imperial policy, it seems most judicious to adopt the working hypothesis that sufetes became more popular after the fall of Carthage and may not even have existed outside western Levantine colonies at all before that period.

As with tophet cult, however, this is not simply a story of the African adoption in the Roman period of a Carthaginian norm: the institution not only appears in new places, but sometimes in new ways. The basic pattern seems to have been to appoint pairs of sufetes, imitating the arrangements at Carthage. But three sufetes appear at Althiburos in texts of the first century CE; at Mactar three sufetes also appear, but one is labeled the *rab ha-shofetim*, the "chief of the judges"; and a *sufes maior* or "senior judge" is recorded in Latin inscriptions at Thugga and Chul.[65] In all these cases, we may be looking at the adaptation or relabeling of earlier local magistracies, or these may be entirely new developments. Either way, the choice made by these particular communities was to adopt the Punic name of an institution rather than the institution itself.

And as with the tophets again, although some reference to Carthage is very likely to have been involved in the adoption of sufetes in these African cities, they respond to each other more than to the past: the towns of the central Maghreb adopted a common language to talk about their political leaders. Furthermore, the double sufeteship mapped neatly onto the standard double magistracy of the *duumvirate* used in Roman *municipia* in the same period, suggesting that the adoption of the institution could also encompass a form of peer polity interaction with the new *Roman* cities and civic organization of Africa. This was an institution that might have seemed familiar to the Roman authorities, even as its foreign origins and above all its variability must have made it difficult to fully comprehend.

MULTILINGUAL STRATEGIES

A final and very obvious example of the persistence and diffusion of the cultural practices of Phoenician colonies is the continuing use of the Punic language across the western Mediterranean. Punic is found on Iberian coinage into the first century BCE, and Ibizan coins into the first century CE; it was still spoken in Sicily in the second century and still used for Sardinian inscriptions in the second or even third.[66] As with the other phenomena I have discussed, however, most of the evidence comes from North Africa, where the language lasted much longer and spread much farther: there are more than seven hundred Punic language inscriptions from the region dating from the second century BCE to the fourth century CE (fig. 8.6).[67]

It is no surprise that Punic continued to be used in the old Levantine settlements in Africa, featuring on the coinage of coastal cities from Tripolitania to the Atlantic coast of Morocco into the Tiberian period,[68] and spoken at least in Tripolitania for considerably longer: as well as the story of Septimius's unfortunate sister, Apuleius tells us that his stepson at Oea in the second century CE "only speaks Punic apart from some words of Greek which come to him from his mother. As for Latin, he neither knows nor wants to speak it."[69] Again, the point is not whether the story is true, but that it was plausible.

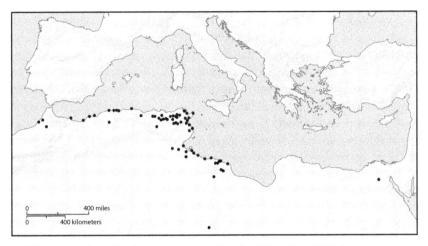

8.6 Findspots of neo-Punic inscriptions in North Africa. Use of this late script seems almost entirely confined to the Roman period.

Punic had also already been adopted in the Numidian and Mauretanian cities and kingdoms before the destruction of Carthage, used there for monumental inscriptions and coin legends from the late third century BCE down to the end of the Hellenistic period, and the royal coinage was also minted on existing weight standards used in the Levantine cities, for obviously practical reasons.[70] It is even possible that it was in a Numidian context that Phoenician was first used to compose literary texts. We are told that the Numidian king Hiempsal, who reigned in the 80s BCE, had "Punic books" (*libri punici*) that Sallust consulted on the history of Africa:[71] if these were in fact written in Punic rather than Greek,[72] there is no reason to ascribe them to Carthaginian rather than Numidian authors, or to assume that these are the same books from Carthage that Pliny tells us the Romans gave to the local kings in 146 BCE.[73] That episode does, however, reveal a Roman taste for Punic: Pliny tells us they kept back twenty-eight volumes by the agricultural author Mago to have them translated from Punic into Latin by Decimus Silanus, who Pliny says was the best at Punic among a number of specialists: it seems that the Punic language was not only appreciated at Rome, but reasonably familiar, a conclusion that might also follow from the lines of transliterated Punic that feature in Plautus's early-second-century BCE comedy *Poenulus* (The little Phoenician).[74]

Punic long survived the Numidian kingdoms in North Africa: although the script is not found after the second century CE, there is plenty of evidence that the language was still spoken in smaller towns and rural areas well into late antiquity. Out of forty-five published inscriptions from the pre-desert region of Tripolitania, dating from the second to fourth centuries CE, just nine are actually in Latin, and thirty-four are "Latino-Punic," where the Punic language is written in Latin script.[75] These Latino-Punic inscriptions also demonstrate that Punic was not only the language of peasants in this period: they are all epitaphs on mausolea or dedications, and so erected by members of the rural elite.[76] And in late-fourth- and early-fifth-century Algeria, Augustine still makes frequent reference to local Punic speakers. In addition to Valerius's encounter discussed in chapter 2, he tells us that the Circumcellions needed a Latin interpreter; that the bishop of Fussala had to speak Punic because the locals did not understand Latin; and, in a sermon given in his own diocese of Hippo, he quotes a proverb in Latin on the grounds that not *all* his listeners could speak Punic.[77]

Punic was not only a thriving language in Roman Africa, but one that was still developing. Almost all Punic inscriptions outside the old Levantine colonies and their territory are written in the cursive neo-Punic script that only appears around about the time of the destruction of Carthage,[78] and over time there were marked changes in the language's pronunciation and in its orthographic conventions, in particular marking more vowels.[79] Punic also came to convey new ideas and understandings: the practice discussed above of using toponyms rather than ethnonyms to describe cities, for instance, still found on all the late republican and early imperial coin legends issued by Levantine settlements in the west, did not survive the broader adoption of the language in Africa: people are described in later Punic inscriptions not, for instance, as "citizen of Mactar," but as "citizen of the Mactarians."[80]

This should not be surprising: as with the tophets and sufetes, it is unlikely that many of the people who now spoke Punic were descended from Phoenician-speaking migrants from the Levant. And while the names people give themselves and their children are no sure guide to origins and descent, they are suggestive.[81] If we compare the names attested in Punic inscriptions in Punic and neo-Punic script—so very roughly before and after the destruction of Carthage—those in the first group are almost entirely Semitic (1,145 names, as opposed to 82 Libyan, 21 Greek, and 13 Latin), while the second includes far more Libyan names (143 Semitic, 264 Libyan, 167 Latin, and 6 Greek).[82] It seems probable that these were in fact people of Libyan descent: while there is plenty of evidence in North Africa for families who originally used Phoenician and Libyan names adopting Roman ones at a certain point in their genealogy, the adoption in Roman Africa of Libyan names in place of originally Phoenician ones would be an unexpected development, and one for which we have no positive evidence.[83]

Despite the expanding use of Punic in African towns, it was not the only or even the most widely employed language in this period. There is, of course, a massive amount of evidence for the adoption of Latin throughout North Africa, at least as an epigraphic language: there are around thirty thousand surviving Latin inscriptions from the region.[84] Latin also seems to have influenced Punic to some extent, with Punic inscriptions acquiring more Latin formulas and vocabulary over time.[85] And 1,225 inscriptions in a variety of related Libyan dialects and scripts from right across the region have also been published, from as early as the fourth century BCE.[86] This language seems however to go out of use around the third century CE: there is no later epigraphic evidence, and no clear reference to its use in late antique authors. Furthermore, new evidence from statistical analyses of modern "Berber" languages used in the Maghreb suggests that they rarely relate to the dialects of these early inscriptions, but almost all descend from another ancestor language closely related to Tuareg, which only split around about the fifth century CE. This implies that a new Libyan-speaking population arrived around that time, probably from the Sahara, and revived a language that had already died out in the region.[87]

So again, while it is certainly the case that the greater the number of languages in play in a region, the harder it is to bring under bureaucratic control, it is difficult to see the use of Punic in Africa as an uncomplicated expression of cultural resistance to Latin, or as an expression of a specifi-cally Phoenician identity, given the widespread use of at least two other languages as well. These different languages tended in fact to be used for different purposes in Africa: euergetistic benefactions were made in Latin from an early date; Punic was used for votive dedications and tombs; Libyan for tombs and royal monuments. And it is striking that while individual dedications in the tophet sanctuaries in central Tunisia were made vari-ously in Punic, Greek, and Latin, the communal offerings and dedications by groups of citizens mentioned above, which were made for the first time in this period, were always in Punic. As at Lepcis, one thing Punic easily represented was a civic identity.

ROMAN AFRICA

There is considerable overlap between the evidence for sufetes, tophets, and the Punic language in the cities of Roman Africa: this was a bundle of insti-tutions that many African communities adopted wholesale, as one aspect of larger and more complex local systems of linguistic, administrative, and religious traditions. As a package, it was not a survival of the pre-Roman period, even in the self-proclaimed Levantine colonies of the Phoenician coast, which are in fact often less committed to the institutions involved than their African neighbors. At Lepcis we find sufetes and the Punic language, but no tophet,[88] while at Sabratha to the west, supposedly another Tyrian colony with a significant number of Punic inscriptions, there is no good evidence for sufetes, and the tophet established in the second century BCE contained only cremated animals.[89] This superficially traditional western Phoenician practice was a recent development at Sabratha, one that it shared with local communities across North Africa rather than with its nearest Levantine neighbor, and even by comparison with some of those it was rather half-hearted.

Nor can this phenomenon be a simple relic of Carthaginian expansion in Africa: the institutions are found a long way from the reach of Carthage's power, even at its height, and they often appear in the surviving evidence not only after the fall of that city, but only once Rome began to take a real political and financial interest in its African territories in the first century BCE.[90] The far-off Mauretanian city of Volubilis in inland Morocco provides a striking example from that period: Punic funerary inscriptions commemorate people with Libyan names, some labeled sufetes, and in an open-air sanctuary small gabled and decorated markers sit atop urns containing the cremated remains of birds and rodents.[91]

These institutions made undeniable connections with Carthage, at least when they were first adopted. In the early stages of Roman imperialism in the region, identifications with Carthage underlined local cultural distance from this new power through the re-created and reimagined institutions of a prestigious African city that no longer presented a potential threat in itself. By adopting a set of institutions closely associated with a recent enemy, they avoided full cultural and political assimilation with the Roman state, and in particular perhaps with the soldiers and colonists it sent to Africa in large numbers. Such arrangements would also have helped to keep the practicalities of Roman power at a distance, by making these African communities difficult to read, both literally and metaphorically: linguistic and cultural complexity, unpredictability, and code-switching helped to maintain civic autonomy on the periphery of state power.

At the same time, attempts to explain the phenomenon in terms of simple resistance to Rome are problematic. As at Lepcis, these Levantine institutions were adopted in tandem with Roman ones, they thrived and expanded under Roman rule, and they often appealed to Roman norms or enthusiasms. As Rome and its provinces merged increasingly into a single system, these towns looked more to each other, developing institutions and practices in new directions, in a decentralized network of African civic communities, in parallel and no doubt in competition. In these African cities, just as at Lepcis, the construction of identifications with past places and powers served contemporary, shifting social and political purposes. They allowed communities to communicate effectively with their own citizens, with each other, and with the dominant powers of the region.

This phenomenon was not, it seems, related to Phoenician group identity. The specific reference of these institutions was Carthage, not the Phoenician world more generally. Besides, they are just one aspect of complex civic cultures: even the Carthaginian identification was only partial. And from the outside, at least, the package must have quickly come to look distinctively African, as these practices died out elsewhere in the western Mediterranean, and the cities in question looked increasingly to each other. There is no doubt that peer polity interaction was a driving factor in cultural change throughout the region, and this can be seen from the architecture of Lepcis to the Volubilis tophet.

This picture does not map easily onto modern ideas about ethnicity, but it does fit in with Roman conceptions of African regional identity. As discussed in chapter 3, the closely related Latin words *poenus* and *punicus* were used regularly from the Late Republic onward to mean not only "Phoenician," but also, it seems, more generally "North African." This usage did not point to shared origins or descent; it did not identify—at least at the beginning—a contemporary political, social, or cultural collective; and it was compatible with Roman rule.

It was also a label that could be accepted by locals: in the early fifth century, Augustine, who was originally from Thagaste in Numidia, embraced the notion of being *poenus* against the abuse of Julian of Aeclanum, leader of the Pelagians, in the early fifth century. In his attacks on Augustine, Julian regularly refers to his African background, calling him, for instance, a "Phoenician disputer" (*poenus disputator*), a "Phoenician preacher" (*poenus tractator*), a "Phoenician orator" (*poenus orator*), and a "Phoenician writer" (*poenus scriptor*).[92] It is clear that Julian does not intend by this to impute to Augustine a fictive Levantine descent or Carthaginian origin; elsewhere he calls him a "Numidian."[93] Instead, the use of *poenus* allows him to dismiss the African provincialism of Augustine and his works with a term that also evokes the deception and untrustworthiness of "Punic faith," which in a Christian context carried the additional implication of paganism.[94] Augustine, however, freely admits to being a *Poenus*, challenging only the derogatory implication given the term by Julian, and claiming that the same label should be applied to Cyprian, the highly respected third-century bishop of Carthage: "Do not despise this *Poenus* who warns and admonishes, puffed up by your geographical origins. Just because Puglia produced you, don't think that you can conquer the *Poeni* with your stock, when you cannot do so with your mind. . . . For blessed Cyprian was also a *Poenus*, who said 'We must boast over nothing when nothing is ours.'"[95]

The meaning of the word *poenus* in this exchange must relate to the region rather than an ethnicity, but it may well relate most directly to the language spoken there. As noted in chapter 2, when Augustine uses the alternative term *punicus*, it is almost always in relation to the Punic language, which he also describes as "African," and to its speakers, and Julian's accusations here also focus on Augustine's activities as a speaker and writer. It makes sense to see the "North African" meaning of these terms as deriving from a fundamentally linguistic ancient notion of "Phoenician" if we accept that, as I have argued in this chapter, the Punic dialect was still in widespread use in North Africa up to late antiquity.

African claims to "Phoenician" identity in these regional and linguistic rather than ethnic senses may, however, have begun much earlier. In the second century BCE, the Numidian King Massinissa (c. 238–158), who used the Punic language at court, depicted a palm frond on one of his coins, and in the early first century CE, Ptolemy II of Mauretania (c. 10 BCE–40 CE), who was descended from Numidian King Juba I, minted coins with palm trees throughout his reign.[96] We might wonder how much the new African implications of the term "Phoenician" in contemporary Roman discourse drew on such local identifiations, as well as how much it was encouraged by the relatively early intertwining of African cultural traditions that we see in the Numidian kings' use of the Punic language as well as in the use of Numidian dating systems in the tophet sanctuary at Cirta. It is also an intriguing fact that almost half of the new African tophet sanctuaries in the Roman period have markers that depict palms and palm branches (fig. 8.7).[97] This may simply have been a well-known symbol associated with Carthage, like the sign of Tanit, but all in all it seems unlikely that Augustine was the first African to proudly call himself a "Phoenician."

Local identifications as "Phoenician" also survived considerably later than Augustine's time, a point vividly illustrated by the reappearance of the palm tree and other Phoenician symbols on Carthage's bronze coinage in the fifth–sixth century CE, minted in the context of the Vandal conquest of the region (fig. 8.8).[98] The imagery is taken from the Siculo-Punic

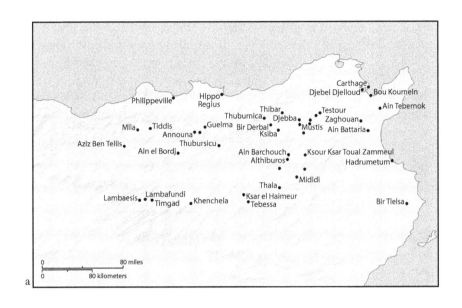

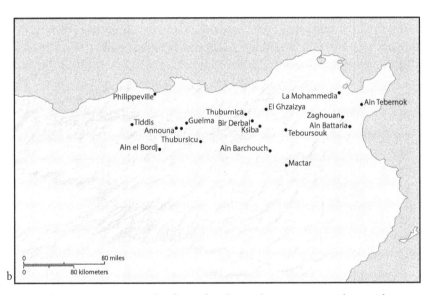

8.7 Findspots in Roman North Africa of tophet-style sanctuary markers with (a) freestanding palm trees and branches and (b) palm branches held by a figure.

8.8 This tiny bronze nummus from fifth- or sixth-century CE Carthage, reproduced here at 4.5x life size, has a head on the obverse and a palm tree on the reverse.

coinage of almost a millennium earlier, creating a fictive colonial identity much more dramatic than that I have suggested for Lepcis, as it completely erases the destruction by Rome of its greatest foe. And as Richard Miles has recently demonstrated, the appearance of the palm on this coinage reflects a host of other references to Phoenician Carthage, to Dido, and even to being Tyrian in contemporary writings by Romano-African authors.[99] This all fits in perfectly with the pattern established in this chapter: once again the distant memory of Carthage and its "Phoenician" networks provided cultural assistance in the face of a new regional power dynamic. This was by no means the last time this happened, and in my final chapter, I will take the story into the modern period.

CHAPTER 9

Phoenician Islands

A thousand years later, we are at a dinner party in the village of Sturry, near Canterbury in Kent. The event takes place at the summer lodgings of John Foche, the last abbot of St. Augustine's of Canterbury before the dissolution of that monastery by Henry VIII in 1538. As well as Foche himself, the company include the abbey's later prior, John Dygon; the dean of Canterbury, Nicholas Wotton, who would later arrange Henry's marriage to Anne of Cleves; and a young man called John Twyne, who became a schoolmaster, mayor of Canterbury, and the local member of Parliament. Dygon and Wotton have just returned from escorting the Spanish humanist scholar Juan Luis Vives from Louvain to Oxford; if this was the journey Vives is known to have made to take up a lectureship at Corpus Christi College, Oxford, we are in the summer of 1524.[1]

John Twyne (c. 1505–81) is the man to whom we owe our account of the event: his *Two Books of Commentaries on Albion, British, and English Affairs* (*De Rebus Albionicis, Britannicis, atque Anglis Commentariorum libri duo*), written in Latin and published posthumously by his son Thomas in 1590, are a record of the dinner conversation, presumably at least partly fictionalized.[2] The commentary concerned is largely that of Foche alone: dinner starts at lunchtime, but the discussion goes on long into the warm evening as the abbot regales his patient, even indulgent, guests with his views on the history of *nostra Britannia*, "our Britain," whose inhabitants he describes as a single *gens* or people.[3]

Foche attacks in particular certain fantasies peddled by Geoffrey of Monmouth in the 1130s that had recently come back into fashion. Geoffrey had traced the history of the kings of Britain—the *Historia Regum Britanniae*, as the work is usually known—from Brutus the Trojan, great-grandson of Aeneas, including the first detailed account of the exploits of King Arthur. He claimed to work from a "very old book" (*vetustissimus liber*), written in Welsh and unavailable for consultation by later scholars. The abbot dismisses Geoffrey's ridiculous story of Trojan origins to conclude instead, on the rational and scientific grounds appropriate to Renaissance humanism, that Britain was in fact first settled by Albion, the son of the god Neptune, and the ancestor of a race of cave-dwelling giants.[4] Foche has many other strongly held opinions, some of them correct, such as his insistence that Britain had once been a peninsula of the European continent.[5] But he also suggests, rather tentatively at first and then with increasing confidence, that after Albion's arrival and the subsequent separation of Britain from France, the first foreigners to reach the island were the Phoenicians.[6]

Twyne's (and perhaps Foche's) interest in the Phoenicians can be explained as part of a more general fascination with the texts and peoples of the classical world in this period. But what is striking here is the suggestion of a Phoenician strand in British history and identity. Phoenicianism in medieval and modern rhetoric has been discussed before, of course, but usually in relation to specific periods or authors, or in countries such as Spain, that have unarguable evidence for ancient Levantine settlement.[7] In this final chapter, I take by contrast the example of Phoenicianism in the north Atlantic islands, where the only evidence for any form of contact with Phoenician-speakers at all is a single graffito on a tile excavated at Holt in Wales, recording in Punic script the name of one "Macrinus"—no doubt a first- or second-century CE African-born solder in Rome's Twentieth Legion that was based at nearby Chester and maintained a pottery at Holt.[8] Given the complete lack of literary or material evidence for Phoenician settlement in Britain or Ireland, I want to explore the role of fictive Phoenicians in developing national consciousness on those islands from the sixteenth to nineteenth centuries.

In Britain, the idea of being Phoenician, literally or metaphorically, appealed to a series of intellectuals as they contributed to the project of developing a national identity that was increasingly formulated in opposition to other nations such as "Roman" France. In Ireland, where the idea of literal Phoenician descent became considerably more popular than it ever was in England, this ancestral identity was a weapon against English cultural and political imperialism: on this model, savage Rome was once again brutalizing the civilized Phoenician race. In both cases, Phoenicianism was developed and discussed by intellectuals in the service of national and imperial political interests: as in the ancient world, "being Phoenician" was an identity imposed on subjects, not chosen by citizens. Both are also examples of the bridges between the Phoenician and Punic games of the Roman Empire and more modern constructions of the Phoenicians as a nation in themselves.

My reading of this material as nationalist may seem surprising: nationalism is widely seen as an eighteenth- or even nineteenth-century phenomenon, a product of (among other things) industrialization, mass communications and the revolutions in France and the United States, reaching its height with the political unification of Germany and Italy.[9] That is the era of nation-states that I discussed in chapter 1, but the language of the "nation" itself, as well as the idea of national character and of personal attachments to particular nations, goes back to medieval times in Europe.[10] In the early modern period, an evolving sense of European "nations" as natural communities with a right to some level of self-government developed alongside widening horizons of power and culture, encompassing the rise of vernacular languages at the expense of Latin and the invention of the printing press in the fifteenth century, both of which allowed much swifter communication of information and ideas to a much larger group of people, as well as the sixteenth-century break with Rome as the ultimate political as well as religious power.[11] This was the period in which kings began gradually to make states out of their subjects, eliminating the influence of the church above them and of the aristocracy below them, a process that culminated in the standing armies and state taxation of the seventeenth century. Supposedly preexisting "nations" were of course attractive to these new rulers, giving their nascent states history, legitimacy, and a ready-made territory.

At the same time, the similarity of the experiences that emerging European nations went through in the medieval and early modern periods makes it unsurprising that although ethnic stereotyping, hostility, and even ideas of genocide can be found in contemporary sources, nationalism as practiced in that era was more positional than oppositional.[12] National identities and allegiances tended not to be exclusive, and one common ingredient in early conceptions of European *nationes* was the notion of their shared descent, either from the heroes of classical myth or, more respectably, the sons of Noah.[13] As early as the mid-ninth century, Trojan origins were attributed to both the Franks and the Britons,[14] but over the following centuries it was the Table of the Nations as laid out in chapter 10 of the Book of Genesis and then expanded upon by Greek and Latin authors that provided a road map for scholars to trace the connections between their own developing nations. As Colin Kidd puts it, "Within the Mosaic scheme, difference mattered less than degrees of consanguinity among a world of nations descended from Noah."[15] Europeans were happy to accept Josephus's claim that the European peoples descended from Noah's son Japheth rather than his brothers, the Semite Shem or the cursed Ham, and made their own amendments as necessary: the Swedes, for instance, considered themselves the descendants of Japheth through his son Magog and then Gotar, the father of the Goths.[16] This is the context in which Twyne introduces the Phoenicians to British history, though by a different route.

BABYLON TO BRITAIN

Twyne's work was a typical example of elite and scholarly nationalism in the sixteenth century: the small octavo format with its 162 pages of dense Latin print, the long list of sources, ancient and modern, at the beginning of the book, the conceit of the dinner party conversation and its Socratic style, the in-jokes and name-dropping in relation to fashionable intellectuals and their Oxford colleges. The role played by court scholars has been one of the central themes of recent scholarship on the discourse of nations in the medieval and early modern periods: early nationalism was very much a project of intellectual elites,[17] and this is a book by a scholar for other scholars, a work of erudite speculation for the secretaries and counselors of the Tudor nobility to chew over while waiting on their lords.[18] Accordingly, it participates in an elite and cosmopolitan discourse about the nation: in his dismissal of Geoffrey of Monmouth, Twyne follows the Italian scholar and Tudor court favorite Polydore Vergil, as well as other Continental humanists,[19] and he emphasizes in a similar spirit the evidence of the classical sources over British historical writing. "Where does Caesar mention Priam?" asks the abbot, and "Where is there a single word about Brutus?" noting that Caesar of all people would scarcely have omitted to mention such a glorious ancestor in his commentaries on his British campaigns.[20] He adds a quotation from Virgil to prove his point and tops this a page later with an appeal to Servius's late antique commentary on the *Aeneid* for a detail of Trojan diaspora history.[21]

The seed of Twyne's Phoenician hypothesis, however, is not directly taken from classical texts, which provided all the information then available on the Phoenicians. Instead, the abbot first suggests that the Phoenicians colonized Cornwall on the basis of a set of remarks about the Phoenicians' mining activities in Iberia by Juan Luis Vives in his recent commentary on Augustine's *City of God*, "which when you read it, friends, surely the thought springs to mind that the same thing could at some point have happened in Britain, on account of course of the metals in which *Cornubia*, vulgarly called *Cornwallia*, abounds?"[22] This does not look like an open and shut case, but Foche goes on to explain that these Phoenicians might in fact have occupied a good part of the island, importing among other things the eastern rites of the druids to Britain,[23] and he lists various words and customs that seem to betray their influence. This theory would explain, for instance, the famous British custom of painting one's body with woad, as an attempt by the faded descendants of the Phoenicians to regain some of their original color.[24] There is also the evidence of the "Punic dress" still worn by some women in Wales, as well as that land's "Punic huts," not to mention the fact that the Welsh word *Caer* means "town" or "city," which must derive from Phoenician, since the third-century CE historian Solinus reports (correctly) that "Carthage" (*Carthago* or *Carthada*) means "the new city" (in fact, Qarthadasht).[25] And from where could the custom of men wearing a moustache have come if not the Babylonians?[26]

This last point is relevant because, as Twyne explains, the Phoenicians originated in Babylonia, before migrating to a variety of other venerable ancient lands, including Egypt, Ethiopia, Syria, Greece, Spain, and finally Albion.[27] Twyne is, of course, much less interested in the precise nature and status of the Phoenicians than in their British descendants, and in describing the former he largely reproduces the fragmentary associations found in ancient texts: "The *Phoenicians* are said to be merchants; the *Phoenicians* [are said to be] red, that is, tinted with colour. The *Phoenicians* are held to be deceitful and cunning, and this is the origin of the proverbial phrases 'Phoenician treaties' and 'Phoenician ways.'"[28] He does not call the Phoenicians a *natio* or even a *gens*, nor does he represent them in other ways as a distinct group related by descent, geography, or culture. With their varied origins and close relations to other places and people, Twyne's Phoenicians fit in comfortably with inclusive contemporary concepts of European nations as related groups of peoples, supporting a version of British nationalism that was not premised on exclusive ethnicity or on difference from others: the Phoenicians came from many places and colonized many countries, and to have them as an element of your ancestry was to be like the other evolving nations of Europe, not to be different from them.

Why introduce Phoenicians into the story of the British nation at all? Twyne's *Commentaries* respond to a specific problem in contemporary historiography. There was undoubtedly an intense scholarly interest in the origins of the nation in the Tudor period, alongside a fledgling antiquarian tradition, helped by the archival and archaeological research opportunities offered by the dissolution of the monasteries.[29] But was the Tudor nation English or British? Politically, the situation was ambiguous: although the kings of England had conquered Ireland in the twelfth century and Wales in the thirteenth, Scotland would still be a separate kingdom until the Union of the Crowns in 1603, and the formal creation of the United Kingdom of Great Britain only took place in 1707. Separate "English" and "British" historical traditions had flourished in the Middle Ages: the English narrative, exemplified by the eighth-century work of the Venerable Bede, focused on England and its Saxon kings, while the British tradition, championed by the ninth-century *Historia Brittonum* and then by Geoffrey of Monmouth, centered on King Arthur, who had supposedly (and temporarily) defeated the island's Saxon conquerors.

Cultural historians have tended to focus on the construction of Englishness and a specifically English past in the early modern era, with "British" identity understood as a largely eighteenth-century development, building on the prior cultural consolidation of component Welsh, Scottish, and Irish, as well as English identities, and on the recent political union of these regions. As a result, "Britishness" is still often seen as a less primitive and therefore better identity than, for example, Scottishness; or alternatively, Scottishness is seen as an earlier and therefore more authentic identity than Britishness.[30] But a "British" past was also embraced in the Tudor period: although the mythical Trojan origins of Britain had largely been discounted by 1450, and there was considerable skepticism about King Arthur, both traditions found a new lease of life in the sixteenth century.[31] By this time, the break with Rome provided another reason for distance from the Anglo-Saxons, who had presided over the importation of the Roman Catholic religion to Britain by St. Augustine of Canterbury; recusant Catholics still championed the "English" version of history, but the newly minted Anglicans needed older roots.[32] Moreover, the Tudors themselves originally came from Wales and were pleased to claim the British King Arthur as an appropriate royal ancestor: in 1486, Henry VII named his oldest son Arthur, and John Leland, Henry VIII's official *antiquarius*, published a trenchant defense of the Arthur legend in 1544.[33] Additionally, the myth of "British" origins suited the imperial ambition of the nascent Tudor state, justifying the "rough wooing" of less powerful kingdoms into the union that was often called in the sixteenth century "the empire of Great Britain," making an old and unified logic of this unequal set of relationships.[34]

In this context, Twyne's move to trump Geoffrey of Monmouth's Brutus with the Phoenicians is ingenious. It provides a new national foundation legend for new kings (whether or not they sought one), and a new past for the whole island of Britain, with a particular emphasis on Wales.[35] It also features credible and creditable protagonists, much better suited to the "New Learning" of the period and the evolving nation-state of Britain than descent from an "unknown and obscure refugee" from Troy,[36] and they are presented as a people of varied origins who could reflect the complex and multilayered local identities in the consolidating Union of the various British kingdoms. This is not to suggest that the *Commentaries* were a straightforward contribution to regime propaganda: Twyne, whose politics were considered somewhat suspect in real life, may have had good reason to arrange for posthumous publication.[37] Instead, like Heliodorus's *sphragis*, this is intellectual game-playing, rearranging and replacing the pieces on the board to suit the new realities of power.

PHOENICIANS AGAINST FRANCE

Twyne's book "was a major work of history, read by Verstegan, Speed and Camden in the seventeenth century,"[38] but his Phoenician proposal did not catch on. In the seventeenth century, Britain was more often seen as "a new Rome in the West,"[39] as Milton put it in 1660, and it was instead the Dutch Republic, Britain's great competitor for control of international trade, that was popularly associated with Phoenician Carthage. The Anglo-Dutch conflicts of 1652–74 were known as "Punic" wars, and Rome's defeat of Carthage's navy was a particular rallying call: in 1673, the Earl of Shaftesbury declared in Parliament that *Delenda est Carthago*, "Carthage must be destroyed,"[40] and in the same year, Dryden's epilogue to his play *Amboyna* extended the point:

> With an ill grace the Dutch their mischiefs do
> They've both ill-nature and ill-manners too.
> Well may they boast themselves an ancient nation
> For they were bred ere manners were in fashion
> And their new commonwealth has set them free,
> Only from honour and civility . . .
> As Cato did his Afric fruits display
> So we before your eyes their Indies lay:
> All loyal English will, like him, conclude,
> Let Cæsar live, and Carthage be subdued![41]

By the mid-1670s, however, the Dutch star was in decline, and it was the French who presented the greatest threat to British interests, as well as competition for the title of new Romans. It was in this context that in 1676 a lawyer named Aylett Sammes published another book-length attempt to establish Phoenician national origins: *Britannia antiqua illustrata, or, The Antiquities of Ancient Britain, Derived from the Phoenicians*, a history of Britain from the first settlers to the Saxon invasion. Little is known about Sammes (c. 1636–79), but unlike Twyne's dense little pocketbook, his is a large folio publication, with detailed maps and illustrations, dedicated to the Lord Chancellor, and written in English for "the Nobility and Gentry"—a work to consult, and more important, display at home.[42]

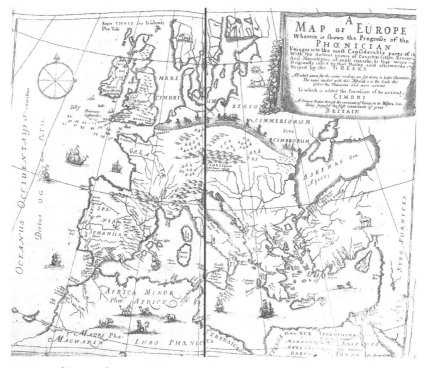

9.1 Map of Europe from Aylett Sammes, *Britannia antiqua illustrata* (1676), depicting the migrations of the Phoenicians and the Cimbri.

According to Sammes, Britons have two sets of ancestors: northern Britain was first settled by the German Cimbri, while the Phoenicians settled in the Isles of Scilly, in Cornwall, and in Devon, mining tin and trading it down to the Mediterranean (fig. 9.1). As a result, "Not only the name of Britain itself, but of most places therein of ancient denomination are purely derived from the Phoenician Tongue, and . . . the Language itself for the most part, as well as the Customs, Religions, Idols, Offices, Dignities of the Ancient Britains are all clearly Phoenician, as likewise their instruments of war."[43]

Like Twyne, Sammes is dismissive of the story of Brutus and the "*British* histories, because their credit in the World is but small" as opposed to "the Authority of *Greek* and *Roman* authors,"[44] but unlike Twyne he actually makes direct use of classical sources to construct his Phoenician hypothesis. He first identifies the Isles of Scilly with the Cassiterides, the ancient "tin islands" that Strabo tells us were exploited and kept secret by the Phoenicians to protect the sources of their trade,[45] then suggests that this Greek name for the islands was a translation of an earlier, unattested

Phoenician name, *Bratanac*, which he would translate as "A Country, or Field *of Tynn*," and finally argues that this name was eventually transferred to the larger island.[46] Further evidence for Phoenician settlement in Britain includes a long list of etymologies for British toponyms and other words from Phoenician names and places, including the name of Cornwall and the word for beer, as well as another survey of the survivals of Phoenician customs and institutions.[47]

Stonehenge is one of the more surprisingly Phoenician sites revealed by Sammes's investigation. Having pointed out that Gerald of Wales and other British authors said that the structure was built by giants with stones brought from Africa, he continues, ". . . to separate Truth from a Fable, and to find out an Ancient Tradition, wrapt up in ignorant and idle Tales; Why may not these Giants, so often mentioned, upon this, and other occasions, be the *Phoenicians*, as we have proved on other occasions, and the Art of erecting these Stones, instead of the STONES themselves, brought from the farthermost parts of *Africa*, the known habitations of the *Phoenicians*?"[48]

Another thing that comes out in the lengthy discussion of Stonehenge is that, as in Twyne's work, Sammes's Phoenicians are still a vaguely defined group, and Sammes himself had a rather open conception of ancient "nations": although Twyne's interest in the mixed ancestry of the Phoenicians themselves is not a feature of Sammes's argument, the latter does see them as the ancestors of a variety of other peoples.[49] So although one surprising objection that he suggests could be made to his theory of Stonehenge's Phoenician origins is "*That the Structure seemeth of* Tuscan *order, and so purely* Italian," he reassures his readers "that the *Tuscans* were (as *Grotius*, and others prove) of *Tyrian* Original, and in all probability brought with them (from *Phoenicia* into *Italy*) that order of building."

An additional complication then arises, however, from the opinion of the monument's restorer, as reported by Sammes, that "in all his Travels, through *Italy* and other Countries, he found no Structure of like Order exactly with this, insomuch that he admires it for its Rarity, and especial difference from all others, it being properly a mixture of the *Tuscan* and *Ionick* Order." This too is swiftly dealt with: "[T]hat the *Ionians* were immediately derived from a Colony of the *Phoenicians, Herodotus* especially, and all Authors with him agree, so that seeing this *Stone-henge* is esteemed in this Age a mixt Building of *Tuscan* and *Ionic* Order, both *Phoenician* Nations, why may not it be accounted a Work of the Ancient *Phoenicians*?"[50]

Although such creative detail is his own, Sammes openly borrows his basic argument about the Phoenicians from Samuel Bochart's *Geographia sacra* (1646), discussed in chapter 1.[51] This book had not only established the possibility of reconstructing their language on the basis of Hebrew and other closely related tongues, but had also addressed among many other things the related questions of the Phoenicians' colonial activities in France, whether they reached America (concluding that it was unlikely), and whether they settled in Britain, Ireland, and the Tin Islands (concluding, in part on the basis of what Bochart saw as the similarities between Hebrew and Welsh, that they did). Bochart, however, was writing not the history of a nation, but a geography of the Phoenicians, in which only two short chapters (41–42) are devoted to his own Gaul, scarcely longer between them than that on the British Isles (39). In none of these is he at all interested in the modern nations, but simply in the evidence for Phoenician activity in the past.

What is new in Sammes's book is the nationalist use to which he puts Bochart's ideas in a work that constantly celebrates the "Nation" of Britain, "the most Renowned Island of the whole World," with its "temperate and blessed Clymate."[52] This motivation for the work is made clear right from the start: the book showcases Britain as a "a Nation great in its Infancy, and like *Hercules* (one of its first discoverers) deserving a History even in its Cradle."[53] And what is particularly interesting for our purposes is that, unlike Twyne, he also calls the Phoenicians themselves a "Nation" and even a "State," although he gives no substantial description of them as such, and "Nation" at least seems here simply to be a translation of Bochart's *gens,* or "people."[54]

Sammes's work also offered a way to think through the ongoing consolidation of England, Scotland, and Ireland in the seventeenth century, and to reconcile the hierarchies it created.[55] In particular, although he asserts that "Nature has set *BRITAIN* such distinct Bounds and Limits, that its Empire is preserved entire," Sammes is sensitive to the differences that remain between the kingdoms, and alert to the hierarchy between "*Britannia Major,* as *ENGLAND,* and *Minor,* as *SCOTLAND, England* being the Greater (and of more particular concern to our present discourse)."[56] His theory that different parts of Britain were colonized by different peoples explains not only their differences, but also the advantages of combination, as well as emphasizing a distinctly racial element in British nationalism: after explaining the somatic distinction between the "sturdier, bigger made" northerners, descended from the Cimbri, and the southern or Phoenician "men of neater strength, and more compact Limbs," he concludes that "Divers Languages, Customes, and Usages . . . are not contrary one to the other, but by the mixture of the Gentry, and the happy union of this Nation under one Monarch, do meet together in the making up of the best compacted Kingdom in the

World."[57] Sammes also takes up Bochart's suggestion that the Phoenicians reached Ireland, uniting the two islands in a convenient fiction during the uneasy peace between them in the years after the Restoration of 1660.[58]

In this narrow sense, Sammes's version of the Phoenician hypothesis still supports an inclusive, if unequal, interpretation of British nationalism. However, in a period during which "a rural and agrarian English society transformed its government in a mercantile and maritime direction under the extreme pressure of war"[59] and was consolidating its imperial possessions at home and in the New World, Sammes distinguishes the British nation-empire much more strongly from other European nations than had Twyne. In particular, and despite his open reliance on Bochart, Sammes is decidedly anti-French.

A major theme in the work is that Britain was not, as Camden had argued in his *Britannia*, founded from ancient Gaul: for Sammes, the similarities between the customs of the ancient Britons and Gauls are to be explained not through kinship but "from their joynt Commerce with the *Phoenicians*."[60] Britain had always been an island and not, as Camden (and before him Twyne) had claimed, a peninsula of northern Europe: "if this *Isthmus* were admitted, then it would seem beyond dispute that the *Gauls* peopled this Nation, which . . . can not be imagined. It seems more glorious for this excellent part of the Earth to have been always a distinct Nation by itself, than to be a dependent member of the Territory to which it hath often given Laws."[61] Although the rhetoric here is somewhat hesitant, the nation of Britannia is presented as an independent law-making polity, and one in the same sort of natural hierarchy to France as England is to Scotland.

Sammes takes one more new direction, in that his association of the British and the Phoenicians is implicitly based on comparison as well as direct contact and kinship. He puts huge emphasis on the fact that the Phoenicians were "great Traders and skilful Mariners, and sent out their Colonies through the World,"[62] but he also emphasizes the parallel qualities of modern Britain as a trading and colonial power—what David Armitage has described as the self-conception of the British Empire in this period as at once "Protestant, commercial, maritime and free."[63] Sammes's work itself does not seem to have been very successful—there is at least no evidence for reprints—but his comparison between the Phoenicians and the British was to prove enduring.

COMPARATIVE PHOENICIANISM

As the hypothesis of direct British descent from the Phoenicians became increasingly hard to maintain in the light of developments in the study of

archaeology, linguistics, and classical literature, it was increasingly confined to the work of local antiquarians, with correspondingly local allegiances and ambitions. In 1700, for instance, Charles Leigh's *The Natural
History of Lancashire, Cheshire and the Peak in Derbyshire, with an Account
of the British, Phoenician, Armenian, Greek and Roman Antiquities in Those
Parts* described how the Phoenicians settled Lancashire, and in particular
Preston, successors there to the giants,[64] and William Stukeley's books
on Stonehenge (1740) and Avebury (1743) followed Twyne in making the
Phoenicians the importers of druidism, his own particular enthusiasm.[65]

Claims of Phoenician settlement remained common in Cornwall well
into the nineteenth century: as Timothy Champion has explained, the coming of the railways and the opening of the Royal Albert Bridge across the
Tamar in 1859, at a time when the Cornish language had basically died out,
meant that "the problem of defining a distinct Cornish identity became
more pressing. . . . the Phoenician heritage was part of the strategy through
which Cornwall sought to resist incorporation into the national unity of an
Anglo-Saxon England."[66]

Even in Cornwall, however, this was a matter for debate. In the October
1866 issue of the *Journal of the Royal Institution of Cornwall*, amid reports on local rainfall, pilchards and the land tortoise, the Reverend John
Bannister contributed an article on "Nomenclature," in which he accepts
that "Melcarth was the original discoverer of Britain, and the first exporter
of tin from our country; and that he was deified by his grateful country-
men for the benefits he conferred on them,"[67] but he is not convinced that
the Phoenician term *qart* (city) of Melqart is behind the Cornish roots *Caer*
and *Car*, or that place names such as Bal-dhu "be derived from the Phoenician God, Baal," as suggested by the Reverend S. Lysons: "I prefer the
simplest rendering, *Black Mine*." More skeptically, Mr. Edward Smirke, the
president of the Royal Institution and vice-warden of the Stannarie (tin
mines), considers whether some "gold gorgets or lunettes found near Pad-
stow" were of local manufacture or foreign import, and concludes that the
"glyptic and plastic arts" of the Tyrian and Sidonian traders are only one
possible source for them: "I well know the favour which this tradition of
Phoenician intercourse finds in the Cornubian mind. It is treated as a sort
of Palladium or idol, any attempt to displace which by sceptical heretics
will be received with marked resentment. But we must not forget that the
interest in this question is not to be limited to Cornwall, or to Ireland; for
I have shown that other, even Scandinavian, regions can shew ornaments
of a like general character, where the influence of Phoenician traffic is not
so satisfactorily established as (we flatter ourselves) it has been in South

Damnonia." The relatively simply decorated examples under discussion are, he concludes, "the work of early British or Irish art."[68] Nonetheless, even in 1906, the president of the Royal Institution of Cornwall, Howard Fox, could claim that the art of clotting cream was "introduced to us by these navigators from Syria."[69]

Outside Cornwall, the preferred mode of association with the Phoenicians in the eighteenth century was comparative. This represents a new stage in intellectual nationalism, less focused on England, Scotland, and Ireland than on the new empire that had been evolving abroad since the East India Company's first charter in 1600 and the first English settlements in North America in 1607. With the domestic imperial project accomplished, establishing the ancient origins of Britain itself was no longer so important, and interest shifted to glorifying British commercial and colonial activity abroad by highlighting its ancient models. And with the "Roman" French now the main military horizon, rather than the "Carthaginian" Dutch, it was not only possible but desirable to compare Britons directly to Rome's great enemy.[70] This Carthaginian comparison was attractive for two further reasons: one was the parallel it provided for the new British colonies in North America, and the other was the focus of the evolving overseas British Empire on trade, along with the significant role played by the British navy in protecting that trade, a situation that coincided with contemporary understandings of Carthaginian imperialism as based on commerce.[71]

Daniel Defoe's *General History of Discoveries and Improvements, in Useful Arts, Particularly in the Great Branches of Commerce, Navigation and Plantation in All Parts of the Known World*, printed in installments over 1725–26, was a long account of world history in which the commercial, scientific, and colonial achievements of the Phoenicians and Carthaginians play a starring role, followed by a stern account of the damage done to innovation and progress by the Romans "having but little Genius to Trade, and but few Merchants among them."[72] For Defoe, the Phoenicians "were not only the Patrons of Commerce, and set Trade first on Foot in the World; but they were, at least, encouragers, (if not the originals) of Arts and Sciences, and the first spreaders of universal Knowledge in the World." In that respect, "it will appear then that the *Phoenicians* were the *Englishmen* of that Age."[73] This parallel applies to colonial activity as well, and Defoe informs us not only that the great explorer and early champion of the plantation of Virginia, Sir Walter Raleigh, was called "the *English Hanno*,"[74] but also that the Carthaginians had already reached and colonized America, as shown by "the Similitude of Manners and Customs, between the *Carthaginians* and the *Americans* . . . particularly, many of their idolatrous Customs, Sacrificings,

Conjurings, and other barbarous usages in the Worship of their Gods."[75] Presumably, he did not see exact parallels with the English in these particulars.

This new, comparative association of the British with the Carthaginians could also, unlike the earlier notions of shared genealogy, be highly oppositional. The most striking example in the eighteenth century is Edward Wortley Montagu's *Reflections on the Rise and Fall of the Antient Republicks Adapted to the Present State of Great Britain*, first published in 1759, when the country was at war with France.[76] Despite its lack of scholarly depth— Polybius is more or less the only ancient source cited in the chapter on Carthage—the work went through four editions by 1778. Montagu's sights are set on Rome, which is to say France: "Of all the free states whose memory is preserved to us in history, Carthage bears the nearest resemblance to Britain, both in her commerce, opulence, sovereignty of the sea, and her method of carrying on her land-wars by foreign mercenaries. If to these we add the vicinity of the Carthaginians to the Romans, the most formidable and most rapacious people at that time in Europe, and the specific difference, as I may term it, of the respective military force of each nation, the situation of Carthage with respect to Rome, seems greatly analogous to that of Britain with respect to France, at least for this last century."[77] For Montagu, the Carthaginians are both commercial and colonial, like Britons, but Britain should learn from the failures of Carthage.[78] The key to success is to exploit nationalist enthusiasm: Carthage relied too much on mercenaries, "strangers to that heart-felt affection, that enthusiastic love of their country, which warms the heart of free citizens, and fires them with the glorious emulation of fighting to the last drop of blood in defence of their common mother."[79]

THE DECLINE OF THE CARTHAGINIAN EMPIRE

Occasional identifications with Carthage were still made in the early years of the nineteenth century, but that particular comparison had become more negative again since it had been enthusiastically adopted by the French as a way to emphasize the untrustworthiness of the British, to the extent that in 1798, in the Conseil des Cinq Cents, Paul Gauran, the deputy from Gers, ended a speech advocating war on the British government in the tradition of the "inflexible" Cato: "Que Carthage soit détruite!"[80] The unflattering parallel spread across the Atlantic, with Thomas Jefferson hesitating to make common cause with Britain against Napoleon in 1810 because of the "*Punica fides* of modern Carthage," a "nation of merchants."[81] The ambivalence of the metaphor even in early-nineteenth-century England is vividly illustrated in the art of Joseph Mallord William Turner.

In the second decade of the nineteenth century, Turner painted Carthage three times in four years. In 1814, he exhibited *Dido and Aeneas: The Morning of the Chase*, depicting the Phoenician queen and the Trojan prince on the heights above Carthage, with the magnificent new town laid out before them. A year later, in the immediate aftermath of the collapse of Napoleon's regime, *Dido Building Carthage; or the Rise of the Carthaginian Empire* brought the queen and the viewer down into the heart of the city. She is depicted striding alongside the shore of the natural harbor, lit from behind by a bright sun, directing the activities as new buildings rise around her. At her feet a group of children play with toy boats. Finally, in *The Decline of the Carthaginian Empire*, exhibited at the Royal Academy in 1817, Carthage itself takes center stage: the same view down what is now an artificial harbor to the sea, past a series of sumptuous buildings and idle citizens, lit from a stormy sky by the setting sun, highlights how much has changed. Between the three paintings, the sun rises and sets on a great state.[82]

The full title of the final work, is *The Decline of the Carthaginian Empire— Rome Being Determined on the Overthrow of Her Hated Rival, Demanded of Her Such Terms as Might Either Force Her into War, or Ruin Her by Compliance: The Enervated Carthaginians, in Their Anxiety for Peace, Consented to Give Up Even Their Arms and Their Children*. The reference to contemporary France, where Napoleon's regime had collapsed after the Battle of Waterloo in 1815, is inescapable and harks back to Turner's 1812 depiction of *Hannibal and His Army Crossing the Alps*, as Napoleon had done in 1800 on his way to defeat the Austrians at the Battle of Marengo.[83] But that's not all there is to it: like Scipio's tears over Carthage, Turner's reflection on the fall of France puts the focus firmly on Britain, a country exhausted by victory. The financial costs of the Napoleonic wars had been enormous, and the government now faced the equally large social problems of demobilizing a huge army. The tensions caused by hunger and unemployment led to a new strand of radical politics and to tensions that would culminate in 1819 in the "Peterloo massacre" of protestors in Manchester. And the dangers illustrated in Turner's image of the ancient city were close to home: luxury, decadence, aggrandizing architecture, but above all the water, washing up through the scene as a slow-moving, inexorable force of invasion. There are no defenses against it, no sea wall as we now know Carthage really had. It isn't Rome that destroys Turner's Carthage, it is Carthage's own success—and the sea.

Despite the problems increasingly associated with Carthage, however, the more general parallel with the Phoenicians as traders and colonists reached its peak of popularity in the nineteenth century, as the revived British Empire reached its greatest extent, fueling the Industrial Revolution.[84] Timothy Champion has discussed at length how the Phoenicians' "reputation for manufactured goods, especially metalwork and textiles, matched the role played by Birmingham and Manchester in Britain's industrial might, and their reputation as sailors paralleled England's claim to be the dominant maritime power of the century."[85] The comparison was now firmly with the English rather than the British, as contemporary nationalist ideology had come to emphasize the primitive nature of the ancient Britons (now the Irish, Scots, and Welsh) and the crucial role played by foreign immigrants in constructing a nation capable of such enormous commercial and imperial success.[86]

The switch to a comparative approach meant that Phoenicianism could now contradict the very "British" nationalism that had created it: on this new model, the Phoenicians were not the literal ancestors of the ancient Britons but the spiritual precursor of the Anglo-Saxons. For Champion, this phase of English Phoenicianism is captured by the fresco painted by Frederic Leighton in 1894–95, *Phoenicians Bartering with Ancient Britons* (fig. 9.2). On the right, four Phoenician traders in fine clothes and distinctive caps show off their sumptuous purple cloth and other luxury commodities; on the left, four young Britons admire the goods while an older man—their father?—offers an animal skin of the kind he wears himself as payment; here the Phoenicians are (like the Anglo-Saxons) "the bringers of civilisation, learning and technical skill to the mostly fur-clad Britons."[87] It is surely no coincidence that the next scene in the sequence of images of commercial history painted along the wall of London's rebuilt Royal Exchange is Frank O. Salisbury's fresco of the Anglo-Saxon King Alfred the Great repairing the walls of the City of London.[88]

This comparison of migrant, maritime peoples was also popular in the newly nationalist scholarship on the Phoenicians that I discussed in chapter 1. At the end of the nineteenth century, George Rawlinson announced in his *History of Phoenicia* that the Phoenicians were "the people who of all antiquity had most in common with England and the English" as well as "the first who discovered the British islands."[89] In France, the less flattering comparison with Carthage continued to play a large part in understandings of the English: in their 1885 volume on Phoenician and Cypriot art, Georges Perrot and Michel Chipiez discuss how the "English of Antiquity" preserved their power by means very similar to "those that England has used for the last two centuries to establish and maintain, with a handful of soldiers and thousands of ships, her vast colonial empire." They

9.2 Frederic Leighton, *Phoenicians Bartering with Ancient Britons* (1894–95),
a fresco painted for the Royal Exchange in London.

continue, however: "The difference is that Tyre never tried to conquer and
govern the peoples living in the lands whose coasts she visited"—a policy
that, they explain, Carthage would have done better to follow—and then
declare that "England has followed the policy of Tyre when circumstances
have not, as they have in India and South Africa, led her further than she
wanted to go."[90] The excellent English translation of the work published
in the same year averts its eyes here, noting simply that "England has followed the policy of Tyre wherever she could."[91]

Occasional examples of the Phoenician settlement hypothesis continue to surface even today,[92] but from the later nineteenth century, the growth of anti-Semitism helped to suppress the appetite for comparisons between the British and Phoenicians, who were increasingly associated both with the Jews and with the practice of child sacrifice highlighted in Gustave Flaubert's hugely successful 1862 novel *Salammbô*.[93] The discovery of the pre-Greek scripts of Linear A and B on Crete was one of the final nails in the coffin of nineteenth-century "Phoenicomania": no longer could the Phoenicians be celebrated as the first great literate civilization of the Iron Age Mediterranean.[94]

PHOENICIAN IRELAND

In Ireland, unlike in Britain, the Phoenicians were not an alternative to medieval legends but an addition to them. Since the medieval search for national origins among the sons of Noah began, Irish works such as the *Lebor Gabála Érenn* (*The Book of the Taking of Ireland*) of around 1100 CE had presented one of the ancestors of the Irish Gaels as Míl the Spaniard, whose ancestors originated in the eastern Mediterranean and were descended from Japheth, son of Noah. They were often associated with Scythia, and before the "discovery" of Indo-European (a model for understanding the development of languages that only became generally accepted in the nineteenth century), all Celtic languages were generally thought to have descended from Scythian.[95]

This Scythian connection was a relatively neutral one in the Irish texts, but contemporary British authors, picking up on descriptions in Greco-Roman writers of the Scythians as a primitive and rather bloodthirsty people, exploited the connection to characterize both the Scythians and the Irish as barbaric, nomadic cannibals.[96] From Gerald of Wales, writing in the twelfth century to justify Henry Plantagenet's invasion and colonization of Ireland in 1171, to the Elizabethan poet Edmund Spenser, a beneficiary of the Tudor phase of colonization or "plantation" of Ireland, British writers take delight in explaining Irish depravity as a result of their Scythian ancestry.[97]

In the seventeenth century, Irish scholars tried to counter such accusations. The Hiberno-Norman priest and poet Seathrún Céitinn (c. 1580–c. 1644), known in English as Geoffrey Keating, and whose *Foras Feasa ar Éirinn* (*Groundwork of Knowledge on Ireland*) circulated in manuscript from around 1634, treated the medieval Irish myths as a source of noble origins, noting among other things that the accomplishments of the Scythians included the introduction of letters to the Egyptians and Greeks.[98] By the late seventeenth century, an explicit notion emerged among Irish intellectuals of a Phoenician component in Irish history.

Aylett Sammes finds his Irish counterpart in Ruaidhrí Ó Flaithbheartaigh (1629–1718; in English, Roderic O'Flaherty), an Irish scholar trained in the bardic tradition whose legendary Irish history *Ogygia*, published in Latin in 1685 and translated into English in 1793, was far more influential than Sammes's book of nine years earlier.[99] The work was a reaction both to the English-language depictions of the Irish and to the ravages of the English "plantation" of the island in the sixteenth and seventeenth centuries. For Ó Flaithbheartaigh, Irish culture was not only more noble than that of Saxon Britain and Rome, it was also older: in his interpretation, the very name *Ogygia* means "very ancient."[100] Drawing on Irish legends, Greco-Roman texts, and contemporary European scholars including Samuel Bochart, who had suggested both that Phoenician was the mother-tongue of the Celtic languages of northwest Europe and that the Phoenicians had reached Ireland, Ó Flaithbheartaigh made the Phoenicians part of Ireland's ancestry, suggesting in particular that the Scythian "Fenius" (Féinus Farsaid) was in fact the "Phoinix" of Greek texts.[101]

This theory of Phoenician origins was part of broader Orientalist and Celticist enthusiasms in Ireland in the seventeenth and eighteenth centuries,[102] and although it continued to be championed by Gaelic Catholic scholars such as Tadhg Ó Neachtain,[103] it became particularly popular among the Protestant Ascendency or "Anglo-Irish" community. These Church of Ireland Anglicans were the political and, to a large extent, the economic elite in the country, as the British consolidated their conquest with Penal Laws that excluded Catholics from, among other things, voting, serving in the army, most public offices, marrying Protestants or inheriting their land, practicing law, and studying abroad or at Trinity College Dublin. Many Ascendency families had been settled in Ireland for centuries, and they often saw themselves as Irish as well as or even instead of English: national identity was, as we have seen, not in this period an exclusive idea or ideal.[104] In the eighteenth century, they won increasing political autonomy from England, but the Anglo-Irish were "caught between dependence on the English connexion and dependence on Irish property,"[105] under pressure both from the Irish, who naturally resented their gains, and the English, for whom they were partially barbarized through long contact and intermarriage with the local population.

The best-known Protestant champion of the theory of Phoenician origins was Charles Vallancey (1721–1812).[106] Vallancey was brought up in England as the son of French Huguenot parents and moved permanently to Ireland in his mid-twenties as a surveyor in the British army, rising to major and then general. A highly respected antiquarian, joint secretary of the Antiquities Committee of the Royal Dublin Society that was established in 1772, and in 1785 a founder member of the Royal Irish Academy, Vallancey used his encyclopedic knowledge of Latin, Greek, and Irish sources to write several long, erudite, and deeply confused works on the Scythian and Phoenician origins of the Irish language, customs, and people.

Building on references in the medieval Irish histories as well as comparisons of the Irish and Phoenician languages, Vallancey's basic thesis was that the Scythians had migrated to Ireland via the Phoenician cities of the Levant and their colonies, especially Carthage, whose merchants brought them and their culture to Spain and thence to both the "British Isles".[107] Vallancey's first publication on the subject in 1772, *An Essay on the Antiquity of the Irish Language*, was advertised on its title page as "being a collation of the Irish with the Punic Languages," addressed to the "literati of Europe." In it, Vallancey proceeded for the most part by analogy, arguing for the "strongest Affinity (nay a perfect Identity in very many Words)" of Gaelic (Irish) with Celtic, Punic, Phoenician, and Hebrew, noting that this relationship "will account for the Irish assuming to themselves the names of Feni or Fenicians, which they have retained through all ages."[108] Later works expanded on these themes: in 1773, his *Grammar of the Iberno-Celtic, or Irish Language* informed the reader that ancient Irish "had such an affinity with the Punic, that it may be said to have been, in great degree, the language of Hannibal, Hamilcar, and of Asdrubal,"[109] and there is also much in his 1786 *Vindication of the Ancient History of Ireland* on linguistic parallels with Phoenician as well as on common customs and cultural survivals.[110]

Vallancey's Phoenicianism was part of a more general romantic Orientalism, in which the Irish also had important, perhaps even more important, connections with the Persians.[111] Indeed, he did not clearly distinguish the two ancient peoples: the Irish round towers, for instance, are described at some points as of Phoenician construction, at others Persian.[112] At the same time, he used the Phoenician hypothesis to reflect on the phenomenon of distinct national consciousness in a pluralistic context: the Scythians, he says, were absorbed into the Phoenicians when they traveled to the Levant, but they kept among themselves awareness of being sons of Japheth.[113]

Vallancey describes himself in the preface to his 1772 essay as "an Irishman,"[114] and he makes it clear that he is elaborating on older Irish histories and collaborating with Irish intellectuals:

> The positive assertions of all the Irish historians, that their ancestors received the use of letters directly from the Phoenicians, and the concurrence of them all in affirming that several colonies from Africa settled in Ireland, induced the author of the following Essay . . . to compare the Phoenician dialect or *bearla Feni* of the Irish with the Punic or language of the Carthaginians. The affinity of the language, worship, and manners of the Carthaginians, with those of the ancient Irish appeared so very strong, he communicated his discoveries from time to time to some gentlemen well skilled in the antiquities of Ireland, and of the eastern nations; their approbation of this rude sketch induced the author to offer it to the consideration of those who have greater abilities and more leisure to prosecute such a work.[115]

He found support for his theories not only from other Ascendency antiquaries, but also from eighteenth-century Irish intellectuals like Charles O'Conor and Sylvester O'Halloran, both members of the Royal Irish Academy, who often offered their Anglo-Irish colleagues very practical help with the language and customs of their country.[116] One of the political attractions of the model for Irish nationalists of all kinds was that it rejected linguistic theories that made Celtic a subgroup of the Teutonic languages, including Anglo-Saxon, advancing instead a more direct route back to the "original" language of Scythian via the Phoenicians.[117]

Vallancey makes a direct parallel in *An Essay on the Antiquity of the Irish Language* between the Carthaginian and Irish experience, pointing out that the Carthaginians' history was similarly "written by their most bitter Enemies, the Greeks and Romans; in this too they resemble the Irish."[118] His theories can also be read against the British, who were at the very same time comparing themselves favorably with the Carthaginians against the "Roman" French.[119] True separatist republicanism was a nineteenth-century phenomenon in Ireland, however, and as with many of his Ascendency peers, Vallancey's nationalism was multiple and complex. He may have been devoted to Irish culture and history, but his *Vindication* is dedicated to the king, and the English are directly criticized only for their misunderstanding of the ancient relationship between the two islands. Like Sammes, and Bochart, Vallancey's model gives the two islands a joint history before the Roman or Anglo-Saxon invasions of England, a vision of common origins that suggests an attachment to an overarching national relationship between the two islands.

Phoenicianism became extremely popular in Ireland in the last two decades of the eighteenth century as, inspired in part by the American Revolution, the patriot movement pushed with some temporary success for the reform of the Penal Laws, free trade, and Irish self-government under the British crown. Some contemporary approaches are straightforwardly oppositional, or at least isolationist: the Irish politician Lawrence Parsons, second Earl of Rosse, wrote a *Defence of the Antient History of Ireland* (1795) in which he argued that "the Irish were a Phoenician colony," largely again on linguistic grounds.[120] Taking a lead from Vallancey, he relied heavily on Plautus's reproduction of "Carthaginian" speech: "Now it is universally admitted, that the Carthaginians originally came from Phoenicia, and spoke the Phoenician language. And a specimen of that language has been preserved by Plautus in one of his plays, which contains some speeches of Hanno, a Carthaginian, in the language of his country. And these speeches appear upon examination to be evidently and undeniably the same language with the Irish."[121]

According to Parsons, the Irish and Carthaginian languages are so similar that the former must have been descended from the latter, or vice versa, or both peoples came from the same country.[122] He also argues that it is lead rather than tin that is implied by the name of the Cassiterides islands mentioned in classical texts, and that the Phoenicians must therefore have been responsible for the lead mines in Ireland, and must therefore have established a colony there "many ages before Herodotus."[123] For him, the Phoenician relationship with the North Atlantic islands starts and ends with Ireland, and Britain is barely involved: the Phoenicians "were sooner and better acquainted with Ireland than with England." Indeed, their only real knowledge of England came from their contact with the Irish, from whom they learned the name "Albion" for the whole island of Britain, which they then passed on to the Greeks, including Aristotle, but which in fact referred properly only to Scotland ("Albin"), the region that had been colonized by the Irish.[124]

Other Anglo-Irish authors embraced the Phoenician hypothesis as offering a useful middle way between the English and the Irish. One of the most interesting exponents of this approach is Charlotte Brooke (c. 1750–93), probably the only survivor of the twenty-two children of the Anglo-Irish novelist and playwright Henry Brooke. Miss Brooke was an enthusiastic Gaelic scholar who published a translation in 1789 of *Reliques of Irish Poetry* accompanied by extensive notes explaining, among other things, the "Phoenician origin" of the Irish: "The Irish in general were frequently called *Fenians*, or *Phenians*, from their great ancestor *Phenius Farsa*, or, perhaps, in allusion to their Phoenician descent."[125] Like Vallancey, Brooke focuses less on criticism than communication, explaining her motivations in her preface: "As yet, we are too little known to our noble neighbour of Britain; were we better acquainted, we should be better friends."[126]

A later example is Sydney Owenson, later Lady Morgan, an author of mixed English and Irish parentage who identified as Irish, Catholic, and a political radical. Her epistolary novel *The Wild Irish Girl: A National Tale*, published in 1806, recounts the romance between an Irish princess and a disguised English aristocrat against the background of dispossessions of Irish land and the Penal Laws. The princess's family teaches the young Englishman about their "nation" and their "national, natural character," and Ireland's Phoenician origins are a recurring theme both in the story and in Owenson's long and learned footnotes, which contain multiple references to Vallancey, Brooke, and other antiquarian scholars.[127] As in Vallancey's account, the Phoenicians here are one among many Irish roots, including the Greeks and Persians.[128]

Owenson had difficulty in publishing her novel, as it was seen as being "opposed to the English interest in Ireland,"[129] although its conclusion is no vindication of Irish autonomy, but rather a marriage between the princess and her lover: Ireland is still the handmaiden of its now more enlightened English lord. As the hero's English father writes, "let . . . the distinctions of English and Irish, of protestant and catholic, [be] for ever buried. And, while you look forward with hope to this family alliance being prophetically typical of a national unity of interests and affections between those who may be factiously severe, but who are naturally allied, lend your *own individual efforts* towards the consummation of an event so devoutly to be wished by every liberal mind, by every benevolent heart."[130] Her hero himself explicitly divorces nationalism from politics: speaking of the Irish "lower orders," he says to a priest, "I am convinced that were endeavours for their improvement more strictly promoted . . . they would be a people as happy, contented, and prosperous, in a political sense, as in a natural and national one."[131]

Owenson was one of the last passionate exponents of Irish Phoenicianism, which barely survived into the nineteenth century after the Patriotic movement came to an abrupt end with the failure of the 1798 rebellion against England led by the more radical United Irishmen. The subsequent Act of Union in 1800 formally created the United Kingdom of Great Britain and Ireland, after which the nationalists were in retreat.[132] It is striking that Owenson's novel is set in the eighteenth century, and her formulation of the "nation" is very much an early modern, inclusive one. A little more than a decade later, Lord Byron pokes fun at the tradition in his description of Don Juan:

> He was what Erin calls, in her sublime
>> Old Erse or Irish, or it may be *Punic*
> (The antiquarians who can settle Time,
>> Which settles all things, Roman, Greek or Runic,
> Swear that Pat's language sprung from the same clime
>> With Hannibal, and wears the Tyrian tunic
> Of Dido's alphabet; and this is rational
>> As any other notion, and not national);—
> But Juan was quite "a broth of a boy,"
>> A thing of impulse and a child of song;[133]

This is accompanied by a note: "See Major Vallancey and Sir Lawrence Parsons." Interest in the Phoenicians continued to wane, and although as late as 1922, Robert Dunlop's *History of Ireland: From the Earliest Times to the Present Day*, published by Oxford University Press, begins with the "discovery" of Ireland by the Phoenicians, he makes it clear that they only established small factories to exploit the natural resources, rather than engaging in a major program of colonization in Ireland, and that "the basic element of its population" was still (in 1922) the "small, dark-haired, and rather long-headed race" called the Ernai, whom the Phoenicians encountered when they arrived.[134] In any case, Dunlop reassures his readers that the Phoenicians "were not, as is generally supposed, a Semitic people. They formed part of a group of peoples, whose centre of civilization was the island of Crete."[135]

The Phoenicians helped British and Irish intellectuals formulate ideas about their own nations and about the nation itself: references to the Phoenician past bolstered a variety of ethnic and political claims in the present, clarified national rivalries, and allowed scholars to negotiate imperialism from above and below. Tudor and Stuart Britain could be characterized as a Phoenician colony against the idea of an Anglo-Saxon England, before eighteenth-century English writers established a cultural comparison with the Phoenicians against the Roman French. At the same time, Irish intellectuals were adopting the idea of Phoenician descent and a parallel with Carthage to combat the British stereotype that they were backward and primitive, as well as to highlight more brutal aspects of British imperialism. As in the Roman period, these Phoenicians were used to play imperial games; their appearance served other places and other sources of power; and their description had more to do with contemporary politics and empire than ancient ethnicity. Once again, we see that far from being spontaneous and liberating popular inventions, identities are often created by and for the benefit of the wealthy and the powerful.

In these stories, however, the Phoenicians are never presented as an exclusive ancestor or universal parallel. Other peoples lie below the contemporary populations of the islands, and the comparison works only in relation to particular military and commercial fields of interest. Nor are the Phoenicians themselves characterized as a full ethnocultural nation of the kind whose emergence I traced in chapter 1. In the language used and the importance attached to the association, however, the authors I have surveyed in this chapter set the stage for the nineteenth-century scholarship that made a modern nation out of the ancient Phoenicians, as well as for the twentieth-century adoption of them as more exclusive forerunners and forebears for modern nation-states. The modern Phoenicians of Lebanon and Tunisia with whom I began can now take their place in a long tradition, as a further stage in the story of the construction of the Phoenician people.

CONCLUSION

In all the exciting work that has been done on "identity" in the past few decades, there has been too little attention paid to the concept of identity itself. We tend to ask how identities are made, vary, and change, not whether they exist at all. But Rogers Brubaker and Frederik Cooper have pinned down a central difficulty with recent approaches: "it is not clear why what is routinely characterized as multiple, fragmented, and fluid should be conceptualized as 'identity' at all."[1] Even personal identity, a strong sense of one's self as a distinct individual, can be seen as a relatively recent development, perhaps related to a peculiarly Western individualism.[2] Collective identities, furthermore, are fundamentally arbitrary: the artificial ways we choose to organize the world, ourselves, and each other. However strong the attachments they provoke, they are not universal or natural facts. Roger Rouse has pointed out that in medieval Europe, the idea that people fall into abstract social groupings by virtue of common possession of a certain attribute, and occupy autonomous and theoretically equal positions within them, would have seemed nonsensical: instead, people were assigned their different places in the interdependent relationships of a concrete hierarchy.[3]

The truth is that although historians are constantly apprehending the dead and checking their pockets for identity, we do not know how people really thought of themselves in the past, or in how many different ways, or indeed how much. I have argued here that the case of the Phoenicians highlights the extent to which the traditional scholarly perception of a basic sense of collective identity at the level of a "people," "culture," or "nation" in the cosmopolitan, entangled world of the ancient Mediterranean has been distorted by the traditional scholarly focus on a small number of rather unusual, and unusually literate, societies.

My starting point was that we have no good evidence for the ancient people that we call Phoenician identifying themselves as a single people or acting as a stable collective. I do not conclude from this absence of evidence that the Phoenicians did not exist, nor that nobody ever called her- or himself a Phoenician under any circumstances: Phoenician-speakers undoubtedly had a larger repertoire of self-classifications than survives in our fragmentary evidence, and it would be surprising if, for instance, they never described themselves as Phoenicians to the Greeks who invented that term; indeed, I have drawn attention to several cases where something very close to that is going on. Instead, my argument is that we should not assume that our "Phoenicians" thought of themselves as a group simply by analogy with models of contemporary identity formation among their neighbors—especially since those neighbors do not themselves portray the Phoenicians as a self-conscious or strongly differentiated collective. Instead, we should accept the gaps in our knowledge and fill the space instead with the stories that we can tell.

The stories I have looked at in this book include the ways that the people of the northern Levant did in fact identify themselves—in terms of their cities, but even more of their families and occupations—as well as the formation of complex social, cultural, and economic networks based on particular cities, empires, and ideas. These could be relatively small and closed, like the circle of the tophet, or on the other hand, they could, like the network of Melqart, create shared religious and political connections throughout the Mediterranean—with other Levantine settlements, with other settlers, and with local populations. Identifications with a variety of social and cultural traditions is one recurrent characteristic of the people and cities we call Phoenician, and this continued into the Hellenistic and Roman periods, when "being Phoenician" was deployed as a political and cultural tool, although it was still not claimed as an ethnic identity.

Another story could go further, to read a lack of collective identity, culture, and political organization among Phoenician-speakers as a positive choice, a form of resistance against larger regional powers. James C. Scott has recently argued in *The Art of Not Being Governed* (2009) that self-governing people living on the peripheries and borders of expansionary states in that region tend to adopt strategies to avoid incorporation and to minimize taxation, conscription, and forced labor. Scott's focus is on the highlands of Southeast Asia, an area now sometimes known as Zomia, and its relationship with the great plains states of the region such as China and Burma. He describes a series of tactics used by the hill people to avoid state power, including "their physical dispersion in rugged terrain, their mobility, their cropping practices, their kinship structure, their pliable ethnic identities . . . their flexible social structure, their religious heterodoxy, their egalitarianism and even the nonliterate, oral cultures." The constant reconstruction of identity is a core theme in his work: "ethnic identities in the hills are politically crafted and designed to position a group vis-à-vis others in competition for power and resources."[4] Political integration in Zomia, when it has happened at all, has usually consisted of small confederations: such alliances, he points out, are common but short-lived, and are often preserved in local place names such as "Twelve Tai Lords" (Sipsong Chutai) or "Nine Towns" (Ko Myo)—information that throws new light on the federal meetings recorded in fourth-century BCE Tripolis ("Three Cities").[5]

In fact, many aspects of Scott's analysis feel familiar in the world of the ancient Mediterranean, on the periphery of the great agricultural empires of Mesopotamia and Iran, and despite all its differences from Zomia, another potential candidate for the label of "shatterzone." The validity of Scott's model for upland Southeast Asia itself —a matter of considerable debate since the book's publication—is largely irrelevant for our purposes;[6] what is interesting here is how useful it might be for thinking about the mountainous region of the northern Levant, and the places of refuge in and around the Mediterranean.

In addition to outright rebellion, we could argue that the inhabitants of the Levant employed a variety of strategies to evade the heaviest excesses of imperial power.[7] One was to organize themselves in small city-states with flimsy political links and weak hierarchies, requiring larger powers to engage in multiple negotiations and arrangements, and providing the communities involved with multiple small and therefore obscure opportunities for the evasion of taxation and other responsibilities—"divide that ye be not ruled," as Scott puts it.[8] A cosmopolitan approach to culture and language in those cities would complement such an approach, committing to no particular way of doing or being or even looking, keeping loyalties vague and options open. One of the more controversial aspects of Scott's model could even explain why there is no evidence for Phoenician literature despite earlier Near Eastern traditions of myth and epic. He argues that the populations he studies are in some cases not so much nonliterate as postliterate: "Given the considerable advantages in plasticity of oral over written histories and genealogies, it is at least conceivable to see the loss of literacy and of written texts as a more or less deliberate adaptation to statelessness."[9]

Another available option was to take to the sea, a familiar but forbidding terrain where the experience and knowledge of Levantine sailors could make them and their activities invisible and unaccountable to their overlords further east. The sea also offered an escape route from more local sources of power, and the stories we hear of the informal origins of western settlements such as Carthage and Lepcis, whether or not they are true, suggest an appreciation of this point. A distaste even for self-government could also explain a phenomenon I have drawn attention to throughout the book: our "Phoenicians" not only fail to visibly identify as Phoenician, they often omit to identify at all.

It is striking in this light that the first surviving visible expression of an explicitly "Phoenician" identity was imposed by the Carthaginians on their subjects as they extended state power to a degree unprecedented among Phoenician-speakers, that it was then adopted by Tyre as a symbol of colonial success, and that it was subsequently exploited by Roman rulers in support of their imperial activities. This illustrates another uncomfortable aspect of identity formation: it is often a cultural bullying tactic, and one that tends to benefit those already in power more than those seeking self-empowerment. Modern European examples range from the linguistic and cultural education strategies that turned "peasants into Frenchmen" in the late nineteenth century,[10] to the eugenic *Lebensborn* program initiated by the Nazis in mid-twentieth-century central Europe to create more Aryan children through procreation between German SS officers and "racially pure" foreign women.[11] Such examples also underline the difficulty of distinguishing between internal and external conceptions of identity when apparently internal identities are encouraged from above, or even from outside, just as the developing modern identity as Phoenician involved the gradual solidification of the identity of the ancient Phoenicians.

It seems to me that attempts to establish a clear distinction between "emic" and "etic" identity are part of a wider tendency to treat identities as ends rather than means, and to focus more on how they are constructed than on why. Identity claims are always, however, a means to another end, and being "Phoenician" is in all the instances I have surveyed here a political rather than a personal statement. It is sometimes used to resist states and empires, from Roman Africa to Hugh O'Donnell's Ireland, but more often to consolidate them, lending ancient prestige and authority to later regimes, a strategy we can see in Carthage's Phoenician coinage, the emperor Elagabalus's installation of a Phoenician sun god at Rome, British appeals to Phoenician maritime power, and Hannibal Qadhafi's cruise ship.

In the end, it is modern nationalism that has created the Phoenicians, along with much else of our modern idea of the ancient Mediterranean. Phoenicianism has served nationalist purposes since the early modern period: the fully developed notion of Phoenician ethnicity may be a nineteenth-century invention, a product of ideologies that sought to establish ancient peoples or "nations" at the heart of new nation-states, but its roots, like those of nationalism itself, are deeper. As origin myth or cultural comparison, aggregative or oppositional, imperialist and anti-imperialist, Phoenicianism supported the expansion of the early modern nation of Britain, as well as the position of the nation of Ireland as separate and respected within that empire; it helped to consolidate the nation of Lebanon under French imperial mandate, premised on a regional Phoenician identity agreed on between local and French intellectuals, but it also helped to construct the nation of Tunisia in opposition to European colonialism.

I will, however, leave the final words to a group of writers who used the Phoenicians to question nationalism rather than to reinforce it, and who will take us back to where we started, in Ireland.

POST-NATIONAL PHOENICIANS

In 1907, the young James Joyce made surprisingly late reference to the Phoenicianist tradition in a lecture he gave in Trieste titled "Ireland, Island of Saints and Sages," and he tied it explicitly to thinking about the nation.[12] He began: "Nations, like individuals, have their egos. It is not unusual for a race to wish to attribute to itself qualities and glories unknown in other races—from the time when our forefathers called themselves Aryans and nobles to the Greeks who were wont to call anyone barbarian that did not live within the sacrosanct land of Hellas. The Irish, with a pride that is perhaps less explicable, love to refer to their land as the island of saints and sages [*santi e savi*]."[13] This is a twist on the standard Latin tag *insula sanctorum et doctorum*, "island of saints and scholars," which was normally used in Ireland to refer to the medieval monastic tradition.[14] Joyce's saints are the usual suspects, including of course St. Patrick, who introduced Catholicism to Ireland. But some at least of his sages are from a quite different, and much earlier, tradition. The Irish language, he tells his audience,

> is eastern in origin, and has been identified by many philologists with the ancient language of the Phoenicians, the discoverers, according to historians, of commerce and navigation. With their monopoly over the sea, this adventurous people established a civilization in Ireland which was in decline and had almost disappeared before the first Greek historian took up his quill. . . . The language that the comic dramatist Plautus puts in the mouth of the Phoenicians in his comedy *Poenula* [*sic*] is virtually the same language, according to the critic Vallancey, as that which Irish peasants now speak. The religion and civilization of that ancient people, later known as Druidism, were Egyptian.[15]

Joyce uses the now outmoded Phoenician theory of Irish origins in a knowing way, not only distancing himself from the hypothesis by attributing it to other scholars, but also exploiting the countertradition that associated the Phoenicians with the British in a later reference to the "Punic faith of the English" in breaking Irish treaties.[16] He explicitly describes himself as a "detached observer" rather than a "convinced nationalist,"[17] and in his hands the Phoenician theory is not the basis for straightforward Irish nationalism either in opposition to the English or in co-operation with them. The English treatment of Ireland over the centuries of occupation comes in for a great deal of criticism in the lecture, but Joyce criticizes the Irish at least as much, and not only for their reactions to British conquest: there is a nice jibe at the native kings who allowed the Danes to conquer much of the island as they "were busy killing one another at the time, occasionally taking a well-earned break for games of chess."[18]

Joyce uses the Phoenicians instead to undermine crude nationalist rhetoric. The version of the story Joyce tells his audience not only credits Irish language and culture to outsiders, but makes that "Phoenician" civilization itself "Egyptian," discrediting claims to Celtic purity and allowing him to celebrate Ireland as a land of many origins:

> Our civilization is an immense woven fabric in which very different elements are mixed, in which Nordic rapacity is reconciled to the Roman law, and new Bourgeois conventions to the remains of a Siriac religion. In such a fabric, it is pointless searching for a thread that has remained pure, virgin and uninfluenced by other threads nearby. What race or language (if we except those few which a humorous will seems to have preserved, such as the people of Iceland) can nowadays claim to be pure? No race has less right to make such a boast than the one presently inhabiting Ireland. Nationality (if this is not really a useful fiction like many others which the scalpels of the present-day scientists have put paid to) must find its basic reason for being in something that surpasses, that transcends and that informs changeable entities such as blood or human speech.[19]

Although the history of ancient Ireland can support an Irish claim to an earlier and greater civilization than that of its Saxon masters, he himself does not believe in making political capital out of such history: "Neither do I see the use in bitter invectives against England, the despoiler, or in contempt for the vast Anglo-Saxon civilization—even though it is almost entirely a materialistic civilization. . . . Just as ancient Egypt is dead, so is ancient Ireland. Its dirge has been sung and the seal set upon its gravestone."[20]

Nationalism is not, for Joyce, the island's only problem: "Ireland prides itself on being in body and soul as faithful to her national traditions as to the Holy See. The majority of Irishmen consider loyalty to these two traditions as their cardinal article of faith."[21] And he applies the traditional contrast between Phoenicians and Romans not to politics but to religion, and in particular the "coherent absurdity that is Catholicism."[22] According to the story of Ireland's origins that he tells, the Phoenicians brought druids to Ireland long before St. Patrick brought Christianity, and Patrick himself found an island already "sacred" through the Phoenicians;[23] and their rivals the Romans are equated by Joyce explicitly not with the English, but with the Church: "I confess that I do not see what good it does to fulminate against English tyranny while the tyranny of Rome still holds the dwelling place of the soul."[24]

In 1922, Joyce found another use for the Phoenicians in his novel *Ulysses*, where he tacitly draws on the French scholar Victor Bérard's theory that the hero of Homer's *Odyssey* was a Phoenician to create a suitably Semitic avatar for his Jewish Irish hero Leopold Bloom. Bloom's own ethnic identity in the novel is, as Elizabeth Cullingford notes, "uncertain," and he "embodies (among many other things) Joyce's affirmation of cultural hybridity."[25] Once again, simple Irish nationalism is trumped by a clear-eyed exploration of the complications and possibilities of unfixed origins and multiple loyalties. It was also in 1922, however, that the Irish Free State was established in the south by the Anglo-Irish treaty, limiting the political and cultural potency of the old Phoenician hypothesis for several decades, until the start of the Troubles.

In August 1969, forty-seven years after the south of Ireland had achieved independence from Britain, tensions in the north between republicans and unionists culminated in the days of rioting in Derry known as the Battle of the Bogside, which ended only with the arrival of British troops on the streets of Derry and Belfast. There they would stay for almost forty years, and that summer, as Seamus Heaney later put it, "the problems of poetry moved from being simply a matter of achieving the satisfactory verbal icon to being a search for images and symbols adequate to our predicament."[26]

Hugh O'Donnell's speech with which this book began is by no means the only example of the old association between the Irish and the Phoenicians being redeployed by poets and playwrights working in the north of Ireland in the 1970s and 1980s.[27] Heaney's own poem "Bog Queen" (1975) was inspired by a long-buried female corpse found on the Moira estate in County Lisburn in 1781, and sold to Lady Moira.[28] In the poem, the dead woman describes her own gradual disintegration and decay:

> My sash was a black glacier
> wrinkling, dyed weaves
> and phoenician stitch work
> retted on my breasts'
> soft moraines. (29–33)

When her body is discovered by a peat-cutter, he is bribed by "a peer's wife" to dig her up,

> and I rose from the dark,
> hacked bone, skull-ware,
> frayed stitches, tufts,
> small gleams on the bank. (53–56)[29]

Like Carthage in Hugh's reading of the *Aeneid*, the Queen's Phoenician handiwork links her land with a more civilized heritage than that of its current occupiers, and the context of her excavation connects her with the old tradition of identification with the Phoenicians against the military might of "Roman" Britain.

In the political context of the Troubles, however, this triple historical perspective of the present, the ancient past, and the eighteenth century provides an appropriate complexity. This is a world in which there are no easy answers. Although Heaney evokes an arresting image of Ireland as a woman defeated and desecrated by a brutal invasion, he uses gender in his poem not to consolidate a simple binary opposition between Ireland and England, weak and strong, right and wrong, but to undermine it: while his queen can be read as the female spirit of Ireland, she is voiced by a man, and desecrated by the English in the person of a woman, and through the agency of an Irishman. At the same time, Phoenicianism itself can be presented as partial and contingent: Friel's schoolmaster is a great devotee of the languages of Greece and Rome as well as an ally of Carthage, but more loyal to his own threatened community than to any flag. These texts are not just postcolonial, but, like Joyce's Phoenician games, post-national.

The intricacy and power of the Phoenician analogy in late-twentieth-century Ireland is most vivid in Frank McGuinness's *Carthaginians*, first performed in Dublin in 1988. The play, set in a Derry graveyard in the present day, opens with the music from Purcell's *Dido and Aeneas*, and plays throughout with an association between Carthage and Derry. As the characters await the resurrection of the dead, they reflect on the city in which they live and look back on the events and repercussions of Bloody Sunday, January 30, 1972, in which twenty-six civilians were shot by the British army. Derry and Carthage are both cities destroyed by Rome, says Paul, a teacher—where Rome recalls not only the British Empire but also the Catholic south and the Roman Church. "I am Carthaginian," says Paul. "This earth is mine, not Britain's, nor Rome's."[30] The play ends with "Dido, queen of Derry," a gay man who was given his nickname by a Lebanese sailor and whose "ambition in life is to corrupt every member of her majesty's forces serving in Northern Ireland,"[31] delivering a monologue over his sleeping companions: "While I walk the earth, I walk through you, the streets of Derry. If I meet one who knows you and they ask, 'How's Dido?' Surviving. How's Derry? Surviving. Surviving. Carthage has not been destroyed."[32]

NOTES

INTRODUCTION

1. *Translations* was the inaugural production of the hugely successful Field Day Theatre Company, formed by Friel and Stephen Rea to apply for grants to produce the play (Carty 2000, 141). On the play's postcolonial context, see Gleitman (1997, 235–36); McGrath (1999, 177–97); Bertha (2006, esp. 158–60); Hinds (2011, 79–83); and Honig (2016, esp. 330n39) on the successful Townlands Campaign, which united the Catholic and Protestant communities in the 1970s against British attempts to remove the Irish townland name from Northern Irish addresses.

2. Friel (1981, 68).

3. Friel himself commented on this: "The sad irony, of course, is that the whole play is written in English. It ought to be written in Irish!" (Carty 2000, 140). The Irish characters speak in a distinctively Irish English dialect, a phenomenon explored by Worthen (1995, 146–48), although Hugh's translation of the *Aeneid* is an adaptation of the 1916 translation for the Loeb Classical Library facing-text series by Henry Rushton Fairclough, a Canadian.

4. Friel (1981, 67).

5. Although the word has its own complicated and often problematic ideological history, I use the term "Levant" in this book as a familiar and usefully vague term for the region of western Asia made up by the modern countries of Syria, Lebanon, and Israel. This includes but is not limited to the area referred to in ancient sources as "Phoenicia."

6. Polyb. 18.35.9.

7. Gellner (1964, 168).

8. On the political and academic enthusiasm for "identity" from the mid-twentieth century, see Rouse (1995, 356–57); Brubaker and Cooper (2000, 2–4, 28–29).

9. See Lucy (2005, 98).

10. For a passionate account of the importance of the multiplicity of identity, see Sen (2006).

11. Foucault (1977; 1978–86; 1980) and Butler (1993; 1999; 2004) are classic sources for the argument that individual identity is not a natural and permanent fact but rather a shifting and temporary effect of actions and interactions.

12. Jonathan Hall has noted that although studies in social psychology suggest that most people have a basic instinct to act as a member of a group, there is "nothing that entitles us to regard all such behaviour as ethnic in nature" (2002, 11); see also Shennan (1989, 11–12). Rogers Brubaker (2002) has made a powerful argument against even the assumption of "groupism," preferring to use "categories" as the basis of analysis. For a summary of the debate over whether the adoption of an ethnic identity is natural or arbitrary, see Ruby (2006, 34–35), with earlier bibliography.

13. Renfrew (1987, 287–88).

14. Brubaker and Cooper (2000, 21–27) discuss the non-ethnic nature of much collective behavior and even conflict in modern Africa and eastern Europe.

15. Ranger (1983, 247–52) summarizes an already large body of scholarship; see also in particular Amselle (1998) and (Scott 2009, 208–9, 256–65), making the point that states fashion tribes as "a coherent object of description and analysis" (209). Eriksen (2010, 13–14) has an interesting discussion of the shift in scholary terminology from the discussion of "tribes," implying a sharp sense of difference between the people writing and the people they are writing about, to "ethnic groups," which emphasizes the cross-cultural similarities of social organization.

16. Remotti (1996, 22); Facci (2009), also noting that the name "Banande" may have originally been given to a group of *bayira* by Zanzibari slave-traders.

17. Remotti (1996, 25). The Tonga may have been the inspiration for Garrison Keillor's *New Yorker* sketch on "Oya Life These Days," which imagines the problems of having neighbors whose name means simply "The Us," and who consider everyone else part of their group as well, and therefore make frequent house calls on their neighbors, often overstaying their welcome (Keillor [1975], with thanks to Greg Woolf for the reference).

18. Vail (1989); cf. Kuper (2005, 203–18) on the more recent phenomenon of indigenous rights movements and the role played within them by descent claims.

19. Scott (2009, 121); Brubaker and Cooper (2000, 25–26).

20. Remotti (1996, 54–56), with Mamdani (2002, 41–102), who also discusses the debated question of the real historical and geographical origin(s) of the two groups encountered by the Belgians and documents the evidence for many generations of intermarriage between them.

21. Mamdani (2002, 98–99) for a useful discussion.

22. Gilroy (1993, 3 and passim).

23. Shennan (1989, 15–17, with earlier bibliography); Rouse (1995, 366–70); Hall (1997, 26–32); Lucy (2005); Eriksen (2010, 80–83, 95–116); cf. Jones (1997, 110).

24. Scott (2009, 25).

25. Malkin (1998, 55–61; 2001b, 15–19); Hall (2002, 9–19); Ruby (2006); Faust (2010); Cifani (2012, 144–46).

26. Moabites: Joffe (2002); Israelites: Faust (2006); Greeks: Hall (1997; 2002); Malkin (1998; 2001a; 2011, quotation at 206); with Ruby (2006) for a critical review of these positions. This is, of course, a tiny selection of the bibliography on these topics.

27. See, e.g., Hall (2002, 168–228). Note that the extent of oppositionalism in the fifth century is contested; see, e.g., M. Miller (1997).

28. D. Thompson (2001, 310–11).

29. Mac Sweeney (2009); Osborne (2012b).

30. Lucy (2005, 98–101).

31. Osborne (2012b).

32. Gruen (2013); with Cifani (2012, 147–148), on the role of "osmosis"; and Conant (2012, 4), both with earlier bibliography.

33. Atlantic Celts: Chapman (1992); James (1999); Collis (2003). Minoans: Papadopoulos (2005).

34. Martin (2017, 38).

35. The "Continental" Celts, who are discussed by ancient authors, might provide an interesting parallel.

36. E.g., Baurain (1986); Pastor Borgoñon (1992); Xella (1995; 2008; 2014); Bonnet (2004; 2009, 296–97); Prag (2006); Sommer (2010); van Dongen (2010); Ferrer Albelda

(2012, 70–71); Vella (2014). In a different register, Tzoroddu (2010) is an idiosyncratic critique of later twentieth-century definitions of "the Phoenicians" and of the standard claim that they settled in Sardinia.

37. Quinn (2010; 2011a; 2013b); Xella et al. (2013); Quinn et al. (2014); Quinn and Vella (2014a); McCarty and Quinn (2015).

CHAPTER 1. THERE ARE NO CAMELS IN LEBANON

1. Joumblatt (1997, 99); I thank Eugene Rogan for advice on my translation. Joumblatt's views evolved into a more straightforward Arab nationalism after the first civil war in 1958: Hazran (2014, 242–47).

2. Kaufman (2004a, 39–48). The major recent work on Lebanese Phoenicianism is Kaufman (2004a), along with Kaufman (2001; 2004b; 2008) and Salameh (2010). There are shorter summaries at Salibi (1988, 170–75) and Morstadt (2015, 25–28).

3. On this passage, see Kaufman (2004a, 39) and Salameh (2010, 78–79); on this author and his work more generally, Salibi (1959, 161–233).

4. Kaufman (2004a, 61–79). "Phoenician Clubs" still exist in the United States from Birmingham and Charlotte to Chicago and Des Moines, affiliated with regional federations of Syrian-Lebanese Clubs.

5. Kaufman (2001, 188). The tradition continues in publications like the management handbook *Negotiate like a Phoenician: Discover Tradeables* (Chamoun-Nicolás 2007).

6. Kaufman (2001, 177, 190).

7. See in particular Kaufman (2004a, 31–33) on Henri Lammens.

8. Kaufman (2004a, 152–53, 222) and for the slogan, Salameh (2010, 63).

9. Joseph (2004, 194–223); Płonka (2006); Salameh (2010, 161–258).

10. Hitti (1957, 154).

11. On the history of Lebanism, see Salameh (2010, 41–73).

12. Kaufman (2001, 185).

13. Kaufman (2001, 188).

14. ". . . ils adoraient tous une Divinité supérieure à laquelle ils sacrificaient des victims humaines" (1). I will return to human sacrifice in part 2.

15. "Abibaal eut réalisé l'unité politique de la Phénicie" (20, with more on his reign on 19). For brief references to the death of Abibaal, see Joseph., *Ap.* 1.113 and 117.

16. ". . . nous voulons . . . cette nation parce qu'elle a toujours eu la priorité dans toutes les pages de notre histoire" (54).

17. For Mediterranean-centred, anti-Arab sentiments among Egyptian Pharaonists, particularly in the work of Taha Husayn, see Salameh (2010, 22–31). On Canaanism, see Shavit (1984; 1987; 1988, 106–12); Wistrich and Ohana (1995); Ohana (2012, 73–100).

18. See Kaufman (2004a, 215–20) on the ideology of Antun Saadeh.

19. Garnand (2001, 48–49); Kaufman (2004a, 197–209; 2004b, 18–19). The relevant passages are Herodotus 1.1 and 7.89, discussed in chapter 3.

20. Kaufman (2004a, 71). Cf. Salibi (1988, 20); Salameh (2010, 7). See also Armstrong (1982, 12): "The territorial principle, slow to emerge, ultimately became the predominant form [of principle on which identity is based] in Europe; the geneaological or pseudo-genealogical principle has continued to prevail in most of the Middle East."

21. Hirschi (2012, 6).

22. Hobsbawm (1997, 270); cf. B. Anderson (1991, 6, 11–12). For the challenges that face modern attempts to construct forms of affect attached to states and other polities rather than nations (so-called constitutional patriotism), see Markell (2000).

23. Kaufman (2001, 173).

24. Scott (2009, 35).

25. Renan (1947, 1:903–4): "Une nation est une âme, un principe spirituel. Deux choses qui, à vrai dire, n'en font qu'une, constituent cette âme, ce principe spirituel. L'une est dans le passé, l'autre dans le present. L'une est la possession en commun d'un riche legs de souvenirs; l'autre est le consentement actuel, le désir de vivre ensemble, la volonté de continuer à faire valoir l'héritage qu'on a reçu indivis."

26. Renan (1947, 1:892): "l'essence d'une nation est que tous les individus aient beaucoup des choses en commun, et aussi que tous aient oublié bien des choses." Renan was referring in particular to the St. Bartholemew's Day massacre in 1572, in which French Catholics slaughtered French Protestants.

27. ". . . la conception de Renan . . . qui ne veut pas envisager la formation d'une nation que dans la volonté des habitants d'être cette nation"; "le principe de libanisme réside dans l'exaltation d'un passé glorieux [et] dans celle d'une toute abstract volonté de cohésion" (*Le Jour*, April 24, 1935, quoted with discussion at Kaufman [2004a, 161–63].)

28. In 1926, the entity was renamed the "Lebanese Republic."

29. Garnand (2001, 57).

30. Traboulsi (2007, 92); Salameh (2010, 54).

31. Cf. Chiha (1964, 152), and see Kaufman (2001, 183–84; 2004b, 6–8). On Berard, see Bernal (1987, 377–82). The third dedicatee was Elias Hoyek, the Maronite Patriarch.

32. Kaufman (2004a, 123).

33. Kaufman (2004a, 138n56).

34. Salibi (1988, 35 [quotation], 183–85).

35. See, for instance, his lecture "Liban d'aujourd'hui," delivered in 1942: Chiha (1964, 23, 35). On Chiha and his versions of Phoenicianism and Lebanism, see Kaufman (2004a, 159–69); Traboulsi (2007, 95).

36. Chiha (1964, 31): "l'étiquette principale des individus qui, sous la domination de Byzance, était nationale (on était ou on n'était pas citoyen de l'Empire) devient confessionnelle."

37. Corm (1987, 53): "nous n'étions au fronton de l'histoire, / Avant de devenir musulmans ou chrétiens, / Qu'un même peuple uni dans une même gloire."

38. Kaufman (2004a, 132).

39. Kaufman (2004a, 230–37).

40. Stone (2008) discusses Phoenician themes in later twentieth-century Lebanese music and theater, including the work of the well-known singer Fairouz.

41. "Da Gheddafi alla Lanterna, i segreti di Preziosa," *La Repubblica*, March 22, 2013. When it became clear over the course of 2011 that Mr. Qadhafi was no longer in a position to take delivery of his boat, it was sold instead to a cruise company, and MSC *Preziosa* came into service in Genoa in March 2013. Potential vacationers will be disappointed to learn that the shark tank is no longer a feature.

42. See Lorcin (2002); Fenwick (2008, 77–79); and Mattingly (2011, 43–72), for the preferred French comparison between Roman and French colonialism in North Africa.

43. For more detailed accounts, see Ardeleanu (2015) and Morstadt (2015, 28–32). For the appeal to the Phoenician past in twentieth-century Algeria, see McDougall (2006, esp. 153–77).

44. This symbol was removed from the sail in 1963.

45. van Dommelen (2014). For the particular role of the World Bank in Tunisian heritage policy, see Samuels (2008), and on the politics of tourism and the role of Carthage in Ben Ali's Tunisia, see Saidi (2008).

46. Saidi (2008, 113); note also the *Saison de Tunisie en France*, which culminated in a hugely successful exhibition on Carthage in Paris (Musée du Petit Palais, 1995).

47. Mellah (1987, 154): "un vagabond indigne de notre Elissa." For a discussion of this and other historical themes in the two novels, see Omri (2000).

48. Hazbun (2007, 27) for the phrase.

49. Charfi and Redissi (2009, esp. 163–72).

50. Hazbun (2007, 27). One could contrast the traditional Moroccan interest in Islamic archaeology, which may relate to the king's status as a descendent of the Prophet. I am very grateful to my Tunisian friends and colleagues, and in particular to Imed Ben Jerbania, for discussion of these topics.

51. "Monument à la gloire d'Hannibal à Carthage", *Mag 14*, May 21, 2013, http://www.mag14.com/actuel/35-societe/1960-monument-a-la-gloire-dhannibal-a-carthage.html.

52. "In Carthage," *LRB Blog*, August 11, 2014, http://www.lrb.co.uk/blog/2014/08/11/josephine-quinn/in-carthage.

53. Kaufman (2004a, 237–40).

54. Kaufman (2004a, 181, 238); Płonka (2006, 429).

55. Tahan (2005, 91), who notes residual Phoenicianism in the heritage and tourism industries. Kaufman (2004a, 240) points out that the museum still has little Arab and Islamic art. The museum fully reopened for the first time only in the autumn of 2016.

56. There are still explicitly Phoenicianist political parties, such as the United Phoenician Party (http://www.unitedphoenicianparty.org/), but they play little role in national politics.

57. Larkin (2011, 61), with examples.

58. "A Geneticist with a Unifying Message," *Nature Middle East* March 31, 2013.

59. "Who Were the Phoenicians?" *National Geographic*, October 2004.

60. On the limitations to the conclusions that can be drawn from this study, see also Morstadt (2015, 37–38), and for more on the problems of studying ancient ethnicity through DNA, see Lucy (2005, 92–93). In an article investigating the problems of using DNA analysis to address questions relating to the origins of the modern British population, Catherine Hills notes that "the premises on which the scientific projects are based, and the interpretation of their results, are strongly conditioned by the models of the history of the period which they have drawn from historians and archaeologists" (Hills 2009, 126).

61. Champion (2001, 455). For the history of the field, see recently Liverani (1998); Bonnet and Krings (2006); and (briefly) Quinn and Vella (2014a).

62. Shalev (2012, 190); cf. 19, 147–49, 190–202 on the enthusiastic reception of Bochart by other European scholars.

63. Shalev (2012, 181), noting at 183–84 that Joseph Scaliger and Samuel Petit had already made the connection.

64. Shalev (2012, 142).

65. Champion (2001, 451).

66. Fénelon (1994, xxxii). See also on the work Chérel (1917) and Hont (2005, 25–27).

67. Fénelon (1997, 31–32): "Vouz voyez, Télémaque, la puissance des Phéniciens. Ils sont redoutables à toutes les nations voisines par leurs innombrables vaisseaux. Le commerce, qu'ils font jusques aux colonnes d'Hercule, leur donne des richesses qui surpassent celles des peuples les plus florissants." The English translation of *Télémaque* by Patrick Riley (Fénelon 1994), itself an adaptation of Tobias Smollet's, is slightly adapted here. Even this vague characterization of Phoenicians as merchants and sailors was dangerous to scholarship: Corinne Bonnet and Véronique Krings have pointed out that as each "people" began to acquire a "character" in this period, investigations of their history tended to focus on those aspects most relevant to that character. It was a well-known fact that the Phoenicians were merchants and sailors, and so scholars of the Phoenician world concentrated on the history of trade and colonies at the expense of less mobile, more agriculturally based communities (Bonnet and Krings 2006, 44).

68. Fénelon (1997, 35): "si célèbres dans toutes les nations connues." Tyre is called both a "nation" and a "people" at 37.

69. Liverani (1998, 5): "Non stupisce perciò di non trovarvi alcun riferimento ad un'immagine complessiva, ad una caratterizzazione dei fenici, né alcun giudizio di valore (al di là dell'implicita, ingenua ammirazione che molti studiosi hanno per l'oggetto dei loro studi). Già allora era puntuale la ricerca delle 'origini,' cioè della provenienza del popolo fenicio (sulla scorta delle notizie dei classici), ma non ancora centrale era la definizione delle 'attitudini,' che è concetto prettamente etnografico e coloniale, implica (e deriva da) rapporti di affari, utilizzazione lavorativa, idiosincrasie culturali e comportamentali nei contatti e nella vita quotidiana."

70. Movers (1841–56, 1:5).

71. Liverani (1998, esp. 5–6), also noting the role of the rise of anti-Semitism.

72. Gilroy (1993, 3, 2); cf. 34 on the role played in nation-building by "romantic conceptions of 'race,' 'people,' and 'nation.' " The work of Johann Herder (1744–1803) was central to the development of the nineteenth-century conception of the world as divided into a hierarchy of different races shaped by the places to which their origins could be traced.

73. Kidd (1999).

74. Braudel (1980, 180, emphasis in original).

75. Kenrick (1855, 250–55, 255–59).

76. Kenrick (1855, 251).

77. Renan (1864, 1).

78. Renan (1864, 815): "[t]out en étant attentif aux intérêts de nos collections."

79. On this work and Renan's expedition, see Bonnet (2013), with earlier bibliography.

80. E.g., Renan (1864, 832).

81. E.g., Renan (1864, 817).

82. Renan (1864, 829): "En géneral, dans leur constructions, les Phéniciens paraissent avoir porté peu d'espirit de suite." He is slightly more polite about their

sculpture, and his letters from Lebanon are more subtle: see, for instance, no. 168, on the modern and ancient races in the area.

83. Renan (1864, 836): "La Phénicie ne fut pas un pays; ce fut une série de ports, avec une banlieue assez étroite. Ces villes, situées à dix ou douze lieues l'une de l'autre, furent le centre d'une vie toute municipale comme les villes greques. La civilisation phénicienne ne rayonna pas dans la montagne et eut peu d'action sur la population de la Syrie."

84. Liverani (1998, 6–8, with references), where he notes that this "contradiction" arose in part from a recourse to rather different sources on the different Semitic "nations."

85. Renan (1864, 830): "l'infériorité des Phéniciens en fait d'art semble, du reste, avoir persisté jusqu'à nos jours dans le pays qu'ils ont habité."

86. Renan (1864, 818): "La race du Liban, soit chrétienne, soit musulmane, est, si j'ose le dire, iconoclaste, inintelligente de l'art. . . . Les églises maronites sont très-sévères et excluent les statues."

87. Renan (1864, 13).

88. Renan (1864, 14): "à demi sauvages ou abruties . . . des races inférieures." Cf. 13 on "the kind and agreeable Maronite peoples" (les douces et bonnes populations maronites). Renan was particularly annoyed by the way that the Muslims and the Greek Orthodox were much less helpful than the Maronites and other Catholic groups when it came to informing him about local epigraphic finds, though he continues, more sympathetically, "to tell the truth, it is the incurable folly and the pervsion of the spirit of these poor races, more than their ill-will, that has made things the Phoenicians difficult for me" (A vrai dire, c'est l'incurable folie et l'aberration d'espirit de ces pauvres races, plûtot que leur mauvais vouloir, qui m'ont créé des difficultés) (14). On Renan's complex orientalism, see Said (1978, 130–48); on his complex anti-Semitism, Bernal (1987, 345–46).

89. Kaufman (2004a, 33).

90. On the stereotypes of this era, see Liverani (1998).

91. Perrot and Chipiez (1885a, 12–13). Although on 18 the Phoenicians have "traditions nationales," on 22 the authors note (in a passage with very strong echoes of the passage by Renan quoted above) that "Phoenicia was not a dense nation, occupying a vast territory in a continuous manner. . . . To tell the truth, it was just a series of ports, each of which had a rather narrow hinterland." (La Phénicie ne fut pas une nation compacte, occupant d'une manière continue un vaste territoire. . . . A vrai dire, ce ne fut qu'une série de ports à chacun desquels tenait une banlieue assez étroite.)

92. Perrot and Chipiez (1885a, 886): "Le Phénicien, a-t-on très bien dit, avait quelques-uns des charactères du juif du moyen âge, mais il était puissant et il appartenait à une race dont on reconnaissait, à certain égards, l'ascendant et la supériorité." There is a short discussion right at the end of the book of Phoenicians "de race pure" (892).

93. E.g., Rawlinson (1889, 49, 51, 61, 64, with 52 on the importance of language in classifying nations by race). As with Perrot and Chipiez, however, these terms are used rather loosely: at 63 the Phoenicians belong by complexion to "the white race," and at 64 some attention is devoted to the fact that the "nation was not a centralized one [but] like Greece, a congeries of homogenous tribes, who had never been amalgamated into a single political entity, and who clung fondly to the idea of separate independence." On this work, see Liverani (1998, 9–10).

94. Rawlinson (2005, 1–2, 20–39). This third edition was reprinted in 2005 as *Phoenicia: History of a Civilization.*

95. Rawlinson (2005, 348–50, quotation at 350).

96. Pietschmann (1889, esp. 96), with the brief discussion in Pastor Borgoñon (1992, 53).

97. Vella (2014, 29–30).

98. Bernal (1987, 367–99, 408–14); Liverani (1998); and Morstadt (2015, 16–23), on the effects of philhellenism, anti-Semitism, orientalism, and the rise of "racial science" on Phoenician historiography from the early nineteenth to mid-twentieth centuries.

99. Moscati (1963, 485): "Chi furono, effectivamente, i Fenici? Quali furono gli elementi distinctivi e caratteristici della loro civiltà, quali I fatti storici, politici, religiosi ed artistici che la definirono e la condizionarono? Perché finora sembra che l'unità, l'autonomia, la consistenza del popolo e della cultura siano state presupposte piuttosto che indagate."

100. Moscati (1963, 486–94): "può emergere la civiltà fenicia come reale oggetto di storia. . . . Nell'insieme, sembra chiaro che il prevalente frazionamento delle città fenicie e la dominante conscienza cittadina non escludono una relativa omogeneità intrinseca all'insieme dell'area e distintiva rispetto all'ambiente."

101. A shift attributed in part by Liverani to Lebanese independence (1998, 18).

102. Moscati (1963, 489): "civiltà"; "popolo"; "nazione fenicia."

103. Space: Moscati (1963, 491) (Antarado to Akko); cf. Moscati (1993c) (Tell Suqas to Carmel, also noting that these geographical limits are conventional and somewhat fuzzy). Time: Moscati (1963, 489–90; cf. 1993c, 11, where he also makes the point, however, that in the west Phoenician history continued for a considerable period, even to late antiquity). For an exhaustive discussion of geographical and chronological definitions of the (eastern) Phoenicians in modern scholarly literature from the mid-nineteenth century to the late twentieth, see Pastor Borgoñon (1992, 39–106, with tables 1–2).

104. Moscati (1963, 488–89): "ma che assumono carattere omogeneo per avere in comune un'area geografica, una lingua ed un processo storico-culturale"; for this definition of a "people" according to "modern science" he cites the second edition of R. Biassuti's *Le razze e i popoli della terra*, published in 1953, though he admits some doubt about the universal relevance of language.

105. Moscati (1988a, 5n6): "a me interessava quale fosse la realtà di un popolo."

106. Moscati (1992a, 16): "la coscienza nazionale risulta assai labile tra le città fenicie, prevalendo in esse l'orizzonte cittadino."

107. Moscati (1993c, 79). On Moscati's views against the background of the developing scholarship on the topic, see the excellent discussion in Pedrazzi (2012, 139–43).

108. Moscati (1990, 77): "Sabatino Moscati ha inventato i Fenici, Gianni Agnelli li ha prodotti"; discussed by Vella (2014, 25).

109. Fontan and Le Meaux (2007).

110. E.g., Aubet (2001; 2009, 16 ["pueblo"]); Bondì et al. (2009, v ["civiltà"]); Woolmer (2011, 11)—all, it should be noted, in the context of thoughtful discussions of the problems of Phoenician identity. Some go further: for Adam-Veleni and Stefani (2012, 26), the Greeks and the Phoenicians are still "two nations."

111. A. Smith (1986, 13, 3). Smith calls these units *ethnies*. See 45 for the earliest evidence for *ethnies* in the third millennium BCE, and 32 for the clarification that "I am not claiming that they [i.e., ethnic groups] have constituted the main mode of socio-cultural organization, let alone the sole one, even in pre-modern eras; only that

they have been at least as important as other forms of organization and culture, and that we therefore ignore them at our peril."

112. A. Smith (1986, 83).

113. A. Smith (1986, 83).

114. A. Smith (1986, 84).

115. It is worth noting that Smith was himself concerned about the extent to which the ethnic culture of the Phoenicians was "insufficiently delineated," a factor in his own view in their disappearance after Alexander's conquest. The judgmental tone of the relevant passage is striking: "Perhaps here we have an *ethnie* that has failed to differentiate itself sufficiently from its neighbours and which has relied too much on their cultures. . . . It would appear that internal strife . . . and an insufficiently delineated culture and sense of solidarity were the main factors contributing to the eventual dissolution of a Phoenician sense of common ethnicity" (A. Smith 1986, 99).

CHAPTER 2. SONS OF TYRE

1. J. Hall (1997, 17–26). Importance of blood: e.g., Ruby (2006, 44); Mac Sweeney (2009, 102); Van der Spek (2009, 102); Eriksen (2010, 81–83). Importance of soil: e.g., J. Hall (1997, 25, 32), with earlier scholarship.

2. On the history of "ethnicity," a term first attested in 1941, see J. Hall (2002, 10, 17).

3. In defense of ancient "nations," see A. Smith (1986, 11–13), and most recently and enthusiastically Gat and Yakobson (2013).

4. A. Smith (1986, 22–31).

5. A. Smith (1986, 23). Cf. Moscati (1966b, 21): "A people defines itself, above all, by its name" (Un popolo si definisce, anzitutto, nel suo nome).

6. For discussion and earlier bibliography, see Prag (2006, 8–10). Dating: Pallottino et al. (1964, 115, by letter forms).

7. Prag (2006, 8).

8. Prag (2006, 9), with references; see also Palmer (1997, 49); Watmough (1997, 46–47); and Pittau (2000, 101–2) for interpretations of Puinel as a personal name, and for examples of the interpretation of *puinel* as an ethnic, see Lancel (1995, 86); Hoyos (2010, 43).

9. Prag also notes the depiction of the Greek Phoinix son of Amyntor on a fresco in the François tomb at Etruscan Vulci, where he is labeled Φuinis, and the Greek phenomenon of *xenia* names, commemorating a family guest friendship (2006, 9), with Jameson and Malkin (1998, 482) for *xenia* names, and Malkin (1990) for examples that were also ethnics, such as Libys, the brother of Lysander, king of Sparta, who was named after a king Libys of Siwa.

10. E.g., Malkin (2011, esp. 63–64, 101–6); contra, J. Hall (2002, 90–124), with earlier bibliography. Hall himself would put the emergence of a broad "Hellenic" identity later, and on the mainland (2002, 168–71).

11. A claim explicitly made of "Canaanites" by Lemche (1991, 152).

12. Prag (2006, 9, 22–23); Arena (1996, no. 63 [Selinus]); Dunant (1978, no. 185.2 [Eretria]); *IDélos* no. 400.11 (Delos: Apollonius Phoinix, second century BCE; *IG* XI.2 no. 163 A 45 (Delos: Herakleides Phoinix, third century BCE); Couillard (1974, no. 477.9 [Rheneia, Megas Phoinix: third to second century BCE]).

13. Prag (2006, 23), following Lacroix (1932, 519n9).

14. The origins and original meanings of the terms "Phoenician" and "Canaanite" are much debated: for the most recent overview, see Ercolani (2015), and for a variety of theories, see Speiser (1936); Bonfante (1941); Astour (1965); Chantraine (1972); Billigmeier (1977); Vandersleyen (1987); Bunnens (1992); Zobel (1995, 213–17); Aubet (2001, 6–13; 2009, 17–23). The suggestion that "Phoenicia" was originally a translation of "Canaan," based on the notion that both terms can mean "red" or "purple," is no longer popular (Bunnens 1992).

15. See Baslez (1987, 270) for a similar point; I thank Scott Scullion for guidance here. Prag (2006, 23) suggests that Herakleides Phoinix, who is said to be a metal worker, "could have got his name from working on the bronze palm tree of the Letoon."

16. Lerat (1952, 1:92, no. 1) = *SEG* 12 no. 295, l.3: 182/1 BCE (ὧι ὄ]νομα Πλεῖστος, τὸ γένος φοίνι[κα]).

17. Couillard (1974, no. 468, l.7): Ἀλίνην ποθὲν Φοίνισσαν, ὡς ἀπ᾽ Ἀσκάλω(ν)?, making a convincing case for reading ὡς ἀπ᾽ Ἀσκάλω(ν) rather than ὡς Ἀπᾶς καλῶ. See Prag (2006, 24n105) for some other examples of people "from Phoenicia."

18. Athens National Musuem, NM 1488 = Clairmont and Conze (1993, 3, no. 410). The inscriptions are catalogued as *CISem.* I no. 115 = *KAI⁵* no. 54 = *IG* II² no. 8388 = *CEG* 596. Recent discussions: Bäbler (1998, 131–42); J. Stager (2005); Tsagalis (2008, 56–58); Osborne (2011, 124–28, 156–57; 2012a, 319–29); Tribulato (2013); Bonnet (2014, 462–72).

19. As Robin Osborne points out, three different methods of converting Phoenician to Greek names are used: "Aphrodisias is a Greek version of Abdashtart (i.e. it employs the name of an equivalent goddess to form a parallel theophoric name), but Antipatros is simply a Greek name instead of Sem, while Domsalôs' names are essentially transliterated" (Osborne 2012a, 319–21); presumably Antipatros had been in Athens for some time, acquiring a local name in addition to his own, while Domsalos has only just arrived on the "sacred ship."

20. J. Stager (2005, 444).

21. There is a full analysis of the text in Tribulato (2013, 466–70). Tsagalis (2008, 58) plausibly suggests that Domsalos wrote it himself. S. Rebecca Martin has pointed out to me that the epigram and epitaph may not be contemporary.

22. J. Stager (2005, 445).

23. Individuals are identified as "Phoenicians" by Athenian authors: Demosthenes, *Against Phormio* 6; Isocrates, *Trapeziticus* 4. Dionysius of Halicarnassus mentions a fourth-century lawsuit brought "by the Phalereans against the Phoenicians" about the priesthood of Poseidon (*Dinarchus* 10), but without further details of what could be a paraphrase, and is in any case presumably a description by the claimants, it is hard to know how much to make of this. Osborne points to the overlap between the imagery on the stele and an idea of "'the Phoenicians' being quintessential sailors from lands of exotic animals" (Osborne 2011, 127). Tribulato notes that death far from home is a "common motif" (Tribulato 2013, 469).

24. *CIL* III no. 4910: *D.M. | Non gravis | hic.texit.tumu|lus te Punica | virgo || Musarum. amor | et.Charitum | Erasina.volup|tas.an.XII.* The reading of another funerary inscription from the start of the Via Latina in Rome and dating from 48 BCE as describing a woman of *natione punica* is admitted by the editor to be much more speculative, since the word is highly abraded (Di Stefano Manzella 1972, 110–13, with *AE* 1972, no. 14). Prag suggests that the word might in fact begin with D (Prag 2006, 29).

25. Among a great many examples, see Speiser (1936, 125); Röllig (1983, 79); Moscati (1988a, 4); Bäbler (1998, 115); Aubet (2001, 9; 2009, 20); Tsirkin (2001, 271); Joffe (2002, 434); Bondì et al. (2009, x); Hoyos (2010, 1); Demetriou (2012, 10). Skepticism is expressed by Baurain and Bonnet (1992, 12). Krahmalkov's speculative and eccentric argument for *pōnnīm* as the standard self-designation for Phoenicians depends entirely on the pseudo-Punic of Plautus's *Poenulus* and an unnecessary textual emendation of Ps. 45:12–14 (Krahmalkov 2000, 11–13; 2001, 2). It has not been widely accepted.

26. Houghton et al. (2002, nos. 1448–50, 1579, 1825–26, 2100, 2185–86, 2251–52, 2326–28). On one issue under Alexander II c. 126–123 BCE (so after the effective collapse of Seleucid power in the region), the city uses its original name "of Beirut" (LBʾRT: Houghton et al. [2002, no. 2252]); others of the same period retain the standard phrase (Houghton et al. [2002, nos. 2250–51]).

27. *EH* no. 102 = *KAI*[5] no. 116. I am very grateful to Robert Kerr and Maria Giulia Amadasi Guzzo for discussion of this inscription.

28. de Vaux (1968, 23n11). I have also confirmed this reading by autopsy at the Musée Cirta Constantine.

29. The inscription leaves it unclear as to which of the men is being given the full description, although parallels (such as the "sons of" phrases discussed below) suggest that such descriptions usually relate to the most recently named individual.

30. *TDOT* 7.228 *TWOT* 1.446; *Hebrew and Aramaic Lexicon of the Old Testament* 2.486. Zeph. 1:11 would provide perhaps the closest parallel for this use of the word כנען in a construct phrase, but see also Isa. 23:8; Ezek. 16:29; 17:3–4; Hos. 12:8; Zech. 14:21; Prov. 31:24; Jerome, *Liber de nominibus hebraicis,* de Exodo, s.v. *Chanani* and de Matthaeo, s.v. *Chanani* and *Chananaei.*

31. Amadasi Guzzo (2013, 258), emphasizing that this is true of plurals as well as singulars; note also Segert (1976, 88, 116) and *PPG*[3] 139, for this norm. See, for example, *KAI*[5] no. 49 l.34: ḤSRY, "the Tyrian" (graffiti from Abydos, fifth to third centuries BCE); Röllig (1972 no. 2): ʾRWDY, "Aradite" (Demetrias, fourth to third century BCE, a bilingual with Masson [1969, no. 5], translating Ἀράδιος); *CISem.* I no. 116 = *KAI*[5] no. 53: ḤSDNY, "the Sidonian" (Athens, fourth to second century BCE, a bilingual with Σιδώνιος in the Greek). Cf. KNʿNY, itself in an Ugaritic inscription: *KTU*[3] no. 4.96, l. 7 (thirteenth century BCE).

32. August. *Ad Rom.* 13.5, according to the text published in Divjak (1971). I translate *punice* here as "in Phoenician" rather than "in Punic," because (as we shall see) while the Latin term *punicus* can mean "Phoenician," "western Phoenician," or more specifically "Carthaginian," Augustine's description in this passage of the Canaanite woman from the area of Tyre and Sidon as a *punica mulier* shows that he is using *punicus* here to mean "Phoenician" in the most general sense.

33. Harden (1962, 22); Moscati (1988b, 24; 1992a, 23); Bunnens (1992); Aubet (2001, 11; 2009, 21); Krahmalkov (2001, 1); Tammuz (2001, 505); Belmonte (2003, 34); J. Stager (2005, 444n100); Sommer (2008, 14); Hoyos (2010, 220); Campus (2012, 310–13), where it is evidence for "collective identity" (310), among many others. Prag strikes a rare note of skepticism (2006, 24), as does (more tentatively) Lemche (1991, 57). Moscati noted in an article on this passage that the context of the line was rarely discussed, despite its relevance, but then failed to do more himself than discuss the first couple of lines of the chapter, missing entirely the role of the Canaanite woman in the argument (Moscati 1984, 529).

34. August. *Ad Rom.* 13.5–6, correcting Divjak's *Punice respondentes*, attested only in B, to *Punice respondent*.

35. August. *Ad Rom.* 13.7 ("sed haec verborum consonantia sive provenerit sive provisa sit, non pugnaciter agendum est, ut ei quisque consentiat, sed quantum interpretantis elegantiam hilaritas audientis admittit"); this interpretation is also supported by the sequence "for . . . for . . . thus . . ." that connects 13.3–6 with 13.1–2.

36. This is an investigation that I undertook with Neil McLynn, Robert Kerr, and Daniel Hadas; we treat the problems of this passage in much greater detail in Quinn et al. (2014), offering only the most tentative solutions. I reproduce parts of that argument, and text, here, as well as our translations, but while my coauthors should be held responsible for anything here of worth, they should not be assumed to support the specific arguments I present in this context.

37. For a fuller version of this discussion, and for the stemma itself, see Quinn et al. (2014, 183–85).

38. E.g. (among many instances), *Conf.* 10.3.3; *C. acad.* 2.7.16. The only use of *quid sint* in something like this sense is at *Enarrationes in Psalmos* 132.3, where the question is about what the Circumcellions do. See for more detail on this point Quinn et al. (2014, 182n16).

39. There are more than thirty-five examples of this usage, most either of *punice* used to mean "in Phoenician" or of *punicus* qualifying language, words, or texts. When *punicus* qualifies a person, the context is almost always linguistic, and the point is to identify the person as a Phoenician speaker. *De peccatorum meritis* 1.34 is arguably an exception. The only other is the phrase *punicum bellum* in *De civitate Dei* (passim), where Augustine is merely using the standard Roman terminology. Full details and references can be found in Quinn et al. (2014, 181–82n15), a list compiled by Daniel Hadas.

40. For all the readings of the two words, see Quinn et al. (2014, 197).

41. Some Christian writings, by contrast, suggest that the concept of Canaan could be rather hazy in late antiquity, as, for instance, in the early fourth-century apologetic treatise by Lactantius, who puts Canaan in Arabia (Lactant. *Div. Inst.* 2 (*De origine erroris*) 14 6), and in his near contemporary Juvencus's harmonization of the gospels as epic poetry, where he appears to confuse Canaan and Cana (Juvencus, *Evangeliorum libri* 2.127–29).

42. Jubilees 9:1.

43. Joseph. *AJ* 1.130–33.

44. Procop. *Vand.* 4.10.18–20.

45. Procop. *Vand.* 4.10.21–22: Ἡμεῖς ἐσμεν οἱ φυγόντες ἀπὸ προσώπου Ἰησοῦ τοῦ λῃστοῦ υἱοῦ Ναυῆ. See Schmitz (2007), with earlier bibliography; Amitay (2011) is another important discussion of the problem that also investigates the relevant rabbinic literature, the significance of Jewish migration to North Africa in the Hellenistic period, and the immediate political and military context in which Procopius was writing.

46. Schmitz (2007, 102). Cf. *Suda*, s.v. Χαναάν.

47. I am grateful to Robert Kerr for suggesting this line of inquiry.

48. It also, of course, contradicts a different modern convention that divides the history of the northern Levant into a "Canaanite" period and people before the regional troubles of c. 1200 BCE, and a "Phoenician" one after that. For skeptical assess-

ment of this conventional model, with relevant bibliography, see Baurain (1986); Bonnet (1988, 2–4); Xella (1995); Aubet (2001, 12; 2009, 22); Bonnet and Krings (2006, 41); Sommer (2010, 121); Tzoroddu (2010, 15–22). It makes very little sense of the considerable evidence for political, religious, and cultural continuity in the region, or the concurrent use of the two sets of terms in sources from the late Bronze Age, and has now largely fallen out of favor.

49. Biblical accounts of the precise extent and specific borders of the land of Canaan vary, as one would expect in a collection of stories, regulations, prophecies, and prayers originally compiled in the seventh or sixth centuries but reflecting successive waves of re-editing down to the second century BCE. For a variety of borders, see Gen. 10:19; 15:18; Num. 34:2–12; Ezek. 47:15–20, 48:1–28. For modern commentary on these borders, as well as the use of Canaan and Canaanites in Near Eastern sources more generally, see Na'aman (1994; 1999); Rainey (1996); Tammuz (2001); and Belmonte (2003, 31–36), all with discussion of earlier scholarship. Canaan is on one occasion described as the "land of the Philistines" (Zeph. 2:5), though Tammuz notes that this is probably a straightforward error based on Josh. 13: 3–4, which simply says that the Philistine territory is Canaanite (2001, 521n82).

50. Tammuz (2001) gives a clear account of "ideological Canaan," summarized at 535–36.

51. Josh. 5:1; Deut. 1:7; cf. Gen. 15:18. See also Gen. 10:19, where the territory of the Canaanites runs from Sidon to Gaza. At Obad. 1:20, the Canaanites possess land as far as Sarepta. On Josh. 13:3–4, a passage confused by multiple later supplements, see Nelson (1997, 164–66). For a counterexample, see Num. 13:17, 13:29.

52. *TDOT* 7.213. Although at Josh. 5:1 the translation "kings of Phoenicia" does seem to map onto a geographical distinction in the Hebrew text between Amorites inland and Canaanites on the coast, the other examples do not suggest that the occasional choice to use "Phoenicia(n)" rather than "Canaan(ite)" in the Bible is related to the specific geographical setting of the story involved (and might therefore be a considered a gloss rather than a translation): see Exod. 16:35 and Josh. 5:12. The woman in the recurring phrase "and Saul the son of the Canaanite woman" is translated into Greek both by "Canaanite woman" (Gen. 46:10) and "Phoenician woman" (Exod. 6:15).

53. Euseb. *Praep. Evang.* 1.10.39 = *BNJ* 790 F 2; see Baumgarten (1981, 232–35) on the difficulties of the text here. This tradition may go back to Alexander Polyhistor, writing in the first century BCE, who attributed to one Eupolemus (the name of a Jewish historian of the second century BCE) a supposedly Babylonian version of the Table of the Nations in which he says that Ham begot Chanaan, "who was the father of the Phoenicians" (Euseb. *Praep. Evang.* 9.17.9 = *BNJ* 724 F 1), although this phrase may simply mean that the people the Greeks called Phoenicians were a subset of the Hebrew Bible's Canaanites. On "pseudo-Eupolemos," see Gruen (1998, 146–50).

54. Hdn. *On Peculiar Style*, 2.912.23–913.2 Lentz. The widespread view that Hekataios of Miletus first said this in the sixth century BCE rests solely on Herodian's citation of Hekataios for a different and unrelated point. *BNJ* 1 (Hekataios) F 21 translates the relevant passage as follows: "No feminine word of more than one syllable ending in -na has a circumflex accent on that syllable, with the sole exception of 'Athena' . . . but someone could object that 'Danae' (Δανᾶ) is pronounced that way in Hekataios: 'Zeus has intercourse with Danae.' One should know that this practice in Hekataios is in accordance with the usage of the Phoenicians, as he himself says, as it was not yet in fact

common practice among Attic writers or in normal usage. . . . I added 'words of more than one syllable' so that we might avoid the exceptions of the common word 'mina' (μνᾶ) and . . . 'Chna' (Χνᾶ), the original name of Phoenicia, which has been imported from abroad." The distinction between Hekataios's contribution and Herodian's addition is also quite clear in Jacoby's edition of the fragments of Hekataios. Cf. the Byzantine grammarian Choiroboscos, later still: "Chnas, from Chna (which is what Agenor was called, and from that Phoenicia is called Ochna)" (Bekker 1814, 1181).

55. City: Frankenstein (1979, 288); Baurain (1986, 20); Xella (1995, 246, 249, and with a useful collection of references to people from the coastal cities from the Ugarit archives at 257–59); Niemeyer (2000, 93); Sommer (2010, 115). Family: Bordreuil and Ferjaoui (1988, 137–39).

56. Some of these were simply "found" on the antiquities market, but others are from the Bekaa valley and (reportedly) the area of Bethlehem in Palestine: Röllig (1995); J. Elayi (2005a); Lemaire (2012, 6–11).

57. For Phoenicians abroad, see Bunnens (1979) (focusing on the textual evidence); Lipiński (2004).

58. *RÉS* no. 604 (HʾRWDY) (m.) and 1226 (HʾRWDT) (f.), both from the Bordj Djedid necropolis. There are many other examples, in addition to those already noted in note 31 above, such as "the Carthaginian," *CISem.* I no. 86B, HQRTHDŠTY, fourth century, from Kition; one Kitian man, or ʾŠ KTY, from Carthage (*RÉS* no. 1225 = *CISem.* I no. 5997), as well as HKTY (m.), fourth to third century, from Demetrias (Röllig 1972, no. 3, a bilingual with Masson 1969, no. 3, translating Κιτέυς); a third-century Sidonian (ṢYDN[Y]) (m.) from Demetrias (Röllig 1972, no. 1, a bilingual with Masson 1969 no. 4, translating Σιδ]ώνιος). All dates given here are based on letter forms. Adjectives seem to be the norm for expressing civic identity (although the Kitian examples ending with "Y" are somewhat ambiguous), but the construct phrase "man of Sidon" (ʾŠ ṢDN) is also frequently found, especially at Carthage. This (often, at least) seems to be a special case with the meaning "freedperson": not only is it in at least one case used of a woman (*CISem.* I, no. 281; cf. 279–80 where the phrase is restored), but it can be found in the phrase ʾŠ ṢDN BD ʾDNY BD [personal name]: "Man of Sidon, emancipated by her/his master, emancipated by [personal name]" (*CISem.* I nos. 269, 272, 276, 280): see further Février [1951–52]; *DNWSI* s.v. ṢDN).

59. *CISem.* I no. 265; *KAI*[5] no. 19 = *TSSI* III no. 31, l. 3 (222 BCE, found in Lebanon; Hammon is modern Umm el-ʿAmed); cf. *KAI*[5] no. 56 (of Byzantium); *KAI*[5] no. 137, l.1 (of Thinissut, Roman period); *KAI*[5] no. 101, l.1 (of Thugga, second century BCE); *EH* no. 102 = *KAI*[5] no. 116 (of ʾYʿRM, third to second century BCE, discussed above). See Sznycer (1975, 59–64) for further references and for discussion of the formal, political sense in which ʿM is used in these inscriptions (perhaps, he suggests, "assembly of the people"); see also *DNWSI* s.v. ʿM$_1$ (p. 866).

60. *KAI*[5] no. 68 (Olbia, third century) and *CISem.* I no. 3778 = *KAI*[5] no. 78 (Carthage). For the more general Phoenician norm of going back several generations in inscriptions, see Crouzet (2012, 41). Where the person was a slave (*abd*), the ancestors of the owner are listed (e.g., *CISem.* I no. 236).

61. I owe this suggestion to Angelos Chaniotis, with thanks; it would be equivalent to the claim that one's ancestors were on the *Mayflower*.

62. The classic discussion is Bordreuil and Ferjaoui (1988), countering on 140–41 arguments that these are personal names rather than references to civic origin. A new

catalogue has been published by Amadasi Guzzo (2012a), to which should be added the "son of Tyre" reported in Ferjaoui (2008b) (as noted at Amadasi Guzzo [2012b]). "Sons of Tyre" is now the name of a Masonic lodge in Texas.

63. Bordreuil and Ferjaoui (1988, 137); for some sons of the land of Canaan, see *AT* 181.9 (Wiseman 1954, 11), and *Ugaritica* V 111–13, 389, no. 36 B 6–8 (DUMU.MEŠ KUR *Ki-na-ʾi / Ki-na-ʾa*$_4$), transliterated, translated, and discussed in Rainey (1996, 5), with Ps. 45:13 for a daughter of Tyre. "Sons" and "daughters" of cities are also found in Greek epigraphic contexts from the later Hellenistic period (Hemelrijk 2015, 252–53, with earlier bibliography), although the connections between this practice and the earlier Near Eastern one are unclear.

64. Ferjaoui (2008b).

65. Prag (2006, 25n108) for the references, not all of which are certain.

66. Prag (2013, 41–45). Cf. Malkin (2011, 117–18) on the emergence of "Sikel" identity among non-Greeks in the fifth century. Prag also notes one possible "Sicilian" at Carthage (*CISem.* I no. 4945), although the word HŠQLNY is unparalleled and difficult to interpret.

67. For Phoenicians in the Aegean from the fourth century onward, see Baslez (1987); Grainger (1991, 205–16).

68. For self-descriptions as Sidonian, see the inscription discussed above erected by Domseleh the Sidonian (ṢDNY) for an Ashkelonite (ʾŠKLNY); and *CISem.* I no. 119 = *KAI*[5] no. 59 (ṢDNT [f.], third century, Athens, a bilingual translating Σιδωνία). For the Athenian evidence in general, see Bäbler (1998, 119–55); Lipiński (2004, 169–73).

69. *IG* II^2 no. 141 = *Syll.*^{3} no. 185 = RO no. 21. The exact date is disputed: see Rhodes and Osborne (2003, 89–90).

70. *IG* II^2 no. 343 = *IG* II^3 1 no. 379.

71. The bulk of the text is in Phoenician (*KAI*[5] no. 60 = *TSSI* III no. 41); the concluding lines are in Greek: *IG* II^2 no. 2946. Both are printed in *KAI*[5], *TSSI*, and Ameling (1990), all with useful discussion; the dating is by letter forms. See also Baslez (1988, 147), pointing out how difficult it is for this group to render their own institutions in Phoenician, suggesting that they have not deliberately preserved homeland customs in their communal practices (Baslez and Briquel-Chatonnet 1991a, 1991b; Lipiński 2004, 171–72).

72. *IG* II^2 no. 342 = *IG* II^3 1 no. 468, with Walbank (1985), and for the theory, J. Stager (2005, 444).

73. *IKition* no. 159 = *IG* II^2 no. 337, ll. 42–45. Baslez (2013, 234n27) points out that members of this group do not appear to be organized into a formal association.

74. *IKition* no. 160 (Aristoklea); cf. no. 161 (fragmentary); for epitaphs of "Kitians" found in Piraeus, including four bilingual examples, see *IKition* nos. 162–68. Much useful bibliography can be found in Parker (1996, 160n29).

75. Dale and Ellis-Evans (2011, 195), discussing *IG* II^2 no. 1290 (mid-third century BCE) and *SEG* 52 no. 135 (334/3?). See Lipiński (2004, 37–107) for the Phoenician evidence from Cyprus.

76. *CISem.* I no. 114 = *IDélos* no. 50.

77. *Syll.*^{3} no. 391 = Bagnall and Derow (2004, no. 73). On Philocles, see Hauben (1987). The phrase "king of the Sidonians" follows the norms of Greek rather than Phoenician, discussed further below, in that it names the king's subjects rather than his city.

78. *IDélos* no. 313 a 34.

79. There is a very clear account of the context at Kay (2014, 199–201).

80. Tréheux (1992); Lipiński (2004, 166–68).

81. *IDélos* no. 1519 (a sanctuary of Melqart established by the association of the Tyrians); cf. no. 1720 (a dedication to Poseidon of Ashkelon set up by Philostratos).

82. Baslez (2013, 230n10), with references.

83. Baslez (1987, 284).

84. *IG* XI 4 no. 1114, with Baslez (2013, 230).

85. *IDélos* no. 1543, with Baslez (1987, 276n59) for the suggested reading.

86. *IDélos* no. 1519.

87. *IDélos* no. 1520, with nos. 1772–82 for other honors and dedications connected with this group. For the date, see Robert (1973, 487), and for the meaning of the term *endocheis*, connected with import-export activity, see Baslez (1987, 276–79). On *IDélos* nos. 1519–20, see Hasenohr (2007, 79–80); Baslez (2013, 232–33).

88. *IDélos* no. 1782. See Grainger (1991, 208) on the varying uses of "Laodikeia in Phoenicia" and "Berytos" in Delian inscriptions. These associations may relate to the Levantine institution of the *marzeah*, a social and funerary club rather like English "friendly societies" (K. Stern 2007).

89. Baslez (1987, 283–84); Lipiński (2004, 167–68); Hasenohr (2007, 78).

90. On Philostratos, see Mancinetti Santamaria (1982), with references.

91. It has been suggested that the Italian "Poseidoniasts," "Hermaiasts," "Apolloniasts," and "Competaliasts" found in inscriptions are different subgroups or magistrates within one Italian association rather than four separate ones (Hasenohr 2007, with earlier bibliography), but the important point for my purposes is their overall identification as Italian rather than as members of individual cities.

92. Hasenohr (2007, 81–88) emphasizes the institutional similarities between the associations and physical buildings of the Italians and the Poseidoniasts of Beirut on Delos, as well as noting some interesting differences.

93. See Dušek (2012, 75–79) for these inscriptions and their interpretation, with references and earlier bibliography.

94. Baslez (2013, 231).

95. For the relevant mid-second-century inscriptions, see Baslez (2013, 234n30).

96. *IDélos* no. 2612. For counterexamples see *IDélos* 1694–6; 1698

97. Grainger (1991, 110).

98. *SEG* 18 no. 450.

99. Thomas (1989, 156–59); Hansen (1996, 171). One unusual exception is Heropythos of Chios, whose fifth-century tombstone gives fourteen generations of ancestry going back to a "Kyprios" (*GDI* no. 5656, missing a generation; for the correct text, see Jeffery (1990, 414 [no. 47])). Rosalind Thomas (1989, 191n96) raises the possibility that this character was from a non-Greek background; I thank her for discussion of these issues. Compare, in the same period, Herodotus's claim that Hekataios (a genealogist, as Thomas points out [1989, 160]) once traced his family tree back sixteen generations to a god (2.143), and Plato on the kind of people who can cite twenty-five generations of their family back to Herakles (*Tht.* 175a); neither account is polite, and Thomas notes that such reports are unusual (159). For (still exceptional) examples of such "genealogical bookkeeping" in Greek in the Roman period (first to third centuries CE), see van Nijf (2010, 171–74) on Termessus; the eight generation ancestry

of Klearchos of Cyrene, going back to a Battos (*GDI* no. 4859, discussed by Thomas [1989, 159n9]); and the twelve generation genealogy of Licinnia Flavilla recorded at Oinoanda (Hall, Milner, and Coulton 1996, with *SEG* 46 no. 1709 for the text). Latin inscriptions normally only give filiation (Adams 2003, 214), though this occasionally extends to three, or in the imperial period four, generations (Hekster 2015, 192–93).

100. Hansen (1996).

101. Byblos: *KAI*[5] nos. 1, 4, 6, 7, 9, 10. Kition: *RÉS* no. 453, and *KAI*[5] nos. 32 (where he is also king of Idalion and Tamessos) and 38 (in which he is also king of Idalion). Sidons: *KAI*[5] no. 14. The only exceptions occur in the Phoenician texts of bilingual inscriptions (with Luwian) from Çineköy, Zincirli, and Karatepe, well north of "Phoenicia" proper (Amadasi Guzzo 2013, 262). It is often claimed that the Phoenician term ṢDNM means "the Sidonians," which would mean that in this case they used the Greek norm in both languages, but Maria Giulia Amadasi Guzzo has recently pointed out that we should expect the "ethnic" plural in Phoenician to be ṢDNYM, and that the word is in fact spelled that way when it is certainly a reference to a community rather than a place (*KAI*[5] no. 60 = *TSSI* III no. 41, recording a decree of the ṢDNYM). ṢDNM is therefore better read as a plural or dual form of the city's name, and we do in fact have evidence from Phoenician inscriptions of the Persian period for a number of "subcities" of Sidon, including "Greater Sidon," "Smaller Sidon," "Sidon of the Sea," and "Sidon of the Fields" (e.g., *KAI*[5] no. 15). An exceptional third-century BCE dedication found on Cos, made by the son of Abdalonymos, calls him "King of the Sidonians" (MLK ṢDNYM; interestingly, the parallel Greek text has "King of Sidon"), but Amadasi Guzzo (2013, 263) suggests that this is a late and unusual spelling of the plural "Sidons."

102. *IG* II² no. 141 = RO no. 21. If the "people of Sidon" in the dating formula of the later inscription from Piraeus discussed above commemorating the crowning of a local official are those of the mother city—although the only known Sidonian era began in 111 BCE, likely to be considerably later than this inscription (see *TSSI* ad loc.)—it would provide an interesting counterexample.

103. The one exception is a shekel issued at Tyre in the first half of the fourth century, of which we have only two specimens, and on which the king's name is briefly replaced by the toponym of the city: ṢR (J. Elayi and A. Elayi 2009, type II.1.2.1.d, with discussion on p. 232).

104. *KAI*[5] no. 60 = *TSSI* III no. 41, l.2 with *IG* II²–III, 2946.

105. *CISem.* I nos. 122 and 122 bis = *KAI*[5] no. 47 = *ICO* Malta no. 1–1 bis = *IG* XIV no. 600. Punic text: L'DNN LMLQRT B'L ṢR 'Š NDR 'BDK 'BD'SR W'ḤY 'SRŠMR ŠN BN 'SRŠMR BN 'BD'SR K ŠM' QLM YBRKM. Greek text: Διονύσιος καὶ Σαραπίων οἱ Σαραπίωνος Τύριοι Ἡρακλεῖ ἀρχηγέτει. Amadasi Guzzo and Rossignani (2002) is a thorough recent treatment, and there are useful brief comments by Yarrow (2013, 357–58) and Bonnet (2015, 289–90). It is worth noting that the fact that the inscription came to light on Malta in the late seventeenth century does not prove that it was originally erected or excavated there: see Amadasi Guzzo and Rossignani (2002, 6–18) for a judicious discussion of the evidence.

106. The use of the word *archegetes* seems to be paralleled in the Greek inscription put up on Delos by the "Herakleists of Tyre" in 153 BCE, which describes "Herakles" as the *archegos tes patridos*, or "founder of the fatherland": *IDélos* 1519, with Bonnet (1988, 372).

107. Hdt. 2.178; Thuc. 6.3.1, with Malkin (2011, 101–6).

108. Hdt. 2.112. By contrast, the Karians based at Memphis lived and worshipped in a collective *Karikon*: Malkin (2011, 89).

109. Bowden (1996, 22–23) for the evidence and its problems, with Malkin (2011, 91).

CHAPTER 3. SEA PEOPLE

1. The classic text on the emic/etic distinction, formulated in relation to the study of language, is Pike (1967, esp. 37–42). On emic and etic labels in the ancient world, see Demetriou (2012, 9–10), with earlier bibliography. Arguing for the prime importance of emic definitions: Shennan (1989, 14); J. Hall (2002, 9). Giuseppe Garbati has noted this "cambiamento di prospettiva" in more recent Phoenician studies (2012, 160).

2. See Eriksen (2010, 77–78) for the importance of external ascriptions in the creation of ethnicity.

3. See Lucy (2005, 95–96) on the problems of the emic vs. etic distinction, given that the construction of ethnic identity often "should be seen as a dialectic . . . rather than a simple binary opposition" (96). Pike himself emphasized that the distinction between emic and etic descriptions was not a dichotomy (Pike 1967, 41–42; cf. Southwood 2012, 97n54).

4. The idea that the Greek word "Phoenician" derives from an Egyptian term of the same meaning (*fenkhu*) is not accepted by most scholars: see, for instance, R. Edwards (1979, 94n88); Aubet (2001, 9).

5. *Ahiqar* l. 207: for this text, see Porten and Yardeni (1993, 24–53).

6. Bagg (2011, 29), with references; see 19–41 for the bigger picture.

7. Van Seters (1972, 67).

8. Hdt. 7.89.2. Although Greek authors use "Erythrean Sea" to mean the Indian Ocean in general, this is probably a reference to the Persian Gulf. For a more specific claim that Tyre and Arados were colonies of islands in the Persian Gulf with the same names (and with "temples like those of the Phoenicians"), see Strabo 16.3.4, who says that this was the view of the inhabitants of those islands rather than the putative colonists. At 16.4.27 and 1.2.35, Strabo himself is skeptical of such a claim in relation to Sidon, noting that there is a contrary claim putting Phoenician settlements in the Gulf. For another report of Tyrian origins in the Erythrean Sea, see Pliny *HN* 4.120. See Salles (1993) for an optimistic account of the plausibility of such accounts, which is not at issue here. Just. *Epit.* 18.3.2–5 reports a different and more complicated migration story, but without a source or a specific starting point.

9. Malkin (2011, 213); cf. Malkin (2001b, 11, 15) on the biblical Exodus and the role of constitutive fictions such as the return of the Heraklids among Greeks, and Malkin (2011, 61) on Thucydides's comment that "before the Trojan War Hellas seems to have engaged in nothing in common" (1.3.1).

10. Hdt. 1.1.1.

11. Fehling (1989, esp. 50–57) on 1.1–5, with Asheri et al. (2007, ad loc.); Fehling dismisses Herodotus's claim at 7.89.2 as "probably no more than an invention" (1989, 36).

12. Hdt. 2.44.

13. Hdt. 3.19.

14. Such an understanding in the sixth or fifth century need not have reflected the precise historical events and relationships of the migration period, which I will explore further in the next section.

15. Mitchell (2007, 182–84), with additional observations at Beekes (2004, 167–69); cf. R. Edwards (1979, 65–86) and Gruen (2011, 233n62). Gruen (2011, 234n67) collects bibliography on the disputed ethnic significance of the Phoinix who makes a brief appearance in the *Iliad* as the father of Europa (*Il.* 14.321; not to be confused with Phoinix the Myrmidon, who has a larger role in the poem); there seems no reason to read him there as Phoenician. Beekes (2004) collects a series of persuasive arguments against theories that the Greek myths associated with Kadmos, or his name, had Levantine origins.

16. For the difference between territorial and land-creation myths, see Malkin (1996, esp. 10–11).

17. For the Greek image of Phoinix more generally, see Tzavellas-Bonnet (1983).

18. Apollod. *Bibl.* 2.1.4.

19. Apollod. *Bibl.* 3.1.1. Apollodorus also notes here an alternative version found in early sources, including Homer, Hesiod, and Bacchylides, that Phoinix was the father rather than the brother of Europa.

20. Eur. fr. 819 (*Phrixos* B). The third named son after Kilix and Phoinix here is named Thasos, but this final sentence of the fragment is preserved only in a scholion on a manuscript copy of another Euripides play, and Thasos is presumably a scribal error for Kadmos, who is after all described a few lines earlier as "son of Agenor."

21. See Gantz (1993, 209–10) on the possibility that Euripides here presents Phoinix and Kadmos as two names for the same person, which would not solve this problem.

22. For Herodotus, Agenor was king of Tyre (Hdt. 1.2.1).

23. Curt. 4.4.15–16; cf. 4.4.19, where Tyre is said to have been founded by Agenor.

24. *BNJ* 790, with the useful commentary of López-Ruiz and Kalledis. Other texts and translations: Attridge and Oden (1981); Baumgarten (1981). See also Barr (1974); Millar (1983, 64–65); M. Edwards (1991); Johnson (2006, 65–74); Gruen (2011, 342–43). On Philo's year of birth, 64 CE, see Kokkinos (2012).

25. Porph. *Abst.* 2.56 (= Eusebius *PE* 4.16.6 = *BNJ* 790 F 3a) with Eusebius *Praep. evang.* 1.9.20–21 (= *BNJ* 790 F 1).

26. Euseb. *Praep. evang.* 1.9.24.

27. On the history of the scholarship, see Baumgarten (1981, 2–6).

28. Euseb. *Praep. evang.* 1.10.7–14.

29. Baumgarten (1981, 140–79) presents the case for an underlying cosmogony and/or theogony, as well as the evidence for Philo's euhemerism and for extensive contamination from Greco-Roman tradition in this passage. For Chousor's identification with Hephaistos, see Euseb. *Praep. evang.* 1.10.11.

30. Byblos: Euseb. *Praep. evang.* 1.10.19; cf. 1.10.15 for another statement of the primacy of Byblos. Attica: Euseb. *Praep. evang.* 1.10.32. Baumgarten (1981, 221) points out that while the association with Attica would make this the Greek Athena, her paternity—since Athena was the daughter not of Kronos but Zeus—evokes the Ugaritic goddess Anat. Beirut: Euseb. *Praep. evang.* 1.10.35.

31. Bendall (forthcoming, sec. 4.7.2 on "Borrowings"), with earlier bibliography; see also Godart (1991). Names or adjectives based on Levantine cities are also found in the Linear B texts, which may be ethnonyms or *xenia* names of the kind discussed above, including *pe-ri-ta* (Beiruti), *tu-ri-jo* (Tyrian) and *a-ra-da-jo* (Aradi) (Cline 2014, 89).

32. Mazza (1988, 556–58). For a convenient collection of Greek sources on Phoenician and Punic matters down to the fourth century, see Mazza et al. (1988). Baurain (1986, 26–27) and Spanò Giammellaro (2004, 28) note the vagueness of the notions that the Greeks held about the origins and geography of the "Phoenicians."

33. Kestemont (1983, 62–63). The Hebrew Bible also associates the individual cities with the sea: for the king of Tyre, "sitting on the throne of the gods in the heart of the seas," see Ezek. 28:2, with 26–28 more generally; cf. 1 Kings 9:27, and on Tyre and Sidon, Isa. 23.

34. *Od.* 15.415.

35. *Il.* 23.740–45. Cf. *Il.* 6.288–95, where Hecuba's robes are Sidonian.

36. On this passage, see Xella (2014, para 25). If, as has sometimes been suggested, "Phoenicians" and "Sidonians" are used as synonyms by Homer—who refers to no other Phoenician cities—this point is even starker (e.g., Winter [1995, 247]; cf. Strabo 1.2.33). Note, however, the curious phrasing at *Od.* 4.83–84, which implies that Sidonians live outside Phoenicia.

37. *Schol. Il.* 23.744. I owe this picturesque translation to Mazza (1988, 640).

38. *Od.* 13.271–86; cf. for other "Phoenicians" met at sea 14.285–307 (a trader who does have a house in "Phoenicia") and 15.403–84 (including a "Phoenician" woman living abroad who says that she originally comes from Sidon).

39. Frankenstein (1979, 288). More recently, Michael Sommer has suggested that the "*ethnikon* 'Phoenicians' may have meant, at that stage, little more than sailor merchants, who brought exotic goods . . . who spoke an exotic language, and who behaved in exotic ways" (Sommer 2010, 118).

40. Gruen (2011, 117). Greedy and deceitful Phoenicians: *Od.* 14.287–307. Good Phoenicians: *Od.* 13.250–86. Ambiguous Phoenicians: *Od.* 15.415–53. For a more traditional picture of a negative Homeric stereotype, see Winter (1995); Camous (2007, 241); Jigoulov (2010, 12–13, focusing on the *Odyssey*).

41. *Od.* 4.83; 14.291.

42. Hdt. 1.2; 2.44, 49, 116; 3.5; 4.39; 7.89.

43. E.g., Hdt. 2.116, where they simply "dwell in Syria," although at 6.3 Histiaeus pretends to the Ionians that Darius has a plan to move the Phoenicians to Ionia, and the Ionians to Phoenicia. On 4.39, which has been read as making Phoenicia an *ethnos* or "people" (How and Wells 1912, ad loc.), see Asheri et al. (2007, ad loc.): the three "peoples" Herodotus refers to here must be Assyrians, Arabs, and Palestinian Syrians.

44. Mavrogiannis (2004, 64); Bondì (1990, 256) makes a similar point. See also Gruen (2011, 118) on the absence of anti-Phoenician prejudice in Herodotus, contra Camous (2007, 241); this is surely related to a weak sense of them as a people at all.

45. Hdt. 1.1.1–2.

46. See Hdt. 2.54–56 for another possible abduction by Phoenicians, and 4.196 for Carthaginian trading practices; for Phoenicians in the Persian fleet, see Hdt. 1.143; 3.19; 5.108–9; 6.6–17, 25, 28, 33–34, 41; 7.23, 25, 96–98; 8.85, 90, 100; cf. 7.165.

47. Hdt. 7.98. Byblos does not seem to have fielded a contingent in the Persian navy until c. 425 (J. Elayi and A. Elayi 2009, 333). At 7.89, where Herodotus briefly describes the equipment carried by the Phoenicians in the Persian fleet as part of his long list of Xerxes's naval allies, he presents them not as a distinct group but in tandem with the "Syrians of Palestine," an area he says now contains both peoples.

48. Expeditions: Hdt. 4.42. Foundations: Hdt. 1.105; 2.4, 112; 4.147; 5.57; 6.47. See Bondì (1990, 273–78), for Herodotus's depiction of the Phoenicians on the Greek seas, making the point that this is largely set in the past (275).

49. Hdt. 2.44.

50. Hdt. 2.49; 5.58.

51. Hdt. 2.104.

52. Hdt. 5.57. See 4.417 for more Phoenician Greeks, as well as Gruen (2011, 341–42).

53. Cf. Pind. *Pyth.* 2.67–68, where Pindar describes his song as being sent like Phoenician merchandise over the sea.

54. Thuc. 1.8.1.

55. Thuc. 6.2.6.

56. Morris (1992, 124–49), paints a vivid picture of extensive interaction in this context; see also, with further bibliography and a wider geographical remit, J. Hall (2002, 93–95). The extent of Levantine presence at the settlement of Pithecusae on Ischia in the Bay of Naples, as opposed to the consumption of Levantine goods, is still a very open question.

57. J. Hall (2002, 111–17, quotations on 115 and 116); he also notes, however, that Herodotus "often regards language as the specific property of an *ethnos*" (191). The term *barbaros* itself is often supposed, on the basis of an etymology given by Strabo (14.2.28), to derive from the harsh pronunciation of non-Greeks.

58. [Pl.] *Epistulae* 8.353e, with Prag (2014, 18).

59. See Millar (1983, 60) for the "Vorhellenismus" of the Phoenician cities in this respect, as well as Malkin (2005, 245–46; 2011, 130–31, 153) and Hodos (2009, 228–33) for other similarities between the people who were colonizing the Mediterranean.

60. Morris (1992, 135), with particular reference to Sparta, for which see also Drews (1979); Murray (2000, 237–38); Niemeyer (2000, 109); for a serious recent study of the proposition, tracing its history from Jacob Burckhardt, see Raaflaub (2004).

61. Malkin (2011, 5, with 218–19), dating this to the Archaic period; Jonathan Hall puts the development of an overall Hellenic identity later than Malkin, in the sixth or even fifth centuries (Hall 1997; 2002). Robin Osborne emphasizes the sense of solidarity between Greek *poleis* in Homer's tales but notes that this is based on the oath that all of Helen's suitors swore to defend her husband and that the "common factor that brings all these Greeks together at Troy is not presented in ethnic terms of ancestry but by reference to common participation in an entirely artificially manufactured bond" (2012b, 26).

62. J. Hall (1997); Malkin (2011, chaps. 2–3).

63. See Quinn (2011, 390–91), with Gruen (2011, 1–5): "The conception of collective identity in terms of (rather than in contrast to) another culture forms a significant ingredient in the ancient outlook" (5). For a slightly different perspective on Greek representations of the Phoenicians, see Morstadt (2015, 12).

64. Malkin (2005, 250; with 2011, 134–35).

65. Pseudo-Skylax 13, 102–4, 111–12, with Shipley (2011, ad loc.).

66. Pseudo-Skylax 100–104. The geographical "titles" of Pseudo-Skylax's chapters, including "Syria and Phoenica" on 104, are later additions (Shipley 2011, 3).

67. J. Hall (1997, 34–36; quotation at 35).

68. Pl. *Rep.* 3.414b–c; Ar. fr. 957 (Kassel-Austin, *PCG*).

69. Gruen (2011, 121–22); Mazza (1988, 560).

70. Strabo 3.5.5.

71. Hermesianax, *Leontion* fr. 2 (= Ant. Lib. *Met.* 39). I am grateful to Aneurin Ellis-Evans for bringing this passage to my attention.

72. J. Hall (2002, 175–205); Malkin notes that "an antithetical 'us' identity could already be observed in the eighth to sixth centuries BCE in Ionia and the Greek colonies in the west" (2001b, 7).

73. Pl. *Menex.* 245d.

74. For a more nuanced account of the satire, see J. Hall (2002, 214–17).

75. J. Hall (2002, 205–26); Isoc., *Paneg.* 50; cf. *Evagoras* 66, with Usher (1993, 142– 43); and J. Hall (2002, 208–10). On the problems of interpreting the famous account of "Greekness" at Hdt. 8.144.2, see Thomas (2001, 214–15), with Malkin (2001b, 6); J. Hall (2002, 190–93).

76. "Phoenician" fleet in the battle off Lade in 494 BCE: Hdt 6.14.1, as pointed out in Morris (1992, 372); Thuc. 1.110, 116 on the defeat of Egypt's Athenian allies by Persia's "Phoenician" fleet c. 454 BCE. Triremes: Hdt. 8.121. See Morris (1992, 371–75) on the role of Phoenicians in the Persian navy in the sixth and fifth centuries, and the importance of those Phoenician ships in contemporary Greek discourse.

77. Martin (2017, 76) notes the curious lack of antipathy for the Phoenicians in Greek sources, despite the prominence of the former in the Persian fleet.

78. Hdt. 6.17.

79. Hdt. 7.166.

80. *BNJ* 70 F 186, with Feeney (2007, 43–46) and skepticism at Arist. *Poet.* 1459a24–27.

81. Prag (2010).

82. Pind. *Pyth.* 1.72 (a poem that makes a connection between Salamis and Himera); Theocr. *Id.* 16.76–81; Diod. Sic. 14.46, 65, 15.15–17. See further Prag (2010, esp. 59, 62; 2014, 17–18). For the way in which sources of the Hellenistic period and later align the barbarian Phoenicians and Carthaginians against the civilized Greeks and later Romans, see Bonnet and Grand-Clément (2010).

83. Arist. *Pol.* 2.8 (1272b–1273b) with Isocrates, *Nikokles* 24; Barceló (1994, 7–8); Gruen (2011, 119–20); Strabo 1.4.9 (quoting Eratosthenes); Polyb. 6.51.2 and 6.52.1, with 1.20.12 and Diodorus 5.20 for similar points.

84. Strabo 16.2.21; Pompon. 1.63; Plin. *HN* 5.66–67, 75–78.

85. Prag (2014, 14n8).

86. Aubet (2001, 12; 2009, 22); Prag (2006, 11–12; 2014).

87. Cic. *Scaur.* 42. See Varro *apud* Plin. *HN* 3.1.8 for another distinction between *Phoenices* and *Poeni* of a similar date, though it is not obvious there what each word means.

88. Cic. *Rep.* 2.9, quoted below; cf. 3.7 for *Poeni* in parallel with "Assyrians" and "Persians," and 3 fr. 3 for *Poeni* who trade in Greece. At Cic. *Fin.* 4.56 the diminutive *poenulus* is used of a Kitian who, it is specified, came originally from Phoenicia: there may be a diasporic implication in the use of the word here.

89. Cic. *Har. resp.* 19.

90. Pompon. 2.96. I thank Jonathan Prag for discussion of this passage.

91. On this text, see Ní Mheallaigh (2012), with earlier bibliography.

92. *Phoenix*: August. *De civ. D.* 4.10; *punica mulier*: August. *Ad Rom.* 13.3.

93. August., *In epistolam Ioannis ad Parthos tractatus decem* 2.3 (407/9 CE); cf. *Ep.* 17.2, and see Courtois (1950, 275–77).

94. See Acquaro (1983, 60); Moscati (1984, 532); Prag (2006, 29n135; 2014, 20–22), though it is of course often hard to tell whether an item would primarily have been associated with Africa in general or Carthage in particular.

95. Sall. *Iug.* 108.3.

96. Cato *Agr.* 7.3; 126.1.

97. Serv. *ad Aen.* 1.108–9.

98. On the picture of Phoenicians and Carthaginians in the Roman literary tradition, see Mazza (1988); Isaac (2004, 324–35); Camous (2007); Erskine (2013, 28–29). Much of the scholarship emphasizes the negative and even oppositional aspects; for a more positive interpretation, see Gruen (2011, 115–40), and chapter 7. *Poenus* tend to retain the negative connotations that *phoinix* had carried in the Western Greek tradition, while *phoenix* was used as a neutral term (Bunnens 1979; Mazza 1988).

99. Plaut. *Poen.* 112f (though see Gruen [2011, 126–28] on the play's basically positive portrayal of the "little Pune" of its title); *Rhet. Her.* 4.20 (where the tone makes the traditional attribution to Cato attractive).

100. Diod. Sic. 30.7.1; Livy puts this as *versutiae Punicae*: 42.47.7.

101. Livy 21.4.9.

102. *Leg. agr.* 2.95, a point noted at Gruen (2011, 132). The two theories are united in Cicero's *De republica*, where the Phoenicians (*Poeni*) import greed into Greece along with their merchandise (*Rep.* 3 fr. 3).

103. Cic. *Rep.* 2.9.

104. As preserved in Festus, *Gloss Lat.* s.v. Tyria maria (484.21 Lindsay); cf. Strabo 3.5.11, 16.2.1.

105. Pompon. 1.65.

106. Lomas (2000, 86).

107. See Baurain (1992), in relation for the most part to Punic "literature" and to Carthage, and see Garbini (1991) for speculation to the contrary, based on an ingenious attempt to connect biblical passages with a wider "Canaanite" literary tradition.

108. Feeney (2005, 229); see also Goody and Watt (1963, 317–18); Woolf (2012, 296–97). I thank Denis Feeney for discussions on this topic.

109. Pompon. 1.56: "litteras et litterarum operas aliasque etiam artes . . . conmenti."

110. Joseph. *AJ* 8.55, 144–49; 9.283–87; *Ap.* 1.106–27. Josephus says that these archives were translated by Menander of Ephesus and Dios; his information about them may in fact be solely from these writers and is not therefore necessarily reliable (Garbini 1980; Boyes 2012, 34). For an argument that Josephus's claims about Tyrian annals were largely rhetorical, designed to give his own work authority, see Mazza (1988, 549). A Phoenician archive has been found at Idalion (Amadasi Guzzo and López Zamora 2016).

111. Strabo 16.2.24; cf. Plin. *HN* 30.9 for a medical text by a Phoenician called Dardanus.

112. Corinne Bonnet notes that Phoenician religion hinges on practice, rite, and cult, not myth, and comments, "Greek myth-making is infinintely more rich and varied" (La mitopoiesi greca è infinintamente più ricca e diversificata) (2005, 22; cf. Ribichini 1985).

113. Plin. *HN* 18.22, with Greene and Kehoe (1995). For the lack of evidence for literary production at Carthage, see Millar (1968, 133); Baurain (1992); Miles (2010, 13), with Kerr (2010, 177) on the preposterous claim that a fourth-century CE Punic inscription from Bir ed-Dreder in Libya is a "three verse metrical Punic poem." For a more positive reading of the evidence, see Hoyos (2010, 105–8). For the huge deposit of clay document seals found in the Temple of Eshmun at Carthage, suggesting the presence of a large documentary archive, see Berges (1997).

114. Feeney (2016, 203–5).

115. Aug. *Ep.* 17.2. I will discuss the evidence for Numidian literature in Punic in chapter 8.

116. This is a version of what Benedict Anderson described as the reliance of imagined communities on a "sociological organism"—a large, coherent group of people who do not necessarily know each other, moving together through time (1991, 26). On the links between literature and identity, see Remotti (1996, 54), and on those between literature and ethnicity in particular, Kristiansen (1998, 402–7); Lucy (2005, 99).

CHAPTER 4. CULTURAL POLITICS

1. 2 Sam. 5:11; 1 Kings 5, 7:13–46, 9:26–28, 10:11, 16:31; 1 Chron. 14:1; 2 Chron. 8:17–18; Joseph. *AJ* 8.141–49.

2. Language: Briquel-Chatonnet (1992a), and see further note 39 below. Architecture: Briquel-Chatonnet (1995, 590); Finkelstein and Silberman (2001, 169– 95); Joffe (2002, 442–44, 448). Temple: Millar (1983, 59). For regional connections between Israel and Phoenicia more generally, see De Geus (1991, 12–14); Briquel-Chatonnet (1992b; 1995).

3. Radner (2006, 62–63).

4. See J. Elayi and Sapin (1998, 14–19) and Jigoulov (2010, 20–30) on the complexities of the ancient sources on this question, with the latter noting that royal Persian inscriptions never mention Phoenicia at all (20).

5. Aubet (2001, 17); cf. Bondì et al. (2009, 1).

6. See, for these cities' natural inclination toward the sea, Malkin (2014b, 138).

7. *ANET*[3] 287–88. Josephus also mentions an "Eloulaios" who ruled at Tyre (*AJ* 9.283–86), but there are significant contradictions between his account and the contemporary Assyrian sources; see Boyes (2012, 39–40). The account in the book of Judges of the Danites' conquest of Laish in upper Galilee might be read as suggesting that Laish, a considerable way inland, was under the (ineffective) protection of Sidon at the time of its alleged conquest by the tribe of Dan (Judges 18:7, 28). For Sidonian control of Sarepta in the ninth century, see 1 Kings 17:9; by the fourth century, it was controlled by Tyre (Pseudo-Skylax 104.3).

8. *KAI*[5] no. 14, l. 18–20 = *TSSI* III no. 28.

9. Pseudo-Skylax 104.

10. Boyes (2012, 40), with 1 Kings 16:31 and Joseph. *AJ* 8.324 (with *Ap.* 1.123) (king of the Tyrians or Tyre), 8.317, 9.138 (king of the Tyrians and Sidonians). Boyes also points out that if Josephus's Tyrian sources on the details of Ittobaal's kingship are entirely reliable, he fathered his first child at the age of nine.

11. *KAI*[5] no. 31 with Amadasi Guzzo (2013) for the reading "of the Sidons," rather than "of the Sidonians" (see chap. 2, n. 101 above). I thank Robin Lane Fox for discussion of this topic.

12. *IG* II[2] no. 141 = RO no. 21. For this date for Strato's death, based on the dating of his coinage, see J. Elayi (2005b, 141).

13. Just. *Epit.* 18.3.

14. *CISem.* I no. 114 = *IDélos* no. 50.

15. J. Elayi (2005b, 95).

16. Pseudo-Skylax 104.2; Diod. Sic. 16.41.1; Strabo 16.2.15.

17. Also noted at Pompon. 1.67. On these and later sources, including independent Arabic ones that seem to confirm that there were three separate fortified sites,

see J. Elayi (1990, 60–62). For a further suggestion of collaboration or co-opted labor between Tyre, Sidon, and Arados (and Byblos), see Ezek. 27:8–9.

18. Strabo 16.2.13.

19. Diod. Sic. 16.41.1.

20. Diod. Sic. 16.41.3. Curiously, the alliance itself is missing in action throughout Diodorus's lengthy account of the subsequent war, in which the Sidonians are the only Phoenician protagonists mentioned until he tells us that after the brutal punishment of Sidon, the other cities went back over to the Persian king (16.45.6). See Maier (1994, 322) and van Dongen (2010, 478n54) for hesitations over the reliability of Diodorus's notice.

21. Jones (1997, 2); cf. Papadopoulos (2005, 127–29) on the work of Vere Gordon Childe.

22. Braudel (1980, 202; 1995, 11, 22). Though he is concerned that his civilizations not be seen as isolated, they are "undeniably . . . distinct" (1995, 7). For the various relationships and the changing hierarchy between "culture(s)" and "civilization(s)" in different European languages see Braudel (1995, 5–6). More recent examples of this approach include Samuel Huntington's theory of the clash of civilizations, and the work of Martin Jacques on the (Han) Chinese "civilization-state": see Huntington (1996); Jacques (2009). For criticism of the models employed by these authors, see Sen (2006, esp. 40–46); P. Anderson (2010); Mac Sweeney (2010).

23. The text of the petition is available at http://macedonia-evidence.org/obama-letter.html. Hobsbawm (1997, 274) conveniently summarizes the history, context, and politics of the dispute over the name of Macedonia.

24. Gilroy (1993, 31). On the waning enthusiasm for this model, see Shennan (1989, 8); further critical assessments are found in J. Hall (1997, 128–31); Jones (1997); Quinn (2003); Lucy (2005, 86–94); Mac Sweeney (2009, 103–4). Not everyone agrees, of course; see, for example, Brett (1996, 9), where an ethnicity is "a social group which shares a culture." Ruby (2006, 28–29); Antonaccio (2010); and Faust and Lev-Tov (2011) provide summaries of the whole debate, with earlier bibliography. Mann (1986) suggests a different and more convincing model of societies "constituted of multiple overlapping and intersecting sociospatial networks of power" (1).

25. Shennan (1989, 13).

26. See Lucy (2005, 91–92), with Osborne (2012b, 28–30), on the lack of consistent matches between similiarities in ancient Greek material culture and known political or ethnic boundaries. For the problems of trying to map the use of the Phoenician language onto "Phoenician" material culture in Cyprus, see Steele (2013, 187).

27. For a typical example of the standard attribution of these artifacts to Phoenicia, see Joffe (2002, 436); for a relatively early summary of the problems, see Harden (1962, 217).

28. van Dongen (2010, 476); for the concept of "international style," see Feldman (2006, 25–58), with (2014, 178–79) on the problems of the stylistic label "Phoenician."

29. Vella (2010; 2014). See Markoe (1985) for the catalogue (updated at Vella [2010, 23n14]), and an argument that they should still be labeled "Phoenician."

30. *Il.* 23.741–45; see Feldman (2014, 111–37) for the most recent discussion of the interpretative problems and possibilities presented by these bowls.

31. Markoe (2000, 147). See, more recently, Feldman (2014, 11–41) on these ivories and their "decentralized production within and across regional borders" (40); she argues that the standard division of Iron Age ivories from the Levant into a "north

Syrian" and a more Egyptianizing "Phoenician" style ignores examples that mix both styles and obscures what is more likely to be a chronological distinction. We could add to this list the colored beads and other glass artifacts often casually labeled Phoenician in museums: despite Pliny's association of glass manufacture with southern Phoenicia (*HN* 36.190–91), the role of other regions including the Aegean, Rhodes, and Egypt in the development of this production is now thought to have been underestimated; see Spanò Giammellaro (2004, 27–28, 35).

32. Martin (2017, 89).

33. van Dongen (2010, 471, 475–76).

34. I take this phrase from the title of Mufwene (2003). On relationships between identity and language, see Joseph (2004). For the importance language can have in the performance of identity, see Adams (2003, 751–53).

35. Terrell (2001).

36. van Dongen (2010, 471–74). For brief overviews of the Phoenician language, see Amadasi Guzzo and Röllig (1995); Hackett (2004); Gzella (2011b); Röllig (2011).

37. Gzella (2011a).

38. Rendsburg (2003b, 72).

39. Briquel-Chatonnet (1992a); Rendsburg (2003a). Garbini argues that the written language was quite simply Phoenician (e.g., Garbini [1988, 27]). The number of uncontroversially Phoenician inscriptions found in the area of the Northern Kingdom show that the language was in any case much used there. For a detailed account of the differences between Hebrew and Phoenician dialects, see Amadasi Guzzo and Rendsburg (2013), and for the region's "dialect continuum" more generally, see Garr (1985, esp. 216–35).

40. Hackett (2004, 366–67); Gzella (2011b, 55; 2013, esp. 175). It is important to note that much of the evidence of and for the different dialects in the cities of "Phoenicia" itself is from different periods, and that the question of the existence of a "northern" dialect spoken at Arados and Amrit is not settled.

41. Sader (2009, 59, 62–63).

42. Van Beek and Van Beek (1981); Sharon (1987); Cecchini (1995, 395–96); E. Stern (1998); Markoe (2000, 71–72).

43. Kamlah (2012); see also Markoe (2000, 125–29); Bondì et al. (2009, 27).

44. The use of pottery as a marker of membership of a particular people rather than, say, membership of a particular class, has attracted particular skepticism: see Dietler and Herbich (1994); Antonaccio (2005, 101–6); cf. Faust and Lev-Tov (2011, 21–23).

45. Bikai (1978); W. Anderson (1990), in particular 36 on the importance of excavations at Tyre and Sarepta in establishing "a referent for all other Phoenician pottery"; Lehmann (1998); Gilboa (1999), making the interesting suggestion that bichrome decoration came over time to signal a regional group identity (12–16; this would not, of course, have necessarily been a "Phoenician" identity); Schreiber (2003); Bondì et al. (2009, 323–35); Jamieson (2011). For a useful brief summary of types, shapes, and chronology, see Markoe (2000, 160–63). I thank S. Rebecca Martin and Barak Monnickendam-Givon for discussion of this material.

46. On, and against, the term "Cypro-Phoenician," see Bourogiannis (2012).

47. For the most recent overview of the evidence and bibliography, see Orsingher (forthcoming).

48. Shennan (1989, 13); see also Faust (2009, 66).

49. On the necessarily subtle use of material culture and social practice in the production of ethnicity and other group identities, see Lucy (2005, 101–8).

50. Barth (1969) is the classic essay; note, however, that Barth does present boundaries as porous. See also Eriksen (2010), esp. 79–80 on "we-hood" and "us-hood." Versions of this approach to the ancient world include Hartog (1988); E. Hall (1989); Cartledge (1993); Isaac (2004).

51. Faust (2010, 58, 62), with specific reference to ethnic identity, and with earlier bibliography. The approach is not universally popular: Irad Malkin argues against a Barthian emphasis on boundaries (Malkin 2011, 99) and his "network" approach to tracing the connections between cultural objects and practices represents a sophisticated new version of Smith's approach, going beyond place-bound notions of civilization, to delineate a "Greek world" in the Mediterranean.

52. J. Hall (2002, 24); see also 19–24 in general, and J. Hall (1998). Along similar lines, see Gunter (2009, 9–195); Malkin (2014a). For a more optimistic account of what can be gleaned from material evidence alone, see Jones (1997) and Faust (2010), with the latter noting that ethnicity should nonetheless be studied alongside other social identities rather than in isolation.

53. Mac Sweeney (2009, 104).

54. Bispham (2013, 47). One phrase I deliberately avoid in this book is "cultural identity," since that term is regularly used in two quite different ways: on the one hand, as an overall name for a set of group identities including ethnicity, gender, class, and so on (e.g., J. Hall [2002, 17]), perhaps better labeled "social identities" (though n.b. Mac Sweeney [2009, 105]); and on the other, to indicate an affiliation to a particular "culture," as in "Roman cultural identity" (e.g., Grahame [1998, 159], there used explicitly as a synonym for "ethnicity"), a concept that, as I have discussed above in relation to Braudel and others, should probably not be used at all. I now think that my attempt to reappropriate the term "cultural identity" to describe identities constructed by means of cultural practices and artifacts (Quinn 2011a, 407n30) only adds to the confusion.

55. Overviews at Sader (1995; 2015); Bondì et al. (2009, 12–67 passim); Dixon (2013); Aubet-Semmler and Trelliso Carreño (2015).

56. Michael Sommer notes a difference between the mixed rites of rural cemeteries and a marked preference for cremation in urban environments on the Levantine coast and suggests that this could be an indication that the city and country were not integrated, as in the Greek city-state, but worked more as an "empire *en miniature*," with a "restricted urban élite that ruled over a politically and socially less privileged, ethnically and culturally diverse periphery" (Sommer 2010, 125–26).

57. Cremation was not entirely unknown on the Israelite side of this "border"; see Bloch-Smith (1992, 52–55).

58. Bondì et al. (2009, 12); Sader (2009, 59).

59. J. Elayi and A. Elayi (1999), also noting signs of close contact with Cyprus.

60. Xella (2008, 70); Bonnet (2014, 157–58).

61. Shrines: Oggiano (2008, 285) with earlier bibliography, including the important article by Bisi (1971). Sanctuary of Eshmoun: Stucky (1984); Stucky et al. (2005); Bondì et al. (2009, 37–43); Bonnet (2014, 211–50). On the varied sculpture from the site, see Stucky (1993). Corinne Bonnet discusses the culture of Sidon (2014, 206–7), and also collects bibliography for Greek cultural references in the Persian period Levant more generally (2014, 287; 2015, 34n67).

62. "Alexander" Sarcophagus: von Graeve (1970); Houser (1998); with discussion by A. Stewart (1993, 290–306). "Mourning Women" Sarcophagus: Fleischer and Schiele (1983). "Satrap" Sarcophagus: Kleemann (1958). "Lycian" Sarcophagus: Schmidt-Dounas (1985); Langer-Karrenbrock (2000). See also the more comprehensive treatment in Ferron (1993). The original publication of the excavation, with beautiful plates, is Hamdi and Reinach (1892).

63. Thanks to Susan Hitch for this observation.

64. S. Hall (1990); Quinn (2011a).

65. See Brubaker and Cooper (2000, 15), on the difference between relational and categorical identification, with 14–17 more generally on cultural identification. I am grateful to Tamar Hodos and S. Rebecca Martin for discussion of these matters.

66. Frede (2000); Lembke (2001, esp. 50–56); Fontan and Le Meaux (2007, 153–57).

67. Lembke (2001, 121–44).

68. Martin (2017, 132, 136).

69. Dixon (2013, 543). The famous sarcophagus of Ahiram from Byblos is the only tomb of this type found in the region that pre-dates the Persian period, going back to perhaps the twelfth or thirteenth century BCE.

70. Bénichou-Safar (1982, 132–35); Tore (1995, 471–73); Frede (2000, 134–49); Lembke (2001, 56–79); Morstadt (2015, 98).

71. Oggiano (2005, 1034–35; 2008, 291–92; 2012, 195).

72. Oggiano (2016, 169).

73. *IG* II³ no. 468 = *IG* II² no. 342, with rather speculative commentary by Walbank (1985).

74. Livy 34.61, with quotations from sections 7 and 12–13. I thank Bruce Hitchner for drawing my attention to this passage.

75. Briscoe (1981, 141).

76. See Renfrew (1986) for the classic statement of the peer polity interaction model; Ma (2003, 15) for its utility in understanding the network of "equipollent, interconnected" Greek cities in the Hellenistic period; and Malkin (2011, 63–64) on the role of peer polity interaction in the formation of conceptions of Greekness in the Archaic period.

77. For recent summaries of Phoenician religion with bibliography, see Bonnet and Xella (1995); Lipiński (1995); Markoe (2000, 115–42); Bondì et al. (2009, 400–405). On the lack of homogeneity: van Dongen (2010, 478–79); Xella (2008, 70–71).

78. Tyre and Sidon may again share more in this respect than other cities: as early as the Bronze Age Epic of King Keret, one of the poems found at Ugarit, a deity called Athirat seems to be called the goddess of the Tyrians and Sidonians, although the reading of both terms has been disputed: *KTU*³ no. 1.14 IV 35–36, with Xella (1995, 261–62).

79. Bonnet (1996).

80. For polythetic and diagnostic sets, see Davis (1990).

81. On the *egersis* ceremony: Joseph. *AJ* 8.146; Bonnet (1988, 33–40, 104–12).

82. Mettinger (2001, 113–65) collects the evidence for Byblos and Sidon; see also Bonnet (1988, 109–10).

83. For the possibility that the *egersis* was celebrated in the west, see Bonnet (1988, 221–22).

84. Child sacrifice: Stavrakopoulou (2004); Xella (2012a); and see further chapter 5. Sacred prostitution: Lipiński (1995, 486–89), emphasizing the variety of customs sub-

sumed under this modern label, with references and earlier bibliography (contra, Markoe 2000, 120). Necromancy: Bénichou-Safar (2012a, 269).

85. The details of this process are difficult to trace; for one attempt, see J. Elayi and A. Elayi (2009, 328–29).

86. For a succinct survey of the various standards and varied designs, see Martin (2017, 123–31), with references and earlier bibliography, and for studies of the coinage of the individual cities of Sidon, Tyre, and Byblos, see J. Elayi and A. Elayi (2004; 2009; 2014).

87. Nitschke (2013, 262–63), with further bibliography.

88. I deliberately say "quotation" here rather than "influence," a concept that, as I and others have argued elsewhere, puts analysis the wrong way round, and in the wrong hands, casting the producers of culture as passive receptacles of cultural influence rather than as active interpreters and manipulators of cultural precedents and models: see Quinn (2013a, 191–92); see also Baxandall (1985, 58–62); Stewart and Korres (2004, 97–98); and Mac Sweeney (2009, 105), on "practices of affiliation."

89. Acquaro (1971).

90. Quinn (2013b, 23–24); Quinn and Vella (2014a, 5–6), both with further bibliography. For more on the problems associated with the term and the concept, see Quinn (2013b), with Prag (2014, 22–23). Some have questioned whether it should be used at all, e.g., López Castro (1995, 9–10).

91. For individual regions, see, for instance, Vincenzo (2013) on Sicily; Roppa (2014) on Sardinia; Papi (2014) on Mauretania. For external relations, see López Castro (1995, 9); Campus (2006); van Dommelen and Gómez Bellard (2008a, 4).

92. On this model and the problems associated with it, see Quinn (2013b, 24–25), with further bibliography.

93. Bondì (2014). Cf. Garbati (2015b, 206) on "Western Phoenician worlds."

94. van Dommelen and Gómez Bellard (2008a, 5). The concept of a cultural "koiné" can be useful in such circumstances, despite the awkwardness of transferring a term from linguistics to broader cultural practice, because it does not necessarily map onto a single group identity but can in fact mediate between them, as Aaron Burke (2014) has observed of what he labels the Amorite koiné in the third to second millennium BCE, drawing on Michael Dietler's (2010) productive investigation of the notion of "entanglement."

95. Fentress (2013, 157–67), with Prag (2011, 5–6); Quinn (2011b; 2013a); Kuttner (2013); A. Wilson (2013); Yarrow (2013, 356n16).

96. Paus. 10.11.3; Carthaginian involvement is doubted by Krings (1998, 25).

97. Hdt. 1.166.

98. Hdt. 5.42.

99. Hdt. 5.46; Pausanias mentions explicitly only Segestans (3.16.4–5), and Diodorus only Carthaginians (4.23.3).

100. Hdt. 7.165; Diod. Sic. 11.21.4, 13.55.1; Jonathan Hall suggests that this information was deliberately suppressed by Herodotus, "whose work is concerned precisely with constructing a sense of Hellenic identity" (2002, 122).

101. Thuc. 6.88.6, 6.34.2, discussed at Prag (2010, 61).

102. Diod. Sic.14.53.4, 18.21.4.

103. Sil. 3.249–53.

104. See Fentress (2013, 159) for the way that "wars created massive potential for communication between the political and ethnic groupings that took part in them, broadening and deepening the networks of relationships between the protagonists."

105. Bechtold (2007; 2013); Bechtold and Docter (2010); A. Wilson (2013); Maraoui Telmini et al. (2014, 131–36). See Wolff (2004) for the amphorae made in Levantine contexts in the western Mediterranean found at sites in Greece, Turkey, and Israel.

106. Quinn (2011b, 15–16).

107. Fentress (2013, 157–58), with Diod. Sic. 14.46.

108. Diod. Sic. 14.77.5.

109. Hamilcar: Hdt. 7.166. For descendants of Syracusans in third-century Carthage, see Polyb. 7.2.4. Sophonisba: Livy 30.11–16. Hannibal and Hasdrubal: Livy 24.41.7; Diod. Sic. 25.12; Sil. 3.66, 97–107. For extensive personal relationships between Greeks and Carthaginians in the west, see the collection of examples at Prag (2010, 53–54). On the mixed population and mixed marriages of Carthage, esp. as seen through onomastics, see Ferjaoui (1991; 1999, 78–81); Xella (2008, 76–78); Crouzet (2012, 41–46).

110. There are exceptions: Sardinia saw very little contact between colonies and the local population in the seventh and sixth centuries (van Dommelen 2005, 149).

111. Bénichou-Safar (1982, esp. 267–68).

112. Maraoui Telmini et al. (2014, 132, 136). For possible evidence for Greek settlement in the area earlier in Carthage's history, see Boardman (2006).

113. Hdn. 5.6.9; Porph. *Abst.* 1.14; Sil. Ital. 3.22–23. There is an increase in pig bones found in "Phoenicia" in this period as well, a detail for which I thank S. Rebecca Martin.

114. Ban: Just. *Epit.* 20.5.13. Hannibal's Greek education: Nepos, *Hannibal* 13.3. González Wagner (1986) and Bonnet (2006a) point out the dangers of overemphasizing the Hellenic elements in Carthaginian culture.

115. Hurst (1994, 291).

116. Acquaro (1971); Dridi (2006, 236).

117. Xella (2008, 76).

118. Diod. Sic. 14.53.2.

119. Bonnet (2006b).

120. Diod. Sic. 14.77.4–5, with Xella (1969).

121. Bonnet (2006a, 373–76).

122. Garbati (2006); van Dommelen and López Bertran (2013).

123. Bisi (1990, 6–7); Prag (2011); Vincenzo (2013, 364); Bondì (2014, 64–65); Frey-Kupper (2014). Prag notes in particular the enormous quantity of "Siculo-Punic" coinage minted by Carthage in Sicily found at Morgantina, well inside the "Greek" part of the island (6), and although Frey-Kupper emphasizes the relative rarity of Punic coinage at many other eastern Sicilian sites (77), she also notes the possibility that some of it was destroyed by Romans. Garbati (2006, 132) traces the extension of Sicilian-Greek terracotta forms to Carthage and the Phoenician-speaking centers of Sardinia.

124. Jenkins (1971, with 1978, 48–58); Manfredi (2009); Prag (2011, 2); Frey-Kupper (2014, 81), noting that this civic coinage ceases entirely c. 300 BCE, after which the only Punic coinage in Sicily is Carthaginian, with Punic legends including "People of the Camp" and "Treasurers." Cf. n149 below.

125. For rare examples of Greek-language "Panormus," see Jenkins (1971), Panormus didrachm no. 2 (p. 38) and tetradrachm no. 1 (p. 45).

126. Francisi (2002); Mezzolani (2009, 407–9). For the beautiful gola cornice discovered on a recently reexcavated Iron Age temple at Tyre, see Badre (2015, 69–70).

127. Wallace-Hadrill (2013, 39–41); Frey-Kupper (2014, 100–102) on the Ebusitan coinage at Pompeii.

128. E.g., Brown (1991, fig. 63a, b), an Etruscan funerary urn.

129. Spanò Giammellaro (2004, 35–38); Bispham (2013, 75).

130. Visonà (2009a, 176).

131. Isid. *Etym.* 20.11.3, noticed by Bispham (2013, 64n109).

132. Keay (2013, 309). Cf. the later "Libyphoenician" coins of southern Spain, whose images link them not with Carthaginian coinage but with other North African cities and Gadir (Jiménez 2010).

133. Irad Malkin's investigations in this area have elucidated the uses of the "colonial middle ground" model for the interpretation of relations between Greeks, Etruscans, and Phoenicians in the Archaic central Mediterranean in a number of works, most notably Malkin (2002; 2011, chap. 5).

134. Coins: Jenkins (1974; 1977; 1978); Mildenberg (1992); Visonà (1998, 4–5). Function: Frey-Kupper (2014, 81): "The fact that these early silver and gold coins have never been found in North Africa clearly attests to their military purpose." It would be more than another fifty years before Carthage started to mint coinage for use at home.

135. Prag (2011, 2, 4–5). When Carthage started minting gold coins in Sicily in the first half of the fourth century, the weight standard was the shekel (Visonà 1998; Frey-Kupper 2014, 81), and the weight standard for the silver coinage shifted to the shekel in the third century (Jenkins 1978, 36–39).

136. Jenkins (1974, 27), for the possibilities; Just. *Epit.* 18.5.16 for the horse's head.

137. Jenkins (1974, series 1).

138. Contra, see Jenkins (1974, 27), objecting to the "rather over-ingenious suggestion" that this is a *type parlant*, in part on the grounds that such an interpretation "would imply that the Carthaginians were bilingual in Greek." This may well often have been true, as noted in chapter 3, but it does not matter: the more important point is that Greek term was the only one on offer to make this particular point. Prag (2006, 26–28) is skeptical on different grounds, pointing out that *phoinix* has several other meanings and associations in Greek. For more on the symbolism of the palm, see Bénichou-Safar (2012b).

139. Visonà (2009a, 173).

140. Visonà (2009a, 176–77).

141. Frey-Kupper (2014, 103), with (2013, 100) and Fine (2005, 141).

142. Whittaker (1978, 63; cf. 60).

143. See López Castro (1991), on Iberia; van Dommelen (1998a, 120–29); van Dommelen and Gómez Bellard 2008a, 8–12; 2008b, 237–39); Roppa (2014), on Sardinia; and Bondì (2006); Prag (2010, 55n17), on Sicily. This does not, of course, mean that Whittaker's interpretation has been universally accepted: see recently, for instance, D'Andrea and Giardino (2011, 133n5).

144. van Dommelen (1998a, 120–24) with Just. *Epit.* 18.7–19.1.

145. Polyb. 3.22–23, with Whittaker (1978, 63).

146. López Castro (1991); Bondì (2006, 132–34); Bondì (2014, 63–66).

147. Diod. Sic. 13.114. On the reading and interpretation of this difficult passage, see Anello (1986).

148. Bondì (2006, 134–36).

149. Jenkins (1978, 7–8, 36–39); Manfredi (1995, 110–11).

150. I discuss the evidence for this in the next chapter.

151. According to Pseudo-Skylax 111.9, all the towns and emporia on the coast of Africa from Euesperides to the Pillars of Herakles were "of the Carthaginians"; cf. Quinn (2014).

152. Álvarez Martí-Aguilar (2014, 32–36), with earlier bibliography; particularly interesting ancient sources on this point include Polyb. 2.1.5 (on the Barcid "recuperation" of Carthaginian possessions in Spain in 237 BCE); [Arist.] *Mir. ausc.* 136 (control of the Gaditan tuna trade); and Pseudo-Skylax 1, saying that there were many Carthaginian commercial establishments along the northern Mediterranean coast from the Pillars of Hercules.

153. Polyb. 1.10; quotation from sections 5 and 8.

154. Frey-Kupper (2014, 77), with Visonà (2006) and *SNG Cop.* 42 nos. 102–19, 124–27.

155. Visonà (2009a, 174).

156. Frey-Kupper (2014, 98).

157. Frey-Kupper (2014, 86–87); *SNG Cop.* 42 nos. 109–19.

158. Jenkins (1971, 74 nos. 4a, 4b, 5, 8, 9 [= Manfredi 1995, SIB nos. 68–69, 73–74, 85]), with Frey-Kupper (2013, 91–92) for the dating of the Motyan coins. I am grateful to Suzanne Frey-Kupper for further discussion of this coinage.

159. Manfredi (1995, SIB no. 97 [with legend BTW'M, and commentary on 117]; SIB no. 98 [= Jenkins (1971, 69 no. 73); cf. SIB nos. 1–2]) for rather different examples from a late-third-century Sicilian mint that may be Morgantina.

160. Mattingly (2011, 226), with McCarty (2011) on the ideological weight that can, but does not have to, be carried by ritual. Michael Sommer has suggested some other bases for mutual identification among Phoenician speakers based on occupation or migration, which could in both cases involve social groups of people from very different places, languages, and cultures (2010, 127).

CHAPTER 5. THE CIRCLE OF THE TOPHET

1. Diod. Sic. 20.14.1–6; cf. Lactant. *Div. Inst.* 1.21.13.

2. For useful general accounts of the phenomenon, see Moscati (1992b); Ciasca (2002); Xella (2012a), and for the most recent commentary, see the essays in Xella (2013b).

3. For another version of this investigation with additional documentation, see Quinn (2013b).

4. For a collection and commentary focusing on the positive evidence the individual passages offer for the sacrificial interpretation, see Xella (2009, 63–88). Garnand (2013) provides another stimulating analysis of this evidence.

5. I use the generic term "marker" to avoid the terminological confusion that surrounds the words "cippus" and "stele." For the relationship between these markers and individual depositions, see Xella (2012b).

6. For some examples, see Morstadt (2014, 96–97).

7. Whitaker (1921, 257–60). The significance of earlier finds at Nora and on Malta had not been understood: see Vivanet (1891); Vella (2013).

8. See Bénichou-Safar (2004, 2) for the circumstances.

9. *CISem*. I no. 338: LRBT LTNT PN BʿL WLʾDN / LBʿL ḤMN ʾŠ NDR ʾRŠ BN / BDʿŠTRT BN BʿLŠLM PʿL / HMGRDM KŠMʿ QLʾ. See Xella et al. (2013), with earlier bibliography, for a fuller argument in favor of the sacrifice hypothesis. Paul Mosca has recently made an interesting case in favor of a simpler ritual killing scenario (Mosca 2013). It is possible that future research will demonstrate that the children buried in these sanctuaries did in fact die of natural causes or that intentional killing was only an occasional aspect of the rites observed there. Even so, there is no question that the tophets were important ritual and votive centers for the communities involved, with a particular focus on birth, death, and descent, and much (though certainly not all) of what I have to say here about them would still stand.

10. For a full set of references, see Xella (2012a, 4–5). Isa. 57:5 states explicitly that the ritual involved killing as well as cremating the child.

11. Lamps: Bénichou-Safar (2004) (Carthage). Masks: Bernardini (2005b, 64 with fig. 4) (Motya), and see the large third- or second-century mask found at the Carthage sanctuary (Musée national de Carthage cat. C1). Incense burner: Musée national de Carthage cat. C3. Dancing figures: Bartoloni (1976, cat. 570–72, 574–75, 597) (Carthage); Bernardini (2005b, 63 with fig. 3) (Motya). Women with drums: Moscati (1986, 63), with Meyers (1991) on the type. Moscati notes that since this image is rarely found in tophets other than Sulcis, the connection with the ritual is insecure, but it still seems a plausible link, at least at that sanctuary.

12. Paolo Bernardini has suggested "sanctuaries of the urn field" as a more appropriate label (2005b, 60).

13. Bondì (1979, 142).

14. See Bénichou-Safar (2004, 144) for this explicitly conservative estimate of the minimum size of the sanctuary, and 188 for the markers; L. Stager (1980, 3) for the estimate of the total number of urns. Recent excavations in the gardens and roads around the site directed by Imed Ben Jerbania for the Institut national du patrimoine have revealed a hitherto unknown extension, with large quantities of urns and markers. Acquaro (2002, 91) conveniently collects the evidence and bibliography for the estimated sizes of the other tophets: 1,500 square meters at Sulcis, 1,000 sq. m. at Motya and Tharros, 500 sq. m. at Monte Sirai. Numbers of markers recovered (so far) from other tophets range from about 140 at Monte Sirai, about 300 at Tharros, more than 1,180 at Motya, and more than 1,500 from Sulcis (Acquaro 2002, 92), where he also notes the considerably larger number of urns that have been found at all these sites.

15. Ferron (1995); Bénichou-Safar (2004, 98–99, 153).

16. P. Smith et al. (2011, 864).

17. Diod. Sic. 13.86.3: *kata to patrion ethos.*

18. Moscati (1972, 206).

19. D'Andrea and Giardino (2011, 137–38). I borrow the phrase "circle of the tophet" from this article. Carthage: Bénichou-Safar (2004), with earlier bibliography. Motya: Ciasca (1992), with earlier bibliography; Bernardini (2005b). Sulcis: Melchiorri (2009), with earlier bibliography.

20. Vella (2005, 9).

21. Vella (2013); on these inscriptions (*CISem.* I no. 123 and no. 123 bis), see also the observations of Frendo (2012).

22. Another plausible candidate for inclusion in this original group is Amathus in Cyprus, if the section of the cemetery there that contains only cremated infants and animals should indeed be identified as an eighth-century tophet: interesting but inconclusive discussions of the hypothesis can be found in Agelarakis et al. (1998) and Christou (1998), and the theory is revisited by Xella (2010, 261n5) and D'Andrea and Giardino (2011, 134n10).

23. Hadrumetum: Cintas (1948); McCarty (2011). For the latest dating, see D'Andrea and Giardino (2011, 136n27), though cf. McCarty (2011, 208n20) on the promised revision of the chronology by Wafa Messaoudi. Tharros: Acquaro (1989), with earlier bibliography. The dating is seventh century: Spanu and Zucca (2011, 46–48). Nora: Moscati (1992b, 24–25). Monte Sirai: Bondì (1995), with earlier bibliography.

24. Pani Loriga: Barreca (1966, 163). Bithia: Moscati (1992b, 31–33). Karales: Tronchetti (1990, 13); Moscati (1992b, 24). I consider Bithia and Karales likely candidates; Pani Loriga must await further investigation.

25. Seven of these markers are presented in Di Stefano (1993, 39–40); an eighth is discussed by Bisi (1967, 50–51). There is an overview in Moscati (1987, 145–46). A single unprovenanced stele with a dedication to Baal Hamon and Tinnit, now in Palermo, is not evidence for a tophet there (De Simone 1997).

26. Amadasi Guzzo (2002, 99); Amadasi Guzzo and Zamora López (2013, esp. figs. 4–7).

27. van Dommelen (2005, 149).

28. Continuities: Bénichou-Safar (2004, 98, 123–24). Child sacrifice in the Levant: Lipiński (1988); Aubet (2001, 246–48); Stavrakopoulou (2004, 141–299); Finsterbusch (2007); Lange (2007). See Xella (2012a, 4–5) for a convenient summary of the biblical sources.

29. Curt. 4.3.23. For possible demographic motivations, see L.Stager and Wolff (1984).

30. Xella (2010, 261). An attempt to identify a tophet at Tyre (Conheeney and Pipe 1991; Sader 1991; Seeden 1991) was comprehensively refuted (Amadasi Guzzo [1993]; Bartoloni [1993]; Moscati [1993b]): the cremated remains were of adults, not children.

31. Bonnet (2011a; 2011b); Quinn (2011a).

32. S. Hall (1990, 226–27).

33. Bonnet (2011b, 382).

34. See Xella (1991, 34–42, 157–60) for a survey of Baal Hammon's appearances in the east, and see also Bordreuil (1986) for the amulet, dated by letter forms.

35. Berthier and Charlier (1955, 167 [cat. 1 GR] and 168–9 [cat. 3 GR]), giving her name as Θινιθ and Θεννειθ.

36. Pritchard (1982).

37. Bordreuil (1987, 80–81), to which one might add a Tyrian example of apparently seventh- to sixth-century date (Sader 2005, no. 13).

38. Garbati (2013, 56–59; 2015a, 343–45).

39. Serv. *ad Aen.* 4.680, with Garbati (2013, 55).

40. *CISem.* I no. 3914; for interpretation and bibliography, see Bordreuil (1987, 79–80).

41. For the ninth-century dating of the settlement at Huelva, see González de Canales et al. (2004), summarized in English in González de Canales et al. (2006): out of 8,009 pottery fragments analyzed, about half were local and half in the "Phoenician tradition," although it is not clear if these were imports or of local manufacture. There

were, by contrast, 33 fragments of Greek pottery. The earliest pottery recovered in the current Tunisian-Spanish excavations at Utica probably points to a ninth-century date, perhaps as early as Huelva and certainly before the earliest ceramic evidence so far found at Carthage (López Castro et al. 2014, 206). Recent bibliography for the early-eighth-century settlements at Lixus and at Castillo de Doña Blanca near Gadir is conveniently collected in Maraoui Telmini et al. (2014, 142–44); new evidence for a ninth-century date for the settlement of Gadir itself is discussed by Celestino and López-Ruiz (2016, 141).

42. Strabo 3.5.3. On the location of this sanctuary, see Maya Torcelly et al. (2014).

43. Acquaro (1989, 15–16).

44. Darius: Just. *Epit.* 19.1.10. It is unclear that Darius had any relevant jurisdiction, and in the same communication he requests an alliance (19.1.12). Prag (2010, 57) sees this as a doublet for the incident involving Gelon, for which see Plut. *Mor.* 175 A and 552 A, and Theophrastus fr. 586 Fortenbaugh *apud Schol.* Pind. *Pyth.* 2.2. I have suggested in the past that the coincidence in Diodorus's account that the rite is celebrated with unusual fervor under attack from Gelon's own city of Syracuse might point to its artifice (Quinn 2011a, 404n10); I now wonder if it might as easily reflect the Carthaginians' sense of an appropriate response to earlier Syracusan interference. Iphikrates: Porph. *Abst.* 2.56.

45. L. Stager (1980, 4–5), also discussed at Melchiorri (2013, 229).

46. D'Andrea and Giardino (2011) discuss the versions of this thesis proposed by Aubet, Acquaro, Bernardini, and Moscati at length, with useful commentary in particular on the eccentricities of the last listed (134–36). Paolo Bernardini has recently proposed an attractive model of Levantine migration based not on the existence of separate regions inhabited by settlers with different aims, but on a settlement hierarchy across the colonial west, with Gadir, Carthage, Sulcis, and Motya all picked out as particularly important settlements controlling and coordinating the activities of smaller mercantile centers (Bernardini 2013).

47. Bechtold (2008, 75) (on Carthage); van Dommelen and Gómez Bellard (2008b, 232–33). This is also true of contemporary Greek colonies in southern Italy: see van Dommelen (2005, 147).

48. Arnaud (2005, 154–55), with 152–53 on the problems of the alternative routes of the Straits of Messina and Bonifaccio, and 158–60 for some example of specific journey-times; Vella (2005, 444), for Malta's strategic value.

49. van Dommelen and Gómez Bellard (2008b, 174–77).

50. D'Andrea and Giardino (2011, 139–40).

51. 2 Kings 23:10. Josiah's moral message is somewhat undermined by the fact that at the same time he himself sacrificed the priests of cults other than Yahweh's (2 Kings 23:20), and his ban was not especially successful, since there are continued references to the practice. I thank Brian Schmidt for discussion of this passage.

52. Euseb. *Praep. evang.* 4.6.11 = Philo *BNJ* 790 F 3b.

53. Just. *Epit.* 18.4–6. The social and religious connections implied by the possible existence of a tophet at Amathus, discussed in note 22 above, would find an interesting echo in the episode related by Justin in which Elissa's boat picks up a priest and eighty young women from Cyprus on the way from Tyre to Carthage.

54. I thank Joseph Greene for suggesting this to me after one of my lectures at Tufts.

55. Shepherd (1995).

56. On the history and culture of the M'zabites, see *Enc. Berb.* s.v. M'zab; Bierschenk (1988); J. Miller (1994); Brett and Fentress (1996). I thank Elizabeth Fentress for suggesting this avenue of investigation and helping me make sense of it.

57. Polyb. 3.22.

58. E.g., Bernardini (1996, 34); Aubet (2001, 255; 2009, 266); Acquaro (2002, 87).

59. Maraoui Telmini et al. (2014).

60. van Dommelen and Gómez Bellard (2008b, 237).

61. Ciasca (2002, 124–26). There are exceptions: the likely tophet at Karales would have been on the coast to the west of the town.

62. For Hadrumetum, see Bénichou-Safar (2010).

63. Bénichou-Safar (2004, 34–66); Bernardini (2005b, 59–60; 2008, 645–49).

64. For more detail on the stratigraphy and development of the markers at Carthage, see Quinn (2011a).

65. Bisi (1967, 23–48; 1971); Moscati (1986, 86–88); Oggiano (2008); Quinn (2011a, 392–96). Baetyls: Mettinger (1995); P. Stewart (2008).

66. On the figurines of women in the east, see E. Stern (2010, 11–15).

67. One example of the bottle idol appears on an undated stele from Akhziv: see Moscati (1965). See Dridi (2004) on the chronology of bottle idol and attempts at interpretation. On the chronology and (more briefly) interpretation of the lozenge motif, see Ruiu (2000).

68. Summary of examples and bibliography at Lipiński (1995, 211–13).

69. Tophet markers have attracted much scholarly attention and a large bibliography: useful summaries include Bisi (1967) and (much more briefly) Moscati (1992c).

70. Ciasca (1992, 135).

71. For more detail and full references, see Quinn (2013b, 35–6).

72. The relevant datasets for Sulcis ($n = 825$) are taken from Bartoloni (1976), and for Carthage from Bartoloni (1986) ($n = 628$) and Brown (1991) ($n = 612$). Gaifman (2008) points out that the term "baetyl" can be misleading, especially when applied indiscriminately to any kind of aniconic object or monument found in the Near East.

73. Carthage: Bartoloni (1986). Motya: Moscati and Uberti (1981). Tharros: Moscati and Uberti (1985). Nora: Moscati and Uberti (1970). For fuller data and references, see Quinn (2013b, 37).

74. The Hadrumetum markers have never been fully published, but there are partial presentations by Cintas (1948); Bisi (1967); Moscati (1996) (with new material), and see, more recently, Bénichou-Safar (2010); Fantar (2012). See also McCarty (2011) for a fuller account of the problems involved in assessing the published evidence from Hadrumetum; Quinn (2013b, 38–9) for a fuller account of the observations presented here.

75. Enthroned deity: McCarty (2011, 217–18). Triple baetyls: Cintas (1948, 24); cf. Moscati and Uberti (1970, 34–35); Moscati and Uberti (1985, 78); Moscati (1996, 251).

76. Moscati (1966a, 198); Moscati and Uberti (1981, 45–46, 50–51).

77. Moscati and Uberti (1981, 62); Bondì (1996: 77–78).

78. Thrones: Moscati and Uberti (1981, 55, nos. 1004 [with seated figure], 1010) Quotation: Moscati (1967, 63–4).

79. Malkin (2011, 26–27).

80. Ciasca (1992, 139).

81. Bondì (1995, 230). For the limited impact of republican Roman imperialism on the island, we might compare the evidence from a Sardinian rural survey that shows striking continuity in settlement patterns and in sites themselves from the late fifth to the first centuries BCE (van Dommelen and Gómez Bellard 2008b, 172).

82. Quinn (2011a, 396–98) for more on this visual shift and its eastern models.

83. Shelby Brown has tried to explain the differences in quality and thickness of the markers by proposing a general deterioration in quality during the Punic Wars, owing to increasing economic problems faced by the city over that period (Brown 1991, 74, 82–89, 108, 113–16). I see no reason to interpret the differences as representing change over time, rather than a range of economic choices, especially as all the evidence now points to increasing prosperity at Carthage in this period: see further discussion at Quinn (2011a, 399–400).

84. Brown (1991). Among the earlier markers there are some leafy branches that also seem likely to be from palms: see, for instance, Bartoloni (1976, nos. 572, 597). There are also two palm trees on markers from Cirta, one sketched, the other very stylized, and neither much like those found at Carthage but both placed at the center of the visual field: *EH* pl. XX, A; XXII, C; see also Bertrandy and Sznycer (1987, 68–69). For occasional palm branches at Hadrumetum, see Moscati (1996, cat. B, discussed on 254); Fantar (2012, 101). Elsewhere, one marker each from Motya (Moscati and Uberti 1981, no. 318) and Monte Sirai (Bondì 1972, no. 55) have palms topped with lunettes standing in for columns of the framing shrine. Bartoloni (1986, no. 1234) is a very fragmentary possible depiction of a palm from Sulcis. The palm also features on contemporary razors from Carthage: Acquaro (1971, 87, 91, 92).

85. Ferjaoui (1991).

86. Bénichou-Safar (2004, 105–6, with 115, 118).

87. Lancel (1995, 117–20). Polybius claims that by the later third century, the voice of the people had become predominant in the city's deliberations (6.51).

88. Greene (1992); Greene and Kehoe (1995). On the methodology of this survey, see Quinn (2003, 12n23).

89. In addition to the examples discussed here, see Quinn (2013b) for discussion of the stelai found at Lilybaeum, founded from Carthage after the destruction of nearby Motya (Diod. Sic. 22.10.4), and the connections they make with both Carthage and Hadrumetum. Since it is not certain that these come from a tophet (see note 25 above), I have left them out of the discussion here.

90. App. *Pun.* 94.

91. Moscati (1996, stele S).

92. Bertrandy and Sznycer (1987, 88–91). For this sanctuary in general, and for catalogues of its markers, see Berthier and Charlier (1955); Bertrandy and Sznycer (1987).

93. McCarty and Quinn (2015, 177).

94. Bertrandy (1993, 7).

95. Cf. Brown (1991, 111).

96. Bertrandy (1993, 7).

97. On the interpretation of this phrase, see Amadasi Guzzo (2007–8, 350–53).

98. A grandfather is sometimes added: Bertrandy and Sznycer (1987, 84).

99. Moscati and Uberti (1985, 51–57); see also Moscati and Uberti (1970, 43–45) (where the argument is based on style).

100. Markers from Monte Sirai: Bondì (1972, 1980).

101. Polyb. 3.24.11; cf. 3.22.9. A notoriously obscure passage in Pseudo-Aristotle mentioning a ban on the planting of fruit trees on the island may also be relevant ([Arist.] *Mir. ausc.* 100). Whittaker, however, points out that the only Carthaginian colonial official after the First Punic War is a boetharch in Sardinia (Whittaker 1978, 72, on Polyb. 1.79.2). See also Bondì (2008).

CHAPTER 6. MELQART'S MEDITERRANEAN

1. Josephus *AJ* 8.146, where the information is said to come from Tyrian records via Menander; cf. *Ap.* 1.118–19 for the same information. On Melqart, see Bonnet (1986; 1988); Bernardini and Zucca (2005).

2. On Melqart and Carthage, see Bonnet (1988, 165–86).

3. Just. *Epit.* 18.7.7; Curt. 4.3.22, with Diod. Sic. 13.108.4.

4. Arr. *Anab.* 2.24.5; Curt. 4.2.10.

5. Livy 33.48.3.

6. Polyb. 31.12.12.

7. Philistos: *BNJ* 556 F 47, with commentary ad loc.

8. *BNJ* 566 F 60 (= Dion. Hal. *Ant. Rom.* 1.74.1), with Feeney (2007, 92–95).

9. *BNJ* 566 F 82. The story of Elissa's rejection of the local African king Hiarbas involves a reversal of the outcome as well as the gender of standard Greek stories told about colonial marriages with (or rapes of) local women, for which see Dougherty (1993, 66–76).

10. App. *Pun.* 1.

11. Haegemans (2000, 280–81), suggesting that these were actually from Carthage, a more obvious source of "Tyrian" knowledge for a Sicilian historian than Tyre itself, with *BNJ* 566 F 81b = Polyb. 12.28a.3 for Timaeus (where, as Haegemans notes, the reading "Tyrian" is not certain).

12. Foundation story: *BNJ* 783 F 1 = Josephus, *Ap.* 1.125. Tyrian sources: *BNJ* 783 T 3a = Josephus, *AJ* 8.144; see also T 3b, 3c, F 1, 4 and 7, all from Josephus. On the plausibly Carthaginian or Tyrian roots of the story of the foundation of Carthage, see also Aubet (2001, 215–17; 2009, 233–34) and Maraoui Telmini et al. (2014), with earlier bibliography, including the important reservations noted by Bonnet (2006a, 370–71).

13. Jenkins (1977, 27), with references, also noting the echo of the murex shell, one source of Tyre's prosperity, in the shape of the headdress. He himself slightly prefers an identification with Artemis, who is occasionally depicted in a similar headdress, and who would provide a connection with the lion on the reverse, or even Tinnit, on the grounds that she appears to be associated with Artemis on a Hellenistic-period bilingual inscription from Athens where one "Abdtinnit," according to the Phoenician text, renders his name as "Artemidoros" in Greek (Jenkins 1977, 28–31, with *CISem.* I no. 116). There is not, however, a regular connection between the imagery on the obverse and reverse of Carthaginian coinage, and "gift of Artemis" is hardly a straightforward translation of "slave of Tinnit."

14. Virg. *Aen.* 1.338–68 and bk. 4; Just. *Epit.* 18.4–6.

15. Just. *Epit.* 18.5.9. The name of the Byrsa hill in Carthage probably derives in fact from the Semitic word BRT, which means "fortress" or "fortified citadel" (Aubet 2001, 216). See Svenbro and Scheid (1985) for a thorough investigation of this "bursa" episode that concludes that it confirms the Greco-Roman origins of the presentation

of Dido as an incarnation of "Punic faith," and the whole story as anti-Punic propaganda (338). It is of course possible that Timaeus did include this detail, but that it was of no interest to the compiler of the treatise *On Women* (as suggested by Svenbro and Scheid [1985, 330]), but since it is one of the most dramatic aspects of the tale, and so strongly associated with the deceptive stereotype of the Phoenicians, it would have been a surprising element to omit.

16. Just. *Epit.* 18.4.15

17. Álvarez Martí-Aguilar (2014, 25–26). For pillars of gold and emerald at Tyre, see Hdt. 2.44; for the sacred olive, see Ach. Tat. 2.14.5; for bronze pillars at Gadir, see Strabo 3.5.5; Porph. *Abst.* 1.25; Philostratos, *Apollonios of Tyana* 5.5, who adds that there was also the "golden olive of Pygmalion."

18. Jenkins (1978, 5–35, series 5), with Prag (2011, 4–5); Nitschke (2013, 265–66); Yarrow (2013, 354–57).

19. BT MLQRT: *CISem.* I nos. 4890, 4894, 5575; there is also one mention of the god in an inscription from the tophet, probably of the third to second century (*CISem.* I no. 5510, with Bonnet [1988, 169–70]). Resuscitators: Bonnet (1988, 174–79); Garbati (2015b, 40), with references.

20. Bonnet (1988, 170–71), with references.

21. Malkin (2005, 243).

22. Vell. Pat. 1.2.3; for this dating of the earliest Phoenician foundations in the west, see also Strabo 1.3.2. While there is no archaeological evidence for settlement at these sites at this very early date, late Bronze Age sediments from Spanish gold mines have been found in the harbor at Sidon (Demand 2011, 221).

23. Strabo 3.5.5. The tale may have come down to Strabo from Ephoros (writing in the fourth century) or Timaeus (writing in the third): Lasserre (1966, 86), though he may simply have gotten it from Posidonius. Pompon. 3.46 also asserts a Tyrian foundation.

24. *Schol. Dionys. Per.* 454.

25. Philostratos, *Apollonios of Tyana* 5.5; Porph. *Abst.* 1.25; Pompon. 3.46; Sil. 3.14–60.

26. Foundation of Utica by Tyrians: Vell. Pat. 1.2.3; see for later encounters Josephus *AJ* 8.146 and *Ap.* 1.119, where the report is attributed to Menander of Ephesus, and Just. *Epit.* 18.4.2, with [Arist.] *Mir. ausc.* 134 on the city's early date. Temple of Apollo: Plin. *HN* 16.216. Shrine at Lixus: Plin. *HN* 19.63.

27. Just. *Epit.* 44.5.1–4: (1) *Post regna deinde Hispaniae primi Karthaginienses imperium provinciae occupavere.* (2) *Nam cum Gaditani a Tyro, unde et Karthaginiensibus origo est, sacra Herculis per quietem iussi in Hispaniam transtulissent urbemque ibi condidissent, invidentibus incrementis novae urbis finitimis Hispaniae populis ac propterea Gaditanos bello lacessentibus auxilium consanguineis Karthaginienses misere. (3) Ibi felici expeditione et Gaditanos ab iniuria vindicaverunt et maiore iniuria partem provinciae imperio suo adiecerunt. (4) Postea quoque hortantibus primae expeditionis auspiciis Hamilcarem imperatorem cum manu magna ad occupandam provinciam misere.*

28. In Strabo's account of the foundation of Gadir, the Tyrian founders of the colony are clearly distinguished from the later Gaditani (3.5.5).

29. Álvarez Martí-Aguilar (2014, 3–5).

30. Polyb. 2.1.5–6.

31. *CIL* II nos. 1927, 1929.

32. Strabo 3.1.7; see Álvarez Martí-Aguilar (2014, 27n19) for frequent confusion between Calpe and Carteia.

33. Sil. 3.1–4.

34. Just. *Epit.* 18.5.12.

35. Álvarez Marti-Aguilar (2014, 20): "una red de ciudades cuyos habitantes reconocían en Tiro a su madre patria y la fuente de legitimidad política y religiosa de sus propias comunidades, vinculadas por lazos de parentesco a través de la figura de Melqart . . . lazos de parentesco que implicaban inherentes obligaciones de auxilio y asistencia."

36. Nonnus, *Dion.* 40.469–534. Unfortunately, it is impossible to pin down a date or context for Nonnus's source (Grottanelli 1972; Bonnet 1988, 31–33). Giuseppe Garbati suggests that the role that Melqart does play in the foundation story of Carthage, even as recorded by Pompeius Trogus in the Augustan period, has been overestimated, suggesting plausibly that the phrase *sacris Herculis . . . repetitis* at Just. *Epit.* 18.4.15 should be understood as a reference to Elissa "reinstating" or "recovering" the *sacra* at Tyre, rather than "bringing" them with her to Carthage (2015b, 198). I suspect that the traditional reading is still the easiest, but the ambiguity is telling in itself, and one wonders to what extent this story is bringing to Carthage elements of tales that already existed at Gadir and Tyre itself.

37. Cf. Garbati (2015b, 200).

38. *ICO* Sard 32: L'DN L'LM ḤQDŠ MLQRT 'L ḤṢR. It is possible that the personal name MQM found in a fourth-century inscription from Tharros (*ICO* Sard 24) is not only related to the phrase MQM 'LM, "Resuscitator of the God," found at Carthage, but also to a Melqart cult at Tharros, and perhaps even the ceremony of the *egersis*: see Bonnet (1988, 260–61). A proposed identification of a Melqart sanctuary at Olbia in northeastern Sardinia (D'Oriano 1994) is based on an ingenious but very speculative juxtaposition of three pieces of evidence: a fragment of a terracotta face of Herakles that was found "near" the foundations of an Archaic temple excavated in 1939; fragments of a life-size, mold-made terracotta statue of Herakles likely to have been of the same or similar type that were discovered in the gulf of Olbia in association with second-century BCE amphorae; and an almost illegible Latin or neo-Punic painted inscription built into the wall of the church that replaced the temple, which might contain a vocalized rendering of the Punic MQR as "Makar."

39. Giuseppe Garbati collects references and earlier bibliography, and a list of similar phrases on several second- to first-century inscriptions from Phoenicia itself, most from Tyre, which refer to Melqart BṢR ("of/on the rock," or simply "in Tyre"): Garbati (2012, 162–63, 167; 2015b). Garbati (2012, 161) also discusses a possible earlier (fifth- to fourth-century) example but notes that the reading is highly disputed.

40. Garbati (2012, 168).

41. See chapter 2 for further discussion.

42. Strabo 3.5.5; 3.4.6; 3.1.7.

43. Abdmelqart: Bonnet (1988, 267). Rosh Melqart coinage: Jenkins (1971, 53–69). It has been argued that the phrase RŠ (or R'Š) MLQRT refers not to a city but to a group of people known as the "Elect" or "Leaders" of Melqart: see Manfredi (1985), with Bonnet (1988, 268n106); Mildenberg (1993). This is hard to reconcile with the epigraphic evidence, which includes inscriptions mentioning "the people of Rosh Melqart" ('M RŠMLQRT) (Lipiński 1995, 237n107; Amadasi Guzzo 1997).

44. Amadasi Guzzo (1997) prefers an identification with Selinus; for a discussion of the various possibilities, see Bonnet (1988, 267–69), where Carthage's hegemony over Herakleia Minoa in the relevant period may be understated. For some of the vicissitudes of Herakleia Minoa from the mid-fourth to mid-third century, see Diod. Sic. 16.9.4 (Carthaginian in 357 BCE; see on this also Plut. *Dion* 25.5); 19.71.7 (confirmed as Carthaginian in 314 BCE); 20.56.3 (taken by Agathokles after an unspecified period of independence from Carthage in 307 BCE); 22.10.2 (taken from the Carthaginians by Pyrrhus in 277 BCE). For the origins of "Minoa" as a colony of Selinus, see Hdt. 5.46. The available evidence suggests that it acquired its additional Greek name of Herakleia when it was taken over by the Spartan Dorieus's supporter Euryleon in the late sixth century: Herodotus says that Dorieus intended to found a colony called Herakleia (5.43), and Diodorus says in a confused passage that he actually did (4.23).

45. Ptol. *Geog.* 4.3.13, with Vella (2002).

46. Diod. Sic. 20.14.1.

47. Hdt. 2.44.

48. Malkin (2011, 8).

49. Hdt. 2.44. He goes on to recount a trip to Thasos itself, where he found a temple of Herakles built by Phoenicians five generations before the birth in Greece of Herakles, the son of Amphitryon. According to Pausanias 5.25.12, the Thasians originally worshipped the same Herakles as the Tyrians, but then, when they became Greek, switched to the cult of (the Greek) Herakles, the son of Amphitryon. For the cult of Herakles on Thasos, which may indeed have incorporated aspects of an earlier Melqart cult, see Bonnet (1988, 351–71) and Malkin (2011, 132–33), with earlier bibliography.

50. Tyrian Herakles: Diod. Sic. 17.40.2; Arr. *Anab.* 2.16.4. For his precedence in relation to Greek Herakles, Hdt. 2.44; Arr. *Anab.* 2.16.1–2; Lucian *Syr. D.* 3. For Egyptian Herakles, who is also said to predate the Greek Herakles: Hdt. 2.43–44; Diod. Sic. 1.24.1–6; 5.76.1–2; Arr. *Anab.* 2.16.2, with Garbati (2010, 172). For Herakles the Dactyl: Bonnet (1988, 380–88); Garbati (2010, 172). For the great variety of gods known as Herakles: Cic. *Nat. D.* 3.42.

51. Miles (2010, 105), with references. On the relationship between Herakles and Melqart, see Bonnet (1988, 346–71; 2005); Jourdain-Annequin (1989); Bonnet and Jourdain-Annequin (1992); Malkin (2005; 2011, 119–41), all with much useful bibliography.

52. Miles (2010, 105), with references.

53. Bonnet (2005, 20); cf. Malkin (2005, 238–41; 2011, 120–24).

54. Jourdain-Annequin (1989, 95–169). It should be noted that the locations of the myths remained very flexible, and Lixus and Gadir were only two of several possibilities in both cases.

55. Malkin (2011, 126).

56. Curt. 4.2.2–3.

57. Arr. *Anab.* 2.15–24; Diod. Sic. 17.40–46; Curt. 4.2–4, with Bosworth (1980), ad 2.15.6. On Alexander's motives, see Amitay (2008).

58. Nitschke (2013, 267) for this suggestion.

59. Sil. 3.32–44; Philostratos, *Apollonios of Tyana* 5.5.

60. Bonnet (1997, nos. 12–26, 37–42), with appropriate caution.

61. Jenkins (1978, 9).

62. Nitschke notes that there are fifth- and fourth-century coins from Kition with Herakles types, but that a specific connection with Melqart is difficult to ascertain in a Cypriot context where (as already noted) Herakles-related imagery is found in the shrines of a variety of different gods (2013, 267n49, with earlier bibliography).

63. See Counts (2008) for these figures (7–9), and for the Near Eastern visual traditions that they exploit (11–12); cf. Jourdain-Annequin and Bonnet (2001, 199–202). This Cypriot iconography also appears at Amrit on the Levantine coast from the fifth century, where Giuseppe Garbati (2010) has made a convincing case that the genre is associated more with Eshmun than Melqart.

64. Counts (2008, 10), noting that Greek depictions of Herakles fighting the Nemean lion depict him naked or wearing armor. Imagery of Herakles's labors does appear in Cypriot art of the early first millennium BCE, and perhaps even earlier: see Jourdain-Annequin and Bonnet (2001, 203).

65. Counts (2008, 10). Similarly, the necropolis at Tharros has yielded late-fifth- or fourth-century scarabs, terracottas, lamps, and incense burners depicting Herakles with his customary Greek attributes, as well as sixth- and fifth-century Greek vases depicting his mythological adventures, but with no accompanying evidence to suggest that they are intended to represent Melqart: Bernardini and Zucca (2005, cat. 23–27); note also cat. 9, a fourth-century statue base from Sulcis depicting Herakles with lion skin and club, and that possible representations of Melqart are also illustrated at cat. 26. Images of Greek Herakles are also found on objects at Carthage: nos. 24 and 25, with Nitschke (2013, 269), suggesting that one of these objects also contains apparent references to a Levantine mythical tradition.

66. Counts (2008, 19–21). A strange, short figure who appears on an eighth-century silver patera from Idalion wearing a lion skin and carrying a lion (Louvre AO 20134, discussed and illustrated at Jourdain-Annequin and Bonnet [2001, 204–5]) seems more likely to be a precursor to this Master of the Lion than a straightforward attempt to render Herakles and/or Melqart.

67. Sil. 3.30–31; Philostratos, *Apollonios of Tyana* 5.5; Hdt. 2.44 might be taken to suggest the same of Tyre.

68. Bonnet (2007, 1). If it is, then there are a few images on sixth- to fifth-century scarabs from Cyprus and Ibiza and a third-century razor from Carthage that could with hesitation be read as representations of the same figure: see Bonnet (1997, nos 3, 4, 7).

69. J. Elayi and A. Elayi (2009, 265–71), with the catalogue at 47–176 (Group II).

70. Nitschke (2013, 263–64).

71. Nitschke (2013, 261n34); less certainly in favor of this identification, J. Elayi and A. Elayi (2009, 269–71); against, Bonnet (1988, 85; 2007).

72. Jenkins (1971, 55), with Nitschke (2013, 265). Two similar images are found on issues from Soluntum (Jenkins 1971, 74, nos. 21–22); these are paired with reverses of a horse and a tuna fish, and the same tuna fish reverse is also paired with a Greek-style head of Herakles (no. 23).

73. The easiest way to survey this numismatic material is through the indices of Manfredi (1995: 463–77), although representations of Herakles are not necessarily representations of Melqart; see also Bonnet (1997, nos. 32, 34, 35), with references and appropriate caution over individual identifications. Nitschke (2013, 267–68) is a useful recent discussion of the problematic male type on the Barcid coinage minted

in Spain in the third century, which at the very least makes reference to Herakles and therefore, we must imagine, to Melqart.

74. *CISem.* I nos. 22 and 22 bis = *KAI*[5] no. 47 = *ICO* Malta no. 1–1 bis = *IG* XIV no. 600.

75. Miles (2010, 108–9).

76. Paus. 10.17.2; with Grottanelli (1973); Bonnet (1988, 160, 250–53; 2005, 23–24), discussing among other things the identification or confusion involved in this account between Tyrian and (an) Egyptian Herakles. For Makeris as a reasonable rendition of the Sardinian way of saying Melqart, see Grottanelli (1973, 153), with Bonnet (1988, 252–53; 2005, 24n32).

77. On Sid Babi, see Garbati (2008, 95–99).

78. Bonnet (2005, 25–27) makes the interesting suggestion that the stories of the Sardinian god Iolaus, also assimilated to Sardus Pater and supposedly the nephew of Herakles, are a Greek countermyth, asserting their own involvement in the story.

79. *CISem.* I no. 256. There are also three SidTinnits: *CISem.* I nos. 247–49.

80. Bonnet (2005, 23) ("la legittimazione del dominio colonial esercitato sulla Sardegna"), with 24–25; see also Miles (2010, 104).

81. Garbini (1997); with Bernardini (2005a, 126).

82. For Carthage, see Miles (2010, 104–5); for a Sardinian city, probably Neapolis, see Bonnet (1988, 254–55); Bernardini (2005a, 126).

83. Manfredi (1995, NB no. 202). Palm branches appear alongside Bes on some Ibizan issues of 125–75 BCE (Manfredi 1995, PIBB nos. 35–39) and on one issue from Malaca of the late first century BCE (Manfredi 1995, PIBB no. 104). I will discuss the coinage of the Numidian kings in chapter 8.

84. Amadasi Guzzo and Xella (2005). For parallels in Cyprus, see Lipiński (1995, 289–92).

85. Cypriot deity: Lipiński (1995, 290–91). Contemporary associations between Eshmun of Sidon and Melqart of Tyre: Garbati (2010, 162).

86. Polyb. 3.22–23 for the first treaty and 24 for the second, with Livy 7.27.3 for the probable date of 348 BCE.

87. Gadir: Sall. *Hist.* 2 fr. 5 Maurenbrecher; Pliny *HN* 4.120; Avienus *Ora Maritima* 85, 265–66. Carteia: Strabo 3.2.14; Pompon. 2.96; Pliny *HN* 3.7. On the debates over the location of Mastia-Tarseion and their relevance to Carthaginian interests in fourth-century Iberia, see Álvarez Martí-Aguilar (2014, 32–33), with references and earlier bibliography.

88. Diod. Sic. 17.40.3, 41.1–2, 46.4; Just. *Epit.* 11.10.12–14; Curt. 4.3.19–20 (for the initial encouragement, see 4.2.11, though it is hard to imagine a reliable source for this report of private conversations). On the inconsistencies in Curtius's account, see Bonnet (2015, 81). On the relationship between Tyre and Carthage more generally, see J. Elayi (1981); Bonnet (1988, 166–67); Ferjaoui (1993, 27–46).

89. Just. *Epit.* 11.10.13. Bonnet (2015, 82), notes how the appeal to a female leader supports the presentation of the Phoenicians and Carthaginians as similarly barbarian.

90. Curt. 4.3.23. Ory Amitay suggests that "Carthaginian influence" was at play here (2008, 101).

91. For skeptical analysis of Greek sources on Greek colonization, see, for instance, Osborne (1998); Yntema (2000).

92. Among many examples of Tyre interpreted as the driving force behind the foundation of "Phoenician colonies," including Carthage and Gadir, see, for instance,

Bunnens (1983); Katzenstein (1997); Aubet 2006, 105–7. Aubet proposes a complex model that subordinates the Tyrian temple of Melqart to the king and government of Tyre and interprets western gifts to Melqart as evidence for ongoing political involvement in a western colonial project on the part of the Tyrian royal house (2001, 152–57, though at 217 she notes the particular complexitites of the foundation of Carthage, and the role that may well have been played in that by Cyprus). For hesitations, see Bondì (1978); Ciasca (1989) (though only on the dubious grounds of mixed pottery assemblages); Bernardini (2013).

93. Multiple civic origins for western Levantine settlements might also explain the story told by Herodotus about the refusal of the "Phoenicians" in the Egyptian navy in 525 BCE to fight against their "children" at Carthage, with whom they have sworn "great oaths" (Hdt. 3.19); the context makes it clear that this is not simply Herodotus's own synonym for "Tyrian." It is also worth noting Pausanias's description, mentioned at note 49 above, of the Thasians who originally worshipped the same Herakles as the Tyrians as coming from Tyre "and other parts of Phoenicia" with Thasos, the son of Agenor (Paus. 5.25.12, not incompatible with Hdt. 2.44). Cf. Malkin (2011, 211) on the informal nature of most western settlement, and Bondì (2014, 61) on the evidence for Cypriot settlement in the west.

94. Herakleides of Lembos, *Excerpta Politiarum*, fr. 59 Dilts.

95. Cf. the rather different interpretation of Malkin (2011, 123–24, 141).

CHAPTER 7. THE FIRST PHOENICIAN

1. For maternal impression, see *Aethiopika* 4.8, with Pliny *HN* 7.52 and Zeitlin (2013, 77–78).

2. Heliodorus 10.41.4: "τοιόνδε πέρας ἔσχε τὸ σύνταγμα τῶν περὶ Θεαγένην καὶ Χαρίκλειαν Αἰθιοπικῶν· ὃ συνέταξεν ἀνὴρ Φοῖνιξ Ἐμισηνός, τῶν ἀφ' Ἡλίου γένος, Θεοδοσίου παῖς Ἡλιόδορος."

3. *C. Ord. Ptol.*[2] *nos.* 21–22 = *C. Ptol. Sklav.* no. 3 = Bagnall and Derow (2004, no. 64); *OGI* no. 230; *SEG* 29 no. 1613 = Austin (2006, no. 193); Rey-Coquais (1989, 614–17), with Bagnall (1976, 14–24); Grainger (1991, 66–67, 102–3); Capdetrey (2007, 248–50). I am grateful to Boris Chrusbasik for discussion of the exiguous evidence for this period.

4. Millar (1983, 60), with chapter 4, note 61. Nitschke (2011, 87) collects the extensive bibliography for the "Hellenization" of Phoenicia, and see Andrade (2013, 47) for a more positive assessment.

5. Local political and institutional continuities: Millar (1983, esp. 62). Architectural models: Boksmati (2009). Umm el-'Amed: Vella (2000); Nitschke (2011). Kharayeb: Xella (2008, 74–75); Bondì et al. (2009, 59–60); Oggiano (2015). Language of inscriptions: Nitschke (2011, 98).

6. Diod. Sic. 33.5.

7. Houghton et al. (2002 nos. 1078–83) (the prow and club types are both minted in two slightly different versions), with commentary at I.I.356, II.I.xix, and II. I.19. The only legend is "King Antiochus," in Greek. For the political and economic context, see Hoover (2004, 486–88), with discussion of earlier Tyrian coins with local iconography that were issued briefly under Ptolemy V.

8. By contrast, the very different palm on the third- and second-century coinage of Delos is a clear reference to the story that Apollo was born there under a palm tree.

9. Hoover (2004, 486) has a similar though not identical interpretation of the image: "a punning symbol of the region in which Tyre was located"; and see also Bonnet (2014, 296) on the palm tree on stamped Tyrian weights.

10. Meleager *Greek Anthology* 7.428.13–14. This is a rather pointed claim, given that Antipater was in fact from Sidon. Meleager's claim that a palm branch as well as a palm tree can carry the broader meaning of *phoinix* may explain the regular appearance of (different) palm branches on the silver coinage of the 140s issued by Beirut, Tyre, and Sidon, and a little later Byblos and Ashkelon, though not as the main motif. On these coins, see Hoover (2004, 493–95).

11. Ach. Tat. 2.14.1–2.

12. For discussion of the general phenomenon, see Mørkholm (1965; 1966, 125–30); Meadows (2001, 59–62); Hoover (2004, 488–92) (especially useful on the political and economic contexts); Sawaya (2004, 109–11); Kosmin (2014, 238–42).

13. For the likelihood that Antiochus IV imposed the quasi-municipal coinage system, see Meadows (2001, 60–62), suggesting that it may have been prompted by Roman practices, and Hoover (2004, 489–90).

14. For Tripolis, see Houghton et al. (2002, vol. 2.1, 79, with 2.2, 367), and for Arados, see Duyrat (2005).

15. Houghton et al. (2002, nos. 1443–47 [Byblos]; nos. 1448–52 [Beirut]; nos. 1453–60 [Sidon]), where the denominations are labelled B (largest) to E (smallest). The contemporary Tyrian types are nos. 1463–71. Byblos had been given the privilege of minting coins with local reverse types from the late 170s, but at first produced only a single denomination depicting Isis Pharia (no. 1442).

16. Houghton et al. (2002, no. 1454 [Sidon]; nos. 1463–69 [Tyre, adopting Amadasi Guzzo's recent reinterpretation of the term ṢDNM discussed above at 225n101]). Sidon's claim to Tyre may relate to the Sidonian belief reported by Curtius Rufus that Agenor founded both cities (4.4.15–16), or to the story that Tyre was founded by refugees from Sidon around the time of the fall of Troy (Just. 18.3.5).

17. Moretti (1953, no. 41), with Bonnet (2014).

18. Houghton et al. (2002, no. 1469); the image is not identical to that used at Sidon, and it appears at Tyre on a higher denomination coin, replacing the usual prow. Later coinage lays claim to particular gods as well: Ashtart, worshipped as the principal goddess at both Sidon and Tyre, is described on Sidonian coinage minted from the 130s BCE in Greek as the "Goddess of Sidon" (Houghton et al. [2002, nos. 2105–2106A for the first examples]).

19. *Scholia* on Apollonius 3.1186; for further detail, see R. Edwards (1979, 23–29); Gantz (1993, 209–10).

20. *BNJ* 788 F 3, from *Etym. Mag.* 219.33, s.v. Gadéira.

21. See Carolina López-Ruiz's commentary on *BNJ* 788 F 3, and Álvarez Martí-Aguilar (2014, 30, 30n28).

22. For the reading "Mother in Canaan" and not, as it is often rendered, "Mother of Canaan," see Bordreuil and Tabet (1985, 180–81); Sawaya (2004, 129–30).

23. For a stronger version of this point, see Andrade (2013, 52–55).

24. Millar (1983); cf. Millar (1993, 286), and see more recently Hirt (2015, 208).

25. *SEG* 2 no. 330 = Curty (1995, no. 12): the Tyrians describe themselves at l. 3 as συγγενεῖς of the Delphians.

26. Houghton et al. (2002, nos. 1441, 1951).

27. Duyrat (2005, nos. 2493–94, 2573–4227).

28. *RPC* 1, 655–657, nos. 4619–706; the equivalent Sidonian autonomous silver coinage has "of the Sidonians" in Greek, with the exception of *RPC* 1 no. 4561, "of Sidon," while Sidon's autonomous bronze coinage in this period uses both locutions.

29. See *IDidyma* 151, l. 9; *IEphesos* III no. 614 (l. 10); VII.1 no. 3033 (ll. 17–18) and 3034 (ll. 16–17); *IPergamon* 2, no. 437, ll. 6–7; 8.3, no. 21, ll. 10–11 (= *AE* 1934, no. 177), with Vitale (2013, 35–41) and Hirt (2015, 206, 213n43) for discussion and further bibliography.

30. *BMC* 361–66, 381–82; for the interpretation of the term *koinon Phoinikes*, see Vitale (2013, 57–63), with further references and bibliography.

31. *CIL* XIV no. 3613 = *ILS* no. 918, with Vitale (2013, 36–37).

32. Dio Cass. 53.12.7, 55.23.2; Ulpian, *Digest* 50.15.1.

33. *RE* XX.1, 369 s.v. Phoiniker (Phoinikia).

34. Semitic names: Millar (1983, 63). Inscription: *IGLS* VII no. 4001 (from Arados), though *KAI*[5] no. 12, a building inscription from Byblos, may be later (Millar 1983, 63). Potsherd: Xella (2014, para. 38). Ulpian: *Digest* 45.1.1.6; for *poenus* here as "Phoenician" rather than "Punic," see Millar's persuasive argument (1983, 66).

35. Millar (1990, 8), and 10–23 on Beirut more generally.

36. Hdn. 3.3.3.

37. Europa at Sidon in the Julio-Claudian period: *RPC* 1, nos. 4562–71, 4604–18; Trajanic period: *BMC* no. 217; Hadrianic period: *BMC* nos. 224–25. Palm tree at Tyre: *RPC* 1, 658: nos. 4733–39; *RPC* 2, nos. 2077–84; *BMC* nos. 284–87, 338–55. Silver coinage was no longer issued in either city after the Julio-Claudian era.

38. Ach. Tat. 1.1.1.

39. Strabo 16.2.22. For Sidonian preeminence in the colonial movement, see Sall. *Iug.* 78.1, Strabo 1.2.33, Just. *Epit.* 18.3.5; in favor of Tyre, Plin. *HN* 5.76, Curt. 4.4.19, Sil. 3.256, and Meleager, *Greek Anthology* 7.428. Millar (1983, 66–67), notes that the maritime role of the Phoenician cities, and especially their colonizing history, were particular topics of comment by classical authors in the early empire.

40. The simple title of *metropolis* first appears on Tyrian coins in 86/87 CE: *RPC* 2, nos. 2063, 2073, with Vitale (2013, 65).

41. *IDidyma* no.151 ll. 9–11: "ἡ βουλὴ καὶ ὁ δῆμος Τυρίων τῆς | ἱερᾶς καὶ ἀσύλου καὶ αὐτονόμου μητροπόλεως Φοινείκης καὶ τῶν κατὰ | Κοίλην Συρίαν καὶ ἄλλων πόλεων καὶ ναυαρχίδος."

42. *OGI* no. 595: "ἐπιστολὴ γραφεῖσα τῇ πόλει | Τυρίων, τῆς ἱερᾶς καὶ ἀσύλου καὶ αὐτονόμου μητροπόλεως Φοινείκης καὶ ἄλλων πόλε|ων καὶ ναυαρχίδος ἄρχουσι, βουλῇ δήμῳ καὶ τῆς κυρίας πατρίδος οἱ ἐν Ποτιόλοις | κατοικοῦντες χαίρειν." I thank Jonathan Prag for discussion of the details of this text.

43. Buckler et al. (1926, 74–75 no. 201) = *AE* 1927, 95, an inscription from Phrygia written in the 130s CE. For an exhaustive discussion of the known variants describing the geographical responsibilities involved, see Vitale (2013, 64–73) with references and earlier bibliography.

44. Ulpian, *Digest* 50.15.1 pr.; for the dating, see Millar (1990, 35). For the possibility that Tyre did see some veteran settlement when it was made a Roman *colonia*, see Hirt (2015, 196).

45. See Hirt (2015, 196–97) on the evidence for this development.

46. Europa: *BMC* nos. 229–35, 293, 295, 311–12. Kadmos: *BMC* nos. 236–41, 287, 296–97, 313. Dido: *BMC* nos. 263–65.

47. Dido: *BMC* nos. 409, 440–41, 447, 470 (and possibly 410, a woman in a galley). Kadmos: *BMC* nos. 411, 425–26, 434, 446, 469, 486–89, 496. Melqart: *BMC* nos. 427, 459, 485. Ambrosial rocks: *BMC* nos. 429–30, 442, 468, 473, with Nitschke (2013, 272–73). Hirt (2015) summarizes the Tyrian bronze coinage produced under Elagabalus at 193–94.

48. Hirt (2015, 197–98), with 199–200 on how the Dido and Kadmos types continued after Tyre's civic titles were restored under Alexander Severus (r. 222–35), with Tyre adding a scene of Kadmos founding Thebes during the reign of Gallienus (r. 260–68) (*BMC* no. 487).

49. Rouvier (1904, no. 2471), in the reign of Trebonius Gallus (r. 251–54); *BMC* no. 468, in the reign of Valerian I (r. 253–60).

50. Butcher (2005, 152).

51. *BMC* no. 442 (minted under Trebonianus Gallus), 473 (minted under Valerian I); for the tales about the dog, see Bonnet (1988, 74–75). Hirt (2015, 200–204) discusses the depiction of the ambrosial rocks on Tyrian coinage and the associated foundation stories, suggesting that they emphasize Tyre's distinct, non-Greek heritage.

52. On the multiple audiences for Tyrian coinage, see Hirt (2015, 205–7).

53. Pompon. 1.65.

54. Batty (2000, esp. 82–85). Contra, Ferrer Albelda (2012).

55. Tingentera: Pompon. 2.96. Claudius's history: Suet. *Claud.* 42.2. See Gruen (2011, 137–38), for Greco-Roman interest in and praise of the Phoenicians in the Imperial period.

56. Dios (*BNJ* 785): Joseph. *Ap.* 1.112; Menander (*BNJ* 783): Joseph. *AJ* 8.144, 9.283; *Ap.* 1.116.

57. Joseph. *AJ* 1.107. For Mochos, see *BNJ* 784; for Hestaios, *BNJ* 786; for Hieronymos, *BNJ* 787.

58. Theodotos (*BNJ* 732) and Hypsikrates: Tatianus *Oratio ad Graecos* 37. Sancuniathon: Athenaeus *Dinner Party Guests* 3.126a, with Carolina López-Ruiz's commentary at *BNJ* 784 (Mochos) F 3b. Klaudios Iolaos (*BNJ* 788): Steph. Byz. s.v. Ake, Doros.

59. Mochus: Strabo 16.2.24 (reporting a claim by Posidonius). Sanchuniathon: Euseb. *Praep. evang.* 1.9.21 = *BNJ* 790 F 1 (reporting a claim by Porphyry).

60. See Johnson (2006, 66) for the term.

61. Berossus: *BNJ* 680; Manetho: *BNJ* 609, both with bibliography.

62. M. Edwards (1991, 214).

63. M. Edwards (1991, 214). For the point that this was a Greek genre, see Baurain and Bonnet (1992, 11).

64. Tatianus *Oratio ad Graecos* 37, on Mochos, Theodotus, and Hipsicrates; the reference at Tert. *Apol.* 19.6, to a Hiram or Hieronymus who was a Phoenician king of Tyre is difficult to interpret: see on this the commentary by Carolina López-Ruiz in *BNJ* 787 T 1b.

65. Millar (1983, 64). For fuller bibliography on Philo, see chapter 3.

66. Johnson (2006, 71); cf. M. Edwards (1991). Brizzi (1980) makes an interesting argument that Philo's work was coherent with Roman imperial policy in the east, even "al serivizio della propaganda imperiale" (128).

67. Euseb. *Praep. evang.* 1.19.29 (= *BNJ* 790 F 2).

68. M. Edwards (1991, 213).

69. Euseb. *Praep. evang* 1.9.20, quoting Porphry (= *BNJ* 790 F 1).

70. Ach. Tat. 1.1 (Sidon); 1.3 (Klitophon's Tyrian origins); 2.14 (Tyre).

71. Ach. Tat. 1.17.3–5, 3.25, with Morgan (2014, 265).

72. Stephens and Winkler (1995, 314–57), dating one of the hands found in the main codex (P. Colon. inv. 3328) to the end of the second century CE (329).

73. Romeo (2010, 82–84) (noting plausible connections with the Severan court); Ní Mheallaigh (2012).

74. Dorotheos fr. 9a Stegemann, with Bohak (2005, 229); Paus. 7.23.7–8.

75. Philostr. *VS* 2.10.

76. On Emesa, see Millar (1993, 300–309).

77. Hdn. 5.3.2–4. Cf. *Epit. de Caes.* 23.2.

78. Dio Cass. 80.11.1; cf., later, SHA *Heliogab.* 8.1–2.

79. Millar (1993, 307); Hdn. 5.5.4; Dio Cass. 80.11.2.

80. Hdn. 5.6.4–5. L. Hall (2004, 136–39) essays a variety of other arguments for the deliberate construction of a "Phoenician" identity on the part of the Severans, focusing in particular on the relationship of this identity with pagan religion and the myths celebrated in the *Aeneid*.

81. Emesa: *BMC* no. 21. Sidon: *BMC* nos. 244–60, 279–86, 291–92, 299–300, 306.

82. Bowie (1998, 14). Morgan adds another possible reference in the *sphragis* itself to Phoinix the Myrmidon of the *Iliad*, "tutor and father-figure to Achilles, as Heliodorus is the creator and director of Achilles' descendant" (2014, 276).

83. An argument for the *Aithoipika* as a centrifugal text "written from the margins of the Greek world" and for its author's self-presentation as an "interloper" is made in Whitmarsh (1998, 97–107; quotations on 97, 107), and reprised in Whitmarsh (2011, 112–16); a counterargument for the novel as an "endorsement, assertion and extension of Hellenism" is made by Morgan (2014, quotation on 264).

84. Whitmarsh (1998).

85. Whitmarsh (2011, 125), with a case presented at 125–28; cf. Whitmarsh (1998); Hilton (2012, 197–205), with much relevant recent bibliography.

86. Whitmarsh (1998, 123), presented as a possibility.

87. Whitmarsh (1998, 100), with references.

88. Whitmarsh (1998, 103), on Heliod. *Aeth.* 2.34.2–8.

89. Heliod. *Aeth.* 4.17.1, 6.3.3.

90. Heliod. *Aeth.* 10.11.3; cf. 4.8.2 for the same claim by her mother. Whitmarsh (2011, 110) notes the centrality of Helios to the narrative. Morgan (2009) argues that the Emesan sun cult is "an essential background element" to the novel (263, with 265) and that Heliodorus wishes to present Emesan religion in a positive light after the bad press brought by Elagabalus's behavior (269–70).

91. Morgan (2014, 260) for the reference of the phrase "descendants of the sun" to the cult of Elagabal; Morgan (2009, 266) for its lack of attestation in relation to the cult. Whether Elagabal was always understood as a sun god at Emesa is unclear: for the probable mismatch between the god's local name, which may well be derived from

the Aramaic words for "god" ('ELAHĀ) and "mountain" (GBL), and the association suggested to Greek-speakers by the pronunciation of the word with "Helios," or sun, see Millar (1993, 301–8); Morgan (2009, 264); Whitmarsh (2011, 109–10). But by the time of Septimius Severus, he was presented even by locals as a sun god: *AE* 1962, no. 229 (from Augsburg) marks the dedication of an altar in Raetia by the Emesene C. Iulius Avitus Alexianus to "his ancestral god of the Sun, Elagabalus" (*deo p[atrio] Soli Ela[gabalo]*). Elagabalus certainly brings Elagabal to Rome as a sun god: contemporary coins call him the "priest of Deus Sol Elagab[al]" (Millar 1993, 308, with references).

92. While the date of Heliodorus is much debated, with many scholars preferring the fourth century, Simon Swain has argued convincingly for the third century on historical grounds (Swain 1996, 423–24), and one plausible view based on parallels with contemporary texts would put him in the 220s or 230s (Bowie 2008, 32–33). A later date would not of course rule out textual references to this period, although later imperial associations evoked by the treatment of Helios in the novel could include the brief resurrection of the cult of Elagabalus by Aurelian (r. 270–75) (Rohde 1914, 496–98; discussed at Bowie 2008, 33), and the "Hymn to King Helios" written by the Roman Emperor Julian (r. 361–63), who elsewhere makes the same claim to descent from the sun (*Or.* 7.229); for a detailed discussion of the parallels between these two texts, which do not of course require them to be contemporary, see Hilton (2012, 210–19).

93. Heliod. *Aeth.* 4.4.2, with Bowie (1998, 5) on the episode.

94. Heliod. *Aeth.* 10.36.3.

CHAPTER 8. A NEW PHOENICIAN WORLD

1. See Quinn (2010) for more detail on these buildings and their Italian associations; for the traditional picture of their role in the "Romanization" of local elites, see MacMullen (2000, 35–42); Bullo (2002, 174); Masturzo (2003, 749).

2. SHA *Sev.* 15.7.

3. Rey-Coquais (1987). I translate here the Latin *Col(onia) Ulpia / Traiana Aug(usta) / Fidelis Lepcis / Magna Tyron et / suam metropolin*; the Greek version includes a little more detail on the circumstances of the dedication, irrelevant to us here, but it is also more fragmentary. Rey-Coquais also notes that another Greek inscription was found in the same excavation of a Roman villa, which also records the dedication, by a city whose name is now lost, of a statue of Tyre to "Tyre which is also its own metropolis" (598, with 601 for the suggestion that this city was Kition).

4. *IRT* no. 437: [*P(ublio) [Septimio]* G*[etae]]/[nobilissimo* Ca*[es(ari)]]/ Septimia Tyros / Colonia Metropolis / Phoenices et aliarum / ciuitatium.* The first two lines were erased after Geta's murder and *damnatio memoriae* in 212.

5. On the political history of Lepcis, see Di Vita (1982, 516–37); Mattingly (1995, 50–53); Quinn (2010, 52), with references.

6. Fontana (2001).

7. A case I first made in Quinn (2010). What follows both draws on and goes beyond that article, especially chronologically, and corrects some minor errors introduced during its admirably swift publication process.

8. Public assembly: Sznycer (1975, 66–67) (on *IPT* no. 31, mid-first-century CE, and *IPT* no. 27, 92 CE). Local priesthoods and sufetes: *IRT*, pp. 79–80.

9. *IPT* no. 31, tentatively dated to the second or early first century BCE: L'DN LŠDRP' WLMLK'ŠTRT RBT 'LPQY. On this inscription and these gods, see Di Vita (1968a, 204–9).

10. See Quinn (2010) for more on these inscriptions and for texts and translations.

11. *IRT*, p. 80.

12. *RPC* 1 nos. 840–41 (Dionysus/Augustus), 842 (Dionysus and Herakles/Augustus), 843–44 (Augustus/thyrsus and club); the only silver issue juxtaposes a lion skin on a club with a panther and thyrsus (*RPC* 1 no. 847).

13. See Di Vita (2005), Quinn (2010, 57–58), and Quinn and Wilson (2013, 154–55) for the identification of the Shadrapa temple, against Niccolò Masturzo's suggestion that it was a Capitolium (Masturzo 2005, building on Musso 1996). The third Augustan-period temple on the forum, also built with a mixed metrology, has been identified as the temple of Milkashtart (Di Vita 1968a), but although this identification has been widely accepted, there is no positive evidence for it, and I have suggested elsewhere that Milkashtart may have "shared" the temple of Shadrapa (Quinn 2010, 58). If Milkashtart was worshipped on the forum in either temple, that would make the juxtaposition of the local and imperial gods even more striking.

14. On the use of the Punic cubit in the Old Forum temples, see Livadiotti and Rocco (2005, 236); Masturzo (2005, 118); Ricciardi (2005, 382).

15. *IPT* no. 24 and *IRT* nos. 321–22, with Quinn (2010, 62), pointing out that the close juxtaposition of the two texts in these cases draws attention to the omission of this information in the Punic; see also *IPT* no. 26 and *IRT* no. 338, with A. Wilson (2012, 287–89).

16. *IPT* no. 21 and *IRT* no. 319. See Adams (2003, 222) on the "linguistic ideology" at work here as "Punic is kept free of Latin words even in reference to distinctively Roman institutions."

17. *IPT* no. 27 and *IRT* no. 318 are the last datable examples.

18. A. Wilson (2012, 272–84).

19. Adams (2003, 301–2) (on "code-switching") discusses the choice of a particular language as, among other things, "accommodation" of or "solidarity" with those for whom it is a first language (convergence), and the expression of dominance over those who cannot use it (divergence).

20. Wallace-Hadrill (2008, 448). For the architecture, see Di Vita (1968b, esp. 46–52; 1982, 565; 1983, 364–67; 1992, 109–10).

21. Livadiotti and Rocco (2005, 204, 216, 222–26, 228–29); Ricciardi (2005, 381). See Alexandropoulos (2000, 256–57) on the influence on Lepcitan coinage of Cyrenaican emissions as well as Numidian ones.

22. Sear (2006, 104, 271–72), with earlier bibliography.

23. Tripolitania: Alexandropoulos (2000, 256). Spain and Mauretania: Alexandropoulos (2000). Callegarin (2011) has recent stratigraphic evidence for Mauretanian cities: Iol minted coins from the end of the third century; Icosium and Lixus from the second: "at the same time as most of their Hispanic equivalents" (46).

24. The editors of *IRT* point out that from this period onward, the use of Ras el-Hammam limestone replaced that of the "soft local sandstone that could only be used . . . under a thick coating of stucco" (p. 82).

25. *IPT* no. 31, discussed above, is generally accepted as pre-Augustan, but it is a personal (if publicly authorized) dedication, and on a rather smaller scale than the later building inscriptions.

26. Sall. *Iug.* 78.4: *eius civitatis lingua modo convorsa conubio Numidarum; legum cultusque pleraque Sidonica, quae eo facilius retinebant, quod procul ab imperio regis aetatem agebant.* There is some exploitation of Libyan in Punic inscriptions: the word for *imperator* used in the market inscription is MYNKD (*IPT* no. 21, l.1), which can be compared with MNKD᾽ in Libyan funerary inscriptions. See Levi Della Vida (1935, 4–7); *IPT* ad loc; and Jongeling (2008, 21–22) (Labdah no. 13) for full discussion.

27. Sall. *Iug.* 78.1: *id oppidum ab Sidoniis conditum est, quos accepimus profugos ob discordias civilis navibus in eos locos venisse.* For local sources, see Sall, *Iug.* 17.7.

28. Pliny, *HN* 5.76; Sil. 3.256. Silius also calls Sabratha Tyrian and says that Sicilians and Africans were involved in the colonization of Oea (3.256–57).

29. Di Vita (1982, 516–17); Malkin (1994, 202–3); Krings (1998, 193–94); Miles (2010, 100).For ongoing commercial ties between the cities, see Quinn (2011b); A. Wilson (2013).

30. *DCPP* s.v. Shadrapha, Milkashtart, with references and bibliography.

31. Milkashtart (originally, at least, "King of [the city of] Ashtarot") became relatively popular in the western Mediterranean in the Hellenistic period, with a temple at Carthage, and the Astarte sanctuary at Tas-Silġ has yielded a cup with the name of the god Milkashtart incised on it, probably in the fourth century BCE (Amadasi Guzzo 1973, 92–94; with 2010, 486–88). The nature of the relationship (if any) that Phoenician speakers understood to exist between this god and Melqart is very unclear and may well have changed over time; see further Lipiński (1995, 271–74).

32. Recent explorations of the theme include Fear (1996, 227–51); van Dommelen (1998a, 174–77; 1998b; 2001; 2007); Quinn (2003); R. Wilson (2005); López Castro (2007); Jiménez (2010); Fantar (2011); Mora Serrano and Cruz Andreotti (2012); R. Wilson (2013, 114–19).

33. van Dommelen (1998b, 32).

34. van Dommelen (1998a, 176; 1998b, 39; 2007, 60).

35. van Dommelen (2007, 66–67).

36. van Dommelen (1998b, quotation on 32; 2001; 2007); for a major revolt in 215, see Livy 23.32–41. Cf., on resistance as an interpretation of culture, Jiménez (2008).

37. Fantar (2011, 464).

38. For a fuller discussion of these three African phenomena, see McCarty and Quinn (2015), where we also argue against the notion that the Numidian kings were primarily responsible for introducing these practices into African towns.

39. Oros. 5.15.6: Jugurtha "yoked almost the whole of Africa, deserting from the Romans, to his kingdom." The scale of this revolt is minimized by Brennan (2000, 540), and it is true that Sallust does not mention a revolt or large-scale defection, but he does describes the antisocial behavior of the Roman army in the *provincia* in the winter of 110/109 (Sall. *Iug.* 39, 43–44), shortly after the passage of the Roman *lex agraria* of 111, with its program of registrations, land distribution, and centuriation, which could only have added to the daily inconvenience of hosting Roman troops in the province.

40. Both my approach and van Dommelen's consciously follow in the footsteps of Marcel Benabou's classic argument for cultural resistance to Rome in North Africa, although his major focus is on continuities in indigenous "Libyan" traditions rather than "Phoenician" ones, and our conclusions are somewhat different: see Bénabou (1976; 1982), and cf. Laroui (1977, 38–66).

41. The most recent summary of the chronology is Xella (2013a, 261). Carthage: Bénichou-Safar (2004, 134–37). Cirta: D'Andrea (2014, 275). Hadrumetum: D'Andrea (2014, 94); McCarty (2011, 208n20) notes that a new study of the site chronology is in progress.

42. For surveys of this phenomenon, see Le Glay (1961–66); Krandel-Ben Younès (2002, 153–282); D'Andrea (2014, 97–290); Ruiz Cabrero and Peña Romo (2010); see also McCarty (2013); McCarty and Quinn (2015, 176–81). For a survey of differences between the African sanctuaries, see Ferjaoui (2007, 64–75). The number of these sanctuaries is seriously underestimated at Quinn (2011a, 402).

43. See McCarty (2013, 94–95) for the relevant bibliography (and exceptions), as well as reflections on the contribution made by archaeology to this impression.

44. Dating: McCarty and Quinn (2015, 177–78). Names: D'Andrea (2014, 320–21). For the preponderance of Libyan over Punic or Latin names at Mididi, see Krandel-Ben Younès (2002, 221).

45. McCarty (2011; 2013).

46. Tert. *Apol.* 9.3.

47. Althiburos: Xella and Tahar 2014; further information has been presented at the International Phoenician and Punic Studies Congress at Sulcis-Carbonia (2014), and is due for publication as Xella and Tahar (forthcoming); I thank the authors for discussion of their findings. Henchir el-Hami: Ferjaoui (2007; 2008a; 2012); Melchiorri (2013, 234–36). Lambafundi: Le Glay (1961–66, 2.114–15), with Rives (1994, 61); D'Andrea (2014, 279).

48. See Jongeling (2008) for the references: Thugga: 76, no. 2; 78, no. 5. Ellès: 78–79, nos. 1–3. Abitina: 81, no. 1. Mactar: 95, no. 11; 106, no. 39; 129, no. 77; 137, no. 105; 139, nos. 110–11; 140, no. 116. Mididi: 149, no. 13; 152, no. 21; 154, no. 26. Thinissut: 65, no. 1.

49. McCarty and Quinn (2015, 179).

50. D'Andrea (2014, 313–18).

51. McCarty (2011).

52. McCarty (2013, 96).

53. McCarty (2013, esp. 98–104), and see 104–7 for an apparent total hiatus in ritual activity of more than a century at Thugga from the early/mid-first century CE.

54. Tinnit: Quodvultdeus, *Liber de promissionibus et praedictionibus Dei* 3.38.44. For the association between Tinnit and Caelestis, which seems clear at the sanctuary of Thinissut (Bir bou Rekba) on Cap Bon where a Punic dedication to Baal Hammon and Tinnit is followed by Latin ones to Saturn and Caelestis, but less certain elsewhere, see Cadotte (2006, 65–71). Henry Hurst has made an ingenious argument that in the Roman colony of Carthage the area of the old tophet became a sanctuary of Caelestis, and he suggests that there are considerable correspondences and perhaps continuities between the "Punic" and "Roman" version of this cult (Hurst 1999, 91–101). Saturn: Hurst (1999, 39–43).

55. McCarty (2010).

56. Tert. *Apol.* 9.2, with Rives (1994, 54n2, 63n20) and Shaw (2016, 266–70) for this reading of the text and the dating it implies. For an argument that the reference in Cicero's speech for Balbus to Julius Caesar's ridding the customs and habits of the Gaditani of "a kind of deep-seated barbarism" (43) when he was provincial governor in Hispania 61/60 BCE relates to another local ban on child sacrifice, see Shaw (2016, 270–71).

57. For the evidence from Africa and Sardinia, see Zucca (2004). Gadir: Livy 28.37.2. Eryx: *ICO* Sicilia Pun. no. 1. The case for Malta, where two "archons" are recorded in a Greek inscription (*IG* XIV no. 953), is less certain. For more on the institution at Carthage, see Ameling (2013, 369), and for its counterpart in the Levant, Manfredi (2003, 341–42).

58. Zucca (2004, 84–101).

59. Zucca (2004, 18–83). The last example is no. 39. See also, for Africa, Belkahia and Di Vita-Évrard (1995).

60. Belkahia and Di Vita-Évrard (1995); Manfredi (2003, 378–86).

61. Picard (1974), envisages a very high level of direct Carthaginian government in Africa, assuming that the institution is already widespread at the point of Roman conquest as "un héritage de Carthage," connecting it with a colonization program that may be mentioned by Aristotle (*Pol.* 2.1273b), and he is uninterested in peer polity interaction as an explanation for the adoption of similar institutions in neighboring settlements.

62. *RIL* no. 2 = *KAI*[5] no. 101, l.1. The term is simply transliterated in the Libyan part of the inscription; see Ghaki (1997, 29, 45) for various other differences between the Punic and Libyan versions.

63. On the magistracies at Thugga, see Février (1964–65), suggesting that some Carthaginian constitutional models had already been adopted in the city of Thugga during the reign of Numidian King Massinissa.

64. *CIL* VIII no. 26517, with Khanoussi and Maurin (2000, 137–42).

65. Althiburos: Jongeling (2008, 155 no. 1); Mactar: Jongeling (2008, 126 no. 75, with 95–96, no. 11). Thugga: *AE* 1966, 509. The inscription from Chul is unpublished but is cited at Belkahia (1994, 1084n56).

66. Coins: Manfredi (1995). Sicily: Apul. *Met.* 11.5, with R. Wilson (2013, 116n103) arguing for the interpretation of the third language mentioned as Punic on the grounds that all other possible candidates were long dead. Sardinia: the latest evidence is Jongeling (2008, 275); Chia 1 = *ICO* Sardegna Neo-Pun no. 8 = *KAI*[5] no. 173, an inscription from Bithia dated by the name of the emperor to the reign of Aurelius or Caracalla.

67. There are 681 catalogued inscriptions from across North Africa in the neo-Punic script, dating between the second century BCE and the second century CE (Jongeling 2008), as well as 69 transliterated Latino-Punic inscriptions from Tripolitania dating from the second to at least the fourth centuries CE (Kerr 2010). For the huge amount of evidence for the use of Punic in Roman Africa, see Millar (1968, 130–32); Adams (2003, 200–245); Jongeling and Kerr (2005, 2–6); Kerr (2010, 13–24); A. Wilson (2012).

68. Manfredi (1995, 58–61, 135–39) catalogues Punic coin legends from North Africa.

69. SHA *Sev.* 15.7; Apul. *Apol.* 98.

70. Inscriptions: Thugga: *KAI*[5] nos. 100–101 with *RIL* 1–2. Cherchel: *KAI*[5] no. 161 = Jongeling (2008, 195, Cherchel no. 2). Volubilis: *IAM* nos. 1, 5–11 = Jongeling (2008, 256–58 [Volubilis nos. 1–7]). Coinage: Alexandropoulos (2000, 137–248, 395–435). For skepticism about the traditional assumption that Punic was the "official" language of the Numidian court, however, see McCarty and Quinn (2015).

71. Sall. *Iug.* 17.7. For *libri punici* later consulted by the Numidian king and historian Juba II for the sources of the Nile, see Amm. Marc. 22.15.8; Solin. 32.2.

72. Likely to be in Greek: Feeney (2016, 203–4), with earlier bibliography. Likely to be in Punic: Gruen (2011, 272n85), with earlier bibliography; Quinn (2014).

73. Plin. *HN* 18.22.

74. On these passages, see Plautus, *The Little Carthaginian. Pseudolus. The Rope*, vol. 4 of *Plautus*, ed. and trans. Wolfgang de Melo, Loeb Classical Library (Cambridge, MA: Harvard University Press, 2012), 173–222.

75. Kerr (2010, 10). There are also two inscriptions from the tophet sanctuary at Cirta that transliterate Punic into Greek (Kerr 2010, 227–28).

76. Kerr (2010, 16, with 195).

77. August. *Ep.* 66.2; 209.3; August. *Serm.* 167.4 (the relevant proverb was "Plague begs for a penny, give him two to go away"); and see Lepelley (2005) with earlier bibliography.

78. The major exception is Cirta, where about half the votive markers are in the older Punic script.

79. Jongeling and Kerr (2005, 2, 7–8); Kerr (2010, 25–130), dealing also with Latino-Punic. Linguistic development is noticed by Jerome in the preface to book 2 of his commentary on Paul's Letter to the Galatians.

80. E.g., Jongeling (2008, 103), Hr. Maktar N32, a dedication by Ahotmilkat, the daughter of Bodmelqart, who is the wife of Iasuktan, the son of Salidio, a citizen of the Mactarians. I thank Robert Kerr for the point and the reference.

81. See Davies (2000) on the importance of onomastics for identity; contra, see, e.g., Van der Spek (2009, 102).

82. Quinn et al. (2014, 181n14), comparing the lists in Benz (1972) and Jongeling (2008).

83. Ferjaoui (2007, 117), notes the phenomenon at the Henchir el Hami tophet sanctuary of a father with a (probably) Libyan name giving his son a Punic name, and a father with a Punic name giving his son a Roman one.

84. A. Wilson (2012, 269).

85. A. Wilson (2012) for the neo-Punic inscriptions; Kerr (2010, 16) for Latino-Punic.

86. *RIL* collects 1,123 inscriptions from Morocco, Algeria, and Tunisia; there is a useful online supplement and index of inscriptions published between 1940 and 2012 compiled by René Rebuffat at HAL archives-ouvertes, https:///halshs.archives-ouvertes.fr/halshs-00841800/document. On this body of material, see Kerr (2010, 21–23); Fentress and Wilson (2016, 50–51), with earlier bibliography.

87. Elizabeth Fentress and Andrew Wilson have related this linguistic analysis to contemporary archaeological evidence for new tomb-types and literary accounts of war and destruction wreaked by people from outside the area of imperial control in a convincing scenario of invasions and conquest from the Sahara in late antiquity (Fentress and Wilson 2016, esp. 51–53 on the new linguistic evidence). For more general observations on the difficulty of establishing a relationship between the Libyan texts and modern Berber dialects, see Kerr (2010, 21–22).

88. The nearest tophet is at Msellata, thirty kilometers inland from Lepcis (Abd Al-Rahman 1995, 155).

89. Tyrian origins: Sil. 3.256. Sufetes: The only evidence for sufetes at all is the appearance of a pair of mysterious two-letter legends on the civic coinage of the Augustan period (Zucca [2004, 27]). Tophet: Brecciaroli Taborelli (1983); Taborelli (1992); D'Andrea (2014, 261–63).

90. On the lack of Roman interest in North Africa during the Republic, see Quinn (2004).

91. Morestin (1980); Brouquier-Reddé et al. (1998).

92. E.g., August. *C. Iul.* 3.32; *C. Iul. imp.* 1.7, 1.48, 1.73. On these and similar passages, see Weber (2003). Julian is not the only interlocutor to refer to Augustine as "Phoenician" in this derogatory fashion: Secundus the Manichean calls him a *punicus* in a letter in which he also begs him to put aside the faithlessless (*perfidia*) of the *gens punica* (Secundinus, *Epistula ad Augustinum*, 2–3; cf. August. *Contra Secundinum* 3).

93. E.g., August. *C. Iul. imp.* 6.6.

94. D. Weber (2003, 81).

95. August. *C. Iul. imp.* 6.18; cf. *C. Iul.* 3.32 and *C. Iul. imp* 1.72 for similar references to Cyprian as a *poenus*.

96. Massinissa's palm frond: Alexandropoulos (2000, 318, no. 23); Ptolemy's palm: Alexandropoulos (2000, 240–41), with useful discussion.

97. I thank Matthew McCarty for compiling the sketches for these figures for me from his comprehensive database.

98. E.g. *BMCV* 26, nos. 68–72. The precise dating and historical context of this coinage is disputed; see most recently Miles (2017).

99. Miles (2017).

CHAPTER 9. PHOENICIAN ISLANDS

1. Vine (2010, 41–2). Vives was a celebrated foreign intellectual in England in the 1520s and a mentor to Princess Mary until he fell out with her father over his support for her mother.

2. For the setting, see Twyne (1590, 6–7 [B3v–B4r]); for the cast of characters, *ODNB*; for an extensive appreciation of the work in the context of English Renaissance scholarship, Ferguson (1969). See also Kendrick (1950, esp. 105–8), and, with a focus on Twyne's interest in material evidence, Vine (2010, 37–43), who notes, "In its published form at least, the work probably dates from the 1560s, as it opens with an apostrophe to Thomas Twyne, and refers to him as a current student at Oxford" (41).

3. Twyne (1590, 1 [B1r]), cf. 63, 65, 66 and see also *gens nostra Britannica* (3 [B2r]), *gens* Britannica (40), *gens* Britannorum (127), Britanni *nostri* (34), *haec nostra insula* (52); cf. the use of the phrase *gens Brittaniarum* in John of Salisbury's *Policraticus* (c. 1159), on which see Afanasyev (2012). The meal is finally served on page 66, and discussion resumes on page 72, as the guests take a walk after dinner with the sun already low in the sky; ninety pages of talking later, the guests leave with scarcely time to reach Canterbury before nightfall.

4. Twyne (1590, 9, 56–59, 64, 76, 94). As Casper Hirschi observes, for early nationalist historians "mythical and critical thinking often went hand in hand. . . . the same methods were normally used for myth criticism and myth creation" (2012, 16).

5. Twyne (1590, 7–9, 15–32, 98–107), with Ferguson (1969, 30–32); Vine (2010, 39).

6. Twyne (1590, 40).

7. See, for example, Ferrer Albelda (1996) on the reconstruction of the Iberian peninsula's Carthaginian past in Spanish historical writing.

8. Thacker and Wright (1955).

9. For classic examples, see Gellner (1983); Hobsbawm (1990); B. Anderson (1991). Kidd (1999, 1–5) and Joseph (2004, 95–98) provide concise summaries of modern approaches to the definition, chronology, and causes of nationalism. Armstrong (1982, 4) argues that the unusual cosmopolitanism of the Enlightenment era makes the subsequent focus on ethnicity and nation seem more novel than it really was.

10. Charles-Edwards (2004); Hirschi (2012, esp. 78–103); Ruddick (2013).

11. Benedict Anderson famously related what he called "the birth of the imagined community of the nation" in the early modern period to the invention of print-capitalism, "which made it possible for rapidly growing numbers of people to think about themselves, and to relate themselves to others, in profoundly new ways" (1991, 24, 36).

12. For more on medieval ideas of genocide, see Scales (2007), and for the collections of ethnic stereotypes made in European monasteries from c. 1000 CE as well as an upsurge in ethnic stereotyping in the twelfth century, see Weeda (2014). Concerning early modern times, Hirschi draws attention to Erasmus's 1517 description of the English hatred of the French, the Scots' of the British, and the Germans' of the French and the Spanish (which led him to ask, "Are we taking the common word 'fatherland' for such a grave cause that one people seeks to annihilate the other?"), as well as the long lists of national characteristics given in sixteenth- and seventeenth-century playwrights' handbooks (*poetics*) (Hirschi 2012, 1, 11).

13. Kidd (1999, 9–33, esp. 30–32).

14. Kendrick (1950, 3–4).

15. Kidd (1999, 10).

16. Joseph. *AJ* 1.122, with Kidd (1999, 29–30).

17. Hirschi (2012, 3): "From the twelfth century onward, legally and philologically trained clerics tried to adapt the legacy of Rome to contemporary politics; the language of the nation was created in the process." Cf. Hirschi (2012, 15–16), and for a similar point about the ancient world, see Lemche (1991, 152–53).

18. Cf. Richard Tuck's description of Thomas Hobbes's life as secretary to Lord Cavendish, a position he assumed in 1608: "Like all such servants, he spent a lot of time sitting in anterooms while his master and other great men discussed state affairs (or merely gossiped), and Aubrey recorded that to while away the time he would read the pocket-sized editions of classical texts produced by the Dutch printers Elzevier" (Tuck 1989, 4, drawing on John Aubrey's *Life of Hobbes*).

19. Vine (2010, 25–26).

20. Twyne (1590, 14): "ubi de *Priamo* sermo? ubi de *Bruto* verbum ullum?" Cf. 76 for a similar point.

21. Twyne (1590, 15); cf. 33 for the abbot's intimate knowledge of Lucan's vocabulary.

22. Twyne (1590, 43–44): "quae cum vos legitis, amici nonne subit in animum idem quoque olim Britanniae contigisse, ob metallicam scilicet rationem, qua Cornubia, quae vulgo Cornwallia dicitur, abundat?" This is followed by a list of metals that can be acquired from other parts of the island as well; see also 56–58, 78. The reference is to Vives's 1522 commentary on Augustine's *City of God*, ad 8.9, summarized at Twyne (1590, 41–43). *Cornubia* is a medieval Latinization of the name of Cornwall.

23. Twyne (1590, 82–83, 134, 144).

24. Twyne (1590, 56–57); cf. 91.

25. Twyne (1590, 81, 107–13), with 110 on the derivation of *Carthago*, drawing on Solin. 27.10.

26. Twyne (1590, 80): "Unde privatim viris barbam abradendi praeterquam in superiore labro consuetudo, nisi ab *Babylonijs*?" (From where in particular do men get the custom of shaving the beard except on the upper lip, if not from the Babylonians?)

27. Twyne (1590, 81): "*Phoenices* primum qui a *Babylone* progressi ad mare rubrum, inde ad *Aegyptum, Aethiopiam, Syriam, Graeciam & Hispaniam* pervenerunt: postea in *Albionem* quae modo *Britannia* dicitur (si quid ego recte conijcio) penetrarunt." [The Phoenicians first proceeded from Babylon to the Red Sea, from there attained Egypt, Ethiopia, Syria, Greece, and Spain, and then reached *Albion*, which is what Britain was called (if I am not mistaken)].

28. Twyne (1590, 41): "*Phoenices* mercatores dicti sunt: *Phoenices* rubri, id est, coloribus tincti. *Phoenices* insidiosi, atque astuti habiti sunt: unde *Phoenicum* pacta, *Phoenicum* mores, proverbia emanarunt." I am grateful to Peta Fowler for discussion of these passages.

29. Vine (2010, 22–50) on sixteenth-century scholars; Kendrick (1950, 18–33) on their predecessors and medieval excavations.

30. Schwyzer (2004, 3–4).

31. Kendrick (1950, 34–44).

32. Schwyzer (2004, 31–33).

33. Cf. Kendrick (1950, 42–43) for some of the ambivalence expressed by Tudor monarchs over connections to the Arthur legend.

34. Armitage (2000, 29–60). The term "British Empire" only regularly referred to the overseas empire after around 1650 (Vance 2000, 213).

35. For praise of the "British" Welsh, see Twyne (1590, 66).

36. Twyne (1590, 33): "ignotus obscurusque profugus."

37. Vine (2010) draws attention to a curious episode in the text in which Foche expresses regret over the loss of an otherwise unattested manuscript of Cicero's *De republica* in a monastery fire, and suggests that he "seems also to be commenting on the dreadful consequences of the Dissolution" (43).

38. Roebuck and Maguire (2010, 42).

39. See Vance (2000) for the complexities and perceived difficulties of this appropriation of Rome and in particular of the Roman Empire. See also Hingley (2008, esp. 59–66).

40. Grey (1763, II, p. 2): February 5, 1673.

41. See also the same author's 1666 poem, *Annus Mirabilis*, a rather awkward celebration of the British commander Albemarle's defeat by the Dutch in a naval battle.

42. Sammes (1676), A1v. Sammes's *ODNB* entry notes that some considered him insufficiently educated to compose the book published under his name. On the work itself, see Parry (1995, 308–23) and on its political contexts, Jonathan Scott (2011, esp. 107–11). Gerritsen (2012) is a useful brief summary, especially interested in the images.

43. Sammes (1676, A3v).

44. Sammes (1676, 2).

45. Sammes (1676, 39–41), for a long and careful demonstration of this identification, which had also been argued by Camden, with reference to Strabo 3.5.11; Sammes also cites Herodotus, Solinus, Diodorus, and Eustathius, among others. Champion (2001, 454) points out that this interpretation of Strabo ignores Diodorus's report that

the tin trade of Cornwall was locally controlled and that tin from Cornwall came overland through France (Diod. Sic. 5.22). The Casseterides of the ancient sources are probably islands off the Atlantic coast of Spain.

46. Sammes (1676, 41–43); cf. 1–2, and Bochart (1646, 720), a debt mentioned on Sammes (1676, 40–41). In this Sammes goes further than Twyne, who had postulated that "Britannia" might be a Phoenician word (*Pritannia*) (1590, 16), but also suggested a derivation from the British "brit," or "piece" (9).

47. See in particular, and at great length, Sammes (1676, 48–70), with 58–59 for Cornwall and 109 for ale. There is a useful summary of the whole argument at Sammes (1676, 70); cf. the varied list of reasons to see the Cimbri as the first arrivals on the island on 10.

48. Sammes (1676, 397).

49. For Sammes, "Tyre *and* Zidon" are the Phoenicians' "*own Native Country*" (1676, 47). On 71, he equates the Phoenicians with the Canaanites (following Bochart).

50. Sammes (1676, 398); see 395–402 for the full treatment of Stonehenge. Although, like Twyne, Sammes acknowledges that the Phoenicians came to Britain via Africa, for both authors it is Phoenicians in general who are national founder figures, not specifically the Carthaginians, wherever their journey may have taken them on the way.

51. Sammes (1676, A3r and passim). Sammes mentions Twyne only in relation to the idea of the isthmus (25).

52. Sammes (1676, 1–2). At the same time, he reflects explicitly, and sometimes perceptively, on the broader phenomenon of "nations," noting, for instance, that "*Nations receive their Names not from themselves, but others*" (44, and see also 45).

53. Sammes (1676, A2v).

54. Sammes (1676, 2); there are many other examples of the Phoenician "Nation" in the text.

55. It was never, of course, the only option: Robert Sheringham, in *De Anglorum gentis origine disceptatio* (1670), believed "that the Saxons, Jutes and Angles virtually obliterated any previous racial cultures in Britain" though he allows for the possibility of Phoenician origins for the German tribes (Parry 1995, 324).

56. Sammes (1676, 36, 4).

57. Sammes (1676, 4).

58. Sammes (1676, 50); the source of the suggestion is again Bochart, with polite disagreement over the precise derivation of the name.

59. Jonathan Scott (2011, xiii); cf. 3–4 for the development of this aspect of the British state from the sixteenth to eighteenth centuries, and 107 for its relevance to Sammes, "a royalist, and a proponent of trade and navigation, offering a prescription for British empire."

60. Sammes (1676, A3v).

61. Sammes (1676, 16); cf. 36–37. As Jonathan Scott puts it, "The point was of course that since 1670 Britain had indeed become a 'dependent member' of that large part of Europe under the influence of France. Specifically Sammes' work, with its high-level patronage, may be contextualized within the campaign of Thomas Osborne, Earl of Danby (both cavalier and Anglican), the purpose of which was to distract attention from this fact" (Scott 2011, 108). Cf. 111: "By the end of 1678 the crown's continuing secret relationship with France had become exposed, precipitating a major crisis."

62. Phoenicians: Sammes (1676, A3v); see also, for instance, 2, 9, 73, 142. Britain: e.g., 1–2.

63. Armitage (2000, 195).

64. Parry (1995, 325–27).

65. See further Parry (1995, 329). Unlike Twyne, Sammes had assigned the druids to later Greek colonists, but says that they nonetheless learned much from earlier Phoenician bards (Sammes 1676, 99–105).

66. Champion (2001, 461). George Smith defends the theory of Phoenician trade with Britain, and in particular Cornwall, in his 1863 book *The Cassiterides: An Enquiry into the Commercial Operations of the Phoenicians in Western Europe, with Particular Reference to the British Tin Trade.*

67. *Journal of the Royal Institution of Cornwall* (October 1866): 106, 115.

68. *Journal of the Royal Institution of Cornwall* (October 1866): 140–42. Smirke returns to this topic the following year: "We have all heard, till we are all well nigh tired of hearing, the names of Strabo, Diodorus, and other Roman and Graeco-Roman writers, who have told us of the Phoenician and Carthaginian traffic with Britain in tin" (*Journal of the Royal Institution of Cornwall* [October 1867]: 284).

69. *Journal of the Royal Institution of Cornwall* (1907–9): 20–21.

70. Cf. Champion (2001, 460).

71. Vance (2000, 216–17); Christopher Brooke (2017).

72. E.g., Defoe (1727, 41, 43, 71); cf. 75 on the Romans' failings in these areas; the quotation is from 105.

73. Defoe (1727, 78).

74. Defoe (1727, 106).

75. Defoe (1727, 107); cf. 75, where the fate of Carthage's American colonies after the mother city's destruction is compared to that of some early British ones. Several of the same passages are noted in Jonathan Scott (2011, 130–31).

76. The *ODNB* entry for this "traveller and criminal" is highly recommended.

77. Montagu (1759, 161); cf. 168, and 163, where "*Punica fides* much more justly . . . may be retorted on the Romans."

78. Montagu (1759, 162–63, 169, 170, 172–73, 179, 198–99).

79. Montagu (1759, 174).

80. *Gazette national de France* (1798): 715. On the sentiment of "perfide Albion" in France, see Schmidt (1953); Bernal (1987, 341–42); Isaac (2004, 330n38). See also the contemporary report in Rawlinson (1889, 62), as well as Christopher Brooke (2017) for French enthusiasm for the notion of the British as defeated Carthage.

81. Schmidt (1953, 611), with references.

82. Butlin and Joll (1984), no. 129, now at Tate Britain; no. 131, now at the National Gallery; no. 135, also at Tate Britain. A rather later painting, *Dido Directing the Equipment of the Fleet, or The Morning of the Carthaginian Empire* (1828) (Butlin and Joll 1984, no. 241), is now in storage at Tate Britain, almost completely destroyed, and four more paintings on Carthaginian themes followed in 1850: *The Departure of the Fleet, Mercury Sent to Admonish Aeneas*, and *The Visit to the Tomb* (all at Tate Britain), and *Aeneas Relating His Story to Dido* (now lost).

83. A painting of *Napoleon Crossing the Alps* made a few months after the event by Jacques-Louis David makes explicit reference to Hannibal, whose name is written on a rock at Napoleon's feet, along with that of Charlemagne. The heroism of

the image is further increased by the substitution of a rearing horse for Napoleon's historical mule.

84. Carthage still retained some cachet: Vance (2000, 217n9) notes that "Liverpool's new classical buildings feature prominently" in Samuel Austin's 1826 picture, *The Arrival of Aeneas at the Court of Dido, Queen of Carthage*, now at the Walker Art Gallery.

85. Champion (2001, 456).

86. Champion (2001, 458–59).

87. Champion (2001, 452); cf. 459.

88. I thank Alex Wilson for this observation.

89. Rawlinson (2005, 23); the quotation is taken from the third edition of the work. The first (1889) edition of the same chapter simply notes the "peculiar capacity for business" shared by "a small number of nations," including the Phoenicians, the English, and the Dutch (1889, 61). Rawlinson also situated a Phoenician colony in the Isles of Scilly (1889, 56; 2005, 69–70).

90. Perrot and Chipiez (1885a, 892): "ceux que l'Angleterre a employés, depuis deux siècles, pour établir et pour maintenir, avec une poignée de soldats et des milliers de vaisseaux, son immense empire colonial. . . . La différence, c'est que Tyr n'a jamais essayé de soumettre et de gouverner les peuples qui habitaient les terres dont elle visitait le côtes. . . . La politique de Tyr était celle que l'Angleterre a suivie là où les circonstances ne l'ont pas, comme dans l'Inde, comme dans l'Afrique australe, menée plus loin qu'elle ne voulait aller."

91. Perrot and Chipiez (1885b, 2:431).

92. Waddell's *Phoenician Origin of the Britons, Scots and Anglo-Saxons* (1924) went into a third edition in 1931, and a recent textbook on the Canaanites still states it as fact that the Phoenicians reached Cornwall (Tubb 1998, 140). One very recent example suggests that Thanet in Kent was the "Isle of Tanit": http://www.caitlingreen.org/2015/04/thanet-tanit-and-the-phoenicians.html.

93. Bernal (1987, 337–99); Champion (2001, 462). Anti-Semitism was not the only prejudice at issue in attitudes toward Carthage, as illustrated by Rudyard Kipling's satirical portrait of a schoolmaster in his 1917 short story "Regulus," who describes the city to his class as "a sort of god-forsaken nigger Manchester." I thank Denis Feeney for the reference.

94. Papadopoulos (2005, 130).

95. Leerssen (1986, 95).

96. Cullingford (1996, 223–24).

97. Cullingford (1996, 223). Spenser's *View of the Present State of Ireland* (written in 1596 and published in 1633) was particularly critical.

98. Kidd (1994, 1199–200); Cullingford (1996); Lennon (2004, 71–72), with the latter author noting that Céitinn did not accept the historical reliability of the ancient tales.

99. O'Flaherty (1685; 1793), with Lennon (2004, 74–80), who again here emphasizes that, like Céitinn, Ó Flaithbheartaigh did not present the legends as literal historical truth.

100. Lennon (2004, 77). The name of the work was taken from Plutarch's description of an island five days' sail west of Britain, identified by some of Ó Flaithbheartaigh's contemporaries with America instead.

101. O'Flaherty (1793, 2:83).

102. Lennon (2004, 62–71).

103. Leerssen (1996, 288).

104. Hayton (2012, 27–28).

105. Hayton (2012, 25).

106. On Vallancey, see Vance (1981, 226–27); Leerssen (1986, 99–100), and then, comprehensively, O'Halloran (1995).

107. Vallancey (1772, iii).

108. Vallancey (1772, 1, ix).

109. Vallancey (1773, iii).

110. For contemporary critique of this "literary mess." see O'Halloran (1995, 168–69).

111. Vallancey (1786, e.g., 11, 58, 60, 244, 252).

112. For an entertaining account of Vallancey's flexible position on this point, see Petrie (1845, 12–30).

113. Vallancey (1786, x).

114. Vallancey (1772, viii).

115. Vallancey (1772, vii).

116. On the limitations of these relationships, see O'Halloran (1995, 167–73), noting the extent to which over time Vallancey's political interests moved "away from Ireland and into the ambit of British scholars in the East India Company" (173). Vallancey's work is also influenced by both Bochart and Stukeley, but departs from both with enthusiasm, especially when he can correct them from Irish sources.

117. Leerssen (1986, 95–96).

118. Vallancey (1772, 3).

119. O'Halloran (1995, 165), points out that other references to the Carthaginians in his work are much less sympathetic.

120. Parsons (1795, 138).

121. Parsons (1795, 139); cf. the criticisms of Vallancey as an extremist on 147, although the argument about Plautus is closely based on the latter's work.

122. Parsons (1795, 158).

123. Parsons (1795, 113–19).

124. Parsons (1795, 116, 119–25).

125. Charlotte Brooke (2009, 27n, 158n). On Brooke, see Leerssen (1996, 363–64).

126. Charlotte Brooke (2009, vii). "Brooke views her role as that of mediator between both countries and aspired to better relations between the Irish, the Anglo-Irish and the English" (Ní Mhunghaile 2009, xxxvii).

127. Owenson ([1806] 1999, 88 107, 143); cf. 21n, 41n, 89n.

128. Owenson debates with her own characters on this point: when the family priest associates the Irish practice of keening with the Greeks, a footnote suggests that it goes back further, to "the lamentations of David for the friend of his soul, and the *conclamatio* breathed over the Phoenician Dido" (Owenson [1806] 1999, 183).

129. Campbell (1988, 63). As her entry in the *ODNB* notes, she later became the first woman writer to receive a pension from the British government.

130. Owenson ([1806] 1999, 250).

131. Owenson ([1806] 1999, 191).

132. Leerssen (1986, 102), though see 103–8 on Vallancey's successors, in particular Sir William Betham (1779–1853).

133. *Don Juan* (1819–24), canto 8, stanzas 23–24.

134. Dunlop (1922, 9).
135. Dunlop (1922, 8).

CONCLUSION

1. Brubaker and Cooper (2000, 6).

2. Rouse (1995) and Brooks (2011) date this development to the seventeenth or eighteenth centuries in European societies, although Taylor (1989) suggests that we can already see a move toward this conception of the self in the late antique period. For a striking critique of contemporary Western models of identity, see Spivak (1988).

3. Rouse (1995, 360); cf. 361–62, where he notes further that the rise of the modern notion of group identities discourages people "from developing a sensitivity to their location in the class structure [and by] privileging issues of prejudice and disenfranchisement, it has either diverted attention from questions of material inequality or obscured processes of exploitation by making these inequalities appear to rest primarily on misplaced attitudes and feelings."

4. James Scott (2009, x, 244).

5. James Scott (2009, 36).

6. For a selection of views, see Sadan (2010); Chatterjee (2011); Dove et al. (2011).

7. Cf. James Scott (2009, x, 9).

8. James Scott (2009, 219).

9. James Scott (2009, 24). On how genealogies in oral cultures can "act as 'charters' of present social institutions rather than as faithful historical records of times past," see Goody and Watt (1963, 310). Useful reflections on the actual as opposed to potential uses of literacy in the government of Greek city-states can be found in Thomas (1992, 128–32).

10. E. Weber (1979).

11. L. Thompson (1971). This initative has become notorious not least for the participation of the Norwegian mother of Abba's Anni-Frid Lyngstad.

12. Joyce (2000, 244–59), with an English translation by Conor Deane at 108–26, from which the text here is taken with minor amendment.

13. Joyce (2000, 108).

14. Cullingford (2000, 222).

15. Joyce (2000, 110).

16. Joyce (2000, 123). As Katherine Mullin has pointed out to me, one of Joyce's key strategies for ironizing nationalism is through drawing attention to awkward overlaps between the English and the Irish varieties.

17. Joyce (2000, 116); see 115 for particular criticism of simple-minded nationalism, tied to the Catholic faith. For the ambiguities in the lecture, see Cullingford (2000), who interprets Joyce's stance in the lecture, by contrast, as "semicolonial." Katherine Mullin notes that the "nationalist tone of Joyce's lecture was in part designed to win the sympathy of an audience of Triestine irredentists" (Mullin 2011, 37).

18. Joyce (2000, 113).

19. Joyce (2000, 118).

20. Joyce (2000, 125).

21. Joyce (2000, 115).

22. Joyce (2000, 121).

23. On the way in which the Phoenician origins of Ireland undermine the island's Catholic identity in the lecture, see Cullingford (2000, 221–22).

24. Joyce (2000, 125).

25. Cullingford (2000, 232–33); cf. 236–37 on how in *Ulysses* "the Phoenicians, legendary voyagers along Mediterranean and Atlantic margins, provide a mythical map of the route to ethnic hybridity." See also, more briefly, Cullingford (1996, 227).

26. Heaney (2002, 23).

27. Cullingford (1996, 227–36).

28. Vendler (1998, 45).

29. Heaney (1975, 32–34).

30. McGuinness (1988, 17). Gleitman (1997) discusses McGuinness's "postmodern" rereadings of Irish history in the context of those of his contemporaries, including Friel.

31. McGuinness (1988, 57, 11).

32. McGuinness (1988, 70).

BIBLIOGRAPHY

Abd Al-Rahman, Ahmed Said. 1995. "Latest Tomb Findings at Leptis Magna and in the Vicinity." *Libya Antiqua*, n.s., 1: 154–55.

Acquaro, Enrico. 1971. *I rasoi punici*. Rome: Consiglio nazionale delle ricerche.

———. 1983. "L'espansione fenicia in Africa." In *Fenici e Arabi nel Mediterraneo: Roma, 12–13 ottobre 1982*, 23–61. Rome: Accademia nazionale dei Lincei.

———. 1989. "Il tofet di Tharros: Note di lettura." In *Riti funerari e di olocausto nella Sardegna fenicia e punica*, 13–22. Cagliari: Edizioni della Torre.

———. 2002. "Il tofet santuario comunitario." In *Otto Eissfeldt: Molk als Opferbegriff im Punischen und Hebräischen und das Ende des Gottes Moloch. Molch como concepto del sacrificio púnico y hebreo y el final del Dios Moloch*, edited by Carlos González Wagner and Luis Alberto Ruiz Cabrero, 87–92. Madrid: Centro de estudios fenicios y púnicos, Universidad Complutense de Madrid.

Adams, J. N. 2003. *Bilingualism and the Latin Language*. Cambridge: Cambridge University Press.

Adam-Veleni, Polyxeni, and Evangelia Stefani. 2012. *Greeks and Phoenicians at the Mediterranean Crossroads*. Thessaloniki: Archaeological Museum of Thessaloniki.

Afanasyev, Ilya. 2012. "'In gente britanniarum, sicut quaedam nostratum testatur historia . . .': National Identity and Perceptions of the Past in John of Salisbury's *Policraticus*." *Journal of Medieval History* 38 (3): 278–94.

Agelarakis, Anagnostis, Athanasia Kanta, and Nikolaos Stampolidis. 1998. "The Osseous Record in the Western Necropolis of Amathus: An Archeo-Anthropological Investigation." In *Eastern Mediterranean: Cyprus-Dodecanese-Crete 16th-6th Cent. B.C.*, edited by Vassos Karageorghis and Nikolaos Stampolidis, 217–32. Athens: University of Crete.

Alexandropoulos, Jacques. 2000. *Les monnaies de l'Afrique antique: 400 av. J.-C.–40 ap. J.-C.* Toulouse: Presses universitaires du Mirail.

Álvarez Martí-Aguilar, Manuel. 2014. "Hijos de Melqart: Justino (44.5) y la Koiné Tiria entre los siglos IV y III A.C." *Archivo español de arqueología* 87: 21–40.

Amadasi Guzzo, Maria Giulia. 1973. "Le iscrizioni puniche." In *Missione archeologica italiana a Malta: Rapporto preliminare della campagna 1970*, edited by Michelangelo Cagiano de Azevedo, Caterina Caprino, and Antonia Ciasca, 87–94. Rome: Consiglio nazionale delle ricerche.

———. 1993. "Osservazioni sulle stele iscritte di Tiro." *Rivista di studi fenici* 21: 157–63.

———. 1997. "Rˤš Mlqrt: Les élus de Melqart?" *Antiquités africaines* 33: 81–85.

———. 2002. "Le iscrizioni dei tofet: Osservazioni sulle espressioni d'offerta." In *Otto Eissfeldt: Molk als Opferbegriff im Punischen und Hebräischen und das Ende des Gottes Moloch. Molch como concepto del sacrificio púnico y hebreo y el final del dios Moloch*, edited by Carlos González Wagner and Luis Alberto Ruiz Cabrero, 93– 119. Madrid: Centro de estudios fenicios y púnicos, Universidad Complutense de Madrid.

Amadasi Guzzo, Maria Giulia. 2007–8. "Il tofet: Osservazioni di un'epigrafista." In *Sepolti tra i vivi: Buried among the Living; Evidenza ed interpretazione di contesti funerari in abitato; Roma, 26–29 aprile 2006* [= *Scienze dell'antichità: Storia archeologia antropologia* 14 (1)], edited by Gilda Bartoloni and M. Gilda Benedettini, 347–362. Rome: Università degli Studi di Roma "La Sapienza."

———. 2010. "Astarte a Malta: Il santuario di Tas Silġ." In *El Carambolo: 50 años de un tesoro*, edited by Maria Luisa de la Bandera Romera and Eduardo Ferrer Albelda, 465–89. Seville: Universidad de Sevilla.

———. 2012a. "Ancora sull'espressione 'Figlio di Tiro' in Fenicio." *Rivista di studi fenici* 40 (1): 107–14.

———. 2012b. "Ancora sull'espressione 'Figlio di Tiro': Nota a *Rivista di studi fenici* 40, 2012, pp. 107–114." *Rivista di studi fenici* 40 (2): 305–8.

———. 2013. " 'Re dei Sidonii?' " In *Ritual, Religion, and Reason: Studies in the Ancient World in Honour of Paolo Xella*, edited by Oswald Loretz, Sergio Ribichini, Wilfred G. E. Watson, and José Ángel Zamora López, 257–65. Münster: Ugarit-Verlag.

Amadasi Guzzo, Maria Giulia, and Gary A. Rendsburg. 2013. "Phoenician/Punic and Hebrew." In *Encyclopedia of Hebrew Language and Linguistics*, edited by Geoffrey Khan, 71–77. Leiden: Brill.

Amadasi Guzzo, Maria Giulia, and Wolfgang Röllig. 1995. "La langue." In *La civilisation phénicienne et punique: Manuel de recherche*, edited by Véronique Krings, 185–92. Leiden: Brill.

Amadasi Guzzo, Maria Giulia, and M. P. Rossignani. 2002. "Le iscrizioni bilingui e gli 'Agyiei' di Malta." In *Da Pyrgi a Mozia: Studi sull'archeologia del Mediterraneo in memoria di Antonia Ciasca* [= *Vicino Oriente* 3 (1)], edited by Maria Giulia Amadasi Guzzo, Mario Liverani, and Paolo Matthiae, 5–28. Rome: Università degli Studi di Roma "La Sapienza."

Amadasi Guzzo, Maria Giulia, and Paolo Xella. 2005. "Eshmun-Melqart in una nuova iscrizione fenicia di Ibiza." *Studi epigrafici e linguistici* 22: 47–57.

Amadasi Guzzo, Maria Giulia, and José Ángel Zamora López. 2013. "The Epigraphy of the Tophet." In *The Tophet in the Phoenician Mediterranean* [= *Studi epigrafici e linguistici* 29–30 (2012–13)], edited by Paolo Xella, 159–92. Verona: Essedue.

Amadasi Guzzo, Maria Giulia, and José Ángel Zamora Lopez. 2016. "L'archivio fenicio di Idalion: stato delle ricerche." *Semitica et Classica* 9: 187–93.

Ameling, Walter. 1990. "Koinon Τῶν Σιδωνίων." *Zeitschrift für Papyrologie und Epigraphik* 81: 189–99.

———. 2013. "Carthage." In *The Oxford Handbook of the State in the Ancient Near East and Mediterranean*, edited by Walter Scheidel and Peter Fibiger Bang, 361–82. Oxford: Oxford University Press.

Amitay, Ory. 2008. "Why Did Alexander the Great Besiege Tyre?" *Athenaeum* 96 (1): 91–102.

———. 2011. "Procopius of Caesarea and the Girgashite Diaspora." *Journal for the Study of the Pseudepigrapha* 20 (4): 257–76.

Amselle, Jean-Loup. 1998. *Mestizo Logics: Anthropology of Identity in Africa and Elsewhere*. Translated by Claudia Royal. Stanford, CA: Stanford University Press.

Anderson, Benedict. 1991. *Imagined Communities: Reflections on the Origin and Spread of Nationalism*. Rev. ed. London: Verso.

Anderson, Perry. 2010. "Sinomania." *London Review of Books*, January 28, 3–6.

Anderson, William P. 1990. "The Beginnings of Phoenician Pottery: Vessel Shape, Style, and Ceramic Technology in the Early Phases of the Phoenician Iron Age." *Bulletin of the American Schools of Oriental Research* 279: 35–54.

Andrade, Nathanael J. 2013. *Syrian Identity in the Greco-Roman World*. Cambridge: Cambridge University Press.

Anello, Pietrina. 1986. "Il trattato del 405/4 a.c. e la formazione della "Eparchia" punica di Sicilia." *Kokalos* 32: 115–79.

Antonaccio, Carla M. 2005. "Excavating Colonization." In *Ancient Colonizations: Analogy, Similarity and Difference*, edited by Henry Hurst and Sarah Owen, 97–113. London: Duckworth.

———. 2010. "(Re)defining Ethnicity: Culture, Material Culture, and Identity." In *Material Culture and Social Identities in the Ancient World*, edited by Shelley Hales and Tamar Hodos, 32–53. Cambridge: Cambridge University Press.

Ardeleanu, Stefan. 2015. "Vom Jugurtha qui a réussi zum Zivilisationendialog Ben Alis: Die Rolle der Antike in der Repräsentation Tunesischer Autokraten nach 1956." *Thersites* 1: 203–48. http://www.thersites.uni-mainz.de/index.php/thr/article/view/11.

Arena, Renato. 1996. *Iscrizioni greche arcaiche di Sicilia e Magna Grecia*. Vol. 1, *Iscrizioni di Megara Iblea e Selinunte*. Pisa: Edizioni dell'Orso.

Armitage, David. 2000. *The Ideological Origins of the British Empire*. Cambridge: Cambridge University Press.

Armstrong, John. 1982. *Nations before Nationalism*. Chapel Hill: University of North Carolina Press.

Arnaud, Pascal. 2005. *Les routes de la navigation antique: Itinéraires en Méditerranée*. Paris: Errance.

Asheri, David, Alan B. Lloyd, and Aldo Corcella. 2007. *A Commentary on Herodotus Books I–IV*. Oxford: Oxford University Press.

Astour, Michael C. 1965. "The Origins of the Terms *Canaan, Phoenician* and *Purple*." *Journal of Near Eastern Studies* 24: 346–50.

Attridge, Harold W., and Robert A. Oden. 1981. *Philo of Byblos, the Phoenician History: Introduction, Critical Text, Translation*. Washington DC: Catholic Bibilical Association of America.

Aubet, Maria Eugenia. 2001. *The Phoenicians and the West: Politics, Colonies and Trade*. 2nd ed. Cambridge: Cambridge University Press.

———. 2006. "On the Organisation of the Phoenician Colonial System in Iberia." In *Debating Orientalism: Multidisciplinary Approaches to Change in the Ancient Mediterranean*, edited by Corinna Riva and Nicholas C. Vella, 94–109. London: Equinox.

———. 2009. *Tiro y las colonias fenicias de Occidente*. 3rd ed. Barcelona: Bellaterra.

Aubet-Semmler, Maria Eugenia, and Laura Trelliso Carreño. 2015. "Pratiques funéraires à l'âge du Fer II au Liban: La nécropole de Tyr Al-Bass." *Archaeology and History in the Lebanon* 40–41: 118–34.

Austin, Michel M. 2006. *The Hellenistic World from Alexander to the Roman Conquest: A Selection of Ancient Sources in Translation*. 2nd ed. Cambridge: Cambridge University Press.

Babelon, Ernest. 1888. *Manuel d'archéologie orientale: Chaldée, Assyrie, Perse, Syrie, Judée, Phénicie, Carthage*. Paris: Maison Quantin.

Bäbler, Balbina. 1998. *Fleissige Thrakerinnen und wehrhafte Skythen: Nichtgriechen im klassischen Athen und ihre archäologische Hinterlassenschaft*. Stuttgart: Teubner.

Badre, Leila. 2015. "A Phoenician Sanctuary at Tyre." *BAAL* 10: 59–82.

Bagg, Ariel M. 2011. *Die Assyrer und das Westland: Studien zur Historischen Geographie und Herrschaftspraxis in der Levante im 1. Jt. v. u. Z.* Leuven: Peeters.

Bagnall, Roger S. 1976. "The Administration of the Ptolemaic Possessions outside Egypt." Leiden: Brill.

Bagnall, Roger S., and Peter S. Derow. 2004. *The Hellenistic Period: Historical Sources in Translation*. 2nd ed. Oxford: Blackwell.

Barceló, Pedro. 1994. "The Perception of Carthage in Classical Greek Historiography." *Acta Classica* 37: 1–14.

Barr, James. 1974. "Philo of Byblos and His 'Phoenician History.'" *Bulletin of the John Rylands Library* 57 (1): 17–68.

Barreca, Ferruccio. 1966. "L'esplorazione topgrafica della regione Sulcitana." In *Monte Sirai III: Rapporto preliminare della missione archaeologica dell'Università di Roma e della Soprintendenza alle Antichità di Cagliari*, 133–70. Rome: Centro di studi semitici, Istituto di studi del Vincino Oriente, Università di Roma.

Barth, Fredrik. 1969. "Introduction." In *Ethnic Groups and Boundaries: The Social Organisation of Ethnic Difference*, edited by Fredrik Barth, 9–38. Boston: Little, Brown.

Bartoloni, Piero. 1976. *Le stele arcaiche del Tofet di Cartagine*. Rome: Consiglio nazionale delle ricerche.

——. 1986. *Le stele di Sulcis*. Rome: Consiglio nazionale delle ricerche.

——. 1993. "Considerazioni sul 'tofet' di Tiro." *Rivista di studi fenici* 21: 153–56.

Baslez, Marie Françoise. 1987. "Le rôle et la place des phéniciens dans la vie économique des ports de l'Égée." In *Phoenicia and the East Mediterranean in the First Millennium B.C.*, edited by Edward Lipiński, 267–85. Leuven: Peeters.

——. 1988. "Les communautés d'orientaux dans la cité grecque: Formes de sociabilité et modeles associatifs." In *L'étranger dans le monde grec*, edited by Raoul Lonis, 139–58. Nancy: Presses universitaires de Nancy.

——. 2013. "Les associations à Délos: Depuis les débuts de l'indépendance (fin du IVe siècle) à la période de la colonie athénienne (milieu du IIe siècle)." In *Groupes et associations dans les cités grecques (IIIe siècle av. J.-C.–IIe siècle ap. J.-C.): Actes de la table ronde de Paris, INHA, 19–20 Juin 2009*, edited by Pierre Fröhlich and Patrice Hamon, 227–49. Geneva: Librairie Droz.

Baslez, Marie Françoise, and Françoise Briquel-Chatonnet. 1991a. "De l'oral `a l'écrit: Le bilinguisme des phéniciens en Grèce." In *Phoinikeia grammata: Lire et écrire en Méditerranée; Actes du Colloque de Liège, 15–18 Novembre 1989*, edited by Claude Baurain, Corinne Bonnet and Véronique Krings, 371–86. Namur: Société des études classiques.

——. 1991b. "Un exemple d'intégration phénicienne au monde grec: Les Sidoniens au Pirée à la fin du IVe siècle." In *Atti del II Congresso internazionale di studi fenici e punici. Roma, 9–14 Novembre 1987*, edited by Enrico Acquaro, 229–40. Rome: Consiglio nazionale delle ricerche.

Batty, Roger. 2000. "Mela's Phoenician Geography." *Journal of Roman Studies* 90: 70–94.

Baumgarten, Albert I. 1981. *The Phoenician History of Philo of Byblos: A Commentary*. Leiden: Brill.

Baurain, Claude. 1986. "Portées chronologique et géographique du terme 'phénicien.'" In *Religio Phoenicia*, edited by Corinne Bonnet, Edward Lipiński, and Patrick Marchetti, 7–28. Namur: Société des études classiques.

———. 1992. "La place des littératures grecque et punique dans les bibliothèques de Carthage." *L'antiquité classique* 61: 158–77.

Baurain, Claude, and Corinne Bonnet. 1992. *Les phéniciens: Marins des trois continents.* Paris: A. Colin.

Baxandall, Michael. 1985. *Patterns of Intention: On the Historical Explanation of Pictures.* New Haven, CT: Yale University Press.

Bechtold, Babette. 2007. "Alcune osservazioni sui rapporti commerciali fra Cartagine, la Sicilia occidentale e la campania (IV-metà del II sec. a.c.)." *Bulletin Antieke Beschaving* 82 (1): 51–76.

———. 2008. *Observations on the Amphora Repertoire of Middle Punic Carthage* [= *Carthage Studies* 2]. Ghent: Ghent University.

———.2013. "Distribution Patterns of Western Greek and Punic Sardinian Amphorae in the Carthaginian Sphere of Influence (6th–3rd century BCE)." *Carthage Studies* 7: 43–119.

Bechtold, Babette, and Roald Docter. 2010. "Transport Amphorae from Punic Carthage: An Overview." In *Motya and the Phoenician Ceramic Repertoire between the Levant and the West 9th–6th Century BC: Proceedings of the International Conference Held in Rome, 26 February 2010*, edited by Lorenzo Nigro, 85–116. Rome: Missione archelogica a Mozia.

Beekes, Robert S. P. 2004. "Kadmos and Europa, and the Phoenicians." *Kadmos* 43: 167–84.

Bekker, Immanuel. 1814. *Anecdota graeca.* Berlin: G. C. Nauckium.

Belkahia, Souraya. 1994. "Les structures politiques pré-romaines dans les cités de la future byzacène." In *L'Africa romana: Atti del X Convegno di studio, Oristano, 11–13 Dicembre 1992*, edited by Attilio Mastino and Paula Ruggieri, 1071–92. Sassari: Editrice archivio fotografico sardo.

Belkahia, Souraya, and Ginette Di Vita-Évrard. 1995. "Magistratures autochtones dans les cités pérégrines de l'Afrique proconsulaire." In *Monuments funéraires: Institutions autochtones en Afrique du Nord antique et médiévale; 6e Colloque international sur l'histoire et l'archéologie de l'Afrique du Nord, Pau, 1993*, edited by Pol Trousset, 255–74. Paris: Éditions du CTHS.

Belmonte, Juan Antonio. 2003. *Cuatro estudios sobre los dominios territoriales de las ciudades-estado fenicias.* Barcelona: Edicions Bellaterra.

Ben Abed, Aicha, and Jean-Jacques Aillagon. 1995. *Carthage: L'histoire, sa trace et son echo; Les Musées de la ville de Paris, Musée du Petit Palais, 9 mars–2 juillet 1995.* Paris: Paris-Musées.

Bénabou, Marcel. 1976. *La résistence africaine à la romanisation.* Paris: François Maspero.

———. 1982. "Les survivances préromaines en Afrique romaine." In *L'Afrique romaine: Les conférences Vanier 1980 / Roman Africa: The Vanier Lectures 1980*, edited by Colin Wells, 13–27. Ottowa: Éditions de l'Université d'Ottowa.

Bendall, Lisa. Forthcoming. *Reading Linear B, Part I.* Cambridge: Cambridge University Press.

Bénichou-Safar, Hélène. 1982. *Les tombes puniques de Carthage: Topographie, structures, inscriptions et rites funéraires.* Paris: Éditions du Centre national de la recherche scientifique.

Bénichou-Safar, Hélène. 2004. *Le tophet de Salammbô à Carthage: Essai de reconstitu-tion.* Rome: École française de Rome.

———. 2010. "Les inscriptions puniques du sanctuaire de Sousse." *Semitica et classica* 3: 99–123.

———. 2012a. "Le statut de l'enfant punique et les objets funéraires." In *L'enfant et la mort dans l'antiquité III: Le matériel associé aux tombes d'enfants; Actes de la table ronde international organisée à la Maison des sciences de l'homme et de la Méditerranée d'Aix-en-Provence, 20–22 janvier 2011,* edited by Antoine Hermary and Céline Dubois, 263–72. Arles: Editions Errance Aix-en-Provence: Centre Camille Jullian.

———. 2012b. "Le vase 'De Sidon' et le symbolisme du palmier." *Semitica et classica* 5: 97–117.

Benz, Frank L. 1972. *Personal Names in the Phoenician and Punic Inscriptions: A Cata-log, Grammatical Study and Glossary of Elements.* Rome: Biblical Institute Press.

Berges, Dietrich. 1997. "Die Tonsiegel aus dem Karthagischen Tempelarchiv." In *Kar-thago II,* edited by Friedrich Rakob, 10–214. Mainz am Rhein: Philipp von Zabern.

Bernal, Martin. 1987. *Black Athena: The Afroasiatic Roots of Classical Civilization.* Lon-don: Free Association Books.

Bernardini, Paolo. 1996. "Giustino, Cartagine e il tofet." *Rivista di studi fenici* 24: 27–45.

———. 2005a. "I Melqart di Sardò." In *Il Mediterraneo di Herakles: Atti del Convegno di studi, 26–28 marzo 2004, Sassari-Oristano, Italia,* edited by Paolo Bernardini and Raimondo Zucca, 125–43. Rome: Carocci.

———. 2005b. "Per una rilettura del santuario tofet—I: Il caso di Mozia." *Sardinia, Corsica et Baleares antiquae* 3: 55–70.

———. 2008. "La morte consacrata: Spazi, rituali e ideologia nella necropolis e nel tofet di Sulky fenicia e punica." In *Saturnia Tellus: Definizioni dello spazio consacrato in ambiente etrusco, italico, fenicio-punico, iberico e celtico; Atti del convegno internazi-onale svoltosi a Roma dal 10 al 12 novembre 2004,* edited by Xavier Dupré Raventós, Sergio Ribichini, and Stéphane Verger, 637–58. Rome: Consiglio nazionale delle ricerche.

———. 2013. "Organised Settlements and Cult Places in the Phoenician Western Expan-sion between the 9th and 7th Centuries BCE: A Reflection on the Tophet." In *The Tophet in the Phoenician Mediterranean* [= *Studi epigrafici e linguistici* 29–30 (2012–13)], edited by Paolo Xella, 1–22. Verona: Essedue.

Bernardini, Paolo, and Raimondo Zucca. 2005. *Il Mediterraneo di Herakles: Studi e ri-cerche.* Rome: Carocci.

Bertha, Csilla. 2006. "Brian Friel as Postcolonial Playwright." In *The Cambridge Com-panion to Brian Friel,* edited by Anthony Roche, 154–65. Cambridge: Cambridge University Press.

Berthier, André, and René Charlier. 1955. *Le sanctuaire punique d'El-Hofra à Constan-tine.* Paris: Arts et métiers graphiques.

Bertrandy, François. 1993. "Les représentations du 'signe de Tanit' sur les stèles vo-tives de Constantine: IIIème–Ier siècles avant J.-C." *Rivista di studi fenici* 21 (1): 3–28.

Bertrandy, François, and Maurice Sznycer. 1987. *Les stèles puniques de Constantine.* Paris: Ministère de la culture et de la communication, Éditions de la Réunion des musées nationaux.

Bierschenk, Thomas. 1988. "Religion and Political Structure: Remarks on Ibadism in Oman and the Mzab (Algeria)." *Studia Islamica* 68: 107–27.

Bikai, Patricia M. 1978. "The Late Phoenician Pottery Complex and Chronology." *Bulletin of the American Schools of Oriental Research* 229: 47–56.

Billigmeier, Jon C. 1977. "Origin of the Greek Word *Phoinix*." *Talanta* 8–9: 1–4.

Bisi, Anna Maria. 1967. *Le stele puniche*. Rome: Istituto di studi del Vicino Oriente, Università di Roma.

——. 1971. "Un naiskos tardo-fenicio del Museo di Beyrut e il problema dell'origine dei cippi egittizzanti nel mondo punico." *Antiquités africaines* 5: 15–38.

——. 1990. *Le terrecotte figurate fenicie e puniche in Italia*. Rome: Libreria dello stato, Istituto poligrafico, e Zecca dello stato.

Bispham, Edward. 2013. "The 'Hellenistics of Death' in Adriatic Central Italy." In *The Hellenistic West: Rethinking the Ancient Mediterranean*, edited by Jonathan R. W. Prag and Josephine Crawley Quinn, 44–78. Cambridge: Cambridge University Press.

Bloch-Smith, Elizabeth. 1992. *Judahite Burial Practices and Beliefs about the Dead*. Sheffield: JSOT.

Boardman, John. 2006. "Early Euboean Settlements in the Carthage Area." *Oxford Journal of Archaeology* 25 (2): 195–200.

Bochart, Samuel. 1646. *Geographiæ sacra seu Phaleg et Canaan*. Caen: P. Cardonelli.

Bohak, Gideon. 2005. "Ethnic Portraits in Greco-Roman Literature." In *Cultural Borrowings and Ethnic Appropriations in Antiquity*, edited by Erich S. Gruen, 207–37. Stuttgart: Franz Steiner.

Boksmati, Nadine. 2009. "Space and Identity in Hellenistic Beirut." In *Inside the City in the Greek World: Studies of Urbanism from the Bronze Age to the Hellenistic Period*, edited by Sara Owen and Laura Preston, 131–40. Oxford: Oxbow.

Bondì, Sandro Filippo. 1972. *Le stele di Monte Sirai*. Rome: Consiglio nazionale delle ricerche.

——. 1978. "Note sull'economia fenicia—I: Impresa privata e ruolo dello stato." *Egitto e Vicino Oriente* 1: 139–49.

——. 1979. "Per una riconsiderazione del tofet." *Egitto e cicino oriente* 2: 139–50.

——. 1980. "Nuove stele da Monte Sirai." *Rivista di studi fenici* 8: 51–70.

——. 1990. "I fenici in Erodoto." In *Hérodote et les peuples non grecs*, edited by Walter Burkert, Giuseppe Nenci, and Olivier Reverdin, 255–300. Geneva: Fondation Hardt.

——. 1995. "Il tofet di Monte Sirai." In *Carbonia e il Sulcis*, edited by Vincenzo Santoni, 225–38. Oristano: S'Alvure.

——. 1996. "Aspetti delle relazioni tra la Fenicia e le colonie d'occidente in età persiana." *Transeuphratène* 12: 73–83.

——. 2006. "Obiettivi e modalità dell'azione militare di Cartagine in Sicilia." In *Guerra e pace in Sicilia e nel Mediterraneo antico (VIII–III sec. a.c.): Arte, prassi e teoria della pace e della guerra*, edited by Maria Adelaide Vaggioli, 131–38. Pisa: Edizioni della Normale.

——. 2008. "Frontières culturelles et frontières administratives dans le monde phénicien d'occident." *Transeuphratène* 35: 71–81.

——. 2014. "Phoenicity, Punicities." In *The Punic Mediterranean: Identities and Identification from Phoenician Settlement to Roman Rule*, edited by Josephine Crawley Quinn and Nicholas C. Vella, 58–68. Cambridge: Cambridge University Press.

Bondì, Sandro Filippo, Massimo Botto, Giuseppe Garbati, and Ida Oggiano. 2009. *Fenici e cartaginesi: Una civiltà mediterranea.* Rome: Istituto poligrafico e Zecca dello stato, Libreria dello stato.

Bonfante, Giuliano. 1941. "The Name of the Phoenicians." *Classical Philology* 36: 1–20.

Bonnet, Corinne. 1986. "Le culte de Melqart à Carthage: Un cas de conservatisme religieux." In *Religio Phoenicia*, edited by Corinne Bonnet, Edward Lipiński, and Patrick Marchetti, 209–22. Namur: Société des études classiques.

——. 1988. *Melqart: Cultes et mythes de l'Héraclès tyrien en Méditerranée.* Leuven: Peeters; Namur: Presses universitaires de Namur.

——. 1996. *Astarte: Dossier documentaire et perspectives historiques.* Rome: Consiglio nazionale delle ricerche.

——. 1997. "Melqart." In *Lexicon iconographicum mythologiae classicae*, 830–34. Zürich: Artemis and Winkler.

——. 2004. *I fenici.* Rome: Carocci.

——. 2005. "Melqart in occidente: Percorsi di appropriazione e di acculturazione." In *Il Mediterraneo di Herakles: Studi e ricerche*, edited by Paolo Bernardini and Raimondo Zucca, 17–28. Rome: Carocci.

——. 2006a. "Identité et altérité religieuses: À propos de l'hellénisation de Carthage." *Pallas* 70: 365–79.

——. 2006b. "La religione fenicia e punica in Sicilia." In *Ethne e religioni nella Sicilia antica*, edited by Pietrina Anello, Giuseppe Martorana, and Roberto Sammartano, 205–16. Rome: L'Erma di Bretschneider.

——. 2007. "Melqart." Electronic pre-publication in *Iconography of Deities and Demons in the Ancient Near East*, edited by Jürg Eggler and Christoph Uehlinger. http://www.religionswissenschaft.uzh.ch/idd/prepublications/e_idd_melqart.pdf (text); http://www.religionswissenschaft.uzh.ch/idd/prepublications/e_idd_illustrations_melqart.pdf (illustrations).

——. 2009. "L'identité religieuse des phéniciens dans la diaspora": Le cas de Melqart, dieu ancestral des tyriens." In *Entre lignes de partage et territoires de passage: Les identités religieuses dans les mondes grec et romain*, edited by Nicole Belayche and Simon Claude Mimouni, 295–308. Paris: Peeters.

——. 2011a. "De Carthage à Salvador de Bahia: Approche comparative des rites du tophet et du candomblé, lieux de mémoire rituels." In *Dans le laboratoire de l'historien des religions: Mélanges offerts à Philippe Borgeaud*, edited by Francesca Prescendi and Youri Volokhine, 469–85. Geneva: Editions Labor et Fides.

——. 2011b. "On Gods and Earth: The Tophet and the Construction of a New Identity in Punic Carthage." In *Cultural Identity in the Ancient Mediterranean*, edited by Erich S. Gruen, 373–87. Los Angeles: Getty.

——. 2013. "Ernest Renan et les paradoxes de la mission de Phénicie." In *Ernest Renan: La science, la religion, la république; Colloque annuel 2012 du Collège de France*, edited by Henry Laurens, 101–19. Paris: Odile Jacob.

——. 2014. "Phoenician Identities in Hellenistic Times: Strategies and Negotiations." In *The Punic Mediterranean: Identities and Identification from Phoenician Settlement to Roman Rule*, edited by Josephine Crawley Quinn and Nicholas C. Vella, 282–98. Cambridge: Cambridge University Press.

——. 2015. *Les enfants de Cadmos: Le paysage religieux de la Phénicie hellénistique.* Paris: De Boccard.

Bonnet, Corinne, and Colette Jourdain-Annequin, eds. 1992. *Héraclès: D'une rive à l'autre de la Méditerranée: Bilan et perspectives; Actes de la Table ronde de Rome, Academia belgica–École française de Rome, 15–16 septembre 1989.* Brussels: Institut historique belge de Rome.

Bonnet, Corinne, and Adeline Grand-Clément. 2010. "La 'barbarisation' de l'ennemi: La parenté entre phéniciens et carthaginois dans l'historiographie relative à la Sicile." In *Alleanze e parentele: Le "affinità elettive" nella storiografia sulla Sicilia antica: Atti del Convegno internazionale (Palermo, 14–15 aprile 2010)*, edited by Daniela Bonanno, Corinne Bonnet, Nicola Cusumano, and Sandra Péré-Noguès, 161–77. Caltanissetta: Salvatore Sciascia Editore.

Bonnet, Corinne, and Véronique Krings. 2006. "Les phéniciens, Carthage et nous: Histoire et représentations." In *Nuevas perspectivas I: La investigación fenicia y púnica*, edited by Juan Pablo Vita and José Ángel Zamora López, 37–47. Zaragossa: Bellaterra.

Bonnet, Corinne, and Paolo Xella. 1995. "La religion." In *La civilisation phénicienne et punique: Manuel de recherche*, edited by Véronique Krings, 316–33. Leiden: Brill.

Bordreuil, Pierre. 1986. "Attestations inédites de Melqart, Baal Hammon et Baal Saphon à Tyr." In *Religio Phoenicia*, edited by Corinne Bonnet, Edward Lipiński, and Patrick Marchetti, 82–86. Namur: Société des études classiques.

———. 1987. "Tanit du Liban." In *Phoenicia and the East Mediterranean in the First Millennium B.C.*, edited by Edward Lipiński, 79–85. Leuven: Peeters.

Bordreuil, Pierre, and Ahmed Ferjaoui. 1988. "À propos des 'Fils de Tyr' et des 'Fils de Carthage.' " In *Carthago*, edited by Edward Lipiński, 137–42. Leuven: Peeters.

Bordreuil, Pierre, and Nehmé Tabet. 1985. "Laodicée 'Mère' en Kanaan." *Syria* 62: 180–81.

Bosworth, A. Brian. 1980. *A Historical Commentary on Arrian's History of Alexander.* Vol. 1, *Commentary on Books I–III.* Oxford: Clarendon Press.

Bourogiannis, Giorgos. 2012. "Pondering the Cypro-Phoenician Conundrum: The Aegean View of a Bewildering Term." In *Cyprus and the Aegean in the Early Iron Age: The Legacy of Nicolas Coldstream*, edited by Maria Iacovou, 183–205. Nicosia: Bank of Cyprus Cultural Foundation.

Bowden, Hugh. 1996. "The Greek Settlement and Sanctuaries at Naukratis: Herodotus and Archaeology." In *More Studies in the Ancient Greek Polis*, edited by Mogens Herman Hansen and Kurt A. Raaflaub, 17–37. Stuttgart: Franz Steiner.

Bowie, Ewen. 1998. "Phoenician Games in Heliodorus' *Aithiopika*." In *Studies in Heliodorus*, edited by Richard Hunter, 1–18. Cambridge: Cambridge Philological Society.

———. 2008. "Literary Milieux." In *The Cambridge Companion to the Greek and Roman Novel*, edited by Tim Whitmarsh, 17–38. Cambridge: Cambridge University Press.

Boyes, Philip J. 2012. " 'The King of the Sidonians': Phoenician Ideologies and the Myth of the Kingdom of Tyre-Sidon." *Bulletin of the American Schools of Oriental Research* 365: 33–44.

Bradley, Guy. 2005. "Aspects of the Cult of Hercules in Central Italy." In *Herakles and Hercules: Exploring a Graeco-Roman Divinity*, edited by Louis Rawlings and Hugh Bowden, 129–51. Swansea: Classical Press of Wales.

Braudel, Fernand. 1980. *On History.* Translated by Sarah Matthews. Chicago: University of Chicago Press.

———. 1995. *A History of Civilizations.* Translated by Richard Mayne. London: Penguin.

Brecciaroli Taborelli, Luisa. 1983. "Il tofet neopunico di Sabratha." In *Atti del I Congresso internazionale di Studi fenici e punici (Roma, 5–10 novembre 1979)*, 543–47. Rome: Consiglio nazionale delle ricerche.

Brennan, T. Corey. 2000. *The Praetorship in the Roman Republic.* Oxford: Oxford University Press.

Brett, Mark G. 1996. "Interpreting Ethnicity: Method, Hermeneutics, Ethics." In *Ethnicity and the Bible*, edited by Mark G. Brett, 3–22. New York: Brill.

Brett, Michael, and Elizabeth Fentress. 1996. *The Berbers.* Oxford: Blackwell.

Briquel-Chatonnet, Françoise. 1992a. "Hébreu du nord et phénicien: Étude comparée de deux dialectes cananéens." *Orientalia Lovaniensia Periodica* 23: 89–126.

——. 1992b. *Les relations entre les cités de la côte phénicienne et les royaumes d'Israël et de Juda.* Leuven: Peeters.

——. 1995. "Syro-Palestine et Jordanie." In *La civilisation phénicienne et punique*, edited by Véronique Krings, 583–96. Leiden: Brill.

Briscoe, John. 1981. *A Commentary on Livy, Books XXXIV–XXXVII.* Oxford: Clarendon Press.

Brizzi, Giovanni. 1980. "Il 'nazionalismo fenicio' di Filone di Byblos e la politica ecumenica di Adriano." *Oriens antiquus* 19: 117–31.

Brooke, Charlotte. 2009. *Reliques of Irish Poetry.* Translated by Lesa Ní Mhunghaile. Dublin: Irish Manuscripts Commission.

Brooke, Christopher. 2017. "Eighteenth-Century Carthage." In *Commerce and Peace in the Enlightenment*, edited by Béla Kapossy, Isaac Nakhimovsky, and Richard Whatmore, 110–24. Cambridge: Cambridge University Press.

Brooks, Peter. 2011. *Enigmas of Identity.* Princeton, NJ: Princeton University Press.

Brouquier-Reddé, Véronique, Abdelaziz El Khayari, and Abdelfattah Ichkhakh. 1998. "Le temple B de Volubilis: Nouvelles recherches." *Antiquités africaines* 34: 65–72.

Brown, Susanna Shelby. 1991. *Late Carthaginian Child Sacrifice and Sacrificial Monuments in Their Mediterranean Context.* Sheffield: JSOT Press.

Brubaker, Rogers. 2002. "Ethnicity without Groups." *European Journal of Sociology* 43: 163–89.

Brubaker, Rogers, and Frederick Cooper. 2000. "Beyond 'Identity.' " *Theory and Society* 29: 1–47.

Buckler, William Hepburn, William M. Calder, and Christopher W. M. Cox. 1926. "Asia Minor, 1924. III.—Monuments from Central Phrygia." *Journal of Roman Studies* 16: 53–94.

Bullo, Silvia. 2002. *Provincia Africa: Le città e il territorio dalla caduta di Cartagine a Nerone.* Rome: L'Erma di Bretschneider.

Bunnens, Guy. 1979. *L'expansion phénicienne en Méditerranée: Essai d'interprétation fondé sur une analyse des traditions littéraires.* Rome: Institut historique belge de Rome.

——. 1983. "Tyr et la mer." In *Redt Tyrus/Sauvons Tyr—Histoire phénicienne/Fenicische geschiedenis*, edited by Eric Gubel, Edward Lipiński, and Brigitte Servais-Soyez, 7–21. Leuven: Peeters.

——. 1992. "Puniques." In *Dictionnaire de la civilisation phénicienne et punique*, edited by Edward Lipiński, 364. Turnhout: Brepols.

Burke, Aaron A. 2014. "Entanglement, the Amorite Koiné, and Amorite Cultures in the Levant." *ARAM* 26: 357–73.

Butcher, Kevin. 2005. "Information, Legitimation, or Self-Legitimation? Popular and Elite Designs on the Coin Types of Syria." In *Coinage and Identity in the Roman Provinces*, edited by Christopher Howgego, Volker Heuchert, and Andrew Burnett, 143–56. Oxford: Oxford University Press.

Butler, Judith. 1993. *Bodies That Matter: On the Discursive Limits of "Sex."* New York: Routledge.

———. 1999. *Gender Trouble: Feminism and the Subversion of Identity*. Rev. ed. New York: Routledge.

———. 2004. *Undoing Gender*. New York: Routledge.

Butlin, Martin, and Evelyn Joll. 1984. *The Paintings of J.M.W. Turner*. Rev. ed. New Haven, CT: Yale University Press.

Cadotte, Alain. 2006. *La romanisation des dieux: L'interpretatio romana en Afrique du Nord sous le Haut-Empire*. Leiden: Brill.

Callegarin, Laurent. 2011. "Coinages with Punic and Neo-Punic Legends of Western Mauretania: Attribution, Chronology and Currency Circulation." In *Money, Trade and Trade Routes in Pre-Islamic North Africa*, edited by Amelia Dowler and Elizabeth R. Galvin, 42–48. London: British Museum Press.

Camous, Thierry. 2007. "Les phéniciens dans l'historiographie romaine et la sous évaluation du rôle joué par les influences phéniciennes dans la république avant les guerres puniques." *Revue des études anciennes* 109: 227–46.

Campbell, Mary. 1988. *Lady Morgan: The Life and Times of Sydney Owenson*. London: Pandora.

Campus, Alessandro. 2006. "Circolazione di modelli e di artigiani in età punica." In *L'Africa romana: Atti del XVI convegno di studio (Rabat, 15–19 dic. 2004)*, edited by Aomar Akerraz, Paola Ruggieri, Ahmed Siraj, and Cinzia Vismara, 185–96. Rome: Carocci.

———. 2012. *Punico—Postpunico: Per una archeologia dopo Cartagine*. Tivoli: TORED.

Capdetrey, Laurent. 2007. *Le pouvoir séleucide: Territoire, administration, finances d'un royaume hellénistique, 312–129 avant J.-C.* Rennes: Presses universitaires de Rennes.

Cartledge, Paul. 1993. *The Greeks: A Portrait of Self and Others*. Oxford: Oxford University Press.

Carty, Ciaran. 2000. "Finding Voice in a Language Not Our Own." In *Brian Friel in Conversation*, edited by Paul Delaney, 138–43. Ann Arbor: University of Michigan Press.

Cecchini, Serena Maria. 1995. "Architecture militaire, civile et domestique *partim* Orient." In *La civilisation phénicienne et punique: Manuel de recherche*, edited by Véronique Krings, 389–96. Leiden: Brill.

Celestino, Sebastián, and Carolina López-Ruiz. 2016. *Tartessos and the Phoenicians in Iberia*. Oxford: Oxford University Press.

Chamoun-Nicolás, Habib. 2007. *Negotiate like a Phoenician: Discover Tradeables*. Kingwood: Keynegotiations.

Champion, Timothy. 2001. "The Appropriation of the Phoenicians in British Imperial Ideology." *Nations and Nationalism* 7: 451–65.

Chantraine, Pierre. 1972. "À propos du nom des phéniciens et des noms de la pourpre." *Studii clasice: Societatea de studii clasice din Republica Socialistă România* 14: 7–15.

Chapman, Malcolm. 1992. *The Celts: The Construction of a Myth*. New York: St Martin's Press.

Charfi, Mohamed, and Hamadi Redissi. 2009. "Teaching Tolerance and Open-Minded Approaches to Understanding Sacred Texts." In *International Perspectives on the Goals of Universal Basic and Secondary Education*, edited by Joel E. Cohen and Martin B. Malin, 145–75. New York: Routledge.

Charles-Edwards, Thomas M. 2004. "The Making of Nations in Britain and Ireland in the Early Middle Ages." In *Lordship and Learning: Studies in Memory of Trevor Aston*, edited by Ralph Evans, 11–38. Woodbridge: Boydell Press.

Chatterjee, Partha. 2011. "Life without the State." *Anthropology Now* 3 (3):111–14.

Chérel, Albert. 1917. *Fénelon au XVIIIe siècle en France, 1715–1820: Son prestige, son influence.* Paris: Hachette.

Chiha, Michel. 1964. *Visage et présence du Liban.* Beirut: Cénacle libanais.

Christou, Demos. 1998. "Cremations in the Western Necropolis of Amathus." In *Eastern Mediterranean: Cyprus-Dodecanese-Crete 16th–6th Cent. B.C.*, edited by Vassos Karageorghis and Nikolaos Stampolidis, 207–15. Athens: University of Crete.

Ciasca, Antonia. 1989. "Fenici." *Kokalos* 34–35: 75–88.

———. 1992. "Mozia, sguardo d'insieme sul tofet." *Vicino Oriente* 8: 113–55.

———. 2002. "Archeologia del tofet." In *Otto Eissfeldt: Molk als Opferbegriff im Punischen und Hebräischen und das Ende des Gottes Moloch; Molch como concepto del sacrificio púnico y hebreo y el final del dios Moloch*, edited by Carlos González Wagner and Luis Alberto Ruiz Cabrero, 121–40. Madrid: Centro de estudios fenicios y púnicos, Universidad Complutense de Madrid.

Cifani, Gabriele. 2012. "Approaching Ethnicity and Landscapes in Pre-Roman Italy: The Middle Tiber Valley." In *Landscape, Ethnicity and Identity in the Archaic Mediterranean Area*, edited by Gabriele Cifani and Simon Stoddart, 144–62. Oxford: Oxbow.

Cintas, Pierre. 1948. "Le sanctuaire punique de Sousse." *Revue africaine* 91: 1–80.

Clairmont, Christoph W., and Alexander Conze. 1993. *Classical Attic Tombstones.* Kilchberg: Akanthus.

Cline, Eric H. 2014. *1177 B.C.: The Year Civilization Collapsed.* Princeton, NJ: Princeton University Press.

Collis, John. 2003. *The Celts: Origins, Myths and Inventions.* Stroud: Tempus.

Conant, Jonathan. 2012. *Staying Roman: Conquest and Identity in Africa and the Mediterranean, 439–700.* Cambridge: Cambridge University Press.

Conheeney, Janice, and Alan Pipe. 1991. "Note on Some Cremated Bone from Tyrian Cinerary Urns." *Berytus* 39: 83–87.

Corm, Charles. 1987. *La montagne inspirée.* Beirut: Éditions de la Revue phénicienne.

Couillard, Marie-Thérèse. 1974. *Les monuments funéraires de Rhénée.* Paris: Dépositaire diffusion de Boccard.

Counts, Derek B. 2008. "Master of the Lion: Representation and Hybridity in Cypriote Sanctuaries." *American Journal of Archaeology* 112: 3–27.

Courtois, Christian. 1950. "Saint Augustin et la survivance du punique." *Revue africaine* 94 (3): 259–82.

Crouzet, Sandrine. 2012. "Des étrangers dans la cité: L'onomastique révélatrice d'échanges et d'intégrations entre grecs et puniques?" In *L'onomastica africana: Congresso della Société du Maghreb préhistorique, antique et médiéval, Porto Conte ricerche (Alghero, 28/29 settembre 2007)*, edited by Antonio Corda and Attilio Mastino, 39–55. Ortacesus (Cagliari): Sandhi.

Cullingford, Elizabeth Butler. 1996. "British Romans and Irish Carthaginians: Anticolonial Metaphor in Heaney, Friel, and McGuinness." *PMLA* 111: 222–39.

——. 2000. "Phoenician Genealogies and Oriental Geographies: Language and Race in James Joyce and His Successors." In *Semicolonial Joyce*, edited by Derek Attridge and Marjorie Howes, 219–39. Cambridge: Cambridge University Press.

Curty, Olivier. 1995. *Les parentés légendaires entre cités grecques: Catalogue raisonné des inscriptions contenant le terme syngeneia et analyse critique.* Geneva: Librairie Droz.

Dale, Alexander, and Aneurin Ellis-Evans. 2011. "A Cypriot Curser at Mytilene." *Zeitschrift für Papyrologie und Epigraphik* 179: 189–98.

D'Andrea, Bruno. 2014. *I tofet del Nord Africa dall'età arcaica all'età romana: VIII sec. a.C.–II sec. d.C.: studi archeologici.* Pisa: Fabrizio Serra.

D'Andrea, Bruno, and Sara Giardino. 2011. "Il tofet dove e perché: Alle origini dell'identità fenicia." *Vicino & Medio Oriente* 15: 133–57.

Davies, Anna Morpurgo. 2000. "Greek Personal Names and Linguistic Continuity." In *Greek Personal Names: Their Value as Evidence*, edited by Simon Hornblower and Elaine Matthews, 15–39. Oxford: Oxford University Press.

Davis, Whitney. 1990. "Style and History in Art History." In *The Uses of Style in Archaeology*, edited by Margaret Wright Conkey and Christine Ann Hastorf, 18–31. Cambridge: Cambridge University Press.

Defoe, Daniel. 1727. *The History of the Principal Discoveries and Improvements in the Several Arts and Sciences Particularly in the Great Branches of Commerce, Navigation, and Plantation in All Parts of the Known World.* London: W. Mears, F. Clay, and D. Browne.

de Geus, C.H.J. 1991. "The Material Culture of Phoenicia and Israel." In *Phoenicia and the Bible*, edited by Edward Lipiński, 11–16. Leuven: Peeters.

Demand, Nancy H. 2011. *The Mediterranean Context of Early Greek History.* Chichester: Wiley-Blackwell.

Demetriou, Denise. 2012. *Negotiating Identity in the Ancient Mediterranean: The Archaic and Classical Greek Multiethnic Emporia.* Cambridge: Cambridge University Press.

De Simone, Rossana. 1997. "La stele punica 'dell'Acquasanta.'" In *Archeologia e Territorio*, 447–450. Palermo: Palumbo.

de Vaux, Roland. 1968. "Le pays de Canaan." *Journal of the American Oriental Society* 88: 23–30.

Dietler, Michael. 2010. *Archaeologies of Colonialism: Consumption, Entanglement, and Violence in Ancient Mediterranean France.* Berkeley: University of California Press.

Dietler, Michael, and Ingrid Herbich. 1994. "Ceramics and Ethnic Identity: Ethnoarchaeological Observations on the Distribution of Pottery Styles and the Relationship between the Social Contexts of Production and Consumption." In *Terre cuite et société: La céramique, document technique, économique, culturel*, edited by Didier Binder and Jean Courtin, 459–72. Juan-les-Pins: Éditions APDCA.

Di Stefano, Carmela A. 1993. *Lilibeo punica.* Rome: Istituto poligrafico e zecca dello stato.

Di Stefano Manzella, Ivan. 1972. "Un'iscrizione sepolcrale romana datata con la seconda dittatura di Cesare." *Epigraphica* 34: 105–30.

Di Vita, Antonino. 1968a. "Shadrapa e Milk'ashtart dèi patri di Leptis ed i templi del lato nord-ovest del Foro Vecchio leptitano." *Orientalia* 37: 201–11.

Di Vita, Antonino. 1968b. "Influences grecques et tradition orientale dans l'art punique de Tripolitaine." *Mélanges d'archéologie et d'histoire* 80: 7–84.

———. 1982. "Gli emporia di Tripolitania dall'età di Massinissa a Diocleziano: Un profilo storico-istituzionale." *Aufstieg und Niedergang der römischen Welt* 2.10.2: 515–95.

———. 1983. "Architettura e società nelle città di Tripolitania fra Massinissa e Augusto: Qualche nota." In *Architecture et société de l'archaïsme grec à la fin de la République romaine: Actes du Colloque international organisé par le Centre national de la recherche scientifique et l'École française de Rome (Rome, 2–4 décembre 1980)*, 355–76. Paris: École française de Rome.

———. 1992. "Influenze alessandrine nel mondo greco e punico del Nord-Africa." In *Roma e l'Egitto nell'antichità classica: Atti del I Congresso internazionale italo-egiziano, Il Cairo, 6–9 febbraio 1989*, 109–20. Rome: Libreria dello stato.

———. 2005. " 'Liber Pater' o *Capitolium*? Una nota." In *I tre templi del lato nord-ovest del Foro Vecchio a Leptis Magna*, edited by Antonino Di Vita and Monica Livadiotti, 14–21. Rome: L'Erma di Bretschneider.

Divjak, J. 1971. *Expositio quarundam propositionum ex epistola ad Romanos; Epistolae ad Galatas expositionis liber unus; Epistolae ad Romanos inchoata expositio*. Vienna: Hoelder-Pichler-Tempsky.

Dixon, Helen. 2013. "Phoenician Mortuary Practice in the Iron Age I–III (ca. 1200–ca. 300 BCE) Levantine 'Homeland'" PhD diss., University of Michigan.

D'Oriano, Rubens. 1994. "Un santuario di Melqart-Ercole ad Olbia." In *L'Africa romana: Atti del X Convegno di studio (Oristano, 11–13 dicembre 1992)*, edited by Attilio Mastino and Paola Ruggieri, 937–48. Sassari: Editrice archivio fotografico sardo.

Dougherty, Carol. 1993. *The Poetics of Colonization: From City to Text in Archaic Greece*. Oxford: Oxford University Press.

Dove, Michael R., Hjorleifur Jonsson, and Michael Aung-Thwin. 2011. "Debate: *The Art of Not Being Governed: An Anarchist History of Upland Southeast Asia* by James C. Scott." *Bijdragen tot de Taal-, Land- en Volkenkunde* 167 (1): 86–99.

Drews, Robert. 1979. "Phoenicians, Carthage and the Spartan *Eunomia*." *American Journal of Philology* 100: 45–58.

Dridi, Hédi. 2004. "À propos du signe dit de la bouteille." *Rivista di studi fenici* 32: 9–24.

———. 2006. *Carthage et le monde punique*. Paris: Belles Lettres.

Dunant, Christine. 1978. "Stèles funéraires." *Eretria* 6: 21–61. Berne: École suisse d'archéologie en Grèce.

Dunlop, Robert. 1922. *Ireland from the Earliest Times to the Present Day*. Oxford: Oxford University Press.

Dušek, Jan. 2012. *Aramaic and Hebrew Inscriptions from Mt. Gerizim and Samaria between Antiochus III and Antiochus IV Epiphanes*. Leiden: Brill.

Duyrat, Frédérique. 2005. *Arados hellénistique: Étude historique et monétaire*. Beirut: Institut français du Proche-Orient.

Edwards, Mark J. 1991. "Philo or Sanchuniathon? A Phoenician Cosmogony." *Classical Quarterly* 41: 213–20.

Edwards, Ruth B. 1979. *Kadmos the Phoenician: A Study in Greek Legends and the Mycenaean Age*. Amsterdam: Adolf M. Hakkert.

Elayi, Josette. 1981. "The Relations between Tyre and Carthage during the Persian Period." *Journal of Ancient Near Eastern Studies* 13: 15–29.

———. 1990. "Tripoli (Liban) à l'époque perse." *Transeuphratene* 2: 59–71.

———. 2005a. "Four New Inscribed Phoenician Arrowheads." *Studi epigrafici e linguistici* 22: 35–45.

———. 2005b. ʿAbdʿaštart *Ier/Straton de Sidon: Un roi phénicien entre Orient et Occident.* Paris: Gabalda.

———. 2013. *Histoire de la Phénicie.* Paris: Perrin.

Elayi, Josette, and Alain G. Elayi. 1999. "Quelques particularités de la culture matérielle d'Arwad au Fer III/Perse." *Transeuphratène* 18: 9–27.

———. 2004. *Le monnayage de la cité phénicienne de Sidon à l'époque perse (Ve–IVe s. av. J.-C.).* Paris: Gabalda.

———. 2009. *The Coinage of the Phoenician City of Tyre in the Persian Period (5th–4th Cent. BCE).* Leuven: Peeters.

———. 2014. *A Monetary and Political History of the Phoenician City of Byblos in the Fifth and Fourth Centuries B.C.E.* Winona Lake, IN: Eisenbrauns.

Elayi, Josette, and Jean Sapin. 1998. *Beyond the River: New Perspectives on Transeuphratene.* Sheffield: Sheffield Academic Press.

Ercolani, Andrea. 2015. "Phoinikes: Storia di un etnonimo." In *Transformations and Crisis in the Mediterranean: "Identity" and Interculturality in the Levant and Phoenician West during the 12th–8th Centuries BCE; Proceedings of the International Conference Held in Rome, CNR, May 8–9, 2013*, edited by Giuseppe Garbati and Tatiana Pedrazzi, 171–82. Pisa: Fabrizio Serra.

Eriksen, Thomas Hylland. 2010. *Ethnicity and Nationalism: Anthropological Perspectives.* 3rd ed. London: Pluto Press.

Erskine, Andrew. 2013. "The View from the East." In *The Hellenistic West: Rethinking the Ancient Mediterranean*, edited by Jonathan R. W. Prag and Josephine Crawley Quinn, 14–34. Cambridge: Cambridge University Press.

Facci, Serena. 2009. "Dances across the Boundary: Banande and Bakonzo in the Twentieth Century." *Journal of Eastern African Studies* 3 (2): 350–66.

Fantar, M'hamed Hassine. 2011. "Death and Transfiguration: Punic Culture after 146." In *A Companion to the Punic Wars*, edited by B. Dexter Hoyos, 449–66. Chicester: Wiley-Blackwell.

———. 2012. "Stèles du tophet de Sousse." *Rivista di studi fenici* 40: 97–106.

Faust, Avraham. 2006. *Israel's Ethnogenesis: Settlement, Interaction, Expansion and Resistance.* London: Equinox.

———. 2009. "How Did Israel Become a People? The Genesis of Israelite Identity." *Biblical Archaeology Review* 201: 62–69, 92–94.

———. 2010. "Future Directions in the Study of Ethnicity in Ancient Israel." In *Historical Biblical Archaeology and the Future: The New Pragmatism*, edited by Thomas Evan Levy, 55–68. London: Equinox.

Faust, Avraham, and Justin Lev-Tov. 2011. "The Constitution of Philistine Identity: Ethnic Dynamics in Twelfth to Tenth Century Philistia." *Oxford Journal of Archaeology* 30: 13–31.

Fear, Andrew T. 1996. *Rome and Baetica: Urbanization in Southern Spain c. 50 BC–AD 150.* Oxford: Clarendon Press.

Feeney, Denis. 2005. "The Beginnings of a Literature in Latin." *Journal of Roman Studies* 95: 226–40.

———. 2007. *Caesar's Calendar: Ancient Time and the Beginnings of History.* Berkeley: University of California Press.

Feeney, Denis. 2016. *Beyond Greek: The Beginnings of Latin Literature*. Cambridge, MA: Harvard University Press.

Fehling, Detlev. 1989. *Herodotus and His Sources: Citation, Invention and Narrative Art*. Leeds: Francis Cairns.

Feldman, Marian H. 2006. *Diplomacy by Design: Luxury Arts and an "International Style" in the Ancient Near East, 1400–1200 BCE*. Chicago: University of Chicago Press.

———. 2014. *Communities of Style: Portable Luxury Arts, Identity, and Collective Memory in the Iron Age Levant*. Chicago: University of Chicago Press.

Fénelon, François de Salignac de La Mothe. 1994. *Telemachus, Son of Ulysses*. Translated by Patrick Riley. Cambridge: Cambridge University Press.

———. 1997. *Oeuvres*. Vol. 2. Paris: Gallimard.

Fentress, Elizabeth. 2013. "Strangers in the City: Élite Communication in the Hellenistic Central Mediterranean." In *The Hellenistic West: Rethinking the Ancient Mediterranean*, edited by Jonathan R. W. Prag and Josephine Crawley Quinn, 157–78. Cambridge: Cambridge University Press.

Fentress, Elizabeth, and Andrew Wilson. 2016. "The Saharan Berber Diaspora and the Southern Frontiers of Byzantine North Africa." In *North Africa under Byzantium and Early Islam*, edited by Susan T. Stevens and Jonathan P. Conant, 41–63. Washington, DC: Dumbarton Oaks Research Library and Collection.

Fenwick, Corisande. 2008. "Archaeology and the Search for Authenticity: Colonialist, Nationalist, and Berberist Visions of an Algerian Past." In *TRAC 2007: Proceedings of the Seventeenth Annual Theoretical Roman Archaeology Conference*, edited by Corisande Fenwick, Meredith Wiggins, and Dave Wythe, 75–88. Oxford: Oxbow.

Ferguson, Arthur B. 1969. "John Twyne: A Tudor Humanist and the Problem of Legend." *Journal of British Studies* 9 (1): 24–44.

Ferjaoui, Ahmed. 1991. "Fonctions et métiers de la Carthage punique à travers les inscriptions." *Reppal* 6: 71–94.

———. 1993. *Recherches sur les relations entre l'Orient phénicien et Carthage*. Fribourg: Vandenhoeck und Ruprecht.

———. 1999. "Les femmes à Carthage à travers les documents épigraphiques." *Reppal* 11: 77–86.

———. 2007. *Le sanctuaire de Henchir El-Hami: De Ba'al Hammon au Saturne africain: Ier s. av. J.-C.–IVe s. apr. J.-C.* Tunis: Institut national du patrimoine.

———. 2008a. "Les pratiques rituelles dans le sanctuaire de Ba'al Hammon en Afrique à l'époque romaine: Le cas de Henchir El-Hami dans le pays de Zama (Tunisie du Nord-Ouest)." In *Saturnia Tellus: Definizioni dello spazio consacrato in ambiente etrusco, italico, fenicio-punico, iberico e celtico; Atti del convegno internazionale svoltosi a Roma dal 10 al 12 novembre 2004*, edited by Xavier Dupré Raventós, Sergio Ribichini, and Stéphane Verger, 397–408. Rome: Consiglio nazionale delle richerche.

———. 2008b. "Y avait-il une communauté de tyriens à Carthage et de carthaginois à Tyr?" In *D'Ougarit à Jerusalem: Recueil d'études épigraphiques et archéologiques offerts à Pierre Bordreuil*, edited by Carole Roche, 183–89. Paris: De Boccard.

———. 2012. "Le témoignage de Tertullien sur le sacrifice d'enfants à Saturne à la lumière des données ostéologiques du sanctuaire de Henchir El-Hami (Tunisie)." *Rivista di studi fenici* 40 (2): 245–50.

Ferrer Albelda, Eduardo. 1996. *La España cartaginesa: Claves historiográficas para la historia de España*. Seville: Universidad de Sevilla.

———. 2012. "Un fenicio apócrifo de época romana: Pomponius Mela." In *La etapa neopúnica en Hispania y el Mediterráneo centro occidental: Identidades compartidas*, edited by Bartolomé Mora Serrano and Gonzalo Cruz Andreotti, 59–74. Seville: Universidad de Sevilla.

Ferron, Jean. 1993. *Sarcophages de Phénicie: Sarcophages à scènes en relief*. Paris: Paul Geuthner.

———. 1995. "Importants travaux de restauration ou d'agrandissement et d'embellissement au tophet de Carthage à partir de la fin du Vè siècle avant l'ère." *Reppal* 9: 73–91.

Février, James Germain. 1951–52. "Vir Sidonius." *Semitica* 4: 13–18.

———. 1964–65. "La constitution municipale de Dougga à l'époque numide." In *Mélanges de Carthage offerts à Charles Saumagne, Louis Poinssot, Maurice Pinard* [= *Cahiers de Byrsa* 10], 85–91. Paris: Paul Geuthner.

Fine, Steven. 2005. *Art and Judaism in the Greco-Roman World: Toward a New Jewish Archaeology*. Cambridge: Cambridge University Press.

Finkelstein, Israel, and Neil Asher Silberman. 2001. *The Bible Unearthed: Archaeology's New Vision of Ancient Israel and the Origin of Its Stories*. London: Simon and Schuster.

Finsterbusch, Karin. 2007. "The First-Born between Sacrifice and Redemption in the Hebrew Bible." In *Human Sacrifice in the Jewish and Christian Tradition*, edited by Karin Finsterbusch, Armin Lange, and Diethard Römheld, 87–108. Leiden: Brill.

Fleischer, Robert, and Wolf Schiele. 1983. *Der Klagefrauensarkophag aus Sidon*. Tübingen: E. Wasmuth.

Fontan, E., and H. Le Meaux. 2007. *La Méditerranée des phéniciens: De Tyr à Carthage*. Paris: Somogy.

Fontana, Sergio. 2001. "Leptis Magna: The Romanization of a Major African City through Burial Evidence." In *Italy and the West: Comparative Issues in Romanization*, edited by Simon Keay and Nicola Terrenato, 161–72. Oxford: Oxbow.

Foucault, Michel. 1977. *Discipline and Punish: The Birth of the Prison*. Translated by Alan Sheridan. New York: Pantheon.

———. 1978–86. *The History of Sexuality*. Translated by Robert Hurley. 3 vols. New York: Pantheon.

———. 1980. *Power/Knowledge: Selected Interviews and Other Writings, 1972–1977*. Edited and translated by Colin Gordon. New York: Pantheon.

Francisi, Maria Teresa. 2002. "Un tipo di gola egizia da Tharros." In *Da Pyrgi a Mozia: Studi sull'archeologia del Mediterraneo in memoria di Antonia Ciasca*, edited by Maria Giulia Amadasi Guzzo, Mario Liverani, and Paolo Matthiae, 239–44. Rome: Università degli Studi di Roma "La Sapienza."

Frankenstein, Susan. 1979. "The Phoenicians in the Far West: A Function of Assyrian Imperialism." In *Power and Propaganda: A Symposium on Ancient Empires*, edited by Mogens Trolle Larsen, 263–94. Copenhagen: Akademisk Verlag.

Frede, Simone. 2000. *Die Phönizischen Anthropoiden Sarkophage*. Mainz: Philipp von Zabern.

Frendo, Anthony J. 2012. "Revisiting Some Phoenician-Punic Inscriptions from the Maltese Archipelago: A Rationale." *Hebrew Bible and Ancient Israel* 1 (4): 525–34.

Frey-Kupper, Suzanne. 2013. *Die Antiken Fundmünzen vom Monte Iato: 1971–1990; Ein Beitrag zur Geldgeschichte Westsiziliens*. Prahins: Éditions du Zèbre.

——.2014. "Coins and Their Use in the Punic Mediterranean: Case Studies from Carthage to Italy from the Fourth to the First Century BCE." In *The Punic Mediterranean: Identities and Identification from Phoenician Settlement to Roman Rule*, edited by Josephine Crawley Quinn and Nicholas C. Vella, 76–110. Cambridge: Cambridge University Press.

Friel, Brian. 1981. *Translations*. London: Faber and Faber.

Gaifman, Milette. 2008. "The Aniconic Image of the Roman Near East." In *The Variety of Local Religious Life in the Near East in the Hellenistic and Roman Periods*, edited by Ted Kaizer, 37–72. Leiden: Brill.

Gantz, Timothy. 1993. *Early Greek Myth: A Guide to Literary and Artistic Sources*. Baltimore, MD: Johns Hopkins University Press.

Garbati, Giuseppe. 2006. "Sul culto di Demetra nella Sardegna punica." In *Mutuare, interpretare, tradurre: Storie di culture a confronto: Atti del 2° Incontro "Orientalisti" Roma, 11–13 dicembre 2002*, edited by Giuseppe Regalzi, 127–43. Rome: Università degli Studi di Roma "La Sapienza."

——. 2008. *Religione votiva: Un'interpretazione storico-religiosa delle terrecotte votive nella Sardegna punica e tardo-punica*. Pisa: Fabrizio Serra.

——.2010. "Immagini e culti: Eshmun ad Amrit." *Rivista di studi fenici* 38 (2): 157–81.

——.2012. " 'Fingere' l'identità fenicia: Melqart 'di/sopra ṣr.' " *Rivista di studi fenici* 40 (2): 159–74.

——.2013. "Baal Hammon and Tinnit in Carthage: The Tophet between the Origin and the Expansion of the Colonial World." In *The Tophet in the Phoenician Mediterranean* [= *Studi epigrafici e linguistici* 29–30 (2012–13)], edited by Paolo Xella, 49–64. Verona: Essedue.

——.2015a. "Le relazioni tra Cartagine e Tiro in età ellenistica: Presente e memoria nel tophet di Salammbô." In *La Phénicie hellénistique: Actes du Colloque international de Toulouse (18–20 février 2013)*, edited by Julien Aliquot and Corinne Bonnet, 335–53. Paris: De Boccard.

——. 2015b. "Tyre, the Homeland: Carthage and Cadiz under the Gods' Eyes." In *Transformations and Crisis in the Mediterranean: "Identity" and Interculturality in the Levant and Phoenician West during the 12th–8th Centuries BCE; Proceedings of the International Conference Held in Rome, CNR, May 8–9, 2013*, edited by Giuseppe Garbati and Tatiana Pedrazzi, 197–208. Pisa: Fabrizio Serra.

Garbati, Giuseppe, and Tatiana Pedrazzi, eds. 2015. *Transformations and Crisis in the Mediterranean: "Identity" and Interculturality in the Levant and Phoenician West during the 12th–8th Centuries BCE: Proceedings of the International Conference Held in Rome, CNR, May 8–9, 2013*. Pisa: Fabrizio Serra

Garbini, Giovanni. 1980. "Gli 'annali' di Tiro e la storiografia fenicia." In *Oriental Studies Presented to Benedikt S. J. Esserlin*, edited by Rifaat Y. Ebied and Michael L. Young, 114–27. Leiden: Brill.

——.1988. *Il semitico nordoccidentale: Studi di storia linguistica*. Rome: Università degli Studi di Roma "La Sapienza."

——. 1991. "La letteratura dei Fenici." In *Atti del II Congresso internazionale di studi fenici e punici: Roma, 9–14 novembre 1987*, edited by Enrico Acquaro, 489–94. Rome: Consiglio nazionale delle ricerche.

——. 1997. "Nuove epigrafi fenicie da Antas." *Rivista di studi fenici* 25: 59–67.

Garnand, Brien K. 2001. "From Infant Sacrifice to the ABC's: Ancient Phoenicians and Modern Identities." *Stanford Journal of Archaeology* 1: http://web.stanford.edu/dept/archaeology/journal/newdraft/garnand/paper.html.

——. 2013. "Phoenicians on the Edge: Geographic and Ethnographic Distribution of Human Sacrifice." In *The Tophet in the Phoenician Mediterranean* [= *Studi epigrafici e linguistici* 29–30 (2012–13)], edited by Paolo Xella, 65–92. Verona: Essedue.

Garr, W. Randall. 1985. *Dialect Geography of Syria-Palestine, 1000–586 B.C.* Philadelphia: University of Pennsylvania Press.

Gat, Azar, and Alexander Yakobson. 2013. *Nations: The Long History and Deep Roots of Political Ethnicity and Nationalism.* Cambridge: Cambridge University Press.

Gellner, Ernest. 1964. *Thought and Change.* London: Weidenfeld and Nicolson.

——. 1983. *Nations and Nationalism.* Oxford: Basil Blackwell.

Gerritsen, Johan. 2012. "Aylett Sammes and the History of Ancient Britain." *Quaerendo* 42 (3–4): 186–92.

Gesenius, Wilhelm. 1837. *Scripturae linguaeque phoeniciae: Monumenta quotquot supersunt edita et inedita ad autographorum optimorumque exemplorum fidem edidit additisque de scriptura et lingua phoenicum commentariis illustravit.* Leipzig: F. Vogel.

Ghaki, Mansour. 1997. "Épigraphique libyque et punique à Dougga." In *Dougga (Thugga): Études épigraphiques*, edited by Mustapha Khanoussi and Louis Maurin, 27–45. Paris: Ausonius.

Gilboa, Ayelet. 1999. "The Dynamics of Phoenician Bichrome Pottery: A View from Tel Dor." *Bulletin of the American Schools of Oriental Research* 316: 1–22.

Gilroy, Paul. 1993. *Black Atlantic: Modernity and Double Consciousness.* London: Verso.

Gleitman, Claire. 1997. "Negotiating History, Negotiating Myth: Friel among His Contemporaries." In *Brian Friel: A Casebook*, edited by William Kerwin, 227–41. New York: Garland.

Godart, Louis. 1991. "I fenici nei testi in Lineare B: Lo stato della questione." In *Atti del II Congresso internazionale di studi fenici e punici, Roma, 9–14 novembre 1987*, edited by Enrico Acquaro, 495–97. Rome: Consiglio nazionale delle ricerche.

González de Canales, Fernando, Leonardo Serrano, and Jorge Llompart. 2004. *El emporio fenicio precolonial de Huelva (ca. 900–770 AC).* Madrid: Biblioteca nueva.

——. 2006. "The Pre-colonial Phoenician Emporium of Huelva, ca. 900–770 BC." *Bulletin Antieke Beschaving* 81: 13–29.

González Wagner, Carlos. 1986. "Critical Remarks concerning a Supposed Hellenization of Carthage." *Reppal* 2: 357–75.

Goody, Jack, and Ian Watt. 1963. "The Consequences of Literacy." *Comparative Studies in Society and History* 5 (3): 304–45.

Grahame, Mark. 1998. "Material Culture and Roman Identity: The Spatial Layout of Pompeian Houses and the Problem of Ethnicity." In *Cultural Identity in the Roman Empire*, edited by Joanne Berry and Ray Laurence, 156–78. London: Routledge.

Grainger, John D. 1991. *Hellenistic Phoenicia.* Oxford: Clarendon Press.

Greene, Joseph A. 1992. "Une reconnaissance archéologique dans l'arrière-pays de la Carthage antique." In *Pour sauver Carthage: Exploration et conservation de la cité punique, romaine et byzantine*, edited by Abdelmajid Ennabli, 195–97. Paris: UNESCO/INAA.

Greene, Joseph A., and Denis P. Kehoe. 1995. "Mago the Carthaginian." In *Actes du IIIe Congrès international des études phéniciennes et puniques, Tunis, 11–16 novembre 1991*, edited by M'hamed Hassine Fantar and Mansour Ghaki, 110–17. Tunis: Institut national de patrimoine.

Grey, Anchitell. 1763. *Debates of the House of Commons from the Year 1667 to the Year 1694*. London: D. Henry, R. Cave, and J. Emonson.

Grottanelli, Cristiano. 1972. "Il mito delle origini di Tiro: Due 'versioni' duali." *Oriens antiquus* 11: 49–63.

——. 1973. "Melqart e Sid fra Egitto, Libia e Sardegna." *Rivista di studi fenici* 1 (2): 153–64.

Gruen, Erich S. 1998. *Heritage and Hellenism: The Reinvention of Jewish Tradition.* Berkeley: University of California Press.

——. 2011. *Rethinking the Other in Antiquity*. Princeton, NJ: Princeton University Press.

——. 2013. "Did the Romans Have an Ethnic Identity?" *Antichthon* 47: 1–17.

Gunter, Ann C. 2009. *Greek Art and the Orient*. Cambridge: Cambridge University Press.

Gzella, Holger. 2011a. "North-West Semitic in General." In *The Semitic Languages: An International Handbook*, edited by Stefan Weninger, 425–51. Berlin: De Gruyter.

—— 2011b. "Phoenician." In *Languages from the World of the Bible*, edited by Holger Gzella, 55–75. Berlin: De Gruyter.

——. 2013. "The Linguistic Position of Old Byblian." In *Linguistic Studies in Phoenician*, edited by Robert D. Holmstedt and Aaron Schade, 170–98. Winona Lake, IN: Eisenbrauns.

Hackett, Jo Ann. 2004. "Phoenician and Punic." In *Cambridge Encyclopedia of the World's Ancient Languages*, edited by Roger D. Woodward, 82–102. Cambridge: Cambridge University Press.

Haegemans, Karen. 2000. "Elissa, the First Queen of Carthage, through Timaeus' Eyes." *Ancient Society* 30: 277–91.

Hall, Alan S., Nicholas P. Milner, and John J. Coulton. 1996. "The Mausoleum of Licinnia Flavilla and Flavianus Diogenes of Oinoanda: Epigraphy and Architecture." *Anatolian Studies* 46: 111–44.

Hall, Edith. 1989. *Inventing the Barbarian: Greek Self-Definition through Tragedy*. Oxford: Clarendon Press.

Hall, Jonathan M. 1997. *Ethnic Identity in Greek Antiquity*. Cambridge: Cambridge University Press.

——. 1998. "Discourse and Praxis: Ethnicity and Culture in Ancient Greece." *Cambridge Archaeological Journal* 8 (2): 266–69.

——. 2002. *Hellenicity: Between Ethnicity and Culture*. Chicago: University of Chicago Press.

Hall, Linda Jones. 2004. *Roman Berytus: Beirut in Late Antiquity*. London: Routledge.

Hall, Stuart. 1990. "Cultural Identity and Diaspora." In *Identity: Community, Culture, Difference*, edited by Jonathan Rutherford, 222–37. London: Lawrence and Wishart.

Hamdi, Osman, and T. Reinach. 1892. *Une nécropole royale à Sidon: Fouilles de Hamdy Bey*. Paris: Leroux.

Hansen, Mogens Herman. 1996. "City-Ethnics as Evidence for Polis Identity." In *More Studies in the Ancient Greek Polis*, edited by Mogens Herman Hansen and Kurt A. Raaflaub, 169–96. Stuttgart: Franz Steiner Verlag.

Harden, Donald B. 1962. *The Phoenicians*. London: Thames and Hudson.

Hartog, François. 1988. *The Mirror of Herodotus: The Representation of the Other in the Writing of History*. Translated by Janet Lloyd. Berkeley: University of California Press.

Hasenohr, Claire. 2007. "Italiens et phéniciens à Délos: Organisation et relations de deux groupes d'étrangers résidents (2e–1er siècles av. J.-C.)." In *Étrangers dans la cité romaine: Actes du Colloque de Valenciennes (octobre 2005)*, edited by Rita Compatangelo-Soussignan and Christian-Georges Schwentzel, 77–90. Rennes: Presses universitaires de Rennes.

Hauben, Hans. 1987. "Philocles, King of the Sidonians and General of the Ptolemies." In *Phoenicia and the East Mediterranean in the First Millennium BC*, edited by Edward Lipiński, 413–427. Leuven: Peeters.

Hayton, David. 2012. *The Anglo-Irish Experience, 1680–1730: Religion, Identity and Patriotism*. Woodbridge: Boydell.

Hazbun, Waleed. 2007. "Images of Openness, Spaces of Control: The Politics of Tourism Development in Tunisia." *Arab Studies Journal* 15–16: 10–35.

Hazran, Yusri. 2014. *The Druze Community and the Lebanese State: Between Confrontation and Reconciliation*. Abingdon: Routledge.

Heaney, Seamus. 1975. *North*. London: Faber and Faber.

——. 2002. *Finders Keepers: Selected Prose 1971–2001*. London: Faber and Faber.

Hekster, Olivier. 2015. *Emperors and Ancestors: Roman Rulers and the Constraints of Tradition*. Oxford: Oxford University Press.

Hemelrijk, Emily Ann. 2015. *Hidden Lives, Public Personae: Women and Civic Life in the Roman West*. Oxford: Oxford University Press.

Hills, Catherine. 2009. "Anglo-Saxon DNA?" In *Mortuary Practices and Social Identities in the Middle Ages: Essays in Burial Archaeology in Honour of Heinrich Härke*, edited by Duncan Sayer and Howard Williams, 123–40. Exeter: University of Exeter Press.

Hilton, Julia L. 2012. "The Sphragis of Heliodoros, Genealogy in the *Aithiopika*, and Julian's Hymn to King Helios." *Ágora* 14: 195–219.

Hinds, Stephen. 2011. "Black-Sea Latin, Du Bellay, and the Barbarian Turn: *Tristia, Regrets, Translations*." In *Two Thousand Years of Solitude: Exile after Ovid*, edited by Jennifer Ingleheart, 59–83. Oxford: Oxford University Press.

Hingley, Richard. 2008. *The Recovery of Roman Britain 1586–1906: A Colony So Fertile*. Oxford: Oxford University Press.

Hirschi, Caspar. 2012. *The Origins of Nationalism: An Alternative History from Ancient Rome to Early Modern Germany*. Cambridge: Cambridge University Press.

Hirt, Alfred. 2015. "Beyond Greece and Rome: Foundation Myths on Tyrian Coinage in the Third Century AD." In *Foundation Myths in Ancient Societies: Dialogues and Discourses*, edited by Naoíse Mac Sweeney, 190–226. Philadelphia: University of Pennsylvania Press.

Hitti, Philip K. 1957. *History of Syria: Including Lebanon and Palestine*. 2nd ed. London: Macmillan.

Hobsbawm, E. J. 1990. *Nations and Nationalism since 1780: Programme, Myth, Reality*. Cambridge: Cambridge University Press.

——. 1997. *On History*. London: Weidenfeld and Nicolson.

Hodos, Tamar. 2009. "Colonial Engagements in the Global Mediterranean Iron Age." *Cambridge Archaeological Journal* 19 (2): 221–41.

Honig, Bonnie. 2016. "What Kind of Thing Is Land? Hannah Arendt's Object Relations, or: The Jewish Unconscious of Arendt's Most 'Greek' Text." *Political Theory* 44 (3): 307–36.

Hont, Istvan. 2005. *Jealousy of Trade: International Competition and the Nation-State in Historical Perspective.* Cambridge, MA: Belknap Press.

Hoover, Oliver D. 2004. "*Ceci n'est pas l'autonomie:* The Coinage of Seleucid Phoenicia as Royal and Civic Power Discourse." *Topoi Supplement* 6: 485–507.

Houghton, Arthur, Catharine Lorber, and Oliver Hoover. 2002. *Seleucid Coins: A Comprehensive Catalogue.* New York: American Numismatic Society.

Houser, C. 1998. "The 'Alexander Sarcophagus' of Abdalonymus: A Hellenistic Monument from Sidon." In *Regional Schools in Hellenistic Sculpture: Proceedings of an International Conference Held at the American School of Classical Studies at Athens, March 15–17, 1996,* edited by Olga Palagia and William Coulson, 281–91. Oxford: Oxbow.

How, W. W., and J. Wells. 1912. *A Commentary on Herodotus.* Oxford: Clarendon Press.

Hoyos, B. Dexter. 2010. *The Carthaginians.* London: Routledge.

Huntington, Samuel P. 1996. *The Clash of Civilizations and the Remaking of World Order.* New York: Simon and Schuster.

Hurst, H. R. 1994. *Excavations at Carthage: The British Mission.* Vol. 2.1, *The Circular Harbour, North Side: The Site and Finds Other Than Pottery.* Oxford: Oxford University Press.

——. 1999. *The Sanctuary of Tanit at Carthage in the Roman Period: A Re-interpretation.* Portsmouth, RI: Journal of Roman Archaeology.

Isaac, Benjamin H. 2004. *The Invention of Racism in Classical Antiquity.* Princeton, NJ: Princeton University Press.

Jacques, Martin. 2009. *When China Rules the World: The Rise of the Middle Kingdom and the End of the Western World.* London: Allen Lane.

James, Simon. 1999. *The Atlantic Celts: Ancient People or Modern Invention?* London: British Museum Press.

Jameson, Michael H., and Irad Malkin. 1998. "Latinos and the Greeks." *Athenaeum* 86 (2): 477–85.

Jamieson, Andrew S. 2011. "The Iron Age Pottery from Tell Beirut 1995—Bey 032: Periods 1 and 2." In *Ceramics of the Phoenician-Punic World: Collected Essays,* edited by Claudia Sagona, 7–276. Leuven: Peeters.

Jeffery, L. H. 1990. *The Local Scripts of Archaic Greece: A Study of the Origin of the Greek Alphabet and Its Development from the Eighth to the Fifth Centuries B.C.* Rev. ed. Oxford: Clarendon Press.

Jenkins, G. Kenneth. 1971. "Coins of Punic Sicily. Part 1." *Schweizerische numismatische Rundschau* 50: 25–78.

——. 1974. "Coins of Punic Sicily. Part 2." *Schweizerische numismatische Rundschau* 53: 23–41.

——. 1977. "Coins of Punic Sicily. Part 3." *Schweizerische numismatische Rundschau* 56: 5–65.

——. 1978. "Coins of Punic Sicily. Part 4." *Schweizerische numismatische Rundschau* 57: 5–68.

Jigoulov, Vadim S. 2010. *The Social History of Achaemenid Phoenicia: Being a Phoenician, Negotiating Empires.* London: Equinox.

Jiménez, Alicia. 2008. "A Critical Approach to the Concept of Resistance: New 'Traditional' Rituals and Objects in Funerary Contexts of Roman Baetica." In *TRAC 2007: Proceedings of the Seventeenth Theoretical Roman Archaeology Conference*, edited by Corisande Fenwick, Meredith Wiggins, and Dave Wythe, 15–30. Oxford: Oxbow.

———, sess. ed. 2010. *Colonising a Colonised Territory: Settlements with Punic Roots in Roman Times*. In *Meetings between Cultures in the Ancient Mediterranean: Proceedings of the 17th International Congress of Classical Archaeology, Rome 22–26 Sept. 2008*, edited by Martina Della Riva and Helga Di Giuseppe. Rome: Bolletino di archaeologia online. www.bollettinodiarcheologiaonline.beniculturali.it/bao _es_a_7.php.

Joffe, Alexander H. 2002. "The Rise of Secondary States in the Iron Age Levant." *Journal of the Economic and Social History of the Orient* 45 (4): 425–67.

Johnson, Aaron P. 2006. *Ethnicity and Argument in Eusebius' Praeparatio Evangelica*. Oxford: Oxford University Press.

Jones, Sian. 1997. *The Archaeology of Ethnicity: Constructing Identities in the Past and Present*. London: Routledge.

Jongeling, Karel. 2008. *Handbook of Neo-Punic Inscriptions*. Tübingen: Mohr Siebeck.

Jongeling, Karel, and Robert M. Kerr. 2005. *Late Punic Epigraphy: An Introduction to the Study of Neo-Punic and Latino-Punic Inscriptions*. Tübingen: Mohr Siebeck.

Joseph, John Earl. 2004. *Language and Identity: National, Ethnic, Religious*. Basingstoke: Palgrave Macmillan.

Joumblatt, Kamal. 1997. "My Mission as a Member of Parliament." In *Les années "Cénacle,"* 91–99. Beyrouth: Dar an-Nahar.

Jourdain-Annequin, Colette. 1989. *Héraclès aux portes du soir: Mythe et histoire*. Paris: Presses universitaires Franche-Comté.

Jourdain-Annequin, Colette, and Corinne Bonnet. 2001. "Images et fonctions d'Héraclès: Les modèles orientaux et leurs interprétations." In *'La questione delle influenze Vicino-Orientali sulla religione greca': Atti del colloquio internazionale, Roma, Maggio 1999*, edited by Maria Rocchi, Sergio Ribichini, and Paolo Xella, 195–223. Rome: Consiglio nazionale delle ricerche.

Joyce, James. 2000. *Occasional, Critical, and Political Writing*. Edited by Kevin Barry. Oxford: Oxford University Press.

Kamlah, Jens. 2012. "Temples of the Levant—Comparative Aspects." In *Temple Building and Temple Cult: Architecture and Cultic Paraphernalia of Temples in the Levant (2.–1. Mill. B.C.E.): Proceedings of a Conference on the Occasion of the 50th Anniversary of the Institute of Biblical Archaeology at the University of Tübingen (28–30 May 2010)*, edited by Jens Kamlah, 507–34. Wiesbaden: Harrassowitz Verlag.

Katzenstein, H. J. 1997. *The History of Tyre: From the Beginning of the Second Millennium B.C.E. until the Fall of the Neo-Babylonian Empire in 538 B.C.E.* Jerusalem: Ben-Gurion University of the Negev Press.

Kaufman, Asher. 2001. "Phoenicianism: The Formation of an Identity in Lebanon of 1920." *Middle Eastern Studies* 37 (1): 173–94.

———. 2004a. *Reviving Phoenicia: The Search for Identity in Lebanon*. London: I. B. Tauris.

———. 2004b. " 'Tell Us Our History': Charles Corm, Mount Lebanon and Lebanese Nationalism." *Middle Eastern Studies* 40 (3): 1–28.

———. 2008. " 'Too Much French but Swell Exhibit': Representing Lebanon at the 1939 New York World's Fair." *British Journal of Middle East Studies* 35: 59–77.

Kay, Philip. 2014. *Rome's Economic Revolution.* Oxford: Oxford University Press.

Keay, Simon. 2013. "Were the Iberians Hellenised?" In *The Hellenistic West: Rethinking the Ancient Mediterranean,* edited by Jonathan R. W. Prag and Josephine Crawley Quinn, 300–319. Cambridge: Cambridge University Press.

Keillor, Garrison. 1975. "Oya Life These Days." *New Yorker,* February 17, 31–32.

Kendrick, Thomas D. 1950. *British Antiquity.* London: Methuen.

Kenrick, John. 1855. *Phoenicia.* London: B. Fellowes.

Kerr, Robert M. 2010. *Latino-Punic Epigraphy: A Descriptive Sudy of the Inscriptions.* Tübingen: Mohr Siebeck.

Kestemont, Guy. 1983. "Tyr et les Assyriens." In *Redt Tyrus / Sauvons Tyr: Histoire phénicienne / Fenicische geschiedenis,* edited by Eric Gubel, Edward Lipiński, and Brigitte Servais-Soyez, 53–78. Leuven: Peeters.

Khanoussi, Mustapha, and Louis Maurin. 2000. *Dougga, fragments d'histoire: Choix d'inscriptions latines, éditées, traduites et commentées (1er–Ive siècles).* Bordeaux: Ausonius and Institut national du patrimoine.

Kidd, Colin. 1994. "Gaelic Antiquity and National Identity in Enlightenment Ireland and Scotland." *English Historical Review* 109 (434): 1197–214.

———. 1999. *British Identities before Nationalism: Ethnicity and Nationhood in the Atlantic World, 1600–1800.* Cambridge: Cambridge University Press.

Kleemann, Ilse. 1958. *Der Satrapen-Sarkophag aus Sidon.* Berlin: Gebr. Mann.

Kokkinos, Nikos. 2012. "A Note on the Date of Philo of Byblus." *Classical Quarterly* 62 (1): 433–35.

Kosmin, Paul J. 2014. *The Land of the Elephant Kings: Space, Territory, and Ideology in the Seleucid Empire.* Cambridge, MA: Harvard University Press.

Krahmalkov, Charles R. 2000. *Phoenician-Punic Dictionary.* Leuven: Peeters.

———. 2001. *A Phoenician-Punic Grammar.* Leiden: Brill.

Krandel-Ben Younès, Alia. 2002. *La présence punique en pays numide.* Tunis: Institut national du patrimoine.

Krings, Véronique. 1998. *Carthage et les grecs, c. 580–480 av. J.-C.: Textes et histoire.* Leiden: Brill.

Kristiansen, Kristian. 1998. *Europe before History.* Cambridge: Cambridge University Press.

Kuper, Adam. 2005. *The Reinvention of Primitive Society: Transformations of a Myth.* 2nd ed. Abingdon: Routledge.

Kuttner, Ann. 2013. "Representing Hellenistic Numidia, in Africa and at Rome." In *The Hellenistic West: Rethinking the Ancient Mediterranean,* edited by Jonathan R. W. Prag and Josephine Crawley Quinn, 216–72. Cambridge: Cambridge University Press.

Lacroix, M. 1932. "Les étrangers à Délos pendant la période de l'independence." In *Mélanges Gustave Glotz II,* 501–25. Paris: Presses universitaires de France.

Lancel, Serge. 1995. *Carthage: A History.* Translated by Antonia Nevill. Oxford: Blackwell.

Lange, A. 2007. "'They Burn Their Sons and Daughters. That Was No Command of Mine' (Jer. 7:31): Child Sacrifice in the Hebrew Bible and in the Deuteronomistic Jeremiah Redaction." In *Human Sacrifice in the Jewish and Christian Tradition,* edited by Karin Finsterbusch, Armin Lange, and Diethard Römheld, 109–32. Leiden: Brill.

Langer-Karrenbrock, Marie-Theres. 2000. *Der Lykische Sarkophag aus der Königsnekropole von Sidon.* Münster: LIT.

Larkin, Craig. 2011. *Memory and Conflict in Lebanon: Remembering and Forgetting the Past.* New York: Routledge.

Laroui, Abdallah. 1977. *The History of the Maghrib: An Interpretive Essay*. Translated by Ralph Manheim. Princeton, NJ: Princeton University Press.

Lasserre, François. 1966. *Strabon, géographie: Tome II (Livres III et IV)*. Paris: Les Belle Lettres.

Leerssen, Joep. 1986. "On the Edge of Europe: Ireland in Search of Oriental Roots, 1650–1850." *Comparative Criticism* 8: 91–112.

———. 1996. *Mere Irish and Fíor-Ghael: Studies in the Idea of Irish Nationality, Its Development and Literary Expression prior to the Nineteenth Century*. 2nd ed. Cork: Cork University Press in association with Field Day.

Le Glay, Marcel. 1961–66. *Saturne africain: Monuments*. Paris: Arts et métiers graphiques.

Lehmann, Gunnar. 1998. "Trends in the Local Pottery Development of the Late Iron Age and Persian Period in Syria and Lebanon, ca. 700 to 300 BC." *Bulletin of the American Schools of Oriental Research* 311: 7–37.

Lemaire, André. 2012. "From the Origins of the Alphabet to the Tenth Century B.C.E.: New Documents and New Directions." In *New Inscriptions and Seals Relating to the Biblical World*, edited by Meir Lubetski and Edith Lubetski, 1–20. Atlanta, GA: Society of Biblical Literature.

Lembke, Katja. 2001. *Phönizische Anthropoide Sarkophage*. Mainz am Rhein: Philipp von Zabern.

Lemche, Niels Peter. 1991. *The Canaanites and Their Land: The Tradition of the Canaanites*. Sheffield: JSOT Press.

Lennon, Joseph. 2004. *Irish Orientalism: A Literary and Intellectual History*. Syracuse, NY: Syracuse University Press.

Lepelley, Claude. 2005. "Témoignages de Saint Augustin sur l'ampleur et les limites de l'usage de la langue punique dans l'Afrique de son temps." In *Identités et cultures dans l'Algérie antique*, edited by Claude Briand-Ponsart, 137–53. Rouen: Presses universitaires de Rouen et du Havre.

Lerat, Lucien. 1952. *Les locriens de l'ouest*. Paris: De Boccard.

Levi Della Vida, Giorgio. 1935. "Due iscrizioni imperiali neopuniche di Leptis Magna." *Africa italiana* 6: 3–15.

Lipiński, Edward. 1988. "Sacrifices d'enfants à Carthage et dans le monde sémitique oriental." In *Carthago*, edited by Edward Lipiński, 151–62. Leuven: Peeters.

———. 1995. *Dieux et déesses de l'univers phénicien et punique*. Leuven: Peeters.

———. 2004. *Itineraria Phoenicia*. Leuven: Peeters.

Livadiotti, Monica, and Giorgio Rocco. 2005. "Il tempio di Roma e Augusto." In *I tre templi del lato nord-ovest del Foro Vecchio a Leptis Magna*, edited by Antonino Di Vita and Monica Livadiotti, 165–308. Rome: L'Erma di Bretschneider.

Liverani, Mario. 1998. "L'immagine dei fenici nella storiografia occidentale." *Studi storici* 39 (1): 5–22.

Lomas, Kathryn. 2000. "Cities, States and Ethnic Identity in Southeast Italy." In *The Emergence of State Identities in Italy in the First Millennium B.C.*, edited by E. Herring and Kathryn Lomas, 79–90. London: Accordia Research Institute.

López Castro, José Luis. 1991. "Cartago y la Península Ibérica: ¿Imperialismo o hegemonía?" In *La caída de Tiro y el auge de Cartago: Jornadas de arqueología fenicio-púnica de Ibiza*, 5: 73–84. Ibiza: Museu arqueologic d'Eivissa.

López Castro, José Luis. 1995. *Hispania poena: Los fenicios en la Hispania romana (206 a.C.–96 d.C.)*. Barcelona: Critica.

——. 2007. "The Western Phoenicians under the Roman Republic: Integration and Persistance." In *Articulating Local Cultures: Power and Identity under the Expanding Roman Republic*, edited by Peter van Dommelen and Nicola Terrenato, 103–25. Portsmouth, RI: Journal of Roman Archaeology.

López Castro, José Luis, Ahmed Ferjaoui, Andrés Adroher Auroux, Fauzzi Arbi, Imed Ben Jerbania, Fathi Dridi, Foued Esaadi, Eduardo Ferrer Albelda, Ivan Fumadó Ortega, Víctor Martínez Hahnmüller, Alfredo Mederos Martín, Carmen Ana Pardo Barrinonuevo, Victoria Peña Romo, and Amparo Sánchez Moreno. 2014. "Proyecto Útica: Investigación en la ciudad fenicio-púnica." *Informes y trabajos* 11: 204–20.

Lorcin, Patricia. 2002. "Rome and France in Africa: Recovering Colonial Algeria's Latin Past." *French Historical Studies* 25 (2): 201–19.

Lucy, Sam. 2005. "Ethnic and Cultural Identities." In *The Archaeology of Identity*, edited by Margarita Díaz-Andreu, 86–109. London: Routledge.

Ma, John. 2003. "Peer Polity Interaction in the Hellenistic Age." *Past and Present* 180: 9–39.

MacMullen, Ramsay. 2000. *Romanization in the Time of Augustus*. New Haven, CT: Yale University Press.

Mac Sweeney, Naoíse. 2009. "Beyond Ethnicity: The Overlooked Diversity of Group Identities." *Journal of Mediterranean Archaeology* 22 (1): 101–26.

——. 2010. Rhetoric and Reality: The Clash of Civilisations from Classical Greece to Today. *Open Democracy*. https://www.opendemocracy.net/naoise-macsweeney/tracing-clash-of-civilisations.

Maier, Franz Georg. 1994. "Cyprus and Phoenicia." In *The Cambridge Ancient History*. 2nd ed. Vol. 6, *The Fourth Century B.C.*, edited by David M. Lewis, John Boardman, Simon Hornblower, and Martin Ostwald, 297–336. Cambridge: Cambridge University Press.

Malkin, Irad. 1990. "Lysander and Libys." *Classical Quarterly* 40 (2): 541–45.

——. 1994. *Myth and Territory in the Spartan Mediterranean*. Cambridge: Cambridge University Press.

——. 1996. "The Polis between Myths of Land and Territory." In *The Role of Religion in the Early Greek Polis: Third International Seminar on Ancient Greek Cult*, edited by Robin Hägg, 9–19. Stockholm: Swedish Institute at Athens.

——. 1998. *The Returns of Odysseus: Colonization and Ethnicity*. Berkeley: University of California Press.

——. 2001a. *Ancient Perceptions of Greek Ethnicity*. Cambridge, MA: Harvard University Press.

——. 2001b. "Introduction." In *Ancient Perceptions of Greek Ethnicity*, edited by Irad Malkin, 1–28. Cambridge, MA: Harvard University Press.

——. 2002. "A Colonial Middle Ground: Greek, Etruscan, and Local Elites in the Bay of Naples." In *The Archaeology of Colonialism*, edited by Claire L. Lyons and John Papadopoulos, 151–81. Los Angeles: Getty.

——. 2005. "Herakles and Melqart: Greeks and Phoenicians in the Middle Ground." In *Cultural Borrowings and Ethnic Appropriations in Antiquity*, edited by Erich S. Gruen, 238–57. Stuttgart: Franz Steiner Verlag.

———. 2011. *A Small Greek World: Networks in the Ancient Mediterranean*. Oxford: Oxford University Press.

———. 2014a. "Between Collective and Ethnic Identities: A Conclusion." In *Culture matérielle et identité ethnique*, edited by Christel Müller and Anne-Emanuelle Veïsse, 283–94. Besançon: Presses universitaries de Franche-Comté.

———. 2014b. "Philistines and Phokaians: Comparative Hinterlands and Middle Grounds." In *Contacts et acculturations en Méditerranée occidentale: Hommages à Michel Bats; Actes du Colloque international d'Hyères-Les-Palmiers (15–18 septembre 2011)*, edited by Réjane Roure, 131–42. Paris: Errance/Centre Camille Jullian.

Mamdani, Mahmood. 2002. *When Victims Become Killers: Colonialism, Nativism, and the Genocide in Rwanda*. Princeton, NJ: Princeton University Press.

Mancinetti Santamaria, Giovanna. 1982. "Filostrato di Ascalona, banchiere in Delo." In *Delo e l'Italia*, edited by Filippo Coarelli, Domenico Musti, and Heikki Solin, 79–89. Rome: Bardi editore.

Manfredi, Lorenza-Ilia. 1985. "Ršmlqrt, R'šmlqrt: Nota sulla numismatica punica di Sicilia." *Rivista italiana di numismatica* 87: 3–8.

———. 1995. *Monete puniche: Repertorio epigrafico e numismatico delle leggende puniche*. Rome: Istituto poligrafico e Zecca dello stato.

———. 2003. "La politica amministrativa di Cartagine in Africa." *Memorie della Accademia nazionale dei Lincei* ser. 9, 16 (3): 329–530.

———. 2009. "Iconografia e leggenda: Il linguaggio monetale di Cartagine." *Mediterranea* 6: 203–18.

Mann, Michael. 1986. *The Sources of Social Power*. Cambridge: Cambridge University Press.

Maraoui Telmini, Boutheina, Roald Docter, Babette Bechtold, Fethi Chelbi, and Winfred Van de Put. 2014. "Defining Punic Carthage." In *The Punic Mediterranean: Identities and Identification from Phoenician Settlement to Roman Rule*, edited by Josephine Crawley Quinn and Nicholas C. Vella, 113–47. Cambridge: Cambridge University Press.

Markell, Patchen. 2000. "Making Affect Safe for Democracy? On 'Constitutional Patriotism.' " *Political Theory* 28 (1): 38–63.

Markoe, Glenn. 1985. *Phoenician Bronze and Silver Bowls from Cyprus and the Mediterranean*. Berkeley: University of California Press.

———. 2000. *Phoenicians*. London: British Museum Press.

Martin, S. Rebecca 2017. *The Art of Contact: Comparative Approaches to Greek and Phoenician Art*. Philadelphia: University of Pennsylvania Press.

Masson, Olivier. 1969. "Recherches sur les phéniciens dans le monde héllenistique." *Bulletin de correspondance hellénique* 93: 694–99.

Masturzo, Niccolò. 2003. "Le città della Tripolitania fra continuità ed innovazione: I fori di Leptis Magna e Sabratha." *Mélanges de l'École française de Rome: Antiquité* 115 (2): 705–53.

———. 2005. "Il tempio occidentale—tempio di 'Liber Pater.' " In *I tre templi del lato nord-ovest del Foro Vecchio a Leptis Magna*, edited by Antonino Di Vita and Monica Livadiotti, 35–164. Rome: L'Erma di Bretschneider.

Mattingly, David J. 1995. *Tripolitania*. London: Batsford.

———. 2011. *Imperialism, Power, and Identity: Experiencing the Roman Empire*. Princeton, NJ: Princeton University Press.

Mavrogiannis, Theodore. 2004. "Herodotus and the Phoenicians." In *The World of Herodotus*, edited by Vassos Karageorghis and Ioannes Taifacos, 53–71. Nicosia: Foundation Anastasios G. Leventis.

Maya Torcelly, Rafael, Gema Jurado Fresnadillo, José-María Gener Basallote, Ester López Rosendo, Mariano Torres Ortiz, and José Ángel Zamora López. 2014. "Nuevos datos sobre la posible ubicación del Kronion de Gadir: Las evidencias de época fenicia arcaica." In *Los fenicios en la Bahía de Cádiz: Nuevas investigaciones*, edited by Massimo Botto, 156–80. Pisa: Fabrizio Serra.

Mazza, Federico. 1988. "The Phoenicians as Seen by the Ancient World." In *The Phoenicians*, edited by Sabatino Moscati, 548–67. Milan: Bompiani.

Mazza, Federico, Sergio Ribichini, and Paolo Xella. 1988. *Fonti classiche per la civiltà fenicia e punica: I. Fonti letterarie greche dalle origini alla fine dell'età classica*. Rome: Consiglio nazionale delle ricerche.

McCarty, Matthew M. 2010. "Soldiers and Stelae: Votive Cult and the Roman Army in North Africa." In *Meetings between Cultures in the Ancient Mediterranean: Proceedings of the 17th International Congress of Classical Archaeology, Rome 22–26 Sept. 2008*, edited by M. Dalla Riva and H. Di Giuseppe. Rome: Bollettino di archeologia online. http://www.bollettinodiarcheologiaonline.beniculturali.it/documenti/generale/4_McCARTY.pdf.

———. 2011. "Representations and the 'Meaning' of Ritual Change: The Case of Hadrumetum." In *Ritual Dynamics in the Ancient Mediterranean: Agency, Emotion, Gender, Representation*, edited by Angelos Chaniotis, 197–228. Stuttgart: Steiner Verlag.

———. 2013. "Continuities and Contexts. The Tophets of Roman Imperial-Period Africa." In *The "Tophet" in the Phoenician Mediterranean*, edited by Paolo Xella, 93–118. Verona: Essedue.

McCarty, Matthew M., and Josephine Crawley Quinn. 2015. "Echos puniques: Langue, culte, et gouvernement en Numidie hellénistique." In *Massinissa, au cœur de la consécration d'un premier état numide*, edited by Dida Badi, 167–98. Algiers: Haut commissariat à l'amazighité Alger.

McDougall, James. 2006. *History and the Culture of Nationalism in Algeria*. Cambridge: Cambridge University Press.

McGrath, Francis Charles. 1999. *Brian Friel's (Post) Colonial Drama: Language, Illusion, and Politics*. Syracuse, NY: Syracuse University Press.

McGuinness, Frank. 1988. *Carthaginians and Baglady*. London: Faber.

Meadows, Andrew. 2001. "Money, Freedom and Empire in the Hellenistic World." In *Money and Its Uses in the Ancient Greek World*, edited by Andrew Meadows and Kirsty Shipton, 53–63. Oxford: Oxford University Press.

Melchiorri, Valentina. 2009. "Le tophet de Sulci (S. Antioco, Sardaigne): État des études et perspectives de la recherche." *Ugarit-Forschungen* 41: 509–24.

———. 2013. "Osteological Analysis in the Study of the Phoenician and Punic Tophet: A History of Research." In *The Tophet in the Phoenician Mediterranean* [= *Studi epigrafici e linguistici* 29–30 (2012–13)], edited by Paolo Xella , 223–58. Verona: Essedue.

Mellah, Fawzi. 1987. *Le conclave des pleureuses*. Paris: Seuil.

Mettinger, Tryggve N. D. 1995. *No Graven Image? Israelite Aniconism in Its Ancient Near Eastern Context*. Stockholm: Almqvist and Wiksell International.

———. 2001. *The Riddle of Resurrection: "Dying and Rising Gods" in the Ancient Near East*. Stockholm: Almqvist and Wiksell International.

Meyers, Carol L. 1991. "Of Drums and Damsels: Women's Performance in Ancient Israel." *Biblical Archaeologist* 54 (1): 16–27.

Mezzolani, Antonella. 2009. "Tharros: 'Membra disiecta' di una città punica." In *Phönizisches und Punisches Städtewesn*, edited by Sophie Helas and Dirce Marzoli, 399–418. Mainz am Rhein: Philipp von Zabern.

Mildenberg, Leo. 1992. "The Mint of the First Carthaginian Coins." In *Florilegium Numismaticum: Studia in Honorem U. Westermark edita*, 289–93. Stockholm: Svenska Numismatika Föreningen.

———. 1993. "Ršmlqrt." In *Essays in Honour of Robert Carson and Kenneth Jenkins*, edited by Martin Price, Andrew Burnett, and Roger Bland, 7–8. London: Spink.

Miles, Richard. 2010. *Carthage Must Be Destroyed: The Rise and Fall of an Ancient Mediterranean Civilization*. London: Allen Lane.

———. 2017. "Vandal North Africa and the Fourth Punic War." *Classical Philology* 112 (3) : 384–410.

Millar, Fergus. 1968. "Local Cultures in the Roman Empire: Libyan, Punic and Latin in Roman Africa." *Journal of Roman Studies* 58 (1–2): 126–34.

———. 1983. "The Phoenician Cities: A Case-Study of Hellenisation." *Proceedings of the Cambridge Philological Society* 29: 55–71.

———. 1990. "The Roman *Coloniae* of the Near East: A Study of Cultural Relations." In *Roman Eastern Policy and Other Studies in Roman History: Proceedings of a Colloquium at Tvärminne, 2–3 October 1987*, edited by Heikki Solin and Mika Kajava, 7–58. Helsinki: Societas Scientiarum Fennica.

———. 1993. *The Roman Near East, 31 BC–AD 337*. Cambridge, MA: Harvard University Press.

Miller, Julie A. 1994. "M'zab Valley (Ghardaïa, Algeria)." In *International Dictionary of Historic Places. Volume 4: Middle East and Africa*, edited by Trudy Ring, Robert M. Salkin, and Sharon La Boda, 533–36. Chicago: Fitzroy Dearborn.

Miller, Margaret C. 1997. *Athens and Persia in the Fifth Century BC: A Study in Cultural Receptivity*. Cambridge: Cambridge University Press.

Mitchell, Lynette G. 2007. *Panhellenism and the Barbarian in Archaic and Classical Greece*. Swansea: Classical Press of Wales.

Montagu, Edward Wortley. 1759. *Reflections on the Rise and Fall of the Antient Republicks Adapted to the Present State of Great Britain*. London: A. Millar.

Mora Serrano, Bartolomé, and Gonzalo Cruz Andreotti, eds. 2012. *La etapa neopúnica en Hispania y el Mediterráneo centro occidental: Identidades compartidas*. Seville: Universidad de Sevilla.

Morestin, Henri. 1980. *Le temple B de Volubilis*. Paris: Éditions du Centre national de la recherche scientifique.

Moretti, Luigi. 1953. *Iscrizioni agonistiche greche*. Rome: A. Signorelli.

Morgan, John R. 2009. "The Emesan Connection: Philostratus and Heliodorus." In *Theios Sophistes: Essays on Flavius Philostratus' Vita Apollonii*, edited by Kristoffel Demoen and Danny Praet, 264–81. Leiden: Brill.

———. 2014. "Heliodorus the Hellene." In *Defining Greek Narrative*, edited by Douglas Cairns and Ruth Scodel, 260–76. Edinburgh: Edinburgh University Press.

Mørkholm, Otto. 1965. "The Municipal Coinages with Portrait of Antiochus IV of Syria." In *Congresso internazionale di numismatica, Roma 1961*, 2:63–67. Rome: Istituto italiano di numismatica.

Mørkholm, Otto. 1966. *Antiochus IV of Syria.* Copenhagen: Gyldendalske Boghandel.

Morris, Sarah P. 1992. *Daidalos and the Origins of Greek Art.* Princeton, NJ: Princeton University Press.

Morstadt, Bärbel. 2014. "Phoenician Sacred Places in the Mediterranean." In *Redefining the Sacred: Religious Architecture and Text in the Near East and Egypt 1000 BC–AD 300*, edited by Elizabeth Frood and Rubina Raja, 75–105. Turnhout: Brepols.

———. 2015. *Die Phönizier.* Darmstadt: Philipp von Zabern.

Mosca, Paul G. 2013. "The Tofet: A Place of Infant Sacrifice?" In *The Tophet in the Punic Mediterranean* [= *Studi epigrafici e linguistici* 29–30 (2012–13)], edited by Paolo Xella, 119–36. Verona: Essedue.

Moscati, Sabatino. 1963. "La questione fenicia." *Rendiconti della Accademia nazionale dei Lincei* 8 (18): 483–506.

———. 1965. "Una stele di Akziv." *Rendiconti dell' Accademia nazionale dei Lincei* 8 (20): 239–41.

———. 1966a. "Due stele di Mozia." *Rendiconti dell'Accademia nazionale dei Lincei* 8 (21): 198–99.

———. 1966b. *Il mondo dei fenici.* Milan: Saggiatore.

———. 1967. "Iconografie fenicie a Mozia." *Rivista degli Studi Orientali* 42 (2): 61–64.

———. 1972. *I fenici e Cartagine.* Turin: Unione tipografico-editrice torinese.

———. 1984. "Unde interrogati rustici nostri . . ." In *Studi in onore di Francesco Gabrieli nel suo ottantesimo compleanno*, edited by Renato Traini, 529–34. Rome: Università degli Studi di Roma "La Sapienza."

———. 1986. *Le stele di Sulcis: Caratteri e confronti.* Rome: Consiglio nazionale delle ricerche.

———. 1987. *L'arte della Sicilia punica.* Milan: Jaca Book.

———. 1988a. "Fenicio o punico o cartaginese." *Rivista di studi fenici* 16: 3–13.

———. 1988b. *The Phoenicians.* Milan: Bompiani.

———. 1990. *Sulle vie del passato: Cinquant'anni di studi, incontri, scoperte.* Milan: Jaca Book.

———. 1992a. *Chi furono i fenici: Identità storica e culturale di un popolo protagonista dell'antico mondo mediterraneo.* Turin: Societa editrice internazionale.

———. 1992b. *Il santuario dei bambini (tofet).* Rome: Libreria dello stato, Istituto poligrafico e Zecca dello stato.

———. 1992c. *Le stele puniche in Italia.* Rome: Libreria dello stato, Istituto poligrafico e Zecca dello stato.

———. 1993a. *Il tramonto di Cartagine: Scoperte archeologiche in Sardegna e nell'area mediterranea.* Turin: Società editrice internazionale.

———. 1993b. "Non è un tofet a Tiro." *Rivista di studi fenici* 21: 147–51.

———. 1993c. *Nuovi studi sull'identità fenicia* [= *Memorie dell' Accademia nazionale di Lincei ser, 9, 4 (1)*]. Rome: Accademia nazionale dei Lincei.

———. 1996. "Studi sulle stele di Sousse." *Rendiconti dell'Accademia nazionale dei Lincei* 9 (7): 247–81.

Moscati, Sabatino, and Maria Luisa Uberti. 1970. *Le stele puniche di Nora nel Museo nazionale di Cagliari.* Rome: Consiglio nazionale delle richerche.

———. 1981. *Scavi a Mozia: Le stele.* Rome: Consiglio nazionale delle richerche.

———. 1985. *Scavi al tofet di Tharros: I monumenti lapidei.* Rome: Consiglio nazionale delle richerche.

Movers, Franz Carl. 1841–56. *Die Phönizier.* Bonn: Eduard Weber.

Mufwene, Salikoko. 2003. "Language Endangerment: What Have Pride and Prestige Got to Do with It?" In *When Languages Collide: Perspectives on Language Conflict, Language Competition, and Language Coexistence*, edited by Brian D. Joseph, Johanna DeStefano, Neil G. Jacobs, and Ilse Lehiste, 324–45. Columbus: Ohio State University Press.

Mullin, Katherine. 2011. " 'Something in the Name of Araby': James Joyce and the Irish Bazaars." *Dublin James Joyce Journal* 4: 31–50.

Murray, Oswyn. 2000. "What Is Greek about the *Polis?*" In *Polis and Politics: Studies in Ancient Greek History, presented to Mogens Herman Hansen on His Sixtieth Birthday, August 20, 2000*, edited by Pernille Flensted-Jensen, Thomas Heine Nielsen, and Lene Rubenstein, 231–44. Copenhagen: Museum Tusculanum Press.

Musso, Luisa. 1996. "Nuovi ritrovamenti di scultura a Leptis Magna: Athena tipo Medici." In *Scritti di antichità in memoria di Sandro Stucchi: La Cirenaica, la Grecia e l'Oriente Mediterraneo*, edited by Lidiano Bachielli, 115–38. Rome: L'Erma di Bretschneider.

Na'aman, Nadav. 1994. "The Canaanites and Their Land: A Rejoinder." *Ugarit-Forschungen* 26: 397–418.

———. 1999. "Lebo-Hamath, Ṣubat-Hamath and the Northern Boundary of the Land of Canaan." *Ugarit-Forschungen* 31: 417–41.

Nelson, Richard D. 1997. *Joshua: A Commentary.* Louisville, KY: Westminster John Knox Press.

Niemeyer, Hans Georg. 2000. "The Early Phoenician City-States on the Mediterranean: Archaeological Elements for Their Description." In *A Comparative Study of Thirty City-State Cultures*, edited by Mogens Herman Hansen, 89–115. Copenhagen: Kongelige Danske Videnskabernes Selskab.

Ní Mheallaigh, Karen. 2012. "The 'Phoenician Letters' of Dictys of Crete and Dionysius Scytobrachion." *Cambridge Classical Journal* 58: 181–93.

Ní Mhunghaile, Lesa. 2009. "Introduction." In *Charlotte Brooke's Reliques of Irish Poetry*, edited by Lesa Ní Mhunghaile, xxi–xliv. Dublin: Irish Manuscripts Commission.

Nitschke, Jessica. 2011. " 'Hybrid' Art, Hellenism and the Study of Acculturation in the Hellenistic East: The Case of Umm El-'Amed in Phoenicia." In *From Pella to Gandhara: Hybridisation and Identity in the Art and Architecture of the Hellenistic East*, edited by Anna Kouremenos, Sujatha Chandrasekaran, and Roberto Rossi, 85–104. Oxford: Archaeopress.

———. 2013. "Interculturality in Image and Cult in the Hellenistic East: Tyrian Melqart Revisited." In *Shifting Social Imaginaries in the Hellenistic Period: Narrations, Practices, and Images*, edited by Eftychia Stavrianopoulou, 253–82. Leiden: Brill.

O'Flaherty, Roderic. 1685. *Ogygia: Seu, rerum hibernicarum chronologia, liber primus, in tres partes distinctus; Quibus accedit carmen chronographicum postremo catalogus regum in Britannia Scotorum, ex hiberniæ monumentis.* London: Typis R. Everingham, sumptibus Ben. Tooke, ad insigne Navis in Coemeterio D. Pauli.

———. 1793. *Ogygia, or, a Chronological Account of Irish Events.* Translated by James Hely. Dublin: W. McKenzie.

Oggiano, Ida. 2005. "Lo spazio sacro a Nora." In *Atti del V Congresso internazionale di studi fenici e punici*, edited by Antonella Spanò Giammellaro, 1029–44. Palermo: Università di Palermo, Facoltà di lettere e filosofia.

Oggiano, Ida. 2008. "Lo spazio fenicio rappresentato." In *Saturnia Tellus: Definizioni dello spazio consacrato in ambiente etrusco, italico, fenicio-punico, iberico e celtico; Atti del convegno internazionale svoltosi a Roma dal 10 al 12 novembre 2004*, edited by Xavier Dupré Raventós, Sergio Ribichini, and Stéphane Verger, 283–300. Rome: Consiglio nazionale delle richerche.

——. 2012. "Architectural Points to Ponder under the Porch of Amrit." *Rivista di studi fenici* 40 (2): 191–210.

——. 2015. "The Question of 'Plasticity' of Ethnic and Cultural Identity: The Case Study of Kharayeb." In *Cult and Ritual on the Levantine Coast and Its Impact on the Eastern Mediterranean Realm*, edited by Anne-Marie Maïla-Afeiche, 507–28. Beirut: Ministère de la culture, Direction générale des antiquités.

——. 2016. "A View from the West: The Relationship between Phoenicia and 'Colonial' Worlds in the Persian Period." In *Finding Myth and History in the Bible: Scholarship, Scholars and Errors*, edited by Łucasz Niesiolowski-Spanò, Chiara Peri, and Jim West, 147–80. Bristol, CT: Equinox.

O'Halloran, Clare. 1995. "An English Orientalist in Ireland: Charles Vallancey (1786–1812)." In *Forging in the Smithy: National Identity and Representation in Anglo-Irish Literary History*, edited by Joep Leerssen, Adriaan van der Veel, and Bart Westerweel, 161–74. Amsterdam: Rodopi.

Ohana, David. 2012. *The Origins of Israeli Mythology: Neither Canaanites nor Crusaders*. New York: Cambridge University Press.

Omri, Mohamed-Saleh. 2000. "Memory and Representation in the Novels of Fawzi Mellah." *International Journal of Francophone Studies* 3 (1): 33–41.

Orsingher, Adriano. Forthcoming. "Ritualized Faces: The Masks of the Phoenicians." In *Proceedings of the International Workshop 'The Physicality of the Other: Masks as a Means of Encounter,' 9–11 November 2015, Leipzig University*. Tübingen: Mohr Siebeck.

Osborne, Robin. 1998. "Early Greek Colonization? The nature of Greek settlement in the West." In *Archaic Greece: New Approaches and New Evidence*, edited by Nick Fisher and Hans van Wees, 251–69. London: Duckworth and Classical Press of Wales.

——. 2011. *The History Written on the Classical Greek Body*. Cambridge: Cambridge University Press.

——. 2012a. "Cultures as Languages and Languages as Cultures." In *Multilingualism in the Graeco-Roman Worlds*, edited by Alex Mullen and Patrick James, 317–34. Cambridge: Cambridge University Press.

——. 2012b. "Landscape, Ethnicity and the Polis." In *Landscape, Ethnicity and Identity in the Archaic Mediterranean Area*, edited by Gabriele Cifani and Simon Stoddart, 24–31. Oxford: Oxbow.

Owenson, Sydney (Lady Morgan). (1806) 1999. *The Wild Irish Girl: A National Tale*. Reprint, Oxford: Oxford University Press.

Pallottino, Massimo, et al. 1964. "Scavi nel santuario etrusco di Pyrgi: Relazione preliminare della settima campagna, 1964, e scoperta di tre lamini d'oro inscrite in etrusco e in punico." *Archeologia classica* 16: 114–15.

Palmer, Robert E. A. 1997. *Rome and Carthage at Peace.* Stuttgart: Franz Steiner.

Papadopoulos, John. 2005. "Inventing the Minoans: Archaeology, Modernity and the Quest for European Identity." *Journal of Mediterranean Archaeology* 18 (1): 87–149.

Papi, Emanuele. 2014. "Punic Mauretania?" In *The Punic Mediterranean: Identities and Identification from Phoenician Settlement to Roman Rule,* edited by Josephine Crawley Quinn and Nicholas C. Vella, 202–18. Cambridge: Cambridge University Press.

Parker, Robert. 1996. *Athenian Religion: A History.* Oxford: Clarendon Press.

Parry, Graham. 1995. *The Trophies of Time: English Antiquarians of the Seventeenth Century.* Oxford: Oxford University Press.

Parsons, Lawrence. 1795. *Observations on the Bequest of Henry Flood, Esq. to Trinity College, Dublin with a Defence of the Ancient History of Ireland.* Dublin: Bonham.

Pastor Borgoñon, Helena. 1992. "Die Phönizier: Eine Begriffsgeschichtliche Untersuchung." *Hamburger Beiträge zur Archäologie* 15–17 (1988–90): 37–142.

Pedrazzi, Tatiana. 2012. "Fingere l'identità fenicia: Confini e cultura materiale in Oriente." *Rivista di studi fenici* 40 (2): 137–57.

Perrot, Georges, and Charles Chipiez. 1885a. *Histoire de l'art dans l'antiquité.* Vol. 3, *Phénicie—Cypre.* Paris: Hachette.

——. 1885b. *History of Art in Phœnicia and Its Dependencies.* Translated by Walter Armstrong. London: Chapman and Hall.

Petrie, George. 1845. *The Ecclesiastical Architecture of Ireland, Anterior to the Anglo-Norman Invasion: Comprising an Essay on the Origin and Uses of the Round Towers of Ireland, Which Obtained the Gold Medal and Prize of the Royal Irish Academy.* Dublin: Royal Irish Academy.

Picard, Gilbert-Charles. 1974. "Une survivance du droit public punique en Afrique romaine: Les cités suffétales." In *I diritti locali nelle province romane,* 125–33. Rome: Accademia nazionale dei Lincei.

Pietschmann, Richard. 1889. *Geschichte der Phönizier.* Berlin: G. Grote.

Pike, Kenneth L. 1967. *Language in Relation to a Unified Theory of the Structure of Human Behavior.* 2nd ed. The Hague: Mouton.

Pittau, Massimo. 2000. *Tabula cortonensis, lamine di Pirgi e altri testi etruschi: Tradotti e commentati.* Sassari: Editrice democratica sarda.

Płonka, Arkadiusz. 2006. "Le nationalisme linguistique au Liban autour de Sa'id 'Aql et l'idée de langue libanaise dans la revue "Lebnaan" en nouvel alphabet." *Arabica* 53 (4): 423–71.

Porten, Bezalel, and Ada Yardeni. 1993. *Textbook of Aramaic Documents from Ancient Egypt.* Vol. 3, *Literature, Accounts, Lists.* Winona Lake, IN: Eisenbrauns.

Prag, Jonathan R. W. 2006. "Poenus plane est—but Who Were the 'Punickes'?" *Papers of the British School at Rome* 74: 1–37.

——. 2010. "Tyrannizing Sicily: The Despots Who Cried 'Carthage!'" In *Private and Public Lies: The Discourse of Despotism and Deceit in the Graeco-Roman World,* edited by Andrew Turner, Kim Ong Chong-Gossard, and Frederik Vervaet, 51–71. Leiden: Brill.

——. 2011. "Siculo-Punic Coinage and Siculo-Punic Interactions." In *Meetings between Cultures in the Ancient Mediterranean: Proceedings of the 17th International Congress of Classical Archaeology, Rome 22–26 Sept. 2008,* edited by M. Dalla Riva and H. Di Giuseppe. Rome: Bollettino di archeologia online. http://www.bollettinodiarcheologiaonline.beniculturali.it/documenti/generale/2_PRAG.pdf.

Prag, Jonathan R. W. 2013. "Sicilian Identity in the Hellenistic and Roman Periods: Epigraphic Considerations." In *Epigraphical Approaches to the Post-classical Polis: Fourth Century BC to Second Century AD*, edited by Paraskevi Martzavou and Nikolaos Papazarkadas, 37–53. Oxford: Oxford University Press.

———. 2014. "Phoinix and Poenus: Usage in Antiquity." In *The Punic Mediterranean: Identities and Identification from Phoenician Settlement to Roman Rule*, edited by Josephine Crawley Quinn and Nicholas C. Vella, 11–23. Cambridge: Cambridge University Press.

Pritchard, James B. 1982. "The Tanit Inscription from Sarepta." In *Phönizier im Westen*, edited by Hans Georg Niemeyer, 83–92. Mainz am Rhein: Philipp von Zabern.

Quinn, Josephine Crawley. 2003. "Roman Africa?" In *Romanization? Digressus Supplement 1*, edited by A. Merryweather and Jonathan R. W. Prag. https://ora.ox.ac.uk/objects/uuid:3531b508–6559–45a8–802b-333f34991990.

———. 2004. "The Role of the Settlement of 146 in the Provincialization of Africa." In *L'Africa romana: Atti del XV convegno di studio, Tozeur, 11–15 dicembre 2002*, edited by Mustapha Khanoussi, Paola Ruggieri, and Cinzia Vismara, 1593–601. Rome: Carrocci.

———. 2010. "The Reinvention of Lepcis." In sess. ed., Alicia Jiménez, *Colonising a Colonised Territory: Settlements with Punic Roots in Roman Times*, in *Meetings between Cultures in the Ancient Mediterranean: Proceedings of the 17th International Congress of Classical Archaeology, Rome 22–26 Sept. 2008*, edited by M. Dalla Riva and H. di Giuseppe. Rome: Bolletino di archeologia Online. http://www.bollettinodiarcheologiaonline.beniculturali.it/documenti/generale/6_Quinn_paper.pdf.

———. 2011a. "The Cultures of the Tophet: Identification and Identity in the Phoenician Diaspora." In *Cultural Identity in the Ancient Mediterranean*, edited by Erich S. Gruen, 388–413. Los Angeles: Getty Research Institute.

———. 2011b. "The Syrtes between East and West." In *Money, Trade and Trade Routes in Pre-Islamic North Africa*, edited by Amelia Dowler and Elizabeth R. Galvin, 11–20. London: British Museum Press.

———. 2013a. "Monumental Power: 'Numidian Royal Architecture' in Context." In *The Hellenistic West: Rethinking the Ancient Mediterranean*, edited by Jonathan R. W. Prag and Josephine Crawley Quinn, 179–215. Cambridge: Cambridge University Press.

———. 2013b. "Tophets in the 'Punic World.'" In *The "Tophet" in the Phoenician Mediterranean* [= *Studi epigrafici e linguistici* 29–30 (2012–13)], edited by Paolo Xella, 23–48. Verona: Essedue.

———. 2014. "A Carthaginian Perspective on the Altars of the Philaeni." In *The Punic Mediterranean: Identities and Identification from Phoenician Settlement to Roman Rule*, edited by Josephine Crawley Quinn and Nicholas C. Vella, 169–79. Cambridge: Cambridge University Press.

Quinn, Josephine Crawley, Neil McLynn, Robert M. Kerr, and Daniel Hadas. 2014. "Augustine's Canaanites." *Papers of the British School at Rome* 82: 175–97.

Quinn, Josephine Crawley, and Nicholas C. Vella. 2014a. "Introduction." In *The Punic Mediterranean: Identities and Identification from Phoenician Settlement to Roman Rule*, edited by Josephine Crawley Quinn and Nicholas C. Vella, 1–8. Cambridge: Cambridge University Press.

———. 2014b. *The Punic Mediterranean: Identities and Identification from Phoenician Settlement to Roman Rule.* Cambridge: Cambridge University Press.

Quinn, Josephine Crawley, and Andrew Wilson. 2013. "Capitolia." *Journal of Roman Studies* 103: 117–73.

Raaflaub, Kurt A. 2004. "Zwischen Ost und West: Phönizische Einflüsse auf die Griechische Polisbildung?" In *Griechische Archaik: Interne Entwicklungen—Externe Impulse,* edited by Robert Rollinger and Christopher Ulf, 271–89. Berlin: Akademie Verlag.

Radner, Karen. 2006. "Provinz. C. Assyrien." In *Reallexikon der Assyriologie und Vorderasiatischen Archäologie,* edited by Michael P. Streck, 42–68. Berlin: de Gruyter.

Rainey, Anson F. 1996. "Who Is a Canaanite? A Review of the Textual Evidence." *Bulletin of the American Schools of Oriental Research* 304: 1–15.

Ranger, Terence. 1983. "The Invention of Tradition in Colonial Africa." In *The Invention of Tradition,* edited by Eric Hobsbawm and Terence Ranger, 211–62. Cambridge: Cambridge University Press.

Rawlinson, George. 1869. *Manual of Ancient History, from the Earliest Times to the Fall of the Western Empire, Comprising the History of Chaldaea, Assyria, Media, Babylonia, Lydia, Phoenicia, Syria, Judaea, Egypt, Carthage, Persia, Greece, Macedonia, Rome, and Parthia.* Oxford: Clarendon Press.

———. 1889. *History of Phoenicia.* London: Longmans, Green, and Co.

———. 2005. *Phoenicia: History of a Civilization.* London: I. B. Tauris.

Remotti, Francesco. 1996. *Contro l'identità.* Rome: Laterza.

Renan, Ernest. 1864. *Mission de Phénicie.* Paris: Imprimerie impériale.

———. 1947. *Œuvres complètes de Ernest Renan.* Edited by Henriette Psichari. Paris: Calmann-Lévy.

Rendsburg, Gary A. 2003a. "A Comprehensive Guide to Israelian Hebrew: Grammar and Lexicon." *Orient* 38: 5–35.

———. 2003b. "Semitic Languages (with Special Reference to the Levant)." In *Near Eastern Archaeology: A Reader,* edited by S. Richard, 71–73. Winona Lake, IN: Eisenbrauns.

Renfrew, Colin. 1986. "Introduction: Peer Polity Interaction and Socio-Political Change." In *Peer Polity Interaction and Socio-Political Change,* edited by Colin Renfrew and John F. Cherry, 1–18. Cambridge: Cambridge University Press.

———. 1987. *Archaeology and Language: The Puzzle of Indo-European Origins.* London: Jonathan Cape.

Rey-Coquais, Jean-Paul. 1987. "Une double dédicace de Lepcis Magna à Tyr." In *L'Africa romana: Atti del IV convegno di studio, Sassari, 12–14 dicembre 1986,* edited by Attilio Mastino, 597–602. Sassari: Dipartimento di storia—Università degli studi di Sassari.

———. 1989. "Apport d'inscriptions inédites de Syrie et de Phénicie aux listes de divinités ou à la prosopographie de l'Égypte hellénistique ou romaines." In *Egitto e storia antica dall'ellenismo all'età araba: Bilancio di un confronto,* edited by Lucia Criscuolo and Giovanna Geraci, 609–19. Bologna: Cooperativa libraria universitaria editrice Bologna.

Rhodes, Peter J., and Robin Osborne. 2003. *Greek Historical Inscriptions, 404–323 BC.* Oxford: Oxford University Press.

Ribichini, Sergio. 1985. *Poenus advena: Gli dei fenici e l'interpretazione classica.* Rome: Consiglio nazionale delle ricerche.

Ricciardi, Maria. 2005. "Il tempio di Milk'ashtart Ercole." In *I tre templi del lato nord-ovest del Foro Vecchio a Leptis Magna*, edited by Antonino Di Vita and Monica Livadiotti, 309–93. Rome: L'Erma di Bretschneider.

Rives, James B. 1994. "Tertullian on Child Sacrifice." *Museum Helveticum* 51 (1): 54–63.

Robert, Louis. 1973. "Sur le décret des Poseidoniastes de Bérytos." In *Études déliennes*, 486–89. Paris: De Boccard.

Roebuck, Thomas, and Laurie Maguire. 2010. "*Pericles* and the Language of National Origins." In *This England, That Shakespeare*, edited by Willy Maley and Margaret Tudeau-Clayton, 23–48. Farnham: Ashgate.

Röllig, Wolfgang. 1972. "Alte und Neue Phönizische Inschrifte aus dem Ägäischen Raum." *Neue Ephemeris für Semitische Epigraphik* 1: 1–8.

——. 1983. "On the Origin of the Phoenicians." *Berytus* 31: 79–93.

——. 1995. "Onomastic and Palaeographic Considerations on Early Phoenician Arrow-Heads." In *Actes du IIIe Congrès international des études phéniciennes et puniques, Tunis 11–16 novembre 1991*, edited by M'hamed Hassine Fantar and Mansour Ghaki, 348–55. Tunis: Institut national du patrimoine.

——. 2011. "Phoenician and Punic." In *The Semitic Languages: An International Handbook*, edited by Stefan Weninger, Geoffrey Khan, Michael P. Streck, and Janet C. E. Watson, 472–79. Berlin: De Gruyter Mouton.

Rollin, Charles. 1730–38. *Histoire ancienne des égyptiens, des carthaginois, des assyriens, des babyloniens, des medes et des perses, des macédoniens, des grecs.* Paris: Chez Jacques Estienne.

Romeo, Ilaria. 2010. "Europa's Sons: Roman Perceptions of Cretan Identity." In *Local Knowledge and Microidentities in the Imperial Greek World*, edited by Tim Whitmarsh, 69–85. Cambridge: Cambridge University Press.

Roppa, Andrea. 2014. "Identifying Punic Sardinia: Local Communities and Cultural Identities." In *The Punic Mediterranean: Identities and Identification from Phoenician Settlement to Roman Rule*, edited by Josephine Crawley Quinn and Nicholas C. Vella, 257–81. Cambridge: Cambridge University Press.

Rouse, Roger. 1995. "Questions of Identity: Personhood and Collectivity in Transnational Migration to the United States." *Critique of Anthropology* 15 (4): 351–80.

Rouvier, Jules. 1904. "Numismatique des villes de la Phénicie: Tyr." *Journal international d'archéologie numismatique* 7: 65–108.

Ruby, Pascal. 2006. "Peuples, fictions? Ethnicité, identité ethnique et sociétés anciennes." *Revue des études anciennes* 108 (1): 25–60.

Ruddick, Andrea. 2013. *English Identity and Political Culture in the Fourteenth Century.* Cambridge: Cambridge University Press.

Ruiu, Pascuale Francesco. 2000. "Per una rilettura del motivo a losanga in ambito votivo fenicio-punico." In *Actas del IV Congreso internacional de estudios fenicios y púnicos*, 669–73. Cádiz: Universidad de Cádiz.

Ruiz Cabrero, Luis Alberto, and Victoria Peña Romo. 2010. "La pervivencia de los tofet como elemento de cohesión territorial tras la caída de Cartago." In *Carthage et les autochtones de son empire du temps de Zama: Hommage à Mhamed Hassine Fantar; Colloque international organisé à Siliana et Tunis du 10 au 13 mars 2004*, edited by Ahmed Ferjaoui, 459–70. Tunis: Institut national du patrimoine.

Sadan, Mandy. 2010. Review of *The Art of Not Being Governed: An Anarchist History of Upland Southeast Asia* by James C. Scott. *Reviews in History*, April 30, 2010: http://www.history.ac.uk/reviews/review/903.

Sader, Hélène. 1991. "Phoenician Stelae from Tyre." *Berytus* 39: 101–26.

——. 1995. "Nécropoles et tombes phéniciennes du Liban." *Cuadernos de arqueología mediterránea* 1: 15–33.

——. 2005. *Iron Age Funerary Stelae from Lebanon*. Barcelona: Edicions Bellaterra.

——. 2009. "Beirut and Tell El-Burak: New Evidence on Phoenician Town Planning and Architecture in the Homeland." In *Phönizisches und Punisches Städtewesen*, edited by Sophie Helas and Dirce Marzoli, 55–67. Mainz am Rhein: Philipp von Zabern.

——. 2015. "Funerary Practices in Iron Age Lebanon." *Archaeology and History in the Lebanon* 40–41: 100–117.

Said, Edward W. 1978. *Orientalism*. London: Routledge and Kegan Paul.

Saidi, Habib. 2008. "When the Past Poses beside the Present: Aestheticising Politics and Nationalising Modernity in a Postcolonial Time." *Journal of Tourism and Cultural Change* 6 (2): 101–19.

Salameh, Franck. 2010. *Language, Memory, and Identity in the Middle East: The Case for Lebanon*. Lanham, MD: Lexington Books.

Salibi, Kamal S. 1959. *Maronite Historians of Mediæval Lebanon*. Beirut: American University of Beirut.

——. 1988. *A House of Many Mansions: The History of Lebanon Reconsidered*. London: Tauris.

Salles, Jean-François. 1993. "Les phéniciens de la mer Erythrée." *Arabian Archaeology and Epigraphy* 4 (3): 170–209.

Sammes, Aylett. 1676. *Britannia antiqua illustrata, or, the Antiquities of Ancient Britain Derived from the Phœnicians, wherein the Original Trade of This Island Is Discovered, the Names of Places, Offices, Dignities, as Likewise the Idolatry, Language and Customs of the Primitive Inhabitants Are Clearly Demonstrated from That Nation, Many Old Monuments Illustrated, and the Commerce with That People, as Well as the Greeks, Plainly Set Forth and Collected out of Approved Greek and Latin Authors: Together with a Chronological History of This Kingdom, from the First Traditional Beginning, until the Year of Our Lord 800, When the Name of Britain Was Changed into England; Faithfully Collected out of the Best Authors, and Disposed in a Better Method Than Hitherto Hath Been Done; with the Antiquities of the Saxons, as Well as Phoenicians, Greeks, and Romans. The First Volume*. London: Tho. Roycroft.

Samuels, Kathryn Lafrenz. 2008. "Value and Significance in Archaeology." *Archaeological Dialogues* 15 (1): 71–97.

Sawaya, Ziad. 2004. "Le monnayage municipal séleucide de Bérytos (169/8–114/3 Av. J.-C.)." *Numismatic Chronicle* 164: 109–46.

Scales, Len. 2007. "Bread, Cheese and Genocide: Imagining the Destruction of Peoples in Medieval Western Europe." *History* 92 (307): 284–300.

Schmidt, H. D. 1953. "The Idea and Slogan of 'Perfidious Albion.'" *Journal of the History of Ideas* 14 (4): 604–16.

Schmidt-Dounas, Barbara. 1985. *Der Lykische Sarkophag aus Sidon*. Tübingen: E. Wasmuth.

Schmitz, Philip C. 2007. "Procopius' Phoenician Inscriptions: Never Lost, Not Found." *Palestine Exploration Quarterly* 139 (2): 99–104.

Schreiber, Nicola. 2003. *The Cypro-Phoenician Pottery of the Iron Age*. Leiden: Brill.

Schwyzer, Philip. 2004. *Literature, Nationalism, and Memory in Early Modern England and Wales*. Cambridge: Cambridge University Press.

Scott, James C. 2009. *The Art of Not Being Governed: An Anarchist History of Upland Southeast Asia*. New Haven, CT: Yale University Press.

Scott, Jonathan. 2011. *When the Waves Ruled Britannia: Geography and Political Identities, 1500–1800*. Cambridge: Cambridge University Press.

Sear, Frank. 2006. *Roman Theatres: An Architectural Study*. Oxford: Oxford University Press.

Seeden, Helga. 1991. "A Tophet in Tyre?" *Berytus* 39: 39–82.

Segert, Stansilaw. 1976. *A Grammar of Phoenician and Punic*. Münich: Beck.

Sen, Amartya. 2006. *Identity and Violence: The Illusion of Destiny*. New York: W. W. Norton; London: Allen Lane.

Sennequier, Geneviève, and Cécile Colonna. 2003. *L'Algerie au temps des royaumes numides: Ve siècle avant J-C–1 siècle après J-C*. Paris: Somogy.

Shalev, Zur. 2012. *Sacred Words and Worlds: Geography, Religion, and Scholarship, 1550–1700*. Leiden: Brill.

Sharon, Ilan. 1987. "Phoenician and Greek Ashlar Construction Techniques at Tel Dor, Israel." *Bulletin of the American Schools of Oriental Research* 267: 21–42.

Shavit, Yaakov. 1984. "Hebrews and Phoenicians: An Ancient Historical Image and Its Usage." *Studies in Zionism* 5 (2): 157–80.

——. 1987. *The New Hebrew Nation: A Study in Israeli Heresy and Fantasy*. London: Frank Cass.

——. 1988. "The Mediterranean World and 'Mediterraneanism': The Origins, Meaning, and Application of a Geo-cultural Notion in Israel." *Mediterranean Historical Review* 3 (2): 96–117.

Shaw, Brent D. 2016. "Lambs of God: An End of Human Sacrifice." *Journal of Roman Archaeology* 29: 259–91.

Shennan, Stephen. 1989. *Archaeological Approaches to Cultural Identity*. London: Unwin Hyman.

Shepherd, Gillian. 1995. "The Pride of Most Colonials: Burial and Religion in the Sicilian Colonies." *Acta Hyperborea* 6: 51–82.

Shipley, D. Graham S. 2011. *Pseudo-Skylax's Periplous: The Circumnavigation of the Inhabited World; Text, Translation and Commentary*. Exeter: Bristol Phoenix Press.

Smith, Anthony D. 1986. *The Ethnic Origins of Nations*. Oxford: Basil Blackwell.

Smith, Patricia, G. Avishai, Joseph A. Greene, and Lawrence E. Stager. 2011. "Aging Cremated Infants: The Problem of Sacrifice at the Tophet of Carthage." *Antiquity* 85 (329): 859–74.

Sommer, Michael. 2008. *Die Phönizier: Geschichte und Kultur*. Münich: Beck.

——. 2010. "Shaping Mediterranean Economy and Trade: Phoenician Cultural Identities in the Iron Age." In *Material Culture and Social Identities in the Ancient World*, edited by Shelley Hales and Tamar Hodos, 114–37. Cambridge: Cambridge University Press.

Southwood, Katherine. 2012. *Ethnicity and the Mixed Marriage Crisis in Ezra 9–10: An Anthropological Approach*. Oxford: Oxford University Press.

Spanò Giammellaro, Antonella. 2004. "Il vetro preromano della Sicilia nella prospettiva mediterranea." In *Glassway: Il vetro: Fragilità attraverso il tempo*, edited by Beatrice Basile, Teresa Carreras Rossell, Caterina Greco, and Antonella Spanò Giammellaro, 25–40. Ragusa: Filippo Angelica editore.

Spanu, Pier Giorgio, and Raimondo Zucca. 2011. "Da Τάρραι Πόλις al portus sancti Marci: Storia e archeologia di una città portuale dall'antichità al medioevo." In *Tharros Felix 4*, edited by Attilio Mastino, Pier Giorgio Spanu, Alessandro Usai, and Raimondo Zucca, 15–103. Rome: Carocci.

Speiser, Ephraim A. 1936. "The Name Phoinikes." *Language* 12 (2): 121–26.

Spivak, Gayatri Chakravorty. 1988. "Can the Subaltern Speak?" In *Marxism and the Interpretation of Culture*, edited by Cary Nelson and Lawrence Grossberg, 271–313. Urbana: University of Illinois Press.

Stager, Jennifer M. S. 2005. " 'Let No One Wonder at This Image': A Phoenician Funerary Stele in Athens." *Hesperia* 74: 427–49.

Stager, Lawrence E. 1980. "The Rite of Child Sacrifice at Carthage." In *New Light on Ancient Carthage*, edited by John G. Pedley, 1–11. Ann Arbor: University of Michigan Press.

Stager, Lawrence E., and Samuel R. Wolff. 1984. "Child Sacrifice at Carthage: Religious Rite or Population Control?" *Biblical Archaeology Review* 10 (1): 30–51.

Stavrakopoulou, Francesca. 2004. *King Manasseh and Child Sacrifice: Biblical Distortions of Historical Realities*. Berlin: Walter de Gruyter.

Steele, Philippa M. 2013. *A Linguistic History of Ancient Cyprus: The Non-Greek Languages and Their Relations with Greek, c.1600–300 BC*. Cambridge: Cambridge University Press.

Stephens, Susan A., and John J. Winkler. 1995. *Ancient Greek Novels: The Fragments*. Princeton, NJ: Princeton University Press.

Stern, Ephraim. 1998. "New Phoenician Elements in the Architecture of Tel Dor, Israel." In *Hesed Ve-Emet: Studies in Honour of Ernest S. Frerichs*, edited by Jodi Magness and Seymour Gitin, 373–88. Atlanta, GA: Scholars' Press.

——. 2010. *Excavations at Dor: Figurines, Cult Objects and Amulets; 1980–2000 Seasons*. Jerusalem: Israel Exploration Society and Institute of Archaeology, Hebrew University of Jerusalem.

Stern, Karen B. 2007. "The Marzeah of the East and the Collegia of the West: Inscriptions, Associations and Cultural Exchange in the Eastern and Western Mediterranean." In *Acta XII Congressus internationalis epigraphiae graecae et latinae: University of Barcelona, Barcelona, Spain, September 2002*, edited by Marc Mayer i Olivé, Giulia Baratta, and Alejandra Guzmán Almagro, 1387–404. Barcelona: University of Barcelona.

Stewart, Andrew F. 1993. *Faces of Power: Alexander's Image and Hellenistic Politics*. Berkeley: University of California Press.

Stewart, Andrew F., and M. Korres. 2004. *Attalos, Athens, and the Akropolis: The Pergamene "Little Barbarians" and Their Roman and Renaissance Legacy*. Cambridge: Cambridge University Press.

Stewart, Peter. 2008. "Baetyls as Statues? Cult Images in the Roman Near East." In *The Sculptural Environment of the Roman Near East: Reflections on Culture, Ideology, and Power*, edited by Yaron Eliav, Elise Friedland, and Sharon Herbert, 297–314. Leuven: Peeters.

Stone, Christopher Reed. 2008. *Popular Culture and Nationalism in Lebanon: The Fairouz and Rahbani Nation*. London: Routledge.

Stucky, Rolf. 1984. *Tribune d'Echmoun: Ein Griechischer Reliefzyklus des 4. Jahrhunderts v. Chr. in Sidon*. Basel: Vereinigung der Freunde antiker Kunst.

Stucky, Rolf. 1993. *Die Skulpturen aus dem Eschmun-Heiligtum bei Sidon: Griechische, Römische, Kyprische und Phönizische Statuen und Reliefs vom 6. Jahrhundert vor Chr. bis Zum 3. Jahrhundert nach Chr.* Basel: Vereinigung der Freunde Antiker Kunst.

Stucky, Rolf, Sigmund Stucky, Antonio Loprieno, Hans-Peter Mathys, and Rudolf Wachter. 2005. *Das Eschmun-Heiligtum von Sidon: Architektur und Inschriften.* Basel: Vereinigung der Freunde Antiker Kunst.

Svenbro, Jesper, and John Scheid. 1985. "Byrsa: La ruse d'Élissa et la fondation de Carthage." *Annales* 40 (2): 328–42.

Swain, Simon. 1996. *Hellenism and Empire: Language, Classicism and Power in the Greek World AD 50–250.* Oxford: Clarendon Press.

Sznycer, Maurice. 1975. "L''Assemblée du peuple' dans les cités puniques d'après les témoignages épigraphiques." *Semitica* 25: 47–68.

Taborelli, Luigi. 1992. *L'area sacra di Ras Almunfakh presso Sabratha.* Rome: Consiglio nazionale delle ricerche.

Tahan, Lina Gebrail. 2005. "Redefining the Lebanese Past." *Museum International* 57 (3): 86–94.

Tammuz, Oded. 2001. "Canaan—A Land without Limits." *Ugarit-Forschungen* 33: 501–44.

Taylor, Charles. 1989. *Sources of the Self: The Making of the Modern Identity.* Cambridge, MA: Harvard University Press.

Terrell, John E. 2001. "Ethnolinguistic Groups, Language Boundaries, and Cultural History: A Sociolinguistic Model." In *Archaeology, Language, and History: Essays on Culture and Identity*, edited by John E. Terrell, 199–221. Westport, CT: Bergin and Garvey.

Thacker, Thomas W., and Richard P. Wright. 1955. "A New Interpretation of the Phoenician Graffito from Holt, Denbighshire." *Iraq* 17 (1): 90–92.

Thomas, Rosalind. 1989. *Oral Tradition and Written Record in Classical Athens.* Cambridge: Cambridge University Press.

———. 1992. *Literacy and Orality in Ancient Greece.* Cambridge: Cambridge University Press.

———. 2001. "Ethnicity, Genealogy, and Hellenism in Herodotus and Fifth-Century Greece." In *Ancient Perceptions of Greek Ethnicity*, edited by Irad Malkin, 213–33. Cambridge, MA: Harvard University Press.

Thompson, Dorothy J. 2001. "Hellenistic Hellenes: The Case of Ptolemaic Egypt." In *Ancient Perceptions of Greek Ethnicity*, edited by Irad Malkin, 301–22. Cambridge, MA: Harvard University Press.

Thompson, Larry V. 1971. "Lebensborn and the Eugenics Policy of the Reichsführer-SS." *Central European History* 4 (1): 54–77.

Tore, G. 1995. "L'art: Sarcophages, relief, stèles. " In *La civilisation phénicienne et punique: Manuel de recherche*, edited by Véronique Krings, 471–93. Leiden: Brill.

Traboulsi, Fawwaz. 2007. *A History of Modern Lebanon.* London: Pluto.

Tréheux, Jacques. 1992. *Les étrangers, à l'exclusion des athéniens de la clérouchie et des romains.* Paris: De Boccard.

Tribulato, Olga. 2013. "Phoenician Lions: The Funerary Stele of the Phoenician Shem/Antipatros." *Hesperia* 82 (3): 459–86.

Tronchetti, Carlo. 1990. *Cagliari fenicia e punica.* Sassari: Chiarella.

Tsagalis, Christos. 2008. *Inscribing Sorrow: Fourth-Century Attic Funerary Epigrams*. Berlin: Walter De Gruyter.

Tsirkin, Juri B. 2001. "Canaan. Phoenica. Sidon." *Aula orientalis: Revista de estudios del Próximo Oriente antiguo* 19 (2): 271–79.

Tubb, Jonathan N. 1998. *Canaanites*. London: British Museum Press.

Tuck, Richard. 1989. *Hobbes*. Oxford: Oxford University Press.

Twyne, John. 1590. *De rebus Albionicis, Britannicis atque Anglicis, commentariorum libri duo*. London: Edm. Bollifantus, pro Richardo Watkins.

Tzavellas-Bonnet, Corinne. 1983. "Phoinix Πρῶτος Εὑρετής." *Études classiques* 51 (1): 3–11.

Tzoroddu, Mikkelj. 2010. *I fenici non sono mai esistiti*. Fiumicino: Zoroddu.

Usher, Stephen. 1993. "Isocrates: *Paideia*, Kingship and the Barbarians." In *The Birth of European Identity: The Europe-Asia Contrast in Greek Thought 490–322 B.C.*, edited by H. Akbar Khan, 131–45. Nottingham: University of Nottingham.

Vail, Leroy. 1989. *The Creation of Tribalism in Southern Africa*. Berkeley, CA: University of California Press.

Vallancey, Charles. 1772. *An Essay on the Antiquity of the Irish Language: Being a Collation of the Irish with the Punic Language; With a Preface Proving Ireland to Be the Thule of the Ancients; Addressed to the Literati of Europe; To Which Is Added, a Correction of the Mistakes of Mr. Lhwyd in Reading the Ancient Irish Manuscript Lives of the Patriarchs; Also, the Mistakes Committed by Mr. Baretti in His Collation of the Irish with the Biscayan Language (Quoted in His Late Publications) Exposed and Corrected*. Dublin: S. Powell.

——. 1773. *A Grammar of the Iberno-Celtic, or Irish Language*. Dublin: R. Marchbank, for G. Faulkner, T. Ewing, and R. Moncrieffe.

——. 1786. *A Vindication of the Ancient History of Ireland*. Dublin: Luke White.

Van Beek, Gus, and Ora Van Beek. 1981. "Canaanite-Phoenician Architecture: The Development and Distribution of Two Styles." *Eretz Israel* 15: 70–77.

Vance, Norman. 1981. "Celts, Carthaginians and Constitutions: Anglo-Irish Literary Relations, 1781–1820." *Irish Historical Studies* 22 (87): 216–38.

——. 2000. "Imperial Rome and Britain's Language of Empire 1600–1837." *History of European Ideas* 26 (3–4): 211–24.

Vandersleyen, C. L. 1987. "L'étymologie de Phoïnix, 'Phénicien.'" In *Phoenicia and the East Mediterranean in the First Millennium B.C.*, edited by Edward Lipiński, 19–22. Leuven: Peeters.

Van der Spek, Bert. 2009. "Multi-ethnicity and Ethnic Segregation in Hellenistic Babylon." In *Ethnic Constructs in Antiquity*, edited by Ton Derks and Nico Roymans, 101–15. Amsterdam: Amsterdam University Press.

van Dommelen, Peter. 1998a. *On Colonial Grounds: A Comparative Study of Colonialism and Rural Settlement in First Millennium BC West Central Sardinia*. Leiden: Rijksuniversiteit te Leiden.

——. 1998b. "Punic Persistence: Colonialism and Cultural Identities in Roman Sardinia." In *Cultural Identity in the Roman Empire*, edited by Ray Laurence and Joanne Berry, 25–48. London: Routledge.

——. 2001. "Cultural Imaginings. Punic Tradition and Local Identity in Roman Republican Sardinia." In *Italy and the West: Comparative Issues in Romanization*, edited by Simon Keay and Nicola Terrenato, 68–84. Oxford: Oxbow.

van Dommelen, Peter. 2005. "Urban Foundations? Colonial Settlement and Urbanization in the Western Mediterranean." In *Mediterranean Urbanization 800–600 BC*, edited by Robin Osborne and Barry Cunliffe, 143–67. Oxford: Oxford University Press.

——. 2007. "Beyond Resistance: Roman Power and Local Traditions in Punic Sardinia." In *Articulating Local Cultures: Power and Identity under the Expanding Roman Republic*, edited by Peter Van Dommelen and Nicola Terrenato, 55–69. Portsmouth, RI: Journal of Roman Archaeology.

——. 2014. "Punic Identities and Modern Perceptions in the Western Mediterranean." In *The Punic Mediterranean: Identities and Identification from Phoenician Settlement to Roman Rule*, edited by Josephine Crawley Quinn and Nicholas C. Vella, 42–57. Cambridge: Cambridge University Press.

van Dommelen, Peter, and Carlos Gómez Bellard. 2008a. "Introduction." In *Rural Landscapes of the Punic World*, edited by Peter van Dommelen and Carlos Gómez Bellard, 1–21. London: Equinox.

——, eds. 2008b. *Rural Landscapes of the Punic World*. London: Equinox.

van Dommelen, Peter, and Mireia López Bertran. 2013. "Hellenism as Subaltern Practice: Rural Cults in the Punic World." In *The Hellenistic West: Rethinking the Ancient Mediterranean*, edited by Jonathan R. W. Prag and Josephine Crawley Quinn, 273–99. Cambridge: Cambridge University Press.

van Dongen, Erik. 2010. " 'Phoenicia': Naming and Defining a Region in Syria-Palestine." In *Interkulturalität in der Alten Welt Vorderasien, Hellas, Ägypten und die Vielfältigen Ebenen des Kontakts*, edited by Robert Rollinger, Birgit Gufler, Martin Lang, and Irene Madreiter, 471–88. Wiesbaden: Harrassowitz Verlag.

van Nijf, Onno. 2010. "Being Termessian: Local Knowledge and Identity Politics in a Pisidian City." In *Local Knowledge and Microidentities in the Imperial Greek World*, edited by Tim Whitmarsh, 163–88. Cambridge: Cambridge University Press.

Van Seters, John. 1972. "The Terms 'Amorite' and 'Hittite' in the Old Testament." *Vetus testamentum* 22: 64–81.

Vella, Nicholas C. 2000. "Defining Phoenician Religious Space: Oumm El-'Amed Reconsidered." *Ancient Near Eastern Studies* 37: 27–55.

——. 2002. "The Lie of the Land: Ptolemy's Temple of Hercules in Malta." *Ancient Near Eastern Studies* 39: 83–112.

——. 2005. "The Western Phoenicians in Malta: A Review of Claudia Sagona, *The Archaeology of Punic Malta*, and Claudia Sagona, *Punic Antiquities of Malta*." *Journal of Roman Archaeology* 18: 436–50.

——. 2010. " 'Phoenician' Metal Bowls: Boundary Objects in the Archaic Period." In *Punic Interactions: Cultural, Technological and Economic Exchange between Punic and Other Cultures in the Mediterranean; Meetings between Cultures in the Ancient Mediterranean; Proceedings of the 17th International Congress of Classical Archaeology, Rome 22–26 Sept. 2008*, edited by M. Dalla Riva and H. Di Giuseppe. Rome: Bolletino di archeologia online. http://www.bollettinodiarcheologiaonline.beniculturali.it/documenti/generale/5_VELLA.pdf.

——. 2013. "Vases, Bones and Two Phoenician Inscriptions: An Assessment of a Discovery Made in Malta in 1816." In *Ritual, Religion and Reason: Studies in the Ancient World in Honour of Paolo Xella*, edited by Oswald Loretz, Sergio Ribichini, Wilfred G. E. Watson, and José Ángel Zamora López, 589–605. Münster: Ugarit-Verlag.

———. 2014. "The Invention of the Phoenicians: On Object Definition, Decontextualization and Display." In *The Punic Mediterranean: Identities and Identification from Phoenician Settlement to Roman Rule*, edited by Josephine Crawley Quinn and Nicholas C. Vella, 24–41. Cambridge: Cambridge University Press.

Vendler, Helen. 1998. *Seamus Heaney*. London: HarperCollins.

Vincenzo, Salvatore de. 2013. *Tra Cartagine e Roma: I centri urbani dell'eparchia punica di Sicilia tra VI e I sec. A.C.* Berlin: De Gruyter.

Vine, Angus Edmund. 2010. *In Defiance of Time: Antiquarian Writing in Early Modern England*. Oxford: Oxford University Press.

Visonà, P. 1998. "Carthaginian Coinage in Perspective." *American Journal of Numismatics* 10: 1–27.

———. 2006. "Prolegomena to a Corpus of Carthaginian Bronze Coins." *Quaderni Ticinesi di Numismatica e antichità classiche* 35: 239–51.

———. 2009a. "Tradition and Innovation in Carthaginian Coinage during the Second Punic War." *Schweizerische numismatische Rundschau* 87: 173–83.

———. 2009b. "The Coins." In *A Cemetery of Vandalic Date at Carthage,* edited by Susan T. Stevens, Mark B. Garrison, and Joann Freed, 173–206. Portsmouth, RI: Journal of Roman Archaeology.

Vitale, Marco. 2013. *Koinon Syrias: Priester, Gymnasiarchen und Metropoleis der Eparchien im Kaiserzeitlichen Syrien*. Berlin: Akademie Verlag.

Vivanet, F. 1891. "Nora: Scavi nella necropoli dell'antica Nora nel comune di Pula." *Notizie degli scavi di antichità* 1891: 299–302.

von Graeve, Volkmar. 1970. *Der Alexandersarkophag und seine Werkstatt*. Berlin: Mann.

Walbank, Michael B. 1985. "Athens, Carthage and Tyre (*IG* II² 342+)." *Zeitschrift für Papyrologie und Epigraphik* 59: 107–11.

Wallace-Hadrill, Andrew. 2008. *Rome's Cultural Revolution*. Cambridge: Cambridge University Press.

———. 2013. "Hellenistic Pompeii: Between Oscan, Greek, Roman and Punic." In *The Hellenistic West: Rethinking the Ancient Mediterranean*, edited by Jonathan R. W. Prag and Josephine Crawley Quinn, 35–43. Cambridge: Cambridge University Press.

Watmough, Margaret. 1997. *Studies in the Etruscan Loanwords in Latin*. Florence: I. S. Olschki.

Weber, Dorothea. 2003. "For What Is So Monstrous as What the Punic Fellow Says?" In *Augustinus Afer*, edited by Pierre-Yves Fux, Jean-Michel Roessli, and Otto Wermelinger, 75–82. Fribourg: Éditions universitaires Fribourg.

Weber, Eugen. 1979. *Peasants into Frenchmen: The Modernization of Rural France, 1870–1914*. London: Chatto and Windus.

Weeda, Claire. 2014. "Ethnic Identification and Stereotypes in Western Europe, circa 1100–1300." *History Compass* 12 (7): 586–606.

Whitaker, Joseph I. S. 1921. *Motya, a Phoenician Colony in Sicily*. London: G. Bell.

Whitmarsh, Tim. 1998. "The Birth of a Prodigy: Heliodorus and the Genealogy of Hellenism." In *Studies in Heliodorus*, edited by Richard Hunter, 93–124. Cambridge: Cambridge Philological Society.

———. 2011. *Narrative and Identity in the Ancient Greek Novel: Returning Romance*. Cambridge: Cambridge University Press.

Whittaker, C. Richard. 1978. "Carthaginian Imperialism in the 5th and 4th Centuries." In *Imperialism in the Ancient World*, edited by Peter Garnsey and C. Richard Whittaker, 58–90. Cambridge: Cambridge University Press.

Wilson, Andrew I. 2012. "Neo-Punic and Latin Inscriptions in Roman North Africa: Function and Display." In *Multilingualism in the Graeco-Roman Worlds*, edited by Alex Mullen and Patrick James, 265–316. Cambridge: Cambridge University Press.

——. 2013. "Trading across the Syrtes: Euesperides and the Punic World." In *The Hellenistic West: Rethinking the Ancient Mediterranean*, edited by Jonathan R. W. Prag and Josephine Crawley Quinn, 120–56. Cambridge: Cambridge University Press.

Wilson, Roger J. A. 2005. "La sopravvivenza dell'influenza punica in Sicilia durante il dominio romano." In *Atti del V Congresso internazionale di studi fenici e punici: Marsala–Palermo, 2–8 ottobre 2000*, edited by Antonella Spanò Giammellaro, 907–17. Palermo: Università degli studi di Palermo.

——. 2013. "Hellenistic Sicily, c. 270–100 BC." In *The Hellenistic West: Rethinking the Ancinet Mediterranean*, edited by Jonathan R. W. Prag and Josephine Crawley Quinn, 79–119. Cambridge: Cambridge University Press.

Winter, Irene J. 1995. "Homer's Phoenicians: History, Ethnography, or Literary Trope?" In *The Ages of Homer: A Tribute to Emily Townsend Vermeule*, edited by Jane P. Carter and Sarah P. Morris, 247–71. Austin: University of Texas Press.

Wiseman, Donald J. 1954. "Supplementary Copies of Alalakh Tablets." *Journal of Cuneiform Studies* 8: 1–30.

Wistrich, Robert S., and David Ohana, eds. 1995. *The Shaping of Israeli Identity: Myth, Memory, and Trauma*. London: Frank Cass.

Wolff, Samuel. 2004. "Punic Amphoras in the Eastern Mediterranean." In *Transport Amphorae and Trade in the Eastern Mediterranean: Acts of the International Colloquium at the Danish Institute at Athens, September 26–29, 2002*, edited by J. Eiring and J. Lund, 451–58. Athens: Danish Institute at Athens.

Woolf, Greg. 2012. *Rome: An Empire's Story*. Oxford: Oxford University Press.

Woolmer, Mark. 2011. *Ancient Phoenicia: An Introduction*. London: Bristol Classical Press.

Worthen, William B. 1995. "Homeless Words: Field Day and the Politics of Translation." *Modern Drama* 38 (1): 22–41.

Xella, Paolo. 1969. "Sull'introduzione del culto di Demetra e Core a Cartagine." *Studi e materiali di storia delle religioni* 40: 215–28.

——. 1991. *Baal Hammon: Recherches sur l'identité et l'histoire d'un dieu phénico-punique*. Rome: Consiglio nazionale delle ricerche.

——. 1995. "Ugarit et les phéniciens: Identité culturelle et rapports historiques." In *Ugarit: Ein Ostmediterranes Kulturzentrum im Alten Orient: Ergebnisse und Perspektive der Forschung*, edited by Manfried Dietrich and Oswald Loretz, 239–66. Münster: Ugarit-Verlag.

——. 2008. "I fenici e gli 'altri': Dinamiche di identità culturale." In *Greci e punici in Sicilia tra V e IV secolo A.C.*, edited by Marina Congiu, Calogero Miccichè, Simona Modeo, and Luigi Santagati, 69–79. Caltanissetta: Salvatore Sciascia.

——. 2009. "Sacrifici di bambini nel mondo fenicio e punico nelle testimonianze in lingua greca e latina—I." *Studi epigrafici e linguistici* 26: 59–100.

——. 2010. "Per un modello interpretativo del tofet: Il tofet come necropoli infantile?" In *Tiro, Cartagine, Lixus: Nuove acquisizioni: Atti del convegno internazionale in onore di Maria Giulia Amadasi Guzzo (Roma, 24–25 novembre 2008)*, edited by Gilda Bartoloni, Paolo Matthiae, Lorenzo Nigro, and Licia Romano, 259–78. Rome: Università degli Studi di Roma "La Sapienza."

———. 2012a. "Il tophet: Un'interpretazione generale." In *Meixis: Dinamiche di stratificazione culturale nella periferia greca e romana: Atti del convegno internazionale di studi 'Il sacro e il profano' (Cagliari, Cittadella dei musei, 5–7 maggio 2011)*, edited by Simonetta Angiolillo, Marco Giuman, and Chiara Pilo, 1–17. Rome: L'Erma di Bretschneider.

———. 2012b. "Urne e stele nel tophet: Contemporanee?" *Rivista di studi fenici* 40 (2): 237–44.

———. 2013a. "'Tophet': An Overall Interpretation." In *The "Tophet" in the Phoenician Mediterranean* [= *Studi epigrafici e linguistici* 29–30 (2012–13)], edited by Paolo Xella, 259–76. Verona: Essedue.

———, ed. 2013b. *The "Tophet" in the Phoenician Mediterranean* [= *Studi epigrafici e linguistici* 29–30 (2012–13)]. Verona: Essedue.

———. 2014. "'Origini' e 'identità': Riflessioni sul caso dei fenici." *MÉFRA online* 126 (2): https://mefra.revues.org/2278.

Xella, Paolo, Josephine Crawley Quinn, Valentina Melchiorri, and Peter van Dommelen. 2013. "Phoenician Bones of Contention." *Antiquity* 87: 1199–207.

Xella, Paolo, and Mohamed Tahar. 2014. "Les inscriptions puniques et néopuniques d'Althiburos. Présentation préliminaire." *Rivista di studi fenici* 42 (1): 123–26.

Xella, Paolo, and M. Tahar. Forthcoming. "Le iscrizioni puniche del tophet di Althiburos (Henchir Médeina, Tunisia): Struttura, terminologia, datazione." In *Atti dell'VIII Congresso internazionale di studi fenici e punici (Carbonia-Sant'Antioco, 21– 26 ottobre 2013)*.

Yarrow, Liv Mariah. 2013. "Heracles, Coinage and the West: Three Hellenistic Case-Studies." In *The Hellenistic West: Rethinking the Ancient Mediterranean*, edited by Jonathan R. W. Prag and Josephine Crawley Quinn, 348–66. Cambridge: Cambridge University Press.

Yntema, Douwe. 2000. "Mental Landscapes of Colonization: The Ancient Written Sources and the Archaeology of Early Colonial-Greek Southeastern Italy." *Bulletin Antieke Beschaving* 75: 1–50.

Zeitlin, Froma. 2013. "Landscapes and Portraits: Signs of the Uncanny and Illusions of the Real." In *The Construction of the Real and the Ideal in the Ancient Novel*, edited by Michael Paschalis and Stelios Panayotakis, 61–87. Groningen: Barkhuis.

Zobel, Hans-Jürgen. 1995. "Canaan." In *Theological Dictionary of the Old Testament*, 211–28. Grand Rapids, MI: Erdmanns.

Zucca, Raimondo. 2004. *Sufetes africae et sardiniae: Studi storici e geografici sul Mediterraneo antico*. Rome: Carocci.

IMAGE CREDITS

Author: 4.2; 5.2; 5.3; 5.4

Courtesy of the Académie des Inscriptions et Belles-Lettres, Paris: 5.5 (*CIS* I no. 5732 [Tab. CI])

Courtesy of the American Numismatic Society: 4.9 (1944.100.10040); 6.2b (1947.98.330); 7.1 (1944.100.77360); 7.2 Beirut B (1944.100.77115); 7.2 Byblos B (1944.100.77142); 7.2 Byblos C (1944.100.77145); 7.2 Sidon B (1948.19.2415); 7.2 Sidon C (1944.100.77159); 7.2 Sidon D (1948.19.2416); 7.2 Tyre B (1948.19.2432); 7.2 Tyre D (1944.100.77384); 7.4c (1948.19.2478); 7.4e (1944.100.81882)

Arts et Métiers Graphiques, Paris (*EH* 102; plate 11A.): 2.2

Ben Abed and Aillagon (1995, 113): 5.6

Bibliothèque nationale de France: 4.5a (1973.1.273); 4.5b (Luynes 3179); 4.5c (Babelon 2022); 4.5d (1966.453.2987); 4.6d (Fonds Général 936); 7.2 Sidon E (Babelon 1041); 7.2 Tyre E (1967.117); 7.4a (Babelon 1807); 7.4b (L 2892); 7.5 (Chandon de Briailles 1526A)

bpk-Bildagentur (Münzkabinett, Staatliche Museen zu Berlin) / Dirk Sonnenwald: 4.6a (18214317); 4.7a (18206025)

bpk-Bildagentur (Münzkabinett, Staatliche Museen zu Berlin) / Reinhard Saczewski: 4.6c (18211779)

The Trustees of the British Museum: 4.6b (RPK,p246B.18.Seg); 4.7b (1900,0601.1); 4.8 (1866,1201.654); 6.1 (1841,0726.223) 6.2a (1908,1111.9); 6.3 (1872,0816.44; 1872,0816.57; 1873,0320.70; 1873,0320.71); 6.5 (1874,0714.99); 7.4d (1908,0110.1400); 8.3 (125117); 8.4 (125098); 8.8 (1846,0711.1).

Courtesy of Catawiki.com: 1.3; 1.4

Courtesy of Direction Générale des Antiquités, République Libanaise: 6.4 (*Bulletin du Musée de Beyrouth* 3 (1939): plate 13)

Courtesy of Nadir Djama: 5.7 (Sennequier and Colonna [2003, 123, no. 114])

Hamdi and Reinach (1892, plate 14): 4.3

Hellenic Ministry of Culture and Sports / Archaeological Receipts Fund: 2.1 (National Archaeological Museum, Athens, 1488)

Courtesy of Arthur Houghton, Catherine Lorber, and Oliver Hoover: 7.2 Beirut C, D, E; Byblos D, E; Tyre C

London Metropolitan Archives: 9.2

Courtesy of the Warden and Fellows of Merton College Oxford: 9.1 (photograph by Jonathan Prag)

Courtesy of Matthew Nicholls: 8.1

Prepared by Princeton University Press: I.1; I.2; 1.1 (modified from Traboulsi [2007, 42]); 1.2 (modified from Traboulsi [2007, 89]); 5.1 (modified from Quinn [2013], fig. 2); 7.3; 8.2 (based on McCarty and Quinn [2015], fig. 3); 8.5 (based on McCarty and Quinn [2015], fig. 5); 8.6 (based on A. Wilson [2012], fig. 11.1); 8.7 (based on maps kindly provided by Matthew McCarty)

Renan (1864, plate 1): 1.5

RMN-Grand Palais (Musée du Louvre) / Christian Larrieu: 4.1 (AO 2060)

RMN-Grand Palais (Musée du Louvre) / Hervé Lewandowski: 4.4 (AO 4801)

INDEX

NOTE: Page numbers followed by *f* indicate a figure.